THE CHILD'S WORLD
OF MAKE-BELIEVE

THE CHILD PSYCHOLOGY SERIES
EXPERIMENTAL AND THEORETICAL ANALYSES OF CHILD BEHAVIOR

EDITOR
DAVID S. PALERMO
DEPARTMENT OF PSYCHOLOGY
THE PENNSYLVANIA STATE UNIVERSITY
UNIVERSITY PARK, PENNSYLVANIA

The Child's World of Make-Believe

EXPERIMENTAL STUDIES OF IMAGINATIVE PLAY

JEROME L. SINGER

Department of Psychology
Yale University
New Haven, Connecticut

With Chapters by

EPHRAIM BIBLOW
Department of Psychology
Nassau County Medical Center
East Meadow, New York

JOAN T. FREYBERG
Postgraduate Center for Mental Health
New York, New York

SYBIL GOTTLIEB
School of Education
City College
City University of New York
New York, New York

MARY ANN PULASKI
Psychological Services
Herricks Public Schools
New Hyde Park, New York

ACADEMIC PRESS   1973
New York   San Francisco   London
A Subsidiary of Harcourt Brace Jovanovich, Publishers

ACADEMIC PRESS, INC.
111 Fifth Avenue, New York, New York 10003

United Kingdom Edition published by
ACADEMIC PRESS, INC. (LONDON) LTD.
24/28 Oval Road, London NW1

LIBRARY OF CONGRESS CATALOG CARD NUMBER: 72-88336

PRINTED IN THE UNITED STATES OF AMERICA

To my sons, Jon, Bruce, and Jeff

Contents

Preface

Observing the spontaneous play of children can be one of the most delightful experiences for an adult. One need not be a devoted grandparent to be caught smiling in a mood of joy and surprise while watching or overhearing children between the ages of 3 and 10 engaging in various aspects of "make-believe." Only a deeply preoccupied, harassed parent or a self-centered Scrooge can resist taking some time out to watch the unfolding of a "story-line," erratic as it may be, played out by a child alone or by a small group of children. Whether the game is "pirates," "cowboys," "school," or "house," one finds a genuine fascination in watching the development of plot sequences, the curious interplay of adult phrases and even bits of wisdom alongside gross "misperceptions" of reality or magical solutions to momentary dilemmas. If the reader will relax a moment and think back to earliest childhood memories of solitary or group play, he will soon realize how frequent imaginary playmates or make-believe roles and characters are part of his own childhood experience.

This book is about the imaginative play of children. It represents an effort to pay special attention to those aspects of the play of preadolescent children which involve "make-believe" or "as-if" elements, the creation from thin air of additional companions in adventure, the attribution of events to different times and places, and the shifting of roles and voices within the same child. Children's play has been classified by Jean Piaget into games of mastery (block construction, reproduction of designs, climbing ladders), games with rules (checkers, marbles, hide-and-seek) and finally "ludic symbolism," games of "make-believe" in which the simplest stick may become the sword "Excalibur," the controls of a rocket ship, and a little baby being rocked to sleep. The focus of our attention will be this "make-believe" category of child's play, the problems it presents for scientific understanding of human development and its implications for the cognitive and emotional growth of the child.

The objective of this book is to present, perhaps for the first time in scientific literature, a detailed examination of the nature of imaginative or symbolic play. There are some fine books on play in general and a small body of systematic research in the area. This book focuses specifically on make-believe play and children's games, and tries to show how such a phenomenon can be studied in a systematic way with appropriate scientific controls. The book also attempts to relate make-believe play to the more general issue of the psychology of day-dreaming, which I have been studying for more than 20 years. It attempts to integrate imaginative behavior in children to a more general body of theory in psychology. Wherever possible, aspects of make-believe are tied back to the works of Piaget, Erikson, Werner among the specialists in child psychology and to the broader theoretical positions of Freud, White, Sullivan, Bandura, and Tomkins, among others.

A special effort is made to present an original integration of the motivationally oriented systems with the cognitive approaches in psychology. In this sense, the cognitive-affective theory of Tomkins seems at once the most general and yet most specific as well for describing details of play behavior in ways that take into account motivation (based on the affect system), information-processing structure and capacities of the child, and the social learning and interpersonal interaction features of the development of make-believe. The important thing is for the reader to see that "as-if" symbolic play in children is not an isolated phenomenon or something mysterious or specific to the psychotherapy play room. It is an intrinsic part of normal growth and subject to careful study and scientific explication.

The format of this book includes chapters on theory and the relevant historical literature, the presentation of examples of formal research carried out on play and imagination under my direction and finally an attempt at a theoretical integration and a more speculative set of practical proposals. Four chapters are contributed by psychologists who have worked with me in this area: Joan T. Freyberg, Sybil Gottlieb, Mary Ann Pulaski, and Ephraim Biblow. Each of these chapters, as well as parts of Chapters II and III, includes fairly detailed examples of specific experiments or systematic researches as models for other investigators or graduate and undergraduate students. By models, however, I do not mean *perfect* experiments, for all have obvious limitations which face every investigator who works in so subtle and complex an area. Rather, they can serve as clear jumping-off points for new studies and it is to be hoped that a generation of further research on make-believe play will be a major outcome of this publication.

A particular method I have employed at various points in this volume may be worth singling out for a brief comment. Wherever possible, we have included specific examples of children's play drawn from research or therapy protocols. This makes all the more vivid the content and also gives some life to material which, if reduced solely to statistical tables of end-products of behavior, defeats much of the intent of making children's play exciting and integral to the total behavior of the child. But I have gone beyond the use of observations of children

to bring in a favorite method of my own, reminiscence about personal experiences and the attempt to recall examples from my own childhood. This
technique is one I have advocated for all psychologists or students of behavior. If
we take the trouble to revive memories about play and recall their setting and
meaning as a child, we can begin to generate new hypotheses about play or in a
sense test on ourselves whether specific statements of Piaget or Freud or any
theorist make sense. Personal introspection cannot substitute for formal research
and experiment, but it is a key part of the total scientific enterprise in a field
like psychology in my opinion. The instances presented herein as well as in my
earlier book on "Daydreaming" should encourage the reader to try it out
anyway. If nothing else, I think it will make reading this book a more enjoyable
experience.

   This book is intended for a fairly wide audience. It has much new material in
it that should be of interest to professionals working in the area of child
development and mental health as well as to graduate and undergraduate
students of psychology, education, or social work. It should also be of use and
interest to specialists and workers in child care and early childhood education
and, finally, to the nonprofessional seeking specific enlightenment about a
fascinating and little-understood facet of the world of childhood. It is a curious
blindspot of psychologists that play which is the main "business" of so much of
childhood (reminisce a little, reader!) gets very little attention from researchers
or textbook authors. A recently published text I examined devoted one page to
children's imagination and another text on adolescence had no references to
daydreams! It seems almost scandalous to me that experiences so integral to our
growing-up as make-believe and fantasy can be so systematically ignored by my
colleagues. I hope this volume can begin to move child research a little toward
scientific work on these phenomena.

Acknowledgments

A word must be said in acknowledgment of the many people who have helped in my research and specifically on this volume. Intellectually, I have been strongly influenced by early reading exposure to Kurt Lewin, Jean Piaget, and Heinz Werner, as well as the inevitable Sigmund Freud. I must thank Gardner Murphy who first encouraged me to grasp their contributions and who as a teacher and theorist showed me how to look for interrelations in the works of great men and draw the best from them. My contacts with Silvan Tomkins have influenced my theoretical thinking greatly and my exposure to psychoanalytic training in the neo-Freudian interpersonal approach of Harry Stack Sullivan has sensitized me to look to the social situation as a key feature of the child's learning environment. Contacts and discussions with Eric Klinger, Brian Sutton-Smith, Mary Engel, Anneliese Riess, Mae Lord, Charles Smith, Herbert Nechin, among many others, have been very useful. My research with children has involved collaborative efforts with John Antrobus, Abram Chipman, Leone Lesser, Richard Rowe, Stanley Feldstein as well as the four contributors to this volume. The many people who have served as observers, raters or judges and research assistants are too numerous to cite individually.

My wife, Dorothy Singer, has served as a research collaborator on the studies of nursery school children mentioned in the book and on a larger study of spontaneous play currently in progress. She has been an endless resource of acute observation and methodological rigor for me as well as serving as an example of a devoted mother of active sons. The many student participants in the Fantasy Play Practicum under her direction at Manhattanville College have been useful indeed in our research. Mary Bundock has helped with statistical analysis of some data on nursery school children referred to in the text. I am indebted to Mrs. Elsie Rothenberg, Director of the Elmwood Country Day School, for her useful advice and for opportunities to visit the school and observe the children. Marcia Guttentag, Director, Harlem Research Center of the City University of New York, has made facilities for observation available and has also been of help in a number of ways. The many specific teachers and schools employed by my four collaborators have been acknowledged in their doctoral dissertations and cannot be specifically cited here.

One can go on endlessly with acknowledgments, for in a sense, a book of this kind is based on a lifetime of personal as well as professional experience. My parents, my childhood friends, the many parents I talk with today socially or professionally, provide one with ideas and examples. My own sons, to whom this book is dedicated, have been a source of numerous observations, not to mention personal joy and interest and occasionally some negative affect as well.

Finally, I am indebted to my secretary, Violet Levine, for invaluable aid in typing the first draft of this manuscript, for helping to assemble the bibliography and for practical and moral support throughout. I also acknowledge with pleasure the work of Terry Conover in typing the final draft and the assistance of David Diamond on the Subject Index and Delores Cotton, Audrey Klein, and Linda Schwartz with proofreading.

CHAPTER I

Theories of Play
and the Origins of Imagination

Introduction

There is a quality of mystery tinged perhaps with humor about the imaginative play of children. We observe these little creatures talking to thin air, treating a bit of blank fluff or a stick like a baby that needs cuddling, having a teddy bear talk on a toy telephone in phrases suspiciously like mother's. Sometimes we see a quiet little boy carrying on bloody and bitter battles punctuated by imitative cannon noises, diving airplanes, with only the help of some props of wooden blocks and perhaps plastic toy soldiers. A 3-year-old girl goes on at great length instructing her invisible friend Mrs. Puffum to be more careful—if she keeps on stepping in puddles she'll ruin her new white shoes. A 5-year-old boy has a toy giraffe of felt and plastic which he declares is a visitor from outer space, a Martian who has a long neck because that's what all the people look like up there.

A child of 4 floats back and forth on a swing at the same time emitting a sound like an airplane engine. Then he reports that he has to change planes and find a new one because he has run out of gas and has to get another plane in order to continue his flight. We cannot be sure that this child has indeed been in his mind's eye picturing in full detail an airplane in flight or its gas tank. It is doubtful that he has any differentiated knowledge of the actual role of gasoline in fueling an airplane, yet one cannot deny that he has far transcended the actual physical situation in which he finds himself—only a small play area and a swing.

One can contrast this type of play with the comparable situation of another child on a swing who might limit his enjoyment to merely swinging as fast or as high as he could. He might enjoy both the mastery of a difficult and frightening task and also the rise and fall and the visual and kinesthetic experiences concurrent with swinging. The former child not only experiences the mastery game, as Piaget would put it, but now has introduced *as-if* elements which are clearly a modification of his environment based on some experiences carried in his memory and which undoubtedly involve some degree of early imagery.

Here then we see the very beginnings of a critically important step in human development. Leading theoreticians and investigators in psychology such as Freud (1959), Lewin (1935), Piaget (1932), and Luria (1932) have all described how the fantasy play of the child may serve as the origin for the later adult daydreaming and other forms of thought.

Most make-believe play also has a social quality in the symbolic sense. It involves interpersonal transactions, events, and adventures that call for other characters and other locations in space and time. While much make-believe play does take place in pairs or even among larger groups of children, there is still the likelihood that there will be introduction of additional invisible characters or the use of inanimate objects to present people or animals not actually present. The story line almost always has a social quality in the sense that it is related in some way to the activities that adults engage in or to adventures that children might have either singly or with others around or in groups.

At a nursery school in the Harlem section of New York City, I watched a group of four young children organizing a game of "picnic." They used some dress-up clothes and had either dolls or makeshift bundles which were to represent children. They lined themselves up on chairs as if they were in automobiles and then proceeded, by making automobile sounds, to drive in the direction of the picnic grounds. In this case, they were acting as if they were adults. They enhanced the effect somewhat by the use of hats and pocketbooks, talked in different voices trying to simulate adult speech. They reprimanded their "children" and they also went on to imagine that they were indeed seated in automobiles and moving from one place to another.

The game thus had a social intent (a picnic); it involved elements of imagery and make-believe, some role-playing and an attempt to simulate adult behavior. Clearly, such play has elements of imagery far more complex than what one observes in games of mastery or rules.

Even games with rules which appear relatively later in childhood can still be incorporated into an imaginative pattern. I quite frequently recall playing games such as bouncing a ball back and forth between my hands or hitting a ball with a paddle over and over again and translating this into an elaborate contest between rival teams. The simple rules of direct physical manipulation involved in these games were considerably amplified by the use of imagery into Olympic contests or championship games with imagined stars all of whom had different personalities. It is possible to observe other young boys using bits of stick, perhaps a ping-pong ball and the faces of baseball players on baseball cards strewn about in baseball positions as a basis for a solitary game that takes on all of the excitement of a crucial series with the accompaniments much like those of the announcers on radio and television. Indeed, there are even pauses for commercials. Lukas (1971) has written charmingly of his fantasies of baseball fame complete with visual imagery and sound effects in the tones of the popular announcer, Mel Allen. The involvement of imagery and make-believe elements may persist in games with rules well into early adolescence. For example, I was part of a group of young boys who formed leagues for sports such as baseball and football played out by various mechanical or board games. These leagues involved the establishment of independent teams with a great variety of fantasy players who had separate personalities and who were given special characteristics by the boy in charge of the particular team.

One of the group had a superstar football player whom he had created, named "Pheneffsonn." Pheneffsonn was supposed to be of Midwest Swedish background and was an incredibly powerful runner and all-around athlete with a certain limited intelligence. Our board games of football consisted of calling a play, throwing dice, and then determining the yardage gain from a table. The boy who was the creator of Pheneffsonn would shout loudly, *Right now this is a crucial moment. It's third down and three to go. This is where they need someone like Pheneffsonn! And sure enough he gets the ball* [casting the dice] *and dives off right tackle. They're struggling to hold him back but he fights forward.* [Meantime the group searches the yardage table.] *That's it, folks, Pheneffsonn has plunged for a 5-yard gain—another powerful run by this great athlete!*

Here, then is an example of a shared fantasy game. Although I had my own stars and rather disliked Pheneffsonn, I also found myself imagining him making the run in question. It did seem to us that the people we chose as our stars somehow did perform better in the games we played, although in actuality these depended very much on chance. We kept elaborate statistics and there was no doubt that Pheneffsonn and some of the others merited the esteem of their proponents.

Probably this type of imaginative play eventually becomes internalized in the form of the daydreams of the adolescent and those fantasies that persist throughout life. Although we have no adequate scientific evidence for this internalization of imaginative play into daydream and fantasy processes, such a possibility has been suggested by a variety of investigators (Luria, 1932; Piaget, 1932; Singer, 1966). Interestingly, even genuine athletes of great stature are not immune to the occurrence of fantasies about their own success or other activities occasionally to their own detriment. Newspaper and magazine articles about Arthur Ashe and Stan Smith, both leading tennis players in the United States, indicate their occasional proneness to daydreaming during matches. For example, Ashe has been known for proclivity to lose concentration and to daydream about meals or dates; opponents tend to take advantage of this. Smith described an incident in an interview in a newspaper: In the finals at Wimbledon he had just scored a dramatic point against the champion, John Newcombe, who fell down in a mock display of rage. This interval permitted Smith to drift into a daydream about receiving the winner's cup and he began picturing the ceremonies of the award. Suddenly he found that his opponent had slipped across several powerful shots. Smith never did recover his momentum and lost the match.

In examining briefly some of the theories and viewpoints proposed over the years that attempt to offer some explanation of the nature of imaginative play, it should be stressed that our emphasis here will be upon the "make-believe" elements. As indicated earlier, there seems to be general agreement among the small number of investigators who have studied play that it is best subdivided into play built around the mastery of the physical feats or of verbal or perceptual tasks with a special emphasis on direct relation to the immediate situation. This would include the child's concentrating on building a tower of blocks as high as possible, putting together a jigsaw puzzle, cutting out paper clothing and dressing up doll figures, riding a tricycle, practicing his skill at checkers or chess. These and dozens of other activities including fighting, tumbling, racing, and jumping rope all represent essentially direct concrete experiences which involve a minimum of make-believe or imaginative elements. Only those most advanced games of skill such as checkers or chess require the development of any degree of imagery.

Games with rules, while they may, as already noted, occasionally incorporate elements of fantasy or imagery, often enough involve direct experiences that call for a minimum usage of symbolic processes. Our concern here will be primarily with the class of play that requires the central generation of imagery and involves pretend elements, changing of voices and roles, changes in time and space. Indeed, some writers on play (Gilmore, 1966; Klinger, 1969) have tended to limit their emphasis on play to the symbolic characteristics. Thus Gilmore uses as his prototype of play a "child putting a blanket to sleep." We really have surprisingly little information of whether the classification I have just described—games of mastery, games with rules, and make-believe games—are all clearly independent and recur with sufficient consistency in different groups of children. Indeed one might propose a series of factor-analytic studies in which direct observations of behavior could be classified along various dimensions and correlated to ascertain if indeed the spontaneous play of children breaks down into three such categories. One wonders why no one as yet has tried something like this.

A Bit of History

Literary and Artistic References to Imaginative Play

Man has been very little interested in the experiences of the child throughout history. Our available literature from classical Western civilization and from other civilizations for which records and literary or artistic products are available suggest a dearth of material describing childhood experiences and the play of children. There are hints of an awareness of the quality of children's play in the Bible or in various ancient writings from different civilizations. These seem on the whole to be of little importance and are sketchy indeed so that we can base little information about the play of children in earlier times. Much of the emphasis until the Renaissance in Europe, suggests that the child was set to work early either in the fields or in the trade of the parents or in housekeeping duties or else began formal education rather early. In the case of nobility about whom we have more information, it is clear that children were early trained in courtly patterns, specific skills relevant to the time such as hunting or sword's play for boys and needlework and housekeeping duties for girls. Children rarely appear in any of the dramas of the ancient times or the Renaissance. There are hints in various passages of Shakespeare that he was sensitive to the imagery and fantasy that characterized childhood, but the few appearances of children in his plays do not involve situations in which we actually observe their games or make-believe. This is all the more noticeable because Shakespeare is characterized by such a great awareness of man's fantasies, images, illusions and the whole inner world of fairies, goblins, and sprites.

One of the few clear indications of attention to the play of children is evident in the famous painting *Children's Play* by Peter Bruegel, and another in the Chinese painting of the Sung Dynasty. Bruegel's painting with its wonderfully vigorous quality includes more than 50 separate childhood games of which only a very small fraction, less than 10%, would appear to have any elements of imagination or make-believe. Without a sufficient basis for comparison, the painting mainly indicates the remarkable continuity of some of the games that have been described by ancient writers and which some of us have already played in our own childhood. As Opie and Opie (1971) point out, one children's game in Bruegel's painting called "Buck Buck" can be traced back to the time of Nero and it is referred to in the famous Satyricon by Petronius. This game is very much the same as a game called "Johnny-on-the-pony" which is still played on American city streets.

By contrast, the Chinese painting is full of sociodramatic play. Almost every one of the children is depicted as involved in some activity ordinarily carried out by an adult, including the dances of Nomads, warriors of the Steppes, a visit from an ambassador, and a figure in an ancient legend. We cannot tell for sure whether the picture has some intention other than the depiction of games and it is indeed possible that it has allegorical meaning. At the same time, it does point up the likelihood that the artist is depicting a group of upper-class or aristocratic children who are already familiar with the roles that adults play and whose play itself mimics these roles. By contrast, the children of the village depicted in Bruegel's painting are much more active and vigorous, much more concerned with direct motor experience and in general also seem to reflect a lower socioeconomic group. Since these two cultures are so far apart in time and space, we cannot be sure whether what is presented is a social class difference, a difference in *genre* painting, or a gross cultural difference in styles of play between Oriental and Western children.

It remained for the nineteenth century romantics to begin opening up the world of childhood and relating it in part to later adult experience in the world of imagination. In Germany, both Goethe and Schiller were especially sensitive to the imaginative component in children's play and also to the implications of play for later adult behavior and especially artistic reaction. Goethe called attention to the fact that his relationship to his mother inspired in him the zest for fantasizing and story telling. Schiller developed an extensive theory of the nature of play which is still cited frequently and has had considerable influence even on modern ethologists.

Among English romantics, Coleridge wrote extensively on the nature of the imagination and Wordsworth idealized the mind of the child in its simplicity and directness. Those early pioneers in the development of educational theory, Froebel and Pestalozzi, both were especially sensitive to the important role of play in the early childhood and made insightful proposals for systematic use of play as part of the child rearing and educational practices they were proposing.

Still, there was very little really effective description of children's play in literature until well into the nineteenth century. Tolstoy, in his recollections of childhood, writes extremely sensitively of the impact of his older brother upon his own development as a very young child. His brother would set up games in which all were to pretend they were "ant people" and then a series of make-believe consequences would follow. Tolstoy's recollections also described vividly the fantasies that he had at a somewhat later age when his misbehavior caused him to be locked up while awaiting punishment from his returning father and grandmother. The elaborate fantasies he describes concerning his feared tutor are surprisingly revealing depictions of the mind of the child around 9 or 10.

In France, Anatole France's *Le livre de mon ami* is a very effective represen-tation of the fantasies and elaborate imaginings of a child alone in his room at night. Flaubert's descriptions of the fantasies of Madame Bovary as a young girl

"Children's Play" by Peter Bruegel. Courtesy of Kunsthistorichen Museum, Vienna, Austria.

"One Hundred Children at Play," anonymous. China. Southern Sung Dynasty. Courtesy of the Cleveland Museum of Art, purchase from the J. H. Wade Fund.

in a convent trying to imagine the lives of the saints and her own future also represent a fine instance of sensitivity to the solitary behavior of children.

Perhaps more than any other writer, Robert Louis Stevenson has glorified the childhood imaginings and make-believe play of children in many little poems and in some of his semiautobiographical essays. Perhaps the earliest most realistic accounts of make-believe play in fiction are those provided by Mark Twain in some of his books and stories. We know very well that Tom Sawyer and Huckleberry Finn and their friends played at being pirates, river boat captains, and many other such games. The charming scene in which Ben Rogers approaches while Tom is painting the fence has been selected for analysis by Erikson (1963) as an especially apt instance of make-believe play that exemplifies the defensive and self-actualizing features of fantasy games.

> Ben Rogers hove in sight presently. . . . Ben's gait was a hop-skip-and-jump, proof enough that his heart was light and his anticipations high. He was eating an apple and giving a long, melodious whoop, at intervals followed by a deeptoned ding-dong-dong, ding-dong-dong for he was personating a steamboat. As he drew near he slackened speed, took the middle of the street, leaned far over to starboard and rounded to ponderously and with glorious pomp and circumstance—for he was personating the *Big Missouri* and considered himself to be drawing nine feet of water. He was boat captain and engine-bells combined so he had to imagine himself standing on his own hurricane-deck giving the orders and executing them.
> "Stop her, Sir! . . . ship up to back! tingalingling," his arm straightened and stiffened down his sides. "Stop the stabbord! tingalingling! Stop the labbord! Come ahead on the stabboard! Stop her! Let your outside turn along slow! tingalingling! Chow-ow! . . . Done with the engines, sir! tingalingling! sh't! sh't! sh't!" (trying the gauge cocks)

Twain also provides some examples of Tom's own fantasies and play in the development of the desire to become a pirate or at the end of *Huckleberry Finn* in the elaborate charade into which Huck and Jim are lured. In *The Prince and the Pauper*, the early description of the poor boy Tom's development, also is characterized by evidence of imaginative play with his companions and with himself as the leader. In a number of instances, Twain also points out that storytelling encouragement by adults has played a role in these tendencies of the children.

It seems unlikely that sociodramatic play started only in the nineteenth century or in the nineteenth century America where we get such good descriptions from Twain. Rather, one might surmise that this type of play was more generally common, but simply went unnoticed, and unrecorded by an adult world that had not yet begun to show a genuine interest in childhood experience.

The importance of adult example and story telling in the eliciting and encouragement of make-believe play in children was explicitly recognized by Mark Twain, but largely neglected by many other writers including most psychologists during the twentieth century. A fairly recent memoir of Auden (1965) provides striking examples of how closeness to a certain type of mother may have fostered the imaginative power of one of the twentieth century's greatest poets. "When I was eight years old, she taught me the words and music of the love potion scene in 'Tristan and Isolde' and we used to sing it together [p. 166]." He also mentions that the novelist Evelyn Waugh's father played charades daily in the course of his life. Movies of the *Our Gang* variety made it all the more clear that children did engage in such play. These films may well have influenced the development of imaginative play in the countless children who enjoyed these antics in the movies and later on television.

Presentations of imaginative play of children are now widespread in the various popular media and literature. During the 1940s and 1950s there was an extremely popular cartoon, "Barnaby," in the newspapers which involved the play of a group of children with the imaginary companion, Mr. O'Malley, in this case, a leprechaun with magical powers. The most popular current children's cartoon, "Peanuts," gives numerous examples of the make-believe play which children engage in and in addition uses the dog Snoopy as a quasi-human figure who is daydreaming frequently about his World War I air battles against the sinister Red Baron.

Theories of Play

Keeping in mind that our focus here is more narrowly on make-believe play, let us quickly examine some of the proposals made by a number of persons in the past 150 years who have seriously sought to understand the nature of children's behavior. More extended reviews of the relevant theories of play in general are available elsewhere (Berlyne, 1969; Gilmore, 1966; Klinger, 1969, 1971; Millar, 1968; and Smilansky, 1968).

Surplus Energy Theory

One major theoretical position was early presented by the poet Schiller and later adopted by the early proponent of evolution theory, Spencer. This theory is known as the *surplus energy* explanation of play and it argues that for children who do not have the necessity of day-to-day survival, the necessary preparatory energies for such action finds an outlet in play behavior rather than work. Schiller was clearly drawn to this theory by observations especially of the boisterous behavior of the young boys and also of some of the creative outlets this behavior later showed. He also was led to compare the work of the artist with its fanciful quality and element of unreality to a continuation of the play of children.

While many theorists today would concur with the relationship of play and creative art, the tying of the theory to excess energy has little support now. Few psychologists still take seriously the notion of a quantum of energy that must be spilled out in some directions. In addition, there is ample evidence that play differs in emphasis upon its make-believe across cultures to a very marked degree that seems related at least in part to the relative emphasis in the culture on make-believe and also to the requirement for early work in the society (Whiting, 1963). Observation does indeed suggest that those societies in which children have less demands upon them for household duties or work in field and factories also show more tendency toward imaginative play. Yet the fact remains that city children who do have imposed upon them specific family responsibilities or work tasks, may engage in a great deal of active physical play with a minimum of fantasy games involved (Smilansky, 1968). It would therefore seem likely that a certain amount of the specific quality of play depends on the society which encourages and provides opportunities for it. It is not at all evident that children will inevitably play if given nothing else to do. This is particularly the case for symbolic play where we have no indications that it is increasingly engaged in simply because children have no work demands made upon them. Animal research provides ample evidence of considerable rough and tumble play, especially on the part of animals who have not reached sexual maturity (Welker, 1961). This cannot however, be attributed to a surplus of energy, since the younger animals have as much responsibility as adults for maintenance of their food supply and it seems more likely that the play behavior has other functions.

Groos's Instinct Theory

A major figure in the development of research on play was Karl Groos. Groos (1901) was perhaps the first person to carry out a truly extensive examination of all the varieties of play both in animals and in humans; and he developed a classification system that is generally comparable to the ones widely accepted today. Groos made observations on his own children, a practice that is still followed by child psychologists. This method has limitations, including small numbers of cases and of the possibilities that the children may reflect particular socioeconomic levels. One cannot overlook the possible influence of parents already inclined in particular directions. Employing evolutionary theory and the then-prevalent emphasis on instincts, Groos proposed that play emerges out of natural selection as a form of necessary practice on the part of the child or immature organism for behaviors that are essential to later survival. In this sense, the playful fighting of animals or the rough and tumble play of children and many of the playful courtship activities of animals and children as well are essentially the practice of skills that will later aid their survival.

Taken simply at the observational level, this view has considerable merit. Play that involves mastery of certain skills of a physical nature, rule games that involve learning of important aspects of social interaction, and make-believe play that might help in the development of imagery or symbolic capacities may all serve the child well in later years. Although Groos collected many examples both from the animal world and from his observations of children and various anecdotal reports, he did not carry out the kind of systematic observation that is necessary to pin down statements so general as those he proposed. In addition, one need not insist upon the concept of instinct to explain play behavior; it seems possible to use notions of a natural exercising of the child's growing capacities that is inherently pleasurable without assuming necessarily that it will lead to any later improved functioning (Bühler's *Funktionlust*, 1930). If anything, one might indeed argue that many of the most interesting features of child's play, the spontaneity, freshness, and novelty are often lost in later life or suppressed; one of the functions of art or of certain forms of psychotherapy is to help the adult recapture the lost capacities and perhaps use them as an adult for later enjoyment or for more effective functioning. We will discuss some of these possibilities later.

Instinct, Recapitulation, and Cultural Theories

A far less plausible theory of play also rooted in the then-current instinct notion was that proposed by a famous psychologist, G. Stanley Hall (1906). Hall felt that the cycle of development involved a recapitulation of the history of the race, a notion also proposed in a number of biological forms at that time. There was presumably a need in mankind to rid himself of more primitive features of behavior. Play, it was felt, with its roots in the ritual of the savage, had to be worked through before one could move on to the realities of adult life.

This rather stern view of man's fate has had other proponents. Wundt (1911–1929), the founder of modern experimental psychology, actually devoted the last 30 years of his life to working on an elaborate theory of social psychology which also emphasized a recapitulation theory and a notion of the group mind. The emphasis placed by Wundt and Hall upon the relationships between early magic and ritual and the play of children is reflected also in a much more recent and much-cited work by the Dutch scholar, Huizinga (1950).

Huizinga's thesis is too extended and complex to discuss at length here, primarily because it focuses on the meaning of play for the adult and deals only peripherally and without much detail with the play of children. For Huizinga, much of man's behavior can be viewed as a continuation of not only childish play, but of the many kinds of rituals and mythic forms that were developed by earlier civilizations. He does not propose that either adult or child play recapitulates earlier forms, but rather that a certain quality of play or "gamesmanship" is essential for effective life in our civilization. Play is viewed as a significant basis for the later competitive strivings that make up many of the major facets of adult civilization. Berlyne (1969) has noted, however, that it is possible that Huizinga's complex view of adult play as an outgrowth of children's play is essentially an orientation toward games of skill and mastery, and that one might better translate the Dutch term as *games* rather than the more general English term of *play*.

Recent Definition

In his attempt to form a theory, Groos particularly emphasized the role of play as practice for later functioning. While it is clear that many aspects of play do have potential value as practice, it remains to be seen whether practice is the *goal* of play or rather a later outcome. In other words, it is important at least at this stage of our attempt to develop any theory of play to distinguish outcomes in play behavior from the initial motivation of play in the child. If one attempts a more careful definition of play, then perhaps some of the difficulties between the origin of the function and its long-range value for the child can be clarified.

An analysis of the definitional problem has been presented by Klinger (1969, 1971). Emphasizing symbolic or make-believe play, Klinger shows that it is best to regard play as the form of behavior that is separated from the usual motivational contexts of work, learning, and problem-solving. This does not mean that beneficial effects cannot accrue from play. If we are to be clear in what we are describing, it is best to approach it from this type of separation of play from normal instrumental activity.

Klinger (1971) writes:

> Play is defined . . . as behavior other than (a) consummatory behavior, (b) instrumental behavior leading detectably to consummatory behavior or to a detectable goal extrinsic to the play activity itself, (c) competition with a standard of excellence, (d) socially prescribed, institutionalized or ritual behavior when it occurs in the context in which the prescription is socially sanctioned and enforced, and (e) behavior constrained by the requirements of social interaction [p. 20].

More concretely, play is behavior that is not obviously associated with direct satisfaction of biological needs such as eating, drinking, overt sexual gratification or the overcoming of immediate obstacles in one's life situation. It is also relatively free of any effort to meet standards set up by society. At least the standards of play, one might say, are established by the player himself within a context that need not be the same as those ordinarily observable in society.

Institutionalized rituals such as a wedding ceremony are quite different from the kind of make-believe or pretend wedding ceremonies depicted in the Bruegel painting. Play behavior in general also is relatively free of the formal requirements of social behavior, in the sense that the child need not be so concerned with proper conventions or with the taboos of society in the course of establishing a make-believe game. This definition of course separates symbolic play from formal rule or mastery games which have standards and also more social interaction possibilities. In the brief reference earlier to the combination of symbolic play with rules play in adolescent make-believe football games, it appears that one may, within the context of play, set up formal rules that are adhered to and still introduce additional make-believe elements that are not subject to formal convention or reality demands. Some of the participants in our make-believe football or baseball leagues had no qualms about using the names of famous players in their games—stars such as Babe Ruth or Lou Gehrig. The boys simply attributed some of the same skills to their created characters, but ignored the fact that these players had independent existences or in fact were already retired from active careers.

This "autotelic" definition of play (Klinger, 1971) has the advantage of freeing us from the difficulty of attempting a comprehensive view of the long-range outcomes of play linked to its origins. From this standpoint, we can mention a number of major efforts to understand how play develops and what its functions *for the child* are, irrespective of what it may later lead to. Gilmore (1966) has called attention to the fact that a number of theorists essentially view play within the general category of cathartic behavior, that is, behavior which represents an effort to *master* situations that were initially overwhelming and difficult to comprehend or which occasioned great fright or conflict.

Psychoanalytic Theory

In this sense, the psychoanalytic theory of play, perhaps the most influential certainly in clinical practice, represents a form of the catharsis theory. In papers published in 1908 (Freud, 1958) and 1911 (Freud, 1959), Freud, the great founder of psychoanalysis, examined the origins of fantasy and the creative processes of adults. He hypothesized that thought originates under conditions when the deprivation of a child's immediate gratification is so great that he is forced to "hallucinate" the image of a satisfying object, such as the mother's breast. This hallucinated image later becomes a source of at least partial drive satisfaction and permits the child to delay or control random restless movements and perhaps cries of distress, which might otherwise occur in the absence of the satisfying object when the drive has been aroused. This brief interval of delay becomes the foundation for the later development of the ego.

In this psychoanalytic view, much of childish play represents an attempt to satisfy drives partially or to resolve conflicts in the absence of a realistic opportunity to do so. Since many of the conflicts indeed are not between actual events and the child's capacity to satisfy needs, there is a great range of unsatisfied wishes in the child which form an increasing basis for an elaborated fantasy and play life. Freud felt that the play represented not merely pure wish-fulfilling tendencies, but also *mastery*—an attempt by repetition to cope with overwhelmingly anxiety-provoking situations. Freud was influenced in this direction by his observation of the so-called traumatic dreams of war veterans. The notion of *mastery* as an important component of play had also been proposed by Bühler (1930). Anna Freud (1937), Peller (1959), and Erikson (1940) have all extended the Freudian notions of the role of conflict and deprivation to play and have also emphasized its defensive functions as well as its role in adaptive mastery of anxiety.

More recently, Erikson (1963) has broadened the view of the role of play to include the mastery of reality and the creation of "model situations." This position is in keeping with the more recent ego psychology and with the formulation of Hartmann (1958) that fantasy may be regarded as an autonomous ego function, that is, a function developed without a conflict having occurred. Such theorizing seems to have opened the way for a more general theory of play. Yet this newer view sabotages in some respects the original Freudian emphasis on conflict, since it can be argued that if play grows out of normal adaptive development, then the so-called conflict uses of play for mastery of anxiety would represent only a special case of a more general function. The advantage of the new ego psychological position is that it brings psychoanalytic observations into line with more general psychological approaches, which makes possible the development of a cognitive orientation to play. Such an orientation is free of the difficult requirement of reducing all play to a very specific set of conflicts between the *id, ego,* and *super-ego* and the elaboration of symbolism and inference that has characterized so much of the clinical literature of play produced by psychoanalysts.

Piaget and Cognitive Theories

A more thoroughly worked out theory of the origins of play has been developed within the framework of a cognitive processing system by Jean Piaget (1962). For Piaget, play derives from the child working out two fundamental characteristics of his mode of experience and development. These are *accommodation*, which represents an attempt to imitate and interact physically with the environment, and *assimilation*, which represents the attempt to integrate externally-derived percepts or motor actions into the relatively limited number of schemata or differentiated motor and cognitive skills available at a particular age. Whereas mastery play clearly involves an attempt to accommodate to the environment as in the case of a child seeking to grasp a rattle or exploring the dimensions of movement of a mobile by pushing it back and forth and laughing at the motion, symbolic play seems more associated with the assimilation process. A child left to its own devices repeats phrases overheard or motor activities observed in adults, but within a framework so limited as to lead to what appear to adults to be quaint or curiously unrealistic actions.

A bright 3½-year-old child I know came back from his first day at nursery school quite downtrodden. His mother asked him what had gone wrong. He said that he had enjoyed the activities at nursery school well enough, but that at the close of the session he asked the teacher if he was now a lawyer. The teacher said that he was not and he was consequently quite disappointed. He then went on to explain that he overheard his father telling about how *he* had gone to school and become a lawyer. The boy thoroughly expected that this would be true for him as well.

On another occasion, the same child was observed in make-believe driving, as if operating a truck selling ice cream. He made the usual ding-a-ling noises and comments about different kinds of ice cream that he was selling. Asked about his game he replied, "I'm playing college." Further inquiry revealed that the child had also heard his father tell about the fact that he had worked as a Good Humor ice cream driver while in college.

Both these examples are instances in which the child overhears a snatch of adult conversation and then later attempts to assimilate this into a limited schema of knowledge with the result a gross distortion of reality, albeit from the adult's standpoint a "cute" one. Piaget would emphasize that much of children's play consists of this ongoing assimilation process. Gradually of course, as the child develops more differentiated schemata, the product of assimilation takes on less and less of the bizarre or fantasy quality and becomes more realistic. To the extent that realism is heavily involved, we are less likely to view the behavior as playful and more likely to see it as ordinary instrumental behavior.

Piaget does not minimize the mastery aspects of such play, but he does not especially focus on it in relation to conflict. In fact, it may be that much of the attribution of mastery of anxiety to certain types of child play may be more truly simple assimilation process, although we cannot be certain of this. For example, one of my children was just 5 years old at the time of the John F. Kennedy assassination. He overheard my wife calling me on the telephone to give me the news and also heard her put on the news broadcast herself. Shortly afterward he set up his phonograph and put on a record which we had acquired some months before—a humorous mimicry of the Kennedy family in the White House. He played this record again and again that afternoon and evening to the considerable distress of my wife and myself. For the adults, the sound of the President's voice as imitated on the record was most painful, immediately reviving the elaborate details of the memory of his death and all of the doubts and fears of the implication of this sudden situation. It seems likely, however, that for the child, all of this complex significance and perhaps indeed all of the meaning of death was less involved than his effort to relate what little he understood about Kennedy about whom so much was now being said, to his own limited schemata which consisted mainly of having heard the record in the past.

Schachtel (1959) has also attempted a similar interpretation of some of the repetitive behavior of children as representing not necessarily a mastery of anxiety, but a fundamental method of a child gradually integrating new information into a limited experiential background. Indeed, one might carry this notion even further and recognize that much of the humorousness and creativity attributed to the child and enjoyed so much in observing children then becomes the basis later for our enjoyment of humor, jokes, and clowning.

For Piaget, symbolic play goes on from about 18 months to the age of 7 when it gradually disappears from the observers' view as the child develops sufficient schemata, or it is transformed to the more obvious overt play of games with rules. Piaget, however, early recognized that the so-called egocentric thought of the child does not completely disappear even as he or she becomes socialized from school age on. Such speech is internalized in the form of fantasies and related private events (Piaget, 1932). There is certainly a good deal of reason to accept some process of this type on the basis of observation as other investigators such as Luria (1932), Freud (1959), Singer (1966), and Klinger (1971) all have noted. At the same time, there are indications that, at least for some children, make-believe play goes on until considerably later in childhood and early adolescence as already noted in the description of boys' make-believe football games.

Klinger (1971) has examined in some detail the possibility that both fantasy in the form of private imagery and make-believe play are discernible in children from a relatively early age, and that the younger child is indeed capable of more private imagery than Piaget seemed to feel. Smilansky (1968) also called attention to the fact that the imaginative play in the child during the school years does not necessarily become completely realistic. If anything, the greater range of experiences with unusual stories, characters from fiction or television, etc. make it possible for children at older ages to engage in even more bizarre and strange stories, albeit more organized from an adult's standpoint. This observation will also be examined in the study by Gottlieb described in a later chapter.

More recently, Millar (1968) and Klinger (1971) have carried further a cognitive view such as that of Piaget. They approach imaginative play with greater emphasis upon our awareness of feedback processes and the coding and signaling characteristics of human behavior. As Millar (1968) notes,

> the pretense of make-believe is not a cloak for something else, or behavior intended to mislead, but thinking (re-coding and rehearsal) in action with real objects as props .... The apparent paradoxes of various kinds of play arise mainly in conditions which leave behavior relatively unorganized, or before it is fully organized, integrated or streamlined [p. 256].

The advantages of positions like those of Piaget, Millar, or Klinger as well as the extension of these viewpoints, which will be described in a subsequent chapter, is that they permit us to view play in a broader context. We are not required to describe play simply as a specific, adaptive function or as a response to conflict, deprivation, or the need for mastery. There seems no question that play can be used for conflict reduction or mastery, but one is hardput to explain all forms of play of a symbolic nature on that basis. It seems more reasonable to view the situation as part of an overall assimilation with a limited range of cognitive schemata and then to move from that point to the ways in which certain defensive or conflict-reducing behavior may also participate in this general process. This approach also opens the way for greater incorporation into the theory of the direct influence of adults who foster imaginative behavior by story telling or establishing situations that children are likely to imitate. It thus becomes possible to relate a relatively pure cognitive theory such as that of Piaget to the kind of social learning theory that is being shown to have powerful impact on child development, as evidenced in recent work by Bandura (1971).

What seems most clear to the student of child psychology at this stage of our development in research is that most of the theories described previously are still far too general as regards their relation to specific play activities. They also lack sufficient basis in formal research, which includes systematic observation under controlled conditions and reasonably controlled experimental study. Piaget's extensive work on the imagery of children is based largely on a small number of specific questions that the child is asked. There is a minimum of formal experimentation or observation of the natural play of children. The extensive experimental work generated by Lewin and his students has focused primarily on the substitute value of a variety of real and fantasy tasks, but again is not focused primarily on the spontaneous play of the children. Much of the remaining information we have is based largely on anecdotal reports often on the observer's own children.

A surprising number of references in the literature of children cite specific examples given by Piaget of his interview of a particular child. Similarly, the psychoanalytic literature refers again and again to Freud's account of Little Hans (whom he hardly observed directly at all). While there are a great many reports in the clinical literature describing diagnostic and treatment use in play observation of children, these also tend to be of individual cases and necessarily of children with severe enough emotional problems to come to the attention of psychoanalysts or child therapists. There is really a paucity of studies set up to test formally kinds of hypothesis raised by the theorists already cited.

A first attempt by Gilmore (1966) may be noted. This study sought to determine which types of toys children would prefer when the toys were varied in terms of novelty or simplicity and their relationship to the anxiety of the children. It represents an attempt to compare Piaget's theory of play with its emphasis on the attraction of novel stimuli to the psychoanalytic theory of play, where the emphasis would be on the conflictful and anxiety-relevant toys. The main point is that at least the beginning has been made toward more systematic observation and tests, although the level of generality of the theories cited makes precise tests very difficult. Another example of an approach to testing specific theories about play can be seen in the chapter by Biblow.

The Work of the Opies

A remarkable collection of information on children's games and lore is currently being assembled by Opie and Opie (1959, 1969). This indefatigable couple has surveyed a good deal of the information on children in the British Empire and much foreign literature. They have carried out extensive observations of the specific games, chants, songs, and related lore of children. They are not greatly concerned with theory or with the development of an integrated point of view. Rather, they are great cataloguers and researchers of the tremendous variety of games and styles of children's play all over the world. Although they quote Bertrand Russell, who refers to the recapitulation theory of play, that is, the child repeating in his play the life of the early human race, this view seems less significant for them than the qualities of exploration, mastery, and sheer enjoyment of fantasy that characterizes most play.

> As long as the action of the game is of a child's own making he is ready, even anxious, to sample the perils of which this world has such plentiful supply. In the security of the game he makes acquaintance with insecurity, he is able to rationalize absurdities, reconcile himself to not getting his own way, assimilate reality (Piaget), act heroically without being in danger. The thrill of a chase is accentuated by viewing the chaser not as a boy in short trousers, but as a bull. It is not a classmate's back he rides upon but a knight's fine charger. It is not a party of other boys but side skirmishes with Indians, Robbers, Men from Mars. And, always provided that the environment is of his own choosing, he—or she—is even prepared to meet the "things that happen in the dark," playing games that would seem strange amusement if it was thought they were being taken literally: "Murder in the Dark," "Ghosties in the Garret," "Moonlight Starlight, Bogie won't come out Tonight." And yet, within the context of the game, these alarms are *taken literally* [Opie & Opie, 1969, p. 300].

The vast majority of the games presented by the Opies are games with rules or games that involve some forms of tag and chase. There is only minimal fantasy, except to the extent that the repetition of various rhymes may in themselves invoke imagery. For example,

Charlie Chaplin
Sat on a pin,
How many inches
Did it go in?
[Opie & Opie, 1969, p. 57]

I'll follow my mother to market
To buy a ha'penny basket;
When she comes home,
She'll break my bones,
For falling over
The cherrystones
[Opie & Opie, 1969, p. 104].

Of the dozens of little poems and quotes that the Opies collect, it seems likely that at least some would indeed evoke imagery along with near repetitive verbal act. I can recall from early childhood my efforts trying to understand a little rhyme, "One little pig went to market, one little pig stayed home . . . " It is my recollection that even though relatively young, I had difficulty truly understanding some of the implications of the poem. I was struggling to visualize what it looked like for the little pig to come running home crying "Wee—Wee—Wee." As I recall, since the only pigs I ever saw were in picture books, they were essentially little animals with long snouts that ran on two legs and seemed more like elves to me.

The problem with attempting to assume imagery in chasing and other relatively structured games is the limitations on inference that a strict scientific operationalism imposes. For serious scientific work, this restriction cannot be taken lightly and it seems best to try to focus primarily on those games and play where the inference of imagery seems at least better established and more reliably judged. This is the case in games the Opies call *acting* and *pretend* games. Acting games would appear to involve somewhat less imagery since the children generally are allotted specific parts and reenact a definite story according to a formula and well-established plot line. Many of the acting games, however, allow ample opportunity for improvisation, and also for the development of sufficient involvement so that the children become quite frightened when the games take on a sinister aspect.

For example, there is a game called variously "Old Man in the Well" or "Ghost in the Well" which the Opies are able to trace around Britain to Australia, Ireland, and over to Austria in almost identical form. It follows a specific line in which the mother sends the child for water. The child finds an old man in the well and calls the mother to see him. Then there follows a specific dialogue such as the following:

Mother:	*What are you doing here?*
Old Man:	*Picking up sand.*
Mother:	*What do you want sand for?*
Old Man:	*To sharpen my needles.*
Mother:	*What do you want needles for?*
Old Man:	*To make a bag.*
Mother:	*What do you want a bag for?*
Old Man:	*To keep my knives in.*
Mother:	*What do you want knives for?*
Old Man:	*To cut off your heads.*
Mother:	*Then catch us if you can.*
	[Opie & Opie, 1969, p. 306].

The Opies quote someone recalling this game from her childhood who indicates that the game was truly terrifying. Even though she had often been the old man and knew that the old man in a given game was just one of the other children, she still became quite frightened in the course of play.

It would appear then that at least some of these acting games, while they are largely ritualistic and mainly involve memory for the lines to be spoken and sequences of steps to be taken, also touch on more complex attitudes and represent a mixture that calls for mastery, fantasies perhaps even of castration fears, and the child's own exploration of the meaning of danger and evil. One wonders to what extent the great variety and charm of these acting games still persists today in the United States. Is it possible that television may have provided an alternative both in filling time and in its presentation of material? Teaching games and passing them along from generation to generation may well be terminated as a result of the information explosion.

The *pretend* games as the Opies call them, are essentially the symbolic play or make-believe play, upon which we are concentrating in this volume. The Opies devote relatively little space to symbolic play perhaps because its essential idiosyncrasy and great variety make it more difficult to classify. Each child is, in effect, playing his own private game. Occasionally, children play fantasy games in small groups, but with the content largely determined by the specific nature of the children and their setting.

The Opies call attention to the practicality of a great deal of group pretend play. Children in Berlin, shortly after the building of the wall, were observed shooting at each other across miniature walls. In the United States, after the assassination of President Kennedy, many children were found playing assassination games. They note that the Roman playwright Seneca observed children mimicking the judges and magistrates and playing out public trials. I recall a brief craze that spread among teenagers in my neighborhood shortly after Pearl Harbor. One young boy, upon seeing another approaching, would spread his arms out and charge at him shouting, "Colin Kelly and the battleship Haruna!" making airplane noises and attempting to knock over the other fellow. The Opies call attention to what they call the game that has proved "the most terrible indictment ever made against man," children in the Auschwitz concentration camp playing "going to the gas chamber."

Among the pretend games that are listed and described by the Opies are "Mothers and Fathers" (or what in America is more likely to be called "Playing House"), "Playing School," "Playing Road Accidents," "Playing Horses," Storybook games based on various stories or television scenes, War Games, Cops and Robbers, and Fairies and Witches. The latter game seems to have gone out of fashion in the United States, but is replaced by games involving vampires and sinister characters, ghouls, zombies, Frankenstein, monsters, etc. which have been available to the children on television or have been communicated to them by older children who have seen them in the movies or on television.

It should be noted that in constrast to the emphasis of Piaget on the fading of symbolic play at around school age, the Opies report considerable fantasy play activity at least among British children through ages 11 and 12 with many of the group fantasy games taking place in the age period from 5 through 12. Undoubtedly, there are a great many factors besides age which determine the choice of games. These must include important cultural differences in the acceptance of

pretend play in children, cultural differences in the necessity for children beginning work at an early age with only a limited opportunity for any spontaneous play, and the opportunities for children to be off by themselves in relatively unsupervised settings, with a physical environment **conducive** to a variety of fantasy activities. The Opies are particularly strong **in their** feelings that children need environments that are not well ordered **and** structured in order to develop a greater flexibility in their play. We shall see an attempt at a beginning study of this problem, the role of the toy structure as part of the physical environment in inducing varied play activities in the chapter by Pulaski.

While the Opies are not much oriented toward theory, they do provide us with a sense of the tremendous range and complexity of children's play activities. They also point to impressive continuities over the centuries in children's play. As hinted earlier, one has the sense perhaps, that some of these continuities will be changed dramatically by the explosion of popular media, especially television, in the past two decades so that the world of play may be considerably different in the centuries to come. The influence may be more upon content of play than upon structural aspects of play and we have as yet no reason to believe that there is any change in the occurrence of make-believe in children's play. If anything, television has probably increased the likelihood of imaginative play for many children who otherwise might not have been provided with the variety of material that becomes the basis of assimilation. It should be noted again that in contrast with the Opies, whose emphasis is largely upon small group games, the focus of the present volume is upon relatively solitary play of children or playing in pairs or extremely small groups. In this sense, we are here concerned more with the relation of symbolic play to the development of imagery in the individual child.

Broader Implications of Imaginative Play: Competence, Exploration, and Creativity

So far, the discussion of the theory has been limited to specific theories about play as a special form of behavior. Another way to approach the problem of play is through attempting to see to what extent it contributes to more general theories of behavior or personality structure. Berlyne (1969) has argued against treating play as a special type of behavior, and has urged that it be viewed within the context of a learning theory model. Certainly any comprehensive personality theory must be able to incorporate so common a behavior as play.

The psychoanalytic theory of personality has drawn heavily on the content of children's play and fantasies in support of particular aspects of the theory. The insights of Freud about the sexual and aggressive concerns of the child are exemplified in many children's games and in the content of much symbolic play. Certainly there are adequately documented instances of children playing games that involve Oedipal conflicts of various kinds, sibling rivalry, and specific references to cutting and killing that certainly support many of the presumed basic psychosexual conflict areas developed from psychoanalysis. Until the 1960s, much of the emphasis in psychoanalytic theory was upon the role of fundamental biological drives such as hunger, thirst, sex (in a somewhat broadened sense of body sensuality), and aggression as fundamental motives of human behavior. From this viewpoint, the stimulus for play would generally be the working out of a drive that could not be directly satisfied.

Analytic theories have stressed energic constructs and the displacement of energies as a consequence of frustrations or conflicts. In his last efforts to systematize psychoanalytic theory, David Rapaport (1960 a, b) still emphasized that the fundamental model of dynamics was the child experiencing the arousal of the drive followed by restlessness, the occurrence of a satisfier such as the bottle or breast, and finally the subsidence of restlessness. The second phase of this development was the occurrence of a hallucinated image of the satisfying object at the time of the arousal of the drive. This hallucinated image delayed the occurrence of the restlessness until consummation was possible. This model, based upon the hunger drive, has proven most unsatisfactory to many theorists who have still sought to preserve some of the insights of psychoanalytic thinking and clinical research. There is, for example, ample evidence that a drive theory expressed in terms of a hunger or thirst model is far from satisfactory as a basis for explaining human motivation. How many children called to supper in the thickening twilight, already well past their usual time for eating, have responded with annoyed shouts of *Wait a minute, Ma, the game isn't over yet!*

The work of the ego psychologists such as Hartmann (1958), has broadened the possibilities of psychoanalysis by emphasizing the degree to which there is much behavior that develops for sheer adaptiveness, rather than out of conflict between basic drives and reality. While most of the ego psychologists still tend to focus primarily on the drive model, its impact is greatly weakened once the notion of autonomous ego functions is introduced. Erikson (1963), in his extension of analytic theory to take into account striking cultural differences in child development, has been forced to recognize greater patterns of adaptation and has tried to preserve the drive notion only at the expense of rechristening the drives under the headings of more general interpersonal constructs such as *trust.*

In 1959, two publications appeared which seem to have tipped the balance away from the drive theories. The limitations of a biologically based theory (in the form proposed by Rapaport as the fundamental psychoanalytic model), have been increasingly evident to theorists even within the psychoanalytic group (Holt, 1967; Klein, 1967). Every parent realizes that even a relatively strong hunger drive can give way before the excitement for play and social activity. Schachtel (1959) has developed an elaborate alternative to a drive-reduction model of behavior based on the affective or emotional and cognitive structure of the child. He stresses the fact that the limited cognitive structure of the child makes his experience essentially different from that of the adult. The repetitive aspects of children's play, for example, are a function of the attempt to assimilate material that is far more novel to the child than it is to the adult. Until a complex new schema is available, the child has a strong motivation to confront the new situation. Schachtel as well as White (1959, 1960, 1964) also call attention to the fact that much of the more exploratory and creative behavior of children is manifested under conditions of relative biological drive satisfaction. Therefore, the more traditional view of all behavior as a consequence of aroused biological drive seems scarcely tenable.

Although White (1959, 1960) stays closer to the psychoanalytic model, he adduces weighty arguments against the basic drive notion. He includes much evidence from animal research that learning is not necessarily a function of drive reduction and that there are learning sets that develop out of the very novelty of a task itself rather than as a function of the relative hunger, thirst, or sexual deprivation state of the animal. White also draws heavily on the work of Berlyne in his studies of curiosity and exploratory behavior and on the observations of Piaget which describe the fundamental role of curiosity and manipulative interest in the child and very young infant.

In a sensitive and subtle analysis, White (1960) examines the psychosexual development model of psychoanalysis, the oral, anal, phallic and genital stages of development and their broadened alternative meanings proposed by Erikson (1940), e.g., *basic trust, autonomy,* etc. White shows that one must make excessive assumptions to derive the complex behavior of the child from the working out of partial sexual drives during oral and anal development in order to justify complex, subsequent behavior. Instead, he proposes that a good deal of the child's striving is part of the normal development of competence. If we regard the child from the standpoint of his attempts to use his own skills and capacities effectively within the limits of his motor and cognitive development, we can encompass a great deal more of the actual behavior of the child.

For example, discussing the development of imagination during the fourth and fifth years, White emphasizes that this is a period when the child has become more aware of different adult roles. His capacities permit him to "clothe plain objects like blocks with all the attributes of airplanes, vehicles, animals and people [White, 1960, p. 123]." As White puts it, "If we consider the bearing of these developments on social competence, it is clear that the child has reached a point of understanding where for the first time he can contemplate his place in the family and his relation to other people in general [p. 123]."

This Oedipal phase in psychoanalytic theory continues to be described on the basis of the child's inferiority to the father in the sexual sphere and his feelings that he will not be able to match the father in sexual relationship to the mother. White points out that this is too narrow a perspective.

From the point of view of competence, . . . sexual inferiority is by no means greater than many other inferiorities such as stature, strength, speed of running, distance one can throw a ball. Father can start the power lawn mower and control it; he can drive the car; for the modern child these must be obvious and hopeless tokens of his superiority [p. 124].

Viewed from this angle, it should be clear that White is posing an important shift in the view of the developmental process and indeed a fundamental shift in our approach to motivation. If we now relate symbolic play to this we see that White comes closer to the position taken by Piaget with the additional emphasis perhaps on the importance of mastery of social roles, something that Piaget does not stress to the same extent. We can now expect that a very careful study of imaginative play of children will help us not only understand the special qualities of play, but will also play a part in the overall development of a theory of human motivation and of behavior theory more generally. The task of the psychologist is not simply to gather systematic observations, although these are sparse enough in the whole area of spontaneous play behavior of children. The problem is still one of finding the best kind of model that will integrate the array of observational data we can encompass. The psychoanalytic model as it developed during the first half of this century was truly exciting because more than any other approach it seemed to cover a tremendous range of behavior, especially pathological forms, and because it did indeed illuminate the special features of disturbance and anxiety that emerge in children's play. But the dependence of the psychoanalytic model upon a hunger drive construct seriously limits its generality and it would appear that psychologists and behavioral scientists more generally are ready to move on to newer models.

Among these new models are those which focus upon competence striving and the development of self actualization. There are also models which place special emphasis upon the interrelationship of information processing (as a key human function) with a differentiated affective system. What is meant by the latter term is that it is likely that man has through natural selection, developed a limited but perhaps reasonably specialized set of emotional responses which are a function of the rate and persistence of his processing of incoming information. This viewpoint has been proposed by theorists as diverse as Schachtel (1959); McClelland, Atkinson, Clark, and Lowell (1953), and Tomkins (1962, 1963).

Within the cognitive-affective framework, one can begin to consider the possibility that the imaginative play of children represents an effort to organize the available experience and at the same time utilize motor and cognitive capacities to their fullest. The consequence of this position is that to the extent that the child interacts with novel material, which is within his capacity for mastery, he will continue to show interest, alertness, and positive emotional reaction. Indeed, as he reaches a peak of familiarity with the material and mastery, he will show the positive emotions of joy and laughter (Tomkins, 1962;

Singer, 1966). If the material that he must deal with is presented too rapidly without an opportunity for him to assimilate it effectively, he will startle or become frightened. If confronted for an excessive period of time with a high rate of unassimilable, unfamiliar material, the child will become angry or depressed. While there is little support in the sense of formal data of this model as it applies to children's play, we shall spell it out in greater detail later, and will attempt to show how it can begin to be approached experimentally as in the chapter by Biblow.

Creativity and Divergent Production

We have thus far emphasized the relationship of play behavior in its more general aspect without specific attention to the matter of individual differences. There is, however, a considerable body of research to which the study of play may also contribute. In view of the extensive work on individual differences in the cognitive and personality spheres, Guilford (1967) has proposed that we regard behavior as encompassing both *convergent* and *divergent* processes.

Convergent processes involve those activities on which the ultimate decision is a single response about which the society agrees, e.g.: Two plus two equals four. Guilford, however, has attempted to show that we must go beyond this relatively limited notion if we are to understand the range of cognitive processes that are of value in normal behavior. Divergent processes are those in which each individual is capable of generating a variety of novel responses which may or may not overlap with those of others. These novel reactions form a basis for what we would ultimately call creative behavior. The advantage of using the term "divergent production," however, is that it makes no automatic value judgment. It simply involves processes such as the ability to think of many different associations to a particular stimulus (the well known "How many uses are there for a brick?"). This type of cognitive fluidity may or may not be a useful function, depending on particular psychological circumstances.

While Getzels and Jackson (1962) have tended to use the word "creativity" in this respect, and Torrance (1962, 1963) has elaborated extensively on this work with many useful techniques applicable to children, there remains the fact that what is ultimately creative is a social judgment that comes in adult life, often enough years after the "creative" person has passed from this earth. In this sense, one is best advised to recognize that there are important and measurable cognitive individual differences characterized by differential capacity toward divergent production rather than referring to differences in creativity.

An intriguing study of a group of English boys carried out by Hudson (1966) yields some evidence in support of the notion that relatively early in childhood one can discern striking differences in style with some boys strongly oriented toward convergent thinking and others more strongly oriented toward divergent processes. The outcome, in terms of school work and patterns of interest, suggests that the "convergent" boys are more likely to move in the direction of scientific types of endeavor, whereas the divergent production groups move more toward artistic and literary types of interest and success. Hudson does not propose that either style has distinct advantages over the other, but that both are essentially parts of the overall human potential.

Similar approaches to the question of early stylistic development in information processing and related behavior by children are presented by Wallach and Kogan (1965). Their data also support the notion of early differences in predisposition to associational fluidity patterns in children. The work on analytic and impulsive styles of information processing by Kagan (1966), which has generated a considerable body of subsequent work on relatively young children, also indicates the importance of stylistic differences in the young child's approach to learning about his world.

The likelihood is that a study of play behavior particularly as it bears on predisposition of certain children toward greater or less imaginative play will contribute to the more general question of the development of convergent and divergent processes and perhaps ultimately of the issue of fundamental cognitive styles. The attempt to study both the issue of individual differences in imaginative play and the general nature of imaginative play is a key feature of this book and will be elaborated in subsequent chapters.

It is of interest to know that in the extensive research of the Bank Street School studies (Minuchin, Biber, Shapiro, & Zimiles, 1969), rather intriguing findings concerning early differences in imaginative play for groups of 9-year-old children in four different types of school settings were observed. The only difference in the general area of imaginative research that emerged between the schools was that those children in the most progressive of the four schools tended to show consistent stylistic differences in their play. Children from the "Conrad School" tended to be rated as invoking more often symbolic and imaginary aspects in their play. They tended to use more supernatural characters and more scenes that were not easily pinned down to the direct reality. The authors feel that it is likely that "The mode of magical and imaginary expression also reflected an educational atmosphere which encouraged a full use of imagination and creative processes without constant commitment to the literal and realistic [Minuchin *et al.*, 1969, p. 239]." Clearly, a more detailed and careful series of studies focusing specifically on imaginative play will also have implications for the overall educational process and, as we shall see in Chapter VI, specific attention to the development of the imaginativeness can yield relatively rapid results.

In conclusion, we can assert that there is no dearth of theoretical material and conceptual models available for dealing with the imaginative play of children.

What we most seriously lack are large bodies of formal data collected under conditions specified in sufficient detail that they can be replicated by others. In addition, we need a set of categories and formal tools for measurement of play behavior. In the subsequent chapters, we shall therefore address ourselves to an approach to the development of tools and then move on to an examination of some specific studies that elaborate on these procedures before finally turning toward some further theoretical suggestions and possibilities for future research.

CHAPTER II

Observing Imaginative Play: Approaches to Recording, Rating, and Categorizing

Although the play of children has been employed for psychotherapeutic and psychodiagnostic purposes for almost 40 years, there has as yet been little formal study of spontaneous play viewed from the perspective of the introduction of imaginary elements. A great variety of useful methods for studying the personality of children through testing and observation have been presented by Murphy (1956) and her collaborators who, in their work at the Sarah Lawrence and Vassar nursery schools in the 1930s and 1940s, pioneered the development of most of the techniques for systematic study of children. Excellent and well-organized reviews of approaches to studying motivation and emotion in children through the use of varied play and projective methods are available in chapters by Miller (1960) and Bronfenbrenner and Ricciuti (1960). A great variety of games, doll and related play techniques with toys, and various methods of rating play behavior of children are available in books such as those by Murphy (1956) and Hartley, Frank, and Goldenson (1952).

Especially important from the standpoint of systematic, psychological observation and theory have been the series of studies carried out by the Sears (and their various collaborators) in which the focus was on doll play, with careful rating for evidence of aggression (Sears, 1951; Sears, Maccoby, & Levin, 1957; Sears, Whiting, Nowlis, & Sears, 1953). Another series of important studies which involves direct observation of children in a variety of play situations has

27

been carried out by Beller (1959). Doll-play studies have been especially fruitful in the testing of specific hypotheses, such as the role of parental attitudes and punishment in influencing aggressive doll-play. At the same time, there is a semistructured quality to most of the doll-play studies which limits their value as basis for describing the more general play behavior of the children. In addition, the emphasis upon aggression within the play situation itself does not tell enough about the degree to which overt and direct aggression against peers or property are characteristic of the spontaneous play of the child.

Another approach to studying aggressive behavior in children's play has emerged in the stimulating work of Patterson and his collaborators (Patterson, 1960; Patterson, Littmen, & Bricker, 1967). These studies are especially intriguing because they involve careful and systematic observation of the reinforcement contingencies that occur spontaneously in the course of play behavior and which foster subsequent, aggressive reactions. Especially important in Patterson's work is the close observation of specific behavior with, at least at the outset, only a minimum of interpretation and with a focus on specific sequences of interaction. If the field of child research, particularly in the area of play, has suffered from anything, it has been excessive overinterpretation of the bits of behavior observed generally speaking in the therapist's office or play room. While it would be impossible to make sense of the natural play of children without some kinds of categorization, it is especially important that we keep elaborate constructs to a minimum and begin by very careful recording and examination of behavioral sequences.

Examples of some of the few studies involving fairly careful direct observation of children may be noted briefly. Furfey (1930) watched the street play of boys and found that two-thirds of his sample of 8-year-olds engaged in make-believe play (certainly a larger figure than Piaget's position would predict). Gump and Sutton-Smith (1955) found that the particular setting, a camp in which the boys played, strongly influenced the kind of play observed by systematic recording. A pioneering study of direct observation of nursery school children was carried out by Parten (1933) who watched the play of 34 nursery schoolers for a minute a day, and obtained 60 behavioral samples. She reported on the size, sex composition, and IQ similarities among play groups. Sandbox play was by far the most preferred and playing "family," "house," or "dolls" (make-believe games) was second in preference. At least for Parten's group (in a university nursery school) make-believe games were highly favored. Sex differences in specific playthings were also documented in an early study by Van Alstyne (1932) who also observed nursery schoolers systematically.

Currently, very extensive observational data have been collected by Eifermann (1971) in her work with Israeli children in the 6–14-year-old age group. Careful sampling in different settings and with multiple observers was employed. Interobserver reliabilities could be obtained in a reasonably controlled fashion.

Records of weather conditions, physical setting, game lengths, number of participants, etc. were recorded on data sheets. Eifermann and her co-workers could
then test hypotheses derived from Piaget about age changes with respect to particular games. Thus, for example, games with rules while increasing sharply
between ages 6 and 10 or 11, show a consistent decline from ages 12 to 14.
Support for Piaget's feeling that make-believe play declines after ages 6—8 was
found, although some persistence of such play into high school age was observed. Contrary to Smilansky's (1968) report on the disadvantaged, poor
children were found to engage in more extensive make-believe play (at older
ages) than middle-class children. The Arabic cultural groups in Israel showed a
very high percentage of symbolic play from ages 6 through 8. Eifermann's
approach is valuable because it permits tests of specific developmental hypotheses. It does not, however, call for continuous recording of actual behavior, but
rather for labeling of one play into certain categories by the observers.

Some Examples of Spontaneous Play

Our concern here of course is the kind of play that involves introduction of
imagery. Let us begin by looking at some examples of the spontaneous play of
some 4-year-olds in a middle-class suburban nursery school. The protocols that
follow were written by college students who were trained to observe and record
play as part of a project under the direction of Dorothy Singer and myself.
Notice that some interpretation of mood is necessary, but beyond that most of
the reports represent careful behavioral description. Since there are always two
observers recording each 10-min sequence of play, we have a way of checking on
the reliability of the observers and evaluating the degree of discrepancy between
them. Only one protocol for each child will be presented here, however.

> Leona is sitting outside near the sandbox with two girls and she says to one girl in
> an annoyed voice, *I don't care.* She walks away indignantly. She then returns and
> says to one of the girls, *If you say that again I'll kick you with the dirt.* She says,
> *I want that*, pointing to an object the girls are playing with. When they object,
> Leona says angrily, *Well, I need it!* The girls in whining voices ask for it back.
> Leona moves over to the swings and she and another girl ask the teacher for the
> swings which are occupied by two boys. The teacher asks the boys to let Leona and
> the other girl have a turn. Leona and the other child run happily over to the swings
> and jump on them. Swinging lightly Leona starts to talk to the girl about a "trailer."
> Her companion says, *We're going the same height.* Leona does not respond. Leona
> gets off the swing but when a boy darts toward it, she seems to change her mind and
> runs back to it. Then she walks away frowning toward the opposite end of the yard
> and climbs on the jungle gym. Leona is in a contorted position and plays on the bars
> alone. The teacher tells her to be careful. She sits on the bars and watches the
> children in the play house. She calls, *Wendy! Wendy!* then resumes her contorted
> position. She asks Lee Ann, *Can you do this?* and demonstrates a new position.

She watches the other children, stretches out on the bars and plays half-heartedly on the jungle gym.

Gena is alone playing with a fire truck, a plastic horse, and an elephant. She is continually changing expressions, talking and singing to her animals, to the truck and to herself. She says, *Hey, Batman, this is a job for you!* Then she begins banging the elephant and screaming softly also in a somewhat singing voice. Then she crawls across the floor to a boy playing nearby and then walks back to the fire engine. She pushes the fire engine backward and settles near the wall. She turns briefly to watch the teacher talking to two girls who are making noise with the blocks. Then she begins playing with plastic animals and singing softly to herself. Then she turns to the boys at the blackboard. *Hey, Batman, you're coming to our house!* Now she is banging the elephant on the floor and again places the elephant and a horse in the fire engine. Then she takes the elephant, climbs him up the ladder. *Down! Up! Put the ladder up!* Next she gets a giraffe plastic toy. She places it on the ladder. Two boys come near her to watch but she is oblivious to them and they leave. She seems completely absorbed in her play. She gets a larger elephant, makes sounds as if the elephant and the giraffe were talking. *Hey, get the giraffe, giraffe, giraffe!* Then singing to herself. Now she holds all three animals and places all in the fire engine pushing it towards the nearest wall. *Hey, Batman.* At this point the teacher tells her to come and sit next to her. She kneels on the bench facing the teacher, fingers in her mouth, and her other hand holding the fire engine ladder. She sits on one leg but then gets up slowly on another. Another girl comes by. Now she is alone because the teacher has become distracted by some other events. The teacher calls her to come back again and she returns quietly. Gena watches the magnet that the teacher is holding, looks around and doesn't seem to be paying attention. She leans on her hand, stands up and sits again with her hand against her cheek, mouth open as she points to the correct answers in a reading discrimination exercise, smiles when told she is correct, now she begins to intently look at the picture still with her fingers in her mouth.

Scott is sitting on the floor playing with tracks and plastic animals. He takes a large hippopotamus with its mouth open and a small one and begins having the larger one be pounced on by the small one. He also makes noises of fighting and growling while he's doing this. The baby hippo is again put on the large one but this time says in a baby voice, *Mommy, mommy!* He next puts the giraffe on the large hippopotamus and says, *Cuckoo, cuckoo.* He then puts the elephant in the pan, lays it down and says, *Ooh, I'm sleepy.* He then bangs another animal together with the elephant hitting another girl in the room at the same time. He starts throwing the animals in the air and says, *Get out before I kick you out the window.* He puts the elephant on the girl's head, watches it fall and says *Boom,* then he takes the elephant and says to a toy lion, *Hey, would you like to come over to my house?* He pounds the lion with the elephant who is saying, *I warned you, I warned you, I warned you.* Then he repeats this same phrase a minute later as he has the two animals confronting each other.

He takes the elephant and then rocks it in his arms and begins singing it a lullaby, *Rock-a-bye-baby on a treetop.* At the end of the song he drops the elephant on the floor forcefully. He becomes aware of the observer, turns, smiles slightly, and winks. Then returns to his animals, picks up the lion and says, *Go see your mama.*

The preceding three samples of 10 min of observation of the children's free play make it clear that there are variations in the degree to which make-believe play can be observed in an almost identical setting, under fairly similar play conditions. All of the children in these particular examples have shown some make-believe play, but it should be obvious to the reader that there is an increase in the amount of time given over to make-believe from the first through the third child. One could, just by examining samples even brief as these, expand extensively on the many aspects of child behavior that are exemplified in this situation.

We see the limited vocabulary and attention span of even these reasonably untroubled youngsters. They seem to play in bursts and then move away partly in response to changing external situation or to noticing new play possibilities like the swings or jungle gym. We also notice the tendency to substitute sound effects and noises for full spoken sentences and the use of phrases in snatches undoubtedly heard from their parents now being assimilated into their limited schemata of knowledge and being attributed to the animals and smaller play things.

Of course, we can question whether the aspects of make-believe shown for example, in having the animals fight with each other or in telling the animal to go to sleep, truly reflect the introduction of imagery here. A strict behaviorist might limit himself simply to the overt spoken expression without making an assumption of implicit language processes. By using their more formal questioning technique, Piaget and Inhelder (1971) have attempted to show that some type of internally generated response for imagery is essential in dealing with more complex material. It is hard to avoid the feeling as one reads the protocols and watches the children that some centrally emitted cognitive material from long-term memory storage is not being produced in the form of auditory and visual imagery at the same time as the child is carrying out a pretend game.

This issue of the occurrence of imagery is extremely important and bears very much on the model of cognitive development and of learning in childhood that must ultimately be proposed. The work of Rohwer (1970) would seem to support the notion that, at least to some extent, the development of imagery as an elaborated symbolic representation of percepts is a skill that depends in part on the child's exposure to certain social experiences. In telling the little elephant to lie down and go to sleep, the child inevitably must not only speak those words, but try to reconstitute from long-term memory the experience of going to sleep in the form of actually seeing his own bed, rehearing the sound of his mother singing the lullaby, and perhaps experiencing some of the kinesthetic sensations associated with snuggling down into the covers and preparing for bed. All of these memories now occur at the same time as he is in a classroom looking at a plastic elephant. These associated images may now become part of a new stimulus situation that the child has created and to which he may react by forming a new schema. In this sense, then, the make-believe play, if it operates in the fashion described, forms the basis for creation of novel environments which then generate their own feedback and further complex memories. If this is the case, then we can begin to see how much learning may indeed take place in the course of spontaneous play, and how much the entire cognitive development of the child may be related to the degree to which the whole series of novel environments of this kind are generated by the child.

Developing Rating Procedures for Play Samples

We now confront the problem of how to take samples of spontaneous behavior and score them systematically according to some reasonably reliable criteria. By reliable, we mean the likelihood that two observers will first record the identical behavior witnessed either directly or perhaps on a videotape and will then proceed to agree on their interpretation of this behavior along certain specified dimensions. Murphy (1956) has indicated a large number of interesting dimensions along which one might attempt to rate the ongoing play or other observed behavior of children.

We can begin at the simplest level and children's movements rate on a 7-point scale for *tempo* or *speed of movements,* for *energy level* beginning with little motor energy and ending with extremely vigorous activities. We can also score for the *area of movement* shown by the child from staying in one place to covering a great deal of ground within the room. One could then proceed to somewhat more interpretative observations such as the degree of *response to people* as measured by interested watching of people, moving toward them, or lack of such reaction. Next, one can move even to more complex interpretations such as *self-enjoyment,* the degree to which the child seems to be enjoying his own body, responding directly to it, or seems to be indifferent to body or clothing and is utterly unself-conscious. Even higher levels of inference are involved in rating introversion—extraversion such as "imposes his own ideas on external reality [Murphy, 1956, p. 402]," or, at the other pole, "rarely stops to daydream."

Inevitably, the decision about which set of ratings to use for a given study already involves some implicit hypotheses about what is worth studying in psychology. In effect, part of the scientific enterprise lies in beginning with the careful examination of what the risks are of limiting oneself to relatively small number of variables which can be reasonably well controlled for the purposes of a delimited experiment for formal investigation. Inevitably, this means giving up some information or some kinds of observation to concentrate on others that are expected to yield useful information within a certain area. In this sense, the present emphasis on imaginativeness in play clearly is eliminating other aspects of cognitive and emotional development. At the same time, unless we do some kind of narrower focusing, we can never be sure of whether we are really touching on reasonably consistent and reliable dimensions along which children vary in their play behavior.

One often hears clinicians talk about the importance of "understanding the whole child." But what is really involved in this? It must mean taking into account a series of separate elements that one observes about the child and forming them into some relationship to each other. This relationship is then made into a set of categories that the observer uses in his attempts to predict the future behavior of the child. If so, obviously some type of implicit dimensional rating is being made by the clinician. How can the "whole child" as understood by a sensitive clinician be described to anybody else if not without some effort at making explicit the specific dimensions that the clinician is employing in his diagnostic understanding? There may be certain outstanding child clinicians or other wise people who seem to show a profound understanding or rapport with children. The task of science continues to be that of making *explicit* just what processes lead to this understanding in some rather than others and in specifying more precisely the capacities that these gifted people have so that their techniques of observation can be taught to others.

The problem in observing play behavior becomes one not so much of rating or not rating, but rather of choosing appropriate dimensions. Some rating schemes may be based on behaviors too petty, so that they ultimately cannot lead to sufficient generalization (as in the case of merely counting the number of movements in one direction or another that a child makes or the number of sentences he speaks irrespective of content). It seems a wiser tactic of research to choose a moderately general behavior pattern that is yet sufficiently specific so that with proper training, a number of raters can agree on its weight along some scale. Examples of this approach will be seen in the chapters by Pulaski, Freyberg, and Biblow.

The systematic approach to studying play behavior calls for a well thought out series of steps. These include careful thought on the kind of behavioral samples to be obtained and their settings, careful consideration in obtaining objective, observational protocols whether by the use of human observers or videotape under conditions where very complete data are obtainable, the careful training of raters along very specifically defined dimensions so that good agreement can be obtained between independent judges reading the protocols. Finally, the choice of ratings should stay as close as feasible to overt observable behavior without risking the danger of trivialization by the microscopic elements that are not likely to be psychologically meaningful.

Examples of Some of the Ratings Employed in These Studies

Imaginativeness of Play

Let us examine more closely some of the specific dimensions that are relevant to our emphasis on make-believe play. An immediate problem that we face is how to delimit what we mean by imaginativeness of play or make-believe play. The puzzling feature especially with very young children is that we have great difficulty ascertaining to what extent the child is merely reciting a verbal formula and to what extent his play includes elements of imagery and internal response. Perhaps we can never truly hit on a solution to this problem, but what we can do is to come as close as possible to obtaining agreement between raters on play that introduces time, space and related features that are not given in the immediate environment of the child. This definition grows out of earlier research which was based on attempts to score projective techniques for imaginativeness.

Weisskopf (1950) proposed a measure called the Transcendance Index for scoring Thematic Apperception Test protocols. Her intention was primarily to evaluate the degree to which particular cards in this picture series were more or less likely to evoke richly varied responses from the subjects. This method essentially called for an examination of the protocol in terms of what elements had been introduced which were not directly given by the objective stimulus. Thus, in the case of the first card of the TAT (the boy staring at the violin) a subject might tell a story such as: *This is a boy. He is sitting at a table. There seems to be a violin on the table. He is looking at the violin. The room is somewhat dark although there appears to be a window in the rear.* This story would yield a score of just about 0 on Transcendence. This subject, despite the instructions to make up a story, has merely described what any observer will perceive to be present in the card. By contrast, another respondent might give the following story: *This boy is trying to decide whether he should take up the violin as a career. His parents and his teacher say he is very gifted. He knows it will involve a lot of work but finally he decides to try. He practices very hard. Years later his parents and teacher come to hear his successful debut in Carnegie Hall.*

This latter story has obviously introduced many elements that are not immediately given in this picture. The mention of the boy's indecision and concern introduces an emotion that is not at all obvious in the picture. The reference to teacher and parents introduces characters who are not in the picture itself. The anticipation of practice and the final happy ending with the introduction of a future dimension and the parents and teacher at Carnegie Hall all contribute to a story that while not highly original, still involves introduction of many elements that are not at all in the stimulus situation.

This technique of using the Transcendence Index as a measure of imagination has been developed further by Singer (Singer & Sugarman, 1955; Singer,

Wilensky, & McCraven, 1956) and various co-workers over the years. It has proven an effective approach in measuring hypothesized, imaginative differences between various adult groups as in the case of a comparison of Italian and Irish schizophrenics carried out in a mental hospital (Singer & Opler, 1956). Essentially, this same principle can be applied to the study of other types of fantasy products such as the dreams and daydreams of blind and sighted children (Singer & Streiner, 1966).

In the case of play or the scoring of dream material, one has less clearly in view a formally structured similar situation as is the case of the TAT protocol. Nevertheless, it is possible to use a fairly delimited setting and to take into account the characteristics of the particular toys that the child is using in helping one to decide on the degree to which imaginative development is involved in a play situation. If a child is swinging on a swing, but refers to the swing as an airplane, it seems quite reasonable to give him credit for imaginativeness or transcendence of the immediate situation. If he is riding a bicycle and referring to it as a space ship, he indeed deserves some credit for transcendence of the immediate situation. If the child behaves in such a way as implies there are other characters in the game who are not visible to the observer, one can again give him credit for transcendence.

In the case of some of the protocols described at the outset, it is obvious that for some of the children, the particular toy they are holding is treated not merely as a toy or as a representation of a particular animal. It has taken on human-like characteristics and is treated really as a child or infant rather than as a baby hippopotamus. In this sense, the introduction of make-believe can scarcely be questioned. It remains to be seen whether rating scales based on this type of analysis are sufficiently capable of reliable scoring by judges and also yield evidence of consistency for young children. We might also go on to attempt to tease out the extent to which the verbalizations upon which we base our inferences of imagery or symbolic elaboration actually *do* reflect such inner processes or whether they are merely verbal clichés or habits.

Imaginativeness of Play and Creativity

In approaching the study of imaginativeness, one is at once confronted with the possible relationship between make-believe play and the dimension of creativity. There has been a considerable body of research in psychology that attempts to tease out the nature of creative processes and their development (Wallach, 1970, 1971). It could be argued that what we have described as imaginativeness of play is simply one aspect of a more general creativity tendency in the child. The problem with this statement is that the term "creativity" has strong socially evaluative features. That is, the decision about what is truly creative in our society ultimately depends on decisions made by co-workers, supervisors, art critics, historians, and society more broadly, often much later in a person's life. It seems more reasonable simply to recognize that there may be a dimension of fluid cognitive activity separate from the intelligence that is measured by the usual intelligence or school achievement measures.

Elaborating upon this notion, we are led to the work of Guilford (1967) who has made a strong argument for the fact that we must distinguish between two major human capacities in the area ordinarily termed "intelligence" or "cognitive skill." One of these is *convergent thinking* by which we ordinarily mean the ability to produce answers rather quickly that reflect the capacities for analysis in abstraction of data yielding a result that society agrees is the "correct" answer. In this sense, convergent processes are those which are measured by intelligence tests and most school achievement grades. *Divergent processes,* on the other hand, are those which tap the capacity to generate a complex and differentiated series of responses to a common stimulus. This is a situation in which it is the production of difference and variability or flexibility that is at a premium. It would appear from our examples of different levels of imaginative play and our earlier discussion of the analysis of fantasy products, that such activities fall within the general category of divergent thinking. The child who develops an interesting story line using just a few plastic toys and indeed often changing the very character of the toys to represent other persons, may well be demonstrating an early trend toward divergent production.

Wallach (1971) has developed the argument that one would be better off to employ the term "ideational fluency" to describe many of the divergent processes that we observe in formal testing with children. While he does not deal with spontaneous activities to any extent, he does elaborate a carefully reasoned argument in favor of viewing ideational fluency as a fundamental human capacity that is to be contrasted to intelligence, at least within the normal and above average range of intelligence. The very important research by Wallach and Wing (1969) is one of the few studies that indicates some relationship between ideational fluency and later achievement that could indeed be classified as creative by society. More specifically, Wallach and Wing found that intelligence test scores predicted academic achievements quite well. When, however, the criterion employed was the ability to have art works exhibited or to win a prize in an art contest, to have writing published in a public newspaper or magazine rather than a school magazine, and the ability to win a prize in a scientific competition or to construct scientific apparatus, the intelligence measures did not predict this criterion. Instead, it was the measures of ideational fluency that were at least moderately successful in predicting this more creative kind of activity. Thus, there were suggestions that ideational fluency among adolescents does have a separate, predictive possibility for specific kinds of products valued by society quite apart from the typical convergent processes that go into ordinary academic grades.

In connection with our references to make-believe games and companions, it should also be noted that Schaefer (1969) found that when high school students were evaluated by teachers in terms of demonstrated creative performance, they turned out not to differ so much in intellectual skill, but rather primarily in their report of having had an imaginary companion or make-believe playmate during childhood. A somewhat similar finding was reported by Helson (1965) in a study of artistic creativity in college women. Here again, one of the few differentiating characteristics based on the retrospective accounts of these women was the fact that the more creative group more frequently reported having engaged extensively in daydreaming in childhood. Therefore, the dimension of imaginativeness which is being utilized in the researches herein clearly bears relationship to an important dimension sometimes known as ideational fluency, now and then called divergent thinking, which may ultimately be linked to certain types of creative activity in adolescence and adult life. For the moment, however, one need not make a commitment in that direction. In fact from our discussion at various points in this volume, it will appear that one could even conceive the possibility that some of the aspects of imaginative play in childhood may contribute also to improved capacity in convergent processes as in the case where the development of imagery may help the child in memorizing tasks of various kinds (Rohwer, 1970).

It can also be argued that make-believe activities as manifested in children and presumably continued into adult life in the form of various types of day-dreaming and imagery skills (Klinger, 1971; Sarbin & Juhasz, 1970; Singer, 1966;) have their own special value as part of living. In the case of young children, they provide a varied and interesting environment to which the child can respond irrespective of whether there may even be any later learning consequences. In addition, the ability to deal with unreality and to generate complex sensitivity to what is fantasy and unreal may have its own ultimate rewarding value in helping to enrich the overall awareness of discovering reality and human possibilities (Bachélard, 1964; Chateau, 1967). We shall return to some of these issues at greater length in our discussion of theoretical implications of imagery and fantasy techniques in childhood. For the moment it seems clear, however, that in studying imaginativeness as a dimension in children's play the work falls generally under the heading of divergent processes as proposed by Guilford (1967) and ideational fluency as presented by Wallach (1970).

Imaginativeness of Play and Fantasy

One can go beyond the simple rating of imaginativeness in terms of introduction of make-believe elements in play and also evaluate this process along a reality-fantasy dimension in the following sense: Some of the make-believe play of children presents situations that are relatively close to their actual life situations. Indeed, much of the play, fantasy and even the dreams of children, studied systematically, turn out to be very closely related to their immediate daily lives, day-to-day problems, and to the parents and children with whom they are associated (Foulkes, Larson, Swanson, & Rardin, 1969; Foulkes & Shepherd, 1971; Klinger, 1971). Still there are ranges in the degree to which children can show a spread of activities along the dimension of relative closeness to the immediate day-to-day situation. Thus, some children may emphasize playing house or school or going on a picnic, all games that are reasonably close to life situations in which they might indeed participate. Other children may play games that are relatively far removed from their life situation or the realistic possibilities in their lives as, for example, playing pirates, or cops and robbers, cowboys, space men and Martians, etc. Snoopy, the childlike dog of the "Peanuts" cartoon series, dreams and fantasies sometimes about bones and quiet places to sleep, but at other times he imagines himself as a World War I fighter pilot pursuing the sinister Red Baron.

One might therefore consider the possibility of another dimension that would be associated presumably only partially with imaginativeness. This scale might represent the degree to which the make-believe elements reflect closeness to the immediate life situation of the child, as contrasted with make-believe elements quite far removed from the day-to-day experience of the child.

In a study by Singer and Streiner (1966), congenitally blind children were compared with sighted children in terms of their fantasy and dream productions. While both groups of children reported a fairly extended degree of fantasy products, it was clear that the sighted children produced many complex and varied imagery products with much more reference to completely unreal characters: monsters, Martians, fairies and witches, all of whom were undoubtedly gleaned from the greater reading and television watching capacities of the sighted children. By contrast, the blind children told stories and reported dreams that involved events much more characteristic of their actual day-to-day life experience. In only one respect did the blind children show more fantasy than the sighted children. Almost all of them reported the occurrence of an imaginary companion, invariably one who was sighted and more or less the same age as the blind child. Even here then in this greater reliance on imagery clearly of a compensatory nature, the fantasy figure was a realistic helper rather than what might be called a magic helper, such as the cartoon character Barnaby's Leprechaun companion.

Measures of Concentration and Emotional Response (Affect)

Some other dimensions that one might study in connection with ongoing play are not directly related to the make-believe, but are employed to increase our understanding of the concomitant cognitive consequences of imaginative play. One dimension we might consider in this connection is *concentration,* a measure originally developed for studying children's play by Hartley, Frank, and Goldenson (1952). This measure refers to the child's capacity to unfold a relatively organized and extended sequence of activities without becoming excessively dependent on each new external stimulus. Concentration need not be identical with imaginativeness of play by any means.

For example, one could conceive of a child concentrating extensively on a mastery game such as building a block tower as high as possible without its tipping over. The child may spend a full 10-min sampling period just engaged in this activity without any indication that any make-believe elements are involved. On the other hand, as seen particularly in the case of make-believe play of 4-year-olds cited earlier in the chapter (see pages 29–30), the make-believe games shown at these early ages are relatively brief and are characterized by very short sequences with interruptions for social interaction or gross motor activity. Therefore, it is an interesting question to ascertain the degree to which the capacity to concentrate one's attention and to focus for relatively extended time periods on a particular task becomes linked to make-believe activities or whether these are fundamentally separate types of measures.

To speculate for a moment, I believe it is quite likely that there is a fundamental relationship between make-believe play and concentration. Children who begin to generate complex and interesting games find these games sufficiently satisfying so that they can spend prolonged periods involved in them and require less direct stimulation from other children or from changing environmental circumstances or gross motor activity. We shall discuss some of the possibilities of this link of concentration and imaginativeness later, but for the moment it seems clear that one ought to try measuring the two variables independently and see what the data reveal before prejudging the linkage.

In addition to the capacity for extended concentration, one is also interested in the emotional reaction of the children as they engage in make-believe games. We can begin by asking in the most general sense whether children seem to show positive affects such as joy and laughter or interest and eagerness while engaging in make-believe or whether their predominant mood may be one of sadness, apathy, or anger. If indeed make-believe and other types of play are inherently rewarding or satisfying activities as Klinger (1971) has argued, then we should observe considerable indication of positive emotion on the part of children when engaged in such activities.

In addition, we might want to move beyond the grossest level of measurement of *positive* versus *negative affect* to studying more precisely the specific mood changes in evidence while the children are engaged in play. Later, we shall attempt to propose some theoretical possibilities about the related differentiated moods to types of play. Suffice it to say at this point that it seems clear we need some estimates of the ongoing mood changes of children associated with different levels of play. Again the research literature is largely silent on this problem.

Part of the reason for this limitation in our knowledge has been the great influence of psychoanalytic theory which has led to an overemphasis on interpreting play in terms of the working out of aggressive or sexual drives. Therefore, the emphasis has been predominantly on measurement of aggressive behavior or aggressive content in fantasy and similarly on sexualized behavior or content in the play situation. The problem with such a focus on sex or aggression is the complex assumption of the underlying appetitive, biological drive system that is the major motivating aspect of behavior, a position strongly taken in most analytic theory and argued perhaps most cogently by Rapaport (1960b). A contrasting position argues that the traditional, biological drives (or even the metapsychological conception of aggression as a biological drive proposed by Freud) have only limited value in a theory of motivation. This has been put forward by a number of recent theorists, (Schachtel, 1959; Tomkins, 1962, 1963; White, 1959). The great importance of a differentiated affect or emotion in man has been strengthened in recent years by experimental research (Ekman, Friesen, & Ellsworth, 1971; Izard, 1971) which points up the significant role played by a variety of emotions as indicators of fundamental trends in man's behavior. This point of view suggests that we had best look more carefully at the ongoing emotional changes in the child during the course of play and this is what is proposed in some of the affect measures which my colleagues and I have been developing. The chapter by Biblow exemplifies a most interesting use of this procedure.

As can be seen from the appended example of rater's instructions, *affect* generally is scored on a 5-point scale with the low end of the scale or the more negative aspect of affect associated with *absence* of interest or of smiling and enjoyment in play activities, tangential behavior, critical or angry remarks concerning the toys or play. At the other extreme, the focus is upon extreme delight in play as evidenced by laughing, singing or smiling and a clear reluctance to interrupt the play situation as well as indications of positive curiosity and interest. This system of measurement can be further differentiated into a series of moods which are based in part on Tomkins' (1962, 1963) development of a fundamental group of emotional possibilities. Thus we can score *angry and annoyed* or *fearfulness* and *a tension* on a 5-point scale. In both cases these are negative affects. We can also consider *ashamed-contrite, contemptuous-disgusted, fatigued and sluggish,* and *downhearted* all as examples of negative moods, each to be separately rated while *lively-excited* and *pleased-elated,* scored on a comparable scale, may be viewed as positive affective states. By staying as close as possible to direct observation ratings of these affects, we are in position to note some of the pattern fluctuation associated with different types of play, specific effects of different toys and particular predisposing personality patterns in relation to their interaction with play behavior.

Still another dimension that one might focus upon that has been used in at least one of these studies has been that of the expression of *overt aggressive behavior.* It is important to stress the word *overt* as much as possible because one of the areas of great confusion in clinical psychology and in research on play has been the tendency to attribute great significance to aggressive fantasies and to equate such fantasies with actual aggressive tendencies or the likelihood of direct violence. The relationship between a great deal of aggression manifested in the form of playful activity or of stories told to pictures of the TAT type and the likelihood of a person engaging in an overt act of aggression or destruction of property, etc., has never been fully resolved. The research evidence suggests that the expression of a great deal of aggressive material in fantasy may be *directly* related to overt aggressive behavior only in the instances where the aggression is not qualified and where there are no indications of inhibition concerning aggression, awareness of the consequences of aggression, or anxiety or guilt in relation to aggression (Klinger, 1971; Singer, 1968).

Certainly at this point in the study of imaginative play, we are not in a position to make the inference that children who show a great deal of make-believe fighting or make-believe incidents of battle or struggles between monsters or Martians, etc., are in any way likely to generate overt, aggressive behavior. This is an area that calls for considerable further study and the work by Biblow represents one approach to the problem with its emphasis particularly on overt, aggressive behavior. We shall also discuss some of the relationships of popular media, which include violence such as television, upon the likelihood of overt, aggressive behavior or aggressive play in children.

Scoring the Content of Play

So far our emphasis has been almost completely upon measuring ongoing play in relation to what might be termed "structural" aspects of the personality: drives, emotions, cognitive factors, and likelihood of overt aggressive or dependent behavior. Actually, most of the available clinical research on ongoing play has focused rather on the *content* of play in an attempt to ascertain the symbolical relationship between the play and presumed underlying fantasies and impulses of the child or to the content of problems in the family relationship of the child. As has been indicated earlier, this is not the central focus of the present volume, but let us briefly discuss some of the issues in relation to content at this point.

By the content of play we mean generally the particular plot lines of the stories that are the subject of make-believe or the types of characters introduced. Reports from child clinicians indicate that the content of children's play psychotherapy sessions frequently reflects the ongoing conflicts in the family situation. At this level, there seems no question that the observation of ongoing play can provide clues as to the particular relationships in the child's experience, the pattern of hostilities and resentments, of rivalries and of special attachment. The child's play activities are to some extent a function of the assimilation of material he is imitating from observation in the world around him. Since the world around him consists of mainly the family figures with whom he is in most contact, then it would be natural that some of the content of a child's play reflects, albeit in necessarily distorted and only partially understood form, the conflicts and characteristics of his immediate family. At the same time, we are not yet sure from available literature whether the indications of serious emotional difficulty in the child or a most problematic situation at home will necessarily be reflected in the content of play under all circumstances. One could propose the hypothesis that in those cases where play is largely limited to representation of family patterns, these are so striking that the child is preoccupied with them and does not draw in other kinds of material gained from stories, overheard contacts with peers, or television material.

In addition to the usefulness of content classifications from children's play for the purposes of evaluating the role of family situations, it might also be valuable to view content as an indicator of the culture of childhood at various age levels from the content material. This of course is a key facet of the psychoanalytically oriented approaches with their emphasis on psychosexual stages (Peller, 1959) or of Erikson's (1963) broader notions of the life cycle stages such as *autonomy* and *basic trust.* We need considerably more research in this direction, particularly as a means of testing the popular hypotheses proposed by Erikson to determine if indeed the pattern of children's play does reflect something like the kind of sequence he proposes. Too often again there is a tendency in psychology and psychiatry to accept the words of wise observers such as Erikson unquestioningly. Such acknowledgement of authority is a substitute for the hard work of careful empirical testing. One of the messages of this book is that we had better get on with the work of formal research in addition to theorizing.

In addition to using content to pin down a life cycle approach, one might also use the content material to gain clues concerning the more general cultural milieu of children. We can also explore the extent to which television has specific or general influences. Does morality reflect particular influences of popular media, cultural problems, problems related to the family group and to the more general ethnic or religious fantasies and myths surrounding this particular cultural setting of the child? In addition, one can begin to discern the special characteristics of peer culture at this particular age, the influence of fantasy on jokes and riddles and general material such as found in the collections by Opie and Opie (1969). The content of play can give us clues as to the major threads of interest in myths and legends that may still pervade the fantasies of children at various age levels. Such content can also provide clues as to the predominant themes that may be partly a function of specific cultural conditions and social class factors and may also represent the more common humanity shared by children across cultural groupings.

The television content of today including the commercials, at least in this country, have generated a new type of mythology and sets of real or fictional "stars" who figure in the children's fantasies. We can use some of the changing occurrences of certain well-established television characters as tracking tags to pinpoint changing fashions in children's approach to certain material, the changing aspects of their identification across class lines and related evidence of the impact of popular media on cognitive development.

Within the past two years, for example, there has been an increasingly widespread and systematic effort on the part of producers of television commercials, and to a somewhat lesser extent, in fictional material presented on television, to include interracial material or to have darker-skinned children and adults appearing with greater frequency at various points in stories and advertisements. Can we detect through children's play whether there has been any increased tolerance or sensitivity across color lines produced by this effort? Can we detect evidences of certain changing patterns of egalitarian values or sensitivity to changing sex role concepts emerging in the course of children's play as a consequence of newer attitudes portrayed in the popular media? The comparative data collected by Sutton-Smith and Rosenberg (in Herron and Sutton-Smith, 1971) points up that girls over the past 60 years are playing more of the boys' games. Some data on this point are presented in the chapter by Pulaski.

It is my impression that television has had a much greater impact than is fully recognized upon the cognitive and fantasy development of poor children. Up until the development of radio, movies, and television, with particular emphasis on television because of its widespread availability, it is striking that there were rarely any opportunities for working class children to be exposed to a great range of legendary stories, scenes of people from other areas of the same city or country let alone historical or mythological episodes. In this sense then, television has tremendously widened the horizons of the poor and provided them with a great deal of material that can be used in the course of make-believe and indeed may even have stimulated greater tendencies toward make-believe play than might have been in evidence in the past. We might get some clues about this from extensive observation of the content of play from children of different social classes. So far, however, we have little formal evidence on this point.

In conclusion, the main thrust of the research described in this volume will be upon the imaginativeness of play of children as manifested from a structural point of view rather than in terms of specific content. The first step would appear to be tying the make-believe play into the more general question of the development of imagery and cognitive functions in children. This type of structural development may more readily cut across gross cultural differences and indeed perhaps differences to exposure in the popular media. This does not mean that we are not interested in content. Developing a more general notion of the function of ongoing play behavior and its implications for personality and cognition involves, as an initial step, careful delineation of what we mean by make-believe play and scoring such play in association with other *structural* dimensions such as mood and aggression, dependency or the effects of external environmental forces.

Ongoing Make-Believe Play in Nursery School Children

The methods described in this chapter are now being applied in an extensive study of nursery school children carried out by Dorothy Singer and myself with the help of students from Manhattanville College. The broader project is far from completed. What will be presented here are some findings from a study of 46 children between the ages of 2 and 5 who were observed in a suburban, middle socioeconomic level, private nursery school.

A group of eight pairs of observers was trained to do continuous 10-min samplings of the play of specific children during both *free play* (in the recreation area) and *structured play* (where specific materials are provided, e.g., paints). Following recording of the children's behavior, the observers proceeded to rate the children on the dimensions already described in accordance with the instructions and definitions provided (see Appendix). Two additional raters rerated all protocols without having directly observed the children. In general, there were relatively few gross differences in ratings (see Tables 1 and 2). Only about 10% of the large number of ratings differed by more than 1 point on a 5-point scale. A final consensus rating on each scale was assigned each child. The children were

TABLE 1

Means and SDs for Observation Ratings of Boys and Girls Combined during Free Play

Observation rating scale	High imaginative predisposition (N = 27)		Low imaginative predisposition (N = 20)			
	M	SD	M	SD	t	p
Imaginativeness	2.59	1.31	1.55	1.59	2.34	<.02
Positive affect	2.93	1.11	2.30	.92	2.07	<.05
Concentration	2.70	1.07	2.35	.81	1.24	ns
Angry	1.70	.88	1.70	1.03	–	ns
Fearful	1.15	.53	1.05	.95	.89	ns
Lively	2.96	1.48	2.30	1.22	1.64	<.20 >.10
Elated	3.65	1.30	2.20	1.00	4.27	<.01
Sad	1.30	.83	1.45	.69	.66	ns
Ashamed	1.22	.80	1.05	.22	1.01	ns
Contemptuous	1.15	.46	1.05	.22	.97	ns
Fatigued	1.15	.36	1.15	.37	0	ns
Aggression	1.89	1.09	2.40	1.31	1.42	<.20 >.10

TABLE 2

t Tests of Observation Rating Differences for Free Play between Boys and Girls

	Boys (N = 21)		Girls (N = 26)			
	M	SD	M	SD	t	p
Imaginative play						
predisposition	1.32	.99	3.69	.93	8.17	<.01
Observation ratings						
Imaginativeness	2.57	1.33	1.81	.98	2.10	<.05
Positive affect	3.09	1.18	2.31	.84	2.52	<.02
Concentration	3.09	.94	2.35	.94	3.70	<.01
Angry	1.85	.81	1.48	1.01	1.37	ns
Fearful	1.12	0	1.00	.43	—	ns
Lively	3.10	1.30	2.35	1.44	1.83	<.10 >.05
Elated	2.76	1.22	2.38	1.17	1.06	ns
Sad	1.19	.51	1.46	.90	.69	ns
Ashamed	1.05	.21	1.02	.10	.60	ns
Fatigued	1.09	.30	1.09	.30	0	ns
Aggression	2.24	1.18	2.00	1.26	.67	ns

also interviewed to establish high and low imaginative play predisposition or high fantasy—low fantasy groups as described in the following chapter.

With respect to the prediction concerning the consistency of play for situations, results of the study make it clear that situational differences between the structured and unstructured situation overrode the likelihood of any consistency in fantasy play tendencies within the children. Correlations between make-believe play in the structured and unstructured settings were negligible. There was a statistically significant difference between the amount of make-believe play observed for both boys and girls in the free as against the structured play situation. Examination of the protocols for the children makes it clear that the structured situation while intended by the staff as one to develop creativity and imaginativeness in the children, did not yield much evidence that the children introduced fantasy elements into the situation. These data bear comparison with the findings of Pulaski (Chapter IV) with kindergärten, first-, and second-grade children which suggested that where playthings are highly structured, children are likely to show a much more limited variety of themes in their play situation. There seems no doubt that situational factors are important in fostering different degrees of imaginativeness, but much more extensive research still is required in this respect. No major sex differences emerged with respect to the degree of imaginative play or the other rating variables as a consequence of the relative structured or unstructured nature of the play. Girls as well as boys seemed, in general, to play more imaginatively and to enjoy the less structured play situation.

If we concentrate primarily on the free-play situation for the balance of our presentation, it is evident that the 3- and 4-year-olds did not show any extensive pattern of make-believe play. Such play constituted only about 10% of the total activities in which they engaged during their free play period. There were group trends toward an increased amount of make-believe play with increasing age for the 3- and 4-year-old children, but while these trends were consistent in both free and structured play, there was considerable individual difference in this sample and none of the differences between the age groups was statistically reliable. It is not possible to make a direct comparison with the data from 5-year-olds obtained by similar rating methods, but different observers, in the study of a middle-class kindergarten by Pulaski (Chapter IV) or by Freyberg (Chapter VI) with lower socioeconomic group kindergarten children. However, indications are that the 3- and 4-year-olds generally show considerably less make-believe than do the 5-year-olds.

The sex differences in this study show an intriguing interrelationship with the differences in imaginative predisposition. In general, the girls report significantly more make-believe play on the basis of the interviews than do the boys. One would, therefore, expect the girls to show more spontaneous, imaginative play than the boys in the free-play situation at least. The reverse turns out to be the case. In the free-play situation the boys showed significantly more make-believe play as well as significantly more concentration and more positive affect than did the girls. This might be taken as an indication that the predictive value of the imaginative play predisposition (IPP) interview is quite limited with such young children. Examining the sexes separately, however, it turns out that for the boys, dividing the group at the median indicates that there is indeed a significant difference between high IPP, and the low IPP boys in the amount of make-believe play with the former group showing ratings higher on this dimension. When the sexes are combined as in Table 1, the differences between high and low IPP groups are significant for imaginativeness, positive affect, and elation as predicted. Clearly, there is some discrepancy between what the girls report and what they do in this specific situation.

An examination of the structure of the free-play setting yields a very likely answer to this dilemma. The setting was a rather open one in which there were swings, seesaws, a sandpile, and bicycles available, as well as a jungle gym. In general, therefore, the setting was conducive to gross motor activity and to the type of play more generally associated with the physical motor direction of boys. This gross difference may well account for the fact that the boys seemed to enjoy themselves more and seemed in general to play more imaginatively here. The girls reported that they preferred to play such make-believe games as house and school—a long tradition with girls that can be dated back to the studies of play at the turn of the century and that has persisted consistently since then (Herron & Sutton-Smith, 1971). The playroom did not present opportunities for this type of play and the girls were very likely simply at loose ends in terms of finding opportunities for the kind of play they preferred. While there is evidence from a number of studies that girls' games are moving more in the direction of boys' games over the years (Roberts & Sutton-Smith, 1971), the kinds of boys' games that girls have adopted tend to be more generally physical and not the make-believe soldier or cowboy games which make so much of boys' active make-believe play.

In the present study, therefore, it seems likely that the observations taking place in a wide open setting with large playthings tended to occur in a situation in which the imagination capacities of boys were challenged more than those of girls. The girls tended somewhat to hold back although they wanted to ride the swings and engage in some of those games. They were somewhat more tentative, somewhat less elated and exhilarated by the situation and certainly less prone to develop elaborated make-believe games. It is of interest, nevertheless, that imaginative play predisposition, at least among the boys, is already in evidence and that the boys who report more make-believe play in general do also show it in the free-play situation here.

The kindergarten boys in Pulaski's study (Chapter IV) generally seemed to show greater overt enjoyment in the course of fantasy than did the girls and also showed a generally higher level of motor activity than did the girls. This was especially true in the situation where the toys available were highly structured. Especially interesting is the fact that more imaginative boys in general showed less gross motor activity than did less imaginative boys. The latter group manifested the most vigorous and uncoordinated motility in that sample.

For the 3- and 4-year-olds in our present study, however, there were relatively few elaborated sequences of play and relatively few really extensive make-believe games that clearly had beginnings and ends. Some of the children with high imaginative predisposition did show bursts of such activity, but these frequently were interrupted by the other children in the course of the almost random movements that took place in the free play yard.

Results of present study make it clear that 3- and 4-year-olds are still in a period of change and growth and much subject to the impact of specific situations on the degree to which they can play various types of imaginative games. Nevertheless, some indications of imaginative play disposition are already in evidence and, in addition, the gross structure of the situation interacts only with sex differences in producing the likelihood that children will carry out make-believe play. Such fantasy games apparently are also strongly associated with their ability to concentrate for long periods of time and to enjoy their play situation. No gross differences in overt aggression appeared in this study between the sexes, but it should be pointed out that the level of overt attack by one child upon another or of overtly destructive behavior for this sample was extremely low during all of the observations made. When the boys were divided into high and low imaginative play predisposition groups, however, there was a significant difference in ratings of overt aggression between the groups. Low IPP boys were distinctly more aggressive than high IPP boys. This finding is comparable to one by Biblow (Chapter V) with 9-year-olds and to Pulaski's (Chapter IV) where imaginative 5-year-olds were less motorically active than children low in fantasy-play predisposition.

CHAPTER III

The Measurement of
Imaginative Predisposition

So far, we have emphasized the tendency toward imaginative play that all children may share in common. In this sense, our emphasis on ongoing play measurement has attempted to find the basis for studying developmental regularities in the emergence of certain types of imagery and cognitive skills in children at different age levels and as a function of different types of external stimulation. Is it possible that against this general background of a developmental trend in children we can discern specific children who show a predominance of imaginative play at very early age and who persist in this pattern through adolescence? If we can show such individual consistencies, do these have any special psychological consequences? Indeed, how does such a predisposition to make-believe get started in the first place? Once one approaches the problem from the standpoint of personality development, the measurement of individual predisposition in imaginative play becomes extremely intriguing and leads to a host of important considerations in the field of personality.

We know, of course, that various people of distinction in adult life had a strong tendency in childhood toward solitary, imaginative play. A well-known example is Robert Louis Stevenson whose make-believe playmates "The Brownies" continued to stay with him in a certain sense right into adult life and to be employed in a semiconscious way by him in the development in some of the plots for his stories. Tolstoy also had documented some of his early childhood imaginary games and thoughts which we cannot help but feel led ultimately (in transformed fashion) to some of the great thoughts he set down in his novels. We have already cited W. H. Auden's description of some of the make-believe play he engaged in as a child in association with his mother, as well as some of his elaborate childhood daydreams. These experiences undoubtedly played a role in the development of his great capacities for imagery and symbolism in poetic expression.

Freud was one of the first psychologists to be sensitive to the relationship of early imaginative play and fantasy and later creative tendencies (Freud, 1959). More recently, Gardner Murphy has written most sensitively on the important role of imaginativeness and daydreaming in early childhood as an influence on later development. He has noted that "Although our culture has tended to disparage the chronic dreamer, it is also true that we have had respect for the boy with 'the long, long thoughts' nor have we been unmindful of the values in daydreaming, provided the daydreams stay within suitable limits [Murphy, 1947, p. 405]." Murphy also calls attention to the early fantasies of people like the Wright brothers who eventually could translate these to action.

The ambivalence of adults to the daydreams and imaginative play of children pervades many periods in society's history. Hamlet refers bitterly to himself as "John-a-dreams." Montaigne, despite his insightful essay on "The Power of Imagination," often writes most disparagingly of adults' indulgence of children's games.

Aries (1962) has described in great detail early Renaissance attitudes toward children and the development of our more modern understanding of children. He quotes a remarkable document published by a physician of Louis XIII which documents the daily development of the prince from infancy through early boyhood and adolescence. In general, the young prince was treated much like a miniature adult and trained very early in courtly practices, hunting, and games that were played as much by adults as children. He did, however, have a set of dolls and toy soldiers which he enjoyed playing with quite extensively, introducing many make-believe elements according to the description. Nevertheless, at about age 6 he was firmly told that he must put aside the dolls he loved so well and take on activities more appropriate to his role: riding, hunting, and swordsmanship. Although dolls were denied him by the age of 7, the young prince still was permitted make-believe play in the company of adults who themselves indulged in some of these activities. He also began to witness many more theatrical performances that involved pantomimes and storytelling. In the court where Louis grew up it was perfectly acceptable for adults, as well as children, to engage in play-acting and make-believe ballets.

Make-Believe Play and Introversion

There are fleeting suggestions at various times in different writings that suggest the continuity between make-believe games and play and the later development of daydreaming as a consistent tendency. It must be said at this point however that the firm evidence on this point is still not available. Suppose we assume that there is indeed such a continuity and that the child who shows a great deal of make-believe elements in his play from a relatively early age gradually internalizes these in the form of daydreams and fantasies. The study of predisposition to make-believe then touches ultimately on a major dimension of personality, that of introversion—extraversion. Introduced initially by Jung (1959), the construct of introversion remains one of the most intriguing notions in the study of personality structure.

Most studies of personality traits in adolescents and adults seem to indicate a limited number of major dimensions along which most people vary. One recurrent dimension is introversion, which may be regarded as the tendency to take pleasure in self-awareness and to spend a great deal of time upon one's own thoughts and fantasies. The person scoring at the introversive end of the scale values thoughtlike activities, while at the other extreme is the person whose major investment is in direct interaction with other people and the objects of the environment. Another pattern of introversion—extraversion has to do with the extent to which the individual greatly values being alone or has a considerable fear of social situations and involvement with other people. By contrast, the extravert constantly seeks the company of others and enjoys conversation, social games, and casual interchanges even with strangers. Eysenck's (1952) factor analytic studies tend to blend the two types of introversion—extraversion together. Eysenck regards introversion—extraversion as a basic dimension of personality along which all humans vary. Guilford's (1959) analyses, on the other hand, suggest two types of introversion—extraversion: One involves greater emphasis on thought and inner experience versus the seeking of external experiences such as social interchange and externally derived stimulation, and the second involves sociability. The social introvert is not necessarily a person who values thought. Rather, he seeks privacy or fears extensive social contact. The social extravert, on the other hand, is a person who may equally well value or discount thought, but who is also inclined toward a considerable amount of social interaction as part of his enjoyment of life.

The evidence supporting the notion that there is indeed a general dimension of introversion—extraversion is by no means conclusive on the basis of inventory and self-report data. We shall not take the time at this point to go into many complex issues surrounding the measurement of introversion—extraversion by various techniques. It is best to limit ourselves for the moment to the task at hand, which is the measurement of a tendency toward make-believe play and imaginativeness in childhood. It will remain a task for other studies and perhaps many later investigators to pin down more precisely whether a consistent tendency toward fantasy play in childhood does indeed become translated into a more pervasive adult trend toward the valuing of inner experience. Needless to say this notion is at the back of the very effort being made in this study to measure imaginativeness of play. Even if one cannot ultimately prove this continuity between childhood play and adult action–thought preferences, the relatively measurable tendency for children at an early age to show consistency in make-believe play seems worth studying in its own right. We can evaluate the implications of this trend for the immediate tasks that face children in their day-to-day lives in order to determine the possible relationship to psychopathological trends as they emerge.

Major questions about the attempt to measure personality traits such as imaginative predisposition are raised by Mischel (1968) in his critique of the limited value of personality traits as long-standing measures. Mischel has argued that there are enormous variations in a given individual's behavior as a function of the different situations in which he finds himself. It is quite important that psychologists study a great variety of situations in order ultimately to make the most effective prediction of human behavior. There still seem to be some patterns of consistency for at least certain traits. The importance of the situation, however, is not sufficient to remove the necessity for measuring what the person brings to a situation in the way of characteristic approaches, understandings, and expectations. If children do differ systematically in their predisposition to make-believe games and play, it seems reasonable to proceed to an exploration of what correlates there may be in other patterns of behavior for this predisposition in a given child.

Projective Technique Measurement of Imaginative Predisposition

A major effort aimed at pinning down more precisely what goes into imaginative tendencies in children and adults has grown out of the use of projective techniques. Projective techniques represent the presentation of relatively ambiguous stimuli to persons who are then required to tell stories to pictures or to give associations to inkblots or to rearrange abstract symbols or to draw human figures or hands, etc. One need not review the well-known history of these techniques at this point. It suffices merely to indicate that projective methods represented, in the late 1930s, 1940s, and 1950s, a movement that generated great excitement on the part of psychologists. The ambiguous testing techniques seemed at that point to offer the hope of behavioral measurement that could tap profound underlying inclinations. While it would be too soon to say that projective techniques have passed from the scene, the fact remains that there is today greater sophistication of the relationship between projective methods and more objective techniques of self-rating or inventories. This has led to a great broadening in the scope of behavioral measurement—the viewing of projective techniques not so much as miracle methods, but merely as techniques to expand our ability to tap ongoing behavioral tendencies in the individual (Singer, 1968).

The use of projective methods for studying imagination has generally involved what the content tells us about specific conflict areas as can be seen from the widespread use of the TAT or various forms of association tests. A somewhat different approach has grown out of the Rorschach inkblot method. One of the major insights which Rorschach (1942) provided was that the tendency to produce movement or color responses when looking at the inkblots tapped not so much the specific content of conflicts or needs, but rather measured a broad trend toward reliance on imagination or on open expression of emotionality as a major tendency. Rorschach proposed that all human experience could be measured along an *introversion–extratension* dimension and that the ratio of the human movement responses in inkblots to the color responses in producing associations was a fundamental way of tapping this predisposition in people.

A person whose response to the 10 Rorschach inkblots was limited at best to one reference to a human in action (*M* response) would be viewed as someone who had not developed very much tendency toward inner living and who tended not to value his own fantasies or attend very much to his own dreams or to engage in planful or creative reconstructions of his experiences. By contrast, a person who produced a great many such *M* responses to the 10 blots would be viewed as an introversive personality much given to awareness of his own thoughts and fantasies, someone who took pleasure in these activities and who could engage in creative and flexible planning. In addition, Rorschach noted that persons who were high in *M* responses were also most likely to be people who showed very little overt motion. That is to say they tended to be inhibited in their motoric expression and to be rather awkward in dancing or perhaps in athletic games, but also somewhat shy in social situations and given perhaps to considerable control of their motor activity so that very little open motor activity was in evidence.

Rorschach felt that one had to measure not only the human movement responses, but also to take into account the relation of the *M* responses to color responses in the Rorschach protocol. Rorschach scored color responses for the degree to which they determined the association given to the response. Thus a response such as "blood" or "fire" were viewed as largely determined by color since neither blood nor fire has a definite physical shape. On the other hand, if one gave a response such as "red butterflies" or "yellow poodle" one was providing an association which had a fairly definite shape, but also was characterized by a definite color. In this latter instance one might surmise that there was a control over the emotionality for which the color stands. In the former case or uncontrolled color responses, one would surmise a great deal of egocentric, uncontrolled emotionality. For Rorschach, the balance of introversive trends as measured by the M responses and the emotional or affective tendencies as measured by the number of C responses and degree of control in color responses, represented a major way of regarding human beings. This view has been continued subsequently by most workers with the Rorschach even though the emphasis has been rather more in recent years on the interpretation of the content of inkblot protocols.

Among the literally thousands of research reports generated by the Rorschach tests, one finds a significant number that have attempted in various ways to examine the implications of Rorschach's emphasis upon introversion–extratension in relation to imaginative behavior, motor controls, and emotionality. On the whole, there seems to be considerable support for at least some aspects of Rorschach's interpretation of the M response as a measure of imaginativeness to some extent and motor inhibition from a great variety of studies with both children and adults (Singer, 1960, 1968). There are also intriguing developmental findings such as those of Ames (1952) which point out the relationship between the emergence of the human movement response in children at around age 7 with the more general inward internalization of overt play behavior. Important relationships at a theoretical level between the child's production of human movement responses and his developmental cycle in relation to control of motor activity and delaying capacity were long ago noted by Werner (1945) and Singer (1955). It is this linkage of the human movement response to the internalization of speech (Piaget's egocentric speech) in the form of heightened imagery and fantasy that lies at the basis for the choice of the inkblot method as one approach in attempting to develop a number of measures for estimating imaginative predisposition in play.

Werner (1945) observed that retarded children characterized by considerable hyperactivity produced relatively few if any M responses to the Rorschach inkblot, whereas retarded children characterized by relatively greater control over motor activity produced significantly more of these human movement reactions. Singer (1960) has reviewed a large number of studies which make it quite clear that there is support for the finding that children or adults who produce relatively few Rorschach human movement responses are inclined to be more active or impulsive in overt behavior. A study by Riess (1957) for example, indicated that children who had numerous human movement responses on a particular set of inkblots were much more likely to remain still or to play quietly during an enforced wait. By contrast, those children who scored relatively low in human movement responses to the inkblots tended to be rather active and to show relatively little ability to sit quietly during the enforced waiting period.

A direct link between the production of movement responses and imaginativeness of play had not yet been demonstrated in the literature despite the various suggestive indications. It is likely that children who sit quietly may indeed be producing fantasies or engaging in imaginative behavior, but this remains to be clearly demonstrated. There are, of course, indications that at least among adolescents, those who produce considerably more Rorschach movement responses are also less likely to be antisocial in their behavior and to show greater general capacity for self-awareness and imagination (Spivak & Levine, 1964).

The tie between production of human movement responses on the inkblots and indications of motor inhibition or control on the one hand and imaginative tendencies on the other has been forged more definitely in studies with a variety of adult groups (Singer, 1960, 1968). In studies with both schizophrenic and normal adult subjects, there are indications that those producing more human movement responses to the inkblots are also likely to show greater imaginative tendencies as measured, for example, by the degree to which they can transcend the stimulus content on TAT cards when telling stories, or give other indications of imaginative trends measured by ratings or by questionnaire responses (Barron, 1955; Schonbar, 1965). Page (1957), found that young adults reporting more frequent daydreaming in response to a questionnaire were also those who produced more Rorschach M responses.

On the basis of the general trend of the literature, therefore, it would appear desirable to continue to use the M response category of the Rorschach or some variant of the measurement of movement tendencies in the Rorschach as an approach to estimating the predisposition of children to daydreaming tendencies or make-believe play.

Normative data with the original set of Rorschach inkblots indicate that children show relatively few such movement responses before the age of 6 or 7. Indeed, it has been argued that the emergence of these responses later in childhood at the time when school attendance enforces greater motor inhibition upon the child, is linked to the internalization of make-believe play and egocentric speech (Singer, 1955). The relative infrequency of M responses in young children can therefore be a problem in using the Rorschach blots in their original form for attempting to tap imaginative predisposition. For this reason, it seems better to move to the employment of inkblots which are likely to invoke greater range of such responses. One such alternative is the Barron Movement Threshold inkblots, a set of 26 blots which show an increasing tendency to invoke movement responses so that one can, in effect, estimate the threshold for producing consistent movement responses on the blots in children (Barron, 1955). These have been used in earlier studies (Singer et al., 1956; Riess, 1957). Their use is also described in the chapters by Freyberg and Pulaski.

Another alternative to the original Rorschach inkblots is the use of the

Holtzman Inkblot technique (1963). Holtzman and his collaborators have developed a valuable research tool as an alternative to the limited information value of the standard Rorschach inkblots and have also provided some of our best available norms on the performance of children on the inkblots at various age levels and along particular determinants. The data from the Holtzman inkblots strongly support the importance of the movement response as an index of ideational tendencies, and also make it clear that there is an increasing trend toward production of M responses with age. The 5-year-olds (lowest in the normative group) show the lowest general scores in movement and college students show the highest scores; older groups show some decline in this response. Examples of the use of the Holtzman blots for scoring imaginative predisposition are found in the chapters by Gottlieb and Biblow. Further discussion of implications of the Rorschach-inkblot-type scoring in measuring imaginative predisposition will be postponed until these later chapters.

The advantage of using a measure such as inkblots as one approach to estimating imaginative predisposition in children lies in the limited degree of verbalization called for in such a procedure. It remains to be proven that the response to the inkblots represents an actual projection of a fundamental tendency to "see movements in the mind's eye" or some translation of motor-inhibited energy into the perception of motion in the environment as Werner (1945) had proposed and as I had earlier emphasized (Singer, 1955). A simpler explanation may be that the likelihood of producing a fantasy cognitive product to an inkblot is almost certainly going to take the form of human or human-like creatures in action. Simple verbalization of such a theme may be sufficient as an estimate of potential make-believe play.

The movement response to the inkblots is perhaps the most clear-cut measure of ideational fluency to the blots themselves, but it is also a part of a general pattern of responses as Holtzman's norms indicate (Holtzman, Thorpe, Swartz, & Herron, 1961). One need not therefore accept the more dubious energic constructs in the interpretation of movement responses to the inkblots to see the value of their use in estimating potential imaginative play. Perhaps the critical element has to do with a certain attitude of playfulness and ideational fluency which the child brings to the inkblot interpretation problem. The child may merely be willing to react as if the blots were interesting people or animals in motion while other children less disposed toward this playfulness may instead focus primarily on trying to be as accurate as possible in describing just what the card resembles.

In any case, the major advantages in the use of the inkblot lie in the fact that their purpose is somewhat disguised from the child, that they provide a reasonably adequate, reliably scored quantitative measure, and finally that the response required of the child involves a relative minimum verbalization so that gross differences in verbal intelligence are held to a minimum. The last is an important consideration. If the movement responses were merely a reflection of general intelligence or vocabulary differences among children, they would be less interesting to us for the purpose of this study. By controlling for verbal intelligence in various ways, one can estimate the degree to which the differences in movement responses are indeed genuine reflections of a divergent production or ideational fluency dimension as discussed by Guilford (1967) or Wallach (1971). The limited number of words necessary to produce human movement responses to inkblots is in contrast with the greater verbalization that is characteristic of some of the other techniques employed to measure imaginative play predisposition such as the Torrance Just-Suppose method or the interview technique.

Additional Approaches to Measuring Imaginative Predisposition

There is ample evidence from many studies of the factor structure of projective scores as well as inventory measurement methods that any investigator who attempts to measure predisposition by the use of contrasting groups should combine a series of measurements rather than rely solely on a specific test. The Torrance Just-Suppose method, for example, is one of a group of measures developed to approach the question of creativity in children. Essentially it is a measure of ideational fluidity or divergent production. Its use is described in the chapter by Gottlieb. Our experience has not included this technique with very young children and so it remains a question as to whether Just-Suppose is completely suitable as part of a battery of tests attempting to estimate imaginative play predisposition. At the same time, it seems conceptually within the same general category and ought at least to be tried in some form, since it involves "an attitude toward the possible," the kind of attitude which the child also brings to his play. We can certainly imagine that there ought to be some relation between the child's ability to conceive of unusual and interesting alternatives for various strange events and the child's ability to take a toy giraffe or elephant and treat it as if it were a human baby.

An approach that may be more suitable for young children, but which has not yet been attempted in any of our own studies is that of the use of the two cognitive styles identified in a series of studies by Kagan (1966) and various collaborators. By using a number of cognitive tests which call for conceptual linkages between pictures, matching of familiar abstract patterns and of familiar figures, and tasks requiring haptic-visual matching, Kagan has identified essentially two dimensions along which extremely young children vary. These he has labeled as the *reflective–impulsive* style and the second as the *analytic* style. The former represents the tendency to give either hasty answers *(impulsive)* or to delay and respond cautiously before yielding the answer *(reflective)*; the second dimension emphasizes the degree to which the child is capable of considering alternative conceptual groupings and for analyzing visual stimuli into smaller components.

It seems likely that the kind of child given to greater make-believe play and who might score high on inkblot movement and on the Torrance Just-Suppose test might also be one who is on the one hand reflective according to measures used by Kagan or analytic at least to some extent on those tests. Kagan reports that a group of 7- to 10-year-old boys who were high in their production of analytic concepts, also showed themselves to less likely be distracted by extraneous stimuli, to be capable of more controlled gross motor behavior in their play, and to prefer sedentary tasks requiring longer periods of concentration. The same boys also indicated a preference for vocations such as scientist or writer, which were clearly more associated with limited motor activity. It seems likely that the employment of measures such as those developed by Kagan and his group, to measure the reflective—impulsive and analytic dimensions could be appropriately applied in a battery attempting to estimate imaginative play predisposition as well. Indeed, it would be most useful at some point to investigate the interrelations among these styles and play behavior.

Still another approach to measurement might be one, as used by Pulaski in Chapter IV, which attempts to use responses of children to their own drawings as an indicator of potential imaginative play tendencies. Pulaski questioned the children about their drawings and rated their responses in terms of indications of make-believe elements. Here the focus is not upon the drawing skill of the child which may, to some extent, limit the generalization one can make. Rather, the emphasis is upon the degree to which the child is attempting to create not just a reproduction of a specific object, but a potential story line. Singer and Whiton (1971) found that kindergarten children high on measures of ideational fluency produce more expressive drawings. This technique merits more extensive study as a possible approach to measuring imaginative play disposition. Winnicott (1971) made extensive use of expressive drawings of "squiggles" as part of his psychiatric interviews with very young children.

Interviewing Children about Their Play Behavior

In attempting to obtain information about the play potentialities of children, there is perhaps an unfortunate overemphasis on the use of tests and techniques which, while seeming to have some ultimate relevant relationships, may take us a bit far afield from our major intention—the study of the play behavior itself. In this sense, it seems reasonable to call upon the most direct observer of the child's play—the child itself. We can get an indication of preference from the child for different kinds of games and a report of the general trend of play as the child perceives it. Naturally, with children below the ages of 3 or 4, there are not likely to be sufficient verbal skills to permit an adequate interview. Thus far, our results suggest that one can obtain adequate data from children of at least kindergarten age by means of a very simple series of questions. A further study employing the same technique in interviewing 3- and 4-year olds was reported in the previous chapter.

Naturally, as in the case of any kind of interview data, one can always question whether the subject himself is the best person to characterize his own behavior. This represents a fundamental problem for all psychologists using inventory or questionnaire approaches as well as interviews in attempting to solicit information on characteristic behavioral tendencies, attitudes, or personality traits. Nevertheless, there is a charming frankness about children. It is often possible to obtain relatively clear reports from them of their own characteristic tendencies, provided that the questions are relatively uncomplicated and that the interviewer shows some sensitivity and skill in throwing out only a limited number of probes to be certain that sufficient data have been obtained.

A suitable interview requires the child simply to state what his favorite games are and what kinds of games he prefers when he is alone. The child's reports can then be evaluated along a dimension of the degree to which fantasy elements are introduced into the games. After experimenting with rather complicated questionnaires and more elaborate questions, I was eventually led to a very simple format which involved the following four questions:

1. What is your favorite game? What do you like to play the most?
2. What game do you like to play best when you are all alone? What do you like to do best when you are all alone?
3. Do you ever have pictures in your head? Do you ever see make-believe things with pictures in your mind or think about them? What sort of things?
4. Do you have a make-believe friend? Do you have an animal or toy or make-believe person you talk to or take along with you? Did you ever have one, even though you don't any more?

Although the interview may include (for some specific purposes of a given study) additional questions in an effort to tease-out correlates of make-believe play, the preceding questions represent the basic items to be scored in using the interview as an approach to estimating imaginative play predisposition. Each question, asked in a number of ways to ensure that the child understands, may be followed by a brief probe if the response is unclear or if there is some hesitation in response. For example, if in response to the first or second question the child indicates the trade name of a commercial game of some type with which the interviewer is not familiar, it is obviously necessary to elicit a description of the game or enough further information to permit subsequent scoring of the item.

The critical feature in the scoring of these items has to do with the degree to which the child's report indicates introduction of symbolic play or make-believe activity. Thus, if a child reports on Item 1 that he prefers to play a game such as hopscotch or jump-rope, the likelihood is that there may not be much fantasy involved, since these are either games with rules or mastery games. A simple probe asking for the descriptions of the games is often sufficient to be certain that the child did not introduce make-believe elements into these traditional games. If, however, the child replies that the favorite game is "cops and robbers," "pirates," "house," or "school," the likelihood is that make-believe elements are involved. The first two items, therefore, are essentially efforts to clarify the self-reports on play preferences with respect to make-believe elements, with the first question being somewhat more ambiguous than the second and permitting the child to report on games that may be played with other children, whereas the second specifies solitary play.

The third question is somewhat more difficult, especially for younger children, but our experience has been that we can get a sufficient range of response even from 3- and 4-year olds for this item. Indeed, one really has to ask why psychologists have not attempted more extensively to generate sets of questions about the symbolic activity of children to clarify the degree to which they can report upon their own private fantasies. The tendency has been all too often to rely almost completely upon test responses or reactions to perceptual situations rather than formalizing at least some effort to make use of the child's own introspective capacities and to clarify the relationship between language development and ability to describe various internal experiences.

The "pictures in the head" question frequently elicits indications of make-believe games or active fantasies, particularly in somewhat older children. Young children respond to this question relatively tersely, but with properly trained judges, scoring can be treated with a reasonably high degree of reliability.

The fourth question has to do with imaginary playmates. As has been indicated earlier, there is a small literature on the role of imaginary playmates and there are indications that approximately a third of children do indeed report such playmates through the early school years. As noted earlier, Schaefer (1969) reported that one of the few retrospective variables that proved to be associated with creativity in college students was the recall of having had an imaginary playmate as a child. In my own case, the stimulus of writing this volume has led me to think back over earlier experiences. While I do not recall any extended imaginary playmates as a very young child, it is certainly true that in high school, as a boy of 13 or 14, or even a bit later, I recall passing the time during solitary rides on the New York City subway imagining that I had as a companion an ancient Roman or Greek who has somehow turned up in the New York City of the late 1930s and to whom I explained all of the marvels and, alas, all of the problems of that particular age. Indeed, I can recall a particular time in May of 1940 at the time when the German Army had broken through the French lines and the Allied cause was in disarray, I found myself sadly walking back from school where I had heard the news and suddenly in my mind explaining to my Roman friend that once again disaster at the hands of German invaders lay ahead for the Western civilization that I valued.

The scoring of a questionnaire of this type depends first of all on obtaining reliable judges who can agree that the answers are indeed make-believe play or fantasy answers. This is relatively simple for these particular interview items. The next step is to score the questionnaire which is essentially a 5-point scale. Thus a child who gives a fantasy answer to all four of these questions would get a score of 4. Our data suggest that, generally speaking, most children do not answer "yes" to more than about two to three items. Frequently, by dividing a group of subjects into those yielding a score of 0 or 1 from those yielding a score of 2 or more, we get rather clear-cut differences in other evidences of imaginativeness of make-believe play. We have not yet been able to carry out any fairly extended repeat reliability studies of this interview measure, but as the reader will see, there are adequate indications that at the very least this interview does show a capacity between different play styles.

A study will now be described which represents the earliest approach to the use of the interview in evaluating the imaginative play behavior and related family background factors of children. From this, it can be seen that the interview is relatively simple to administer, requiring no clinical skills or special professional qualities other than reasonable maturity and sensitivity to establishing rapport with children. For this reason, a simple interview technique like this ought to become a basis for more extended studies to be used with student interviewers. The report that follows is a modified version of a study published in 1961. It is repeated here to indicate some of the correlates of imaginative predisposition based on interviewing and as a basis for the use of the measure in the subsequent studies in this volume.

Some Correlates of Children's Self-Reported
High- and Low-Fantasy Predisposition

How Fantasy Play May Develop

The tendency to engage in imaginative play, fantasied role-shifting, or daydreaming may be looked on as a particular skill that can be developed in a given child as a consequence of the interaction of constitutional brain capacities (e.g., for symbolization) with a particular set of early environmental circumstances that provides stimulation and encouragement for practice. One of the environmental factors that seems particularly important appears to be an opportunity for regular contact with at least one benign adult whose movements, speech patterns, attitudes, and values are available for mimicry by the child. In the subsequent absence of the adult, faced by either an unsatisfied need or, more significantly, the anxiety or ambiguity of sheer empty time to fill, the child has available a repertory of movements, words, or postures that briefly relieve his loneliness and also provide new sources of pleasure.

The exploration that occurs through fantasy play seems likely to generate its own satisfaction in competence and environmental exploration and may result in the formation of what Rapaport has called a new hierarchical level of thought. It should be noted, however, that parental absence need not imply rejection or loss. This absence may merely represent the normal absorption of the adults in household chores or personal recreation. The greatly overprotected child who is constantly under adult scrutiny and who is smothered by attention or enforced interaction may not develop fantasy skills for lack of opportunity to practice. Such children may indeed become as dependent on the adults to think for them as they are dependent on parents for physical care.

An optimal balance of benign parental contact and opportunity to be alone seems therefore essential to the development of a rich imaginative life. This optimal situation probably occurs most readily where the child's mother is relatively warm, devoted, willing, and capable of spending time with the child, but not so emotionally involved that she cannot at times leave the child to its own devices. This particular set of circumstances seems also most likely to occur in the case of an only or first child or where the birth spacing produces similar conditions.

The preceding considerations suggest a number of related hypotheses which can be tested by comparing relatively imaginative and unimaginative children. It may be anticipated, for example, that children who report considerable fantasy play or daydreaming also report greater closeness or identification with their mothers, as well as generally greater contact with their parents. Support for the linkage of maternal identification and daydreaming or introceptive tendencies have indeed been reported in a number of studies with adults (Singer & Schonbar, 1961; Singer & McCraven, 1961; Singer & Opler, 1956; Sharef, 1959).

If stimulation from other children or adults or communication media is ever-present, the child seems much less likely to practice and perfect fantasy play. It seems reasonable to deduce that only children, first-born children, or children distantly spaced from other siblings might show greatest daydreaming tendencies. The child with many real playmates is less likely to invent an imaginary one. Schachter's (1959) work on ordinal position and need for affiliation is suggestive although it is not directly related to the *degree* of fantasy activity here referred to.

The mere availability of an adult is undoubtedly not enough, however, to foster a continuous development of a fantasy dimension in the child. It seems likely that several other factors must be considered. Parents who are verbally expressive, whose vocabularies are varied and colorful, who read and tell the children stories, must certainly contribute to the development of imagination. Such parents provide the raw materials, e.g., variety of topics, past and future references, verbal imagery, and accounts from which the child can fashion his fantasies of fictional and historical personalities. It is likely that parents who spend time with children through the medium of games of skill or chance such as cards, Parcheesi, checkers, or model building would not necessarily foster daydreaming tendencies to the same extent. They might of course help the child to develop well in games of mastery and other cognitive skills.

The very unreality for the child of many of an imaginative adult's conversations or references may result in efforts by the child to integrate this imaginative or abstract material in his own unique fashion. One might expect that children raised chiefly in adult company and with minimal peer contacts would reveal greater evidence of ruminative or imaginative behavior. This was, in fact, the observation of McCurdy (1960) in his study of the childhood of geniuses. This again suggests the hypothesis that children who report considerable imaginative play will also report greater parental contact, greater maternal identification, and less involvement with siblings or fewer siblings.

Given a moderate development of imaginative ability, daydreaming or fantasy play may become available for defensive purposes to the youngster who experiences failure or frustration either in the family constellation or in peer associations. To the extent that an imaginary world gains excessive value, the child's failure to practice and learn social skills by direct contact may cause him ultimate misery, although the world has often profited from the imaginative products of unhappy persons with such backgrounds who possessed literary, graphic, or musical talent as well. Under optimal circumstances, a capacity for daydreaming and fantasy afford both child and adult a useful and pleasurable medium for handling anxiety and for creative exploration of the future by means of "experimental action," to use Freud's felicitous phrase. There is no evidence to assume that daydreaming or introversive tendencies are inherently maladaptive (Carrigan, 1960). Instead, it seems reasonable to consider that some development of daydreaming ability is useful for all persons. Beyond that, the relative richness of development of this capacity represents a life-style dimension along which people may vary in their day-to-day approach to both problems and pleasures.

Viewed as a manifestation of a cognitive and affective style, imagination or daydreaming capacity might well be associated with a pattern of development and personality organization in which thinking is valued and affective and motor control are somewhat more emphasized. From the vantage point of psychopathology, one might suspect that high daydreamers might show more manifestations of defenses associated with obsessional characteristics, while children who show little daydreaming might well exhibit patterns more like those of hysterical personalities with less self-consciousness and greater use of mechanisms such as denial or repression. Indeed it seems likely that daydreaming or imagination are ego functions autonomously developed, but particularly available for dealing with certain types of conflicts that arise in development or, perhaps, that are further fostered by certain particular kinds of parent—child conflicts. The reasoning concerning the relationship to the parents which enhances imaginative skill leads then to the possibility that children who report more daydreaming will also reveal different patterns of psychological conflicts than children who report minimal fantasy play. The closeness to mother or to both parents suggests that daydreamers are more likely to have difficulties surrounding adult identification problems, Oedipal conflicts, aggression specifically directed toward their fathers, achievement pressures, and rivalries with younger siblings. Children with relatively less fantasy may manifest problems less involved with adult identification and more with specific deprivations or impulse manifestations, e.g., oral deprivation, diffuse aggression, passivity or dependency, feelings of rejection, etc. While precise evaluation of these complex differences in defense structure and conflict areas was beyond the scope of the present investigation, a clinical estimate of differences between high- and low-fantasy children in conflict areas and defense mechanisms was attempted.

If daydreaming or fantasy tendencies grow chiefly out of conflict and deprivation, one might expect imaginative children to show a greater degree of conflict or more manifestations of psychological difficulties than less imaginative children. Indeed Freud (1959) wrote, " . . . A happy person never phantasies, only an unsatisfied one [p. 146] ." The present study could provide no final answer to the issue of whether fantasy or daydreaming arises chiefly as a consequence of conflict. It was felt, however, that evidence of differing patterns rather than degrees of conflict in children differing in self-reported imaginative tendencies might offer some indication that fantasy tendencies represent an autonomously developed cognitive style rather than merely an indication of greater frustration or anxiety.

An important behavioral consequence of the differential development of fantasy or daydreaming tendencies in children might well be expected to be manifested in waiting ability. Given a situation in which the child must either defer gratification or inhibit his natural motor expressive tendencies, it might be expected that a highly imaginative child could rely more on his fantasy-making capacity to pass the time. The less imaginative child might have to resort more to direct perceptual and physical contact with his environment. In a preliminary effort to evaluate this possibility, high- and low-fantasy children were exposed to two simple waiting situations in the present study. To the extent that day-dreaming affords a satisfying medium for filling time, it could be predicted that high-fantasy children would function more effectively in a situation calling for them to wait quietly for long periods. One might also expect group differences in creativity of storytelling and possibly in other personality characteristics or preferences.

Method

An investigation of the predictions previously outlined called for child interviews, storytelling tasks, and behavioral observations in waiting situations. All procedures were administered in one session lasting approximately one hour. Following collection of protocols from all *Ss*, the children were divided at the median into high- and low-fantasy groups on the basis of their responses to the four questions concerning fantasy and daydreaming activities. These high- and low-fantasy groups served as the basic comparison groups for testing the hypotheses concerning differences between imaginative and less imaginative children.

Subjects The *Ss* were 40 children between the ages of 6 and 9 attending a small private school and a summer day camp. They were all from middle socioeconomic backgrounds and were of somewhat above-average intelligence. The range of intelligence or socioeconomic status was too narrow to permit testing of some of Jersild, Markey, and Jersild's (1933) reports concerning the relationships between daydreaming and intelligence or social class. The choice of this age group grew out of a number of considerations, most important being school attendance and the frequent reports in the literature (Singer, 1955) that internalization of fantasy play as thought and imagery begins in this age range. Since one of the purposes of this study was to explore the possibilities of direct interviews with children concerning their daydreaming or imaginative behavior, the frankness and spontaneity of the children's responses to questions about their private worlds proved refreshing and encouraging for further approaches of this sort.

The children were divided into high- and low-fantasy groups on the basis of the number of positive responses to the four questions which were asked as part of the interview procedure. Inspection of the distribution of scores for the total sample revealed that dividing the groups at a score of 2 or more positive fantasy replies yielded an almost even split into high and low groups of 19 and 21, respectively. Assignment of positive or negative fantasy scores for each of the four items proved relatively simple and there was complete agreement on scoring responses to the four items by two independent raters.

A comparison of high- and low-fantasy children on a number of variables is presented in Table 1. Inspection of this table reveals that the two groups did not differ significantly in age or sex composition. Although formal IQs were available for only a much smaller sample of *Ss*, no significant difference in the comparison groups emerged here either. The mean IQ for the high-fantasy *Ss* ($N = 11$) was 116, while that for the low-fantasy *Ss* ($N = 10$) was 114.

Interview In order to obtain direct information from the children concerning the extent and character of their fantasy and other play activities, a structured, clinical interview schedule was prepared. This schedule included (in addition to background identification data) questions concerning the child's favorite games (e.g., "verbal, athletic, gambling, skill, or fantasy"), amount of time spent watching television, favorite programs, reading activities, parents' reading habits, type of play when alone, etc. The questions covered the general pattern of the child's play and permitted scoring for relative prominence of fantasy play or indications of degree of physical activities or hobbies of a nonfantasy nature. The questionnaire included a variety of questions concerning the degree of parental contact with the children. Children were asked if their parents read to them, if they told stories and if they played with the children. Degree of parental contact was then scored on a scale of 0–3 by two independent raters without knowledge of S's group classification. The children were also asked to indicate which parent they most resembled and which they liked best. Results were treated in terms of whether they chose, "Father, Mother, or Both." Data such as television and movie favorites, wishes that a "Magic Man" could transform them, etc., were analyzed qualitatively.

Storytelling and Color Choice

In order to obtain additional clinical information as well as to score for creativity of stories, need achievement, and psychological defense patterns, the children were asked to tell stories to verbally administered stimuli, e.g., "a mother and her son. They look worried." This procedure was based directly on an approach to achievement motive measurement in children described in Atkinson (1958). Color choice involved asking children's preferred crayon from four: red, yellow, blue and green. Previous research has suggested the red and yellow are more often associated with low need for achievement and blue and green with high need for achievement (Atkinson, 1958).

The stories were then rated independently by two clinicians without knowledge of the daydream status of each S. Agreement on need achievement, scored from 0–5, was obtained in 87% of the cases and the final scores of the remaining Ss were settled by rating of a third judge. The creativity rating of 0–5 was based on originality of content, variety of characters, or changes in space and time. Two judges agreed in 75% of their ratings of creativity with final scores of disagreements based on a third judge's decision.

Finally, a clinician with experience in child diagnosis read all protocols carefully, including the clinical interviews and thematic stories, and prepared a brief summary of the major defense structure, e.g., obsessional, hysterical, schizoid, etc., and of major problem areas, e.g., controlling diffuse aggression, Oedipal problem, oral deprivation, etc. These clinical reports, while admittedly of unknown reliability, were used to provide at least some greater tentative enrichment of the material available on each child. Based on these clinical reports, each S was classified in terms of major defense operation and major level of conflict, Oedipal (involving adult identification problems, aggression directed toward father, etc.) or pre-Oedipal (involving oral deprivation, diffuse aggression, penis envy, rejection feelings). Also scored here were total number of conflict areas indicated in the clinical ratings. Finally, the clinician indicated specific protocols that suggested severe disturbance.

Waiting Behavior In order to obtain a simple quantitative measure of relative motor control and capacity for delay, each child was asked to cooperate in a situation calling for him or her to remain quietly in one spot as long as possible. The child could sit or stand as he wished, but could not keep changing position. To interest the children in the procedure, the instructions indicated that a study of persons suitable for space flight with its long periods of solitary confinement in a narrow space was involved. An attempt was made to obtain maximum motivation by emphasizing the importance of space travel and the selection of "space men of the future." Two forms of this procedure were used with each child, one calling for him to wait indefinitely until he could not continue further, the other calling for him to wait quietly for a 15-min period. Both conditions were employed with each child and were alternated throughout to control for sequence effects. The child's score was the length of time in seconds he sat or stood quietly in place before signaling that he could not continue or that he felt the 15 min had passed. Each child was required to remain standing or seated in a narrowly circumscribed area. Following a description of the strictures of rocket travel and of the need for finding suitable candidates, the child was told that he would have to remain standing or seated with minimal movement as long as possible or for 15 min (depending on the condition). During the waiting time, E carefully avoided conversation or any clues which might encourage the child to stop or to converse. The definite time period condition was employed to ascertain whether any differences might emerge as a result of specifying for the child the length of his wait.

Results

Inspection of results in Table 1 suggests that children divided into high- and low-fantasy groups do indeed differ on a number of variables relevant to the theoretical formulations outlined in the introduction. For simplicity of presentation, these findings will be presented in general groupings with a review of the hypotheses involved.

Background Variables and Parental Relationships

The theoretical considerations outlined earlier suggest that the backgrounds of high-fantasy Ss may be expected to differ from those of low-fantasy Ss in terms of a combination of birth order, degree of parental contact, identification

TABLE 1

Experimental and Background Variables for High- and Low-Fantasy Children

Variables	High fantasy (N = 19)			Low fantasy (N = 21)			Significance tests	
	$\bar{x}$	SD	Freq.	$\bar{x}$	SD	Freq.	Test	p values
Background variables								
Age	7.87	1.06		7.64	1.06		t = .68	.50
Sex			11F, 8M			8F, 13M		.50
Birth Order	1.32	.58		1.67	.81		t = 1.49	.50
Siblings								
Older Siblings			6			15	$x^2 = 4.33$	<.05 >.02
Younger Siblings			17			13		
No. of Only or First-Born Children			14			11		
Other birth Positions			5			10	$x^2 = 1.71$	.20
Parental Contact	1.82	1.17		1.14	.75		t = 2.26	.05
Parental Preference								
Father			12			3		
Mother			4			2	$x^2 = 14.19$	.001
Both			3			15		

Parents' Reading

No.	9	12			
1 per week	2	2	$\chi^2 = .36$	.90
2–3 per week or more	7	6			

TV Watching Time

Daily	13	17			
2–3 per week	2	1	$\chi^2 = 3.88$	.20
1 per week or less	3	0			

Experimental variables

Waiting Time

(15' Ext.)	486.10 sec	307.72	235.52	247.12	$t = 2.82$	.01
Waiting Time (Indef.)	592.68 sec	447.06	241.62	223.02	$t = 3.09$	.01
Creativity	3.10	1.02	1.90	.87	$t = 3.97$	.01
Need Achievement	2.79	1.23	2.28	1.26	$t = 1.28$	.50

Color Choice

blue–green	12	3	$\chi^2 = 6.96$	.01
red–yellow	5	13		

Type of Conflict

Oedipal	16	7	$\chi^2 = 12.50$	.001
Pre-Oedipal	2	17		

Defense Structure

Obsessional	9	2	$\chi^2 = 7.27$	.01
Hysterical	1	8		

Note—In some instances children refused to respond, confused instructions, or data were not available, thus yielding different frequencies in certain choice categories or in clinical ratings. In the Type of Conflict category a few Ss showed both types, thus altering frequencies.

with mother or at least one stable parental figure, and relative absence of many other siblings. Examination of Table 1 reveals that although the high-fantasy Ss tend to obtain lower birth order scores, the difference between the groups is not significant. It should be noted, however, that for some reason children in this total sample showed a high percentage of first-born or only children, thus severely limiting the range of birth-order scores. There was a trend also towards a greater frequency of only children in the high-fantasy group. If the frequencies of older and younger siblings for each S in the two groups are compared, a significant chi-square emerges, with high-fantasy Ss showing fewer older siblings and more younger siblings. These results generally suggest some support for the notion that fantasy development is related to lessened opportunities for peer contact and earlier birth order.

If we next consider parental relationships, some interesting findings emerge. The ratings of degree of contact with parents indicate that high-fantasy Ss report significantly greater association between themselves and their parents ($p = .05$) than do the low-fantasy Ss. The data indicate that this greater parental contact is general. When a separate analysis by number of fantasy-play contacts was made, the groups were not differentiated. Closer examination indicates a possible limitation of the questioning since high-fantasy Ss are more likely to be read to by parents. The data therefore do not offer support for the hypothesis concerning the nature of the parent—child contact, but do indicate a generally greater frequency of interaction between the high-fantasy Ss and their parents.

When the children were asked to state their preferred parent, a striking difference emerged between the groups. The low-fantasy group refused, as a rule, to choose between them and indicated both parents as equally liked, while the high-fantasy children far more often singled out one parent. A chi-square for choice of both or a single preferred parent was significant at $p = .001$. Despite the anticipated relationship between maternal closeness and daydreaming, the father was actually much more often chosen by the high-fantasy Ss. Although girls slightly outnumbered boys in the high group, this result could not be attributed to opposite-sex preferences since the boys made as many father choices as the girls. No differences emerged between the groups in the parent described as the disciplinarian nor in the type of punishment reported. Physical punishment was common in both groups. No difference in parents' reported reading habits emerged, but children's observations in this area are of questionable value.

It seems likely from these findings that high-fantasy children orient themselves clearly toward one parent and that this focus on a single individual may enhance identification possibilities and ultimate fantasy tendency. The emphasis on the father by the high-fantasy Ss is certainly contrary to expectation and to previous reports. These results may represent a particular characteristic of the fathers of this sample who tended on the whole to be in the professional or managerial class (for both high and low groups) and who might transfer their own intellectual interests to the children.

Waiting Behavior

Examination of Table 1 reveals that, as hypothesized, high-fantasy children were able to remain seated or standing quietly for significantly longer time periods before giving up than the low-fantasy Ss. This result held for both types of waiting, one calling for a definite time, the other an indefinite wait. The two procedures proved to be significantly correlated ($r = .64$). The general mean wait was only a little more than 6 min. Qualitatively, it was apparent that remaining in this situation was not uncomfortable or upsetting, yet most children seemed to require some activity to help fill the time. After initial visual exploration of the room, scanning the E's face for a clue, they lapsed into apathy for brief periods, only to begin visual search or minor fidgeting again. The children who generally showed longest delays were those who fairly soon transformed the waiting situation into a fantasy game and rolled their eyes, muttered under their breath (to imitate engines or radio orders), or occasionally turned an imaginary steering wheel. Interviewed after the study, they revealed that they had helped pass the time by "playing a rocket game" or "I made believe I was flying an airplane and bad guys were after me."

It is possible, of course, that the waiting situation only demonstrates that children who say they play fantasy games enter more quickly or effectively into the spirit of a fantasy game. Qualitative observation suggested, however, that all the children were quite intrigued by the element of competition and seemed quite eager to demonstrate that they had the ability to meet the standards for an astronaut by waiting quietly. Obviously, other types of waiting or deferred gratification situations would appear appropriate to develop the theory further. The interview data suggest that children who reported extensive fantasy play felt less awareness of the passage of time. These observations suggest the value of further exploration of the relation of fantasy or daydreaming to time experience. A study with adults also suggests that fantasy activity makes time appear to pass more quickly (Wheeler, 1969).

Personality Characteristics

The third group of results bears on differences between high- and low-fantasy Ss in various personality measures. The two groups did not differ significantly in achievement motivation, as measured by the storytelling technique, although the imaginative play group showed a somewhat higher mean need for achievement. As noted above, there seemed to be no qualitative differences reported in the eagerness with which children approached the waiting room situation. Very striking differences emerged in the color choices of the Ss, however. The high-fantasy Ss most often chose green or blue crayons while the low-fantasy Ss most often chose red or yellow. These color preferences present an intriguing confirmation of frequently cited personality differences in responses to cool or warm colors (Gerard, 1958; Colvin, 1953). Knapp and McClelland (Atkinson, 1958) have reported in separate studies that choices of red and yellow were more closely associated with low need for achievement while blue and green were more closely linked to high need for achievement. The finding in the present investigation may therefore imply a difference in achievement motivation between high- and low-fantasy Ss after all. The color choice proved to be significantly associated both with need for achievement ($\chi^2 = 6.3, p = .02$) and with waiting time ($\chi^2 = 4.5, p = .05$) for this sample. The preference for the blue—green end of the spectrum thus again appears to be associated with a more controlled orientation to living, greater fantasy, waiting ability, and achievement motivation. In general, the high- and low-fantasy Ss showed no differences in occupational choices. No differences in favorite television characters or programs emerged either.

If we turn next to ratings of creativity or imaginativeness of story telling, the high-fantasy group shows significantly higher scores, as predicted. This result confirms for children the findings reported in earlier studies with adults (Singer & McCraven, 1961; Singer & Schonbar, 1961) that suggest that frequent day-dreamers are more ingenious and flexible in their story telling. There is no reason, of course, to believe (as yet) from the present series of studies that they are actually more creative in other areas. The extent to which daydreaming frequency might be associated with general originality in nonliterary fields is an intriguing area for study. One might well further consider whether particular types of reverie content (e.g., interpersonal versus abstract or physical form) are associated with occupational choice or creativity.

The final group of findings must be considered with caution since they involve greater clinical speculation, particularly in view of the limited data available. Relying upon a brief clinical summary of the total protocol for each child, an attempt was made to test the notion of more pervasive personality differences between the two groups. It was felt that Ss who resort to fantasy are more likely to have formed greater adult identifications or are at least more likely to have reached a stage of attempted identification. Perhaps children with minimal daydream tendencies are more likely to manifest signs of fixations or deprivations of part-functions, e.g., orality, diffuse aggression, or rejection. Roughly, using a psychoanalytic model, the latter problems correspond to personality problems or conflict areas which occur in the pre-Oedipal period of development while the identification strivings seem more likely to emerge as an effort to deal with Oedipal problems in childhood. When the clinical reports were rated for Oedipal and pre-Oedipal conflict areas, rather striking differences emerge. The high-fantasy Ss showed greater Oedipal involvements, aggression toward the father, rivalry with adults, identification conflicts, etc., while the low-fantasy children more often were reported to have conflicts centering on oral deprivation, fear of loss of love and generalized aggression ($\chi^2 = 16.28, p = .001$). This intriguing result obviously merits more intensive scrutiny under better-controlled conditions.

Finally, in terms of general defense structure, it had been predicted that obsessional mechanisms would be more conspicuous in the protocols of high-fantasy Ss while hysterical mechanisms such as repression and denial of difficulties would be more often evident in low-fantasy Ss' records. For those Ss on whom this data could be rated ($N = 10$ in each group), the result proved to be significant ($\chi^2 = 7.26, p = .01$). It is admittedly difficult to avoid the possibility that halo effects or contamination of information entered into these judgments. However, the clinician who prepared the original reports was unfamiliar with the intent of the analysis or with these hypotheses. It should be noted that the two groups were not significantly different in total number of conflict areas cited nor in number of children cited for overall degree of pathology.

Some Conclusions

In general, it appears clear both from quantitative and qualitative findings that children who report differences in daydreaming or fantasy play frequency show a consistent pattern of differences in terms of other variables which have theoretical relevance. The support afforded the hypotheses in this study represents a promising beginning for a more systematic evaluation of the origins and concomitants of imaginative play in children. Most encouraging was the directness and simplicity of children's reports in the interviews.

It should be noted that the relative homogeneity of this sample in intelligence, cultural background, socioeconomic status, and parental education, while limiting some of the findings, also makes the significance of positive results more noteworthy. The overall qualitative impression which emerges from the experience of this investigation is that the tendency toward fantasy behavior represents not so much a defensive maneuver in the "conflictual ego-sphere" as a more general pattern or life style. It seems to be a dimension of experience and exploration available to most children, but one whose richness and frequency of employment grows from a set of optimal conditions including parental interest and acceptance of imagination, availability of adults for identification, and opportunity or occasion for practice of fantasy through being alone. The next group of studies (Chapters IV through VII) will provide additional evidence with varying age groups of the importance of the predisposition to fantasy play.

CHAPTER IV

Toys and Imaginative Play

Mary Ann Pulaski

Introduction

So far in this volume we have emphasized the development of measures for ongoing play and for assessing predisposition to play. However, the child also plays in a physical environment which generates a set of possibilities in its own right. The following study represents one of the few efforts until now to examine what effects the structure of the toys available to a child may have upon his level of make-believe play. It also makes use of an evaluation of fantasy predisposition and studies some possible interactions between what a child brings to the playroom in expectations and style and what impact the kind of materials he finds there can have on his play. By presenting this material in detail, we hope to stimulate considerable further exploration of the relationship of toy characteristics and the environmental setting more generally to the development of make-believe or other forms of play.

What the child brings to any play situation is also of critical importance. The research described here by Dr. Pulaski brings out very clearly an approach to measuring predisposition to fantasy or make-believe play and how to observe it in the playroom. While any effort to control all the complexities of children's play necessarily involves some limitations and compromises, the following report is remarkably thorough in its effort to take into account many possibilities. The reader seriously concerned with developing further research in this field can find many basic components upon which to build further in this work.

JEROME L. SINGER

One of the characteristics that distinguishes human from animal play in childhood is the capacity for make-believe. Piaget (1962) noted the rudiments of fantasy play in his children at ages of a year to 15 months. Church's (1966) mothers reported it in two of the "Three Babies" as early as 14 months. Usually such fantasy play is accompanied by laughter and manifestations of delight. In older children, it takes the form of storytelling and dramatic role-playing. In still older children, it can be observed in the ability to produce varied and fanciful responses to school tasks: to write a composition, paint a picture, or compose poetry that has the quality of imagination and originality. Yet not all children have this make-believe ability; in fact, after many years of teaching and observing children, some of us wonder if it is not gradually decreasing among children today.

There could be many reasons for such a decrease in fantasy ability. For one thing, there is much less need for many children of this generation to exercise fantasy. In the movies, on television, and in their toys, they are provided with the utmost in prefabricated fantasy materials. Corncob dolls and scrapwood guns are things of the past; children today have dolls as well-dressed and sophisticated as Vogue models, and war toys so realistic as often to be gruesome. Nothing is left to the imagination; thus, it is conceivable that imagination and fantasy may decline in some groups for lack of practice.

Singer (1966, p. 148) has raised the intriguing question of whether realistic toys might not actually impede fantasy development. At least, it might be expected that children would tire of them more quickly because they have such limited possibilities. Conversely, unstructured toys, being less clearly defined, could give rise to a greater variety of fantasy themes. There has been some research, reviewed in what follows, which indicates that the structure of toys has an effect upon play behavior. In other areas of study, the role of stimulus characteristics in influencing behavior has come under observation. Berkowitz and Le Page (1967) found that the sight of guns in their experimental room elicited much stronger aggressive responses from already angry, aroused young men than were observed when no guns were present. Lieberman (1964), in a recent study of playfulness, stated, "It might be worth exploring whether some play materials more than others would encourage playfulness in the child . . . it might aid in selecting play materials that stimulate creative thinking [p. 98]."

The Issue of Fantasy: Constructive or Compensatory

In recent years, there has been a move toward a view of fantasy as a constructive cognitive ability. Piaget (1962) considered "ludic symbolism," the make-believe fantasies of children, an indispensable step in their cognitive development. The imaginative symbol was the means by which the child moved beyond the concrete and immediately present to the realm of operational thought. Werner (1948) spoke of the oscillation between fantasy and everyday reality that characterizes children's play, and regarded it as a necessary part of the child's development. " . . . the older the child grows, the more he becomes aware of the fictitious character of his play fantasies. A sign of this development is the fluctuation of his attitude toward the creations of his own fancy [p. 398]." McClelland and his associates (1953), particularly Atkinson (1958), have pointed out the role of fantasy in achievement motivation. Marshall (1961) and Marshall and Doshi (1965) have reported that doll-play fantasies in nursery school children are related to pleasant experiences, and that pleasant and stimulating home relations are directly associated with the use of fantasy in play with peers.

The dichotomy between fantasy as constructive and the psychoanalytic view of fantasy as compensatory is found also in the attitudes of educators toward the fantasy play of children. In the nineteenth century, Froebel described the child as a self-active, creative being who should be educated by self-expression. But half a century later Dr. Maria Montessori created a system which frowned upon imaginative play as a "somewhat unfortunate pathological tendency of early childhood [Hill, in Garrison, 1926, p. xiv]." Her materials were designed to suppress fantasy and imaginative play. Children should not make believe, Montessori declared; "to encourage them along such lines was to encourage defects of character [Gross & Gross, 1965, p. 34]." The fact that Montessori's theories and materials are enjoying such a revival today may be contributing to a decrease in fantasy play.

On the other hand, the researchers in creativity (Getzels & Jackson, 1962; Guilford, 1956; Tayler, 1964; Torrance, 1962; Wallach & Kogan, 1965) all seem to be searching for ways to increase imaginative, divergent thinking. One psychologist (de Mille, 1967) has recently published a book of games designed to exercise children's imagination, which he regards as "an intellectual ability that can be improved by practice [p. 19]." He further states:

> Television and comic book fantasy can hardly be expected to cultivate the imagination, because it is already completely formed, on the screen or on the page. Nothing is left for the child to do but absorb it. The experience of the child is passive. It is not *his* imagination that is being exercised, but that of some middle-aged writer in Hollywood, New York, or Chicago [p. 18].

The Effect of Toys as a Variable

The earliest fantasy play, as observed by Piaget and others, is in relation to objects—the toys and materials the child has at hand. The effect of such materials upon the development of fantasy thus becomes an important experimental variable. There have been a number of research studies which have shown the differential effects of different kinds of toys upon children's behavior in a variety of situations. The well-known work of Barker, Dembo, and Lewin (1941) demonstrated the regressive responses of preschool children to mutilated or incomplete toys before and after they had had access to more elaborate and attractive toys. In an unpublished dissertation, Riess (1957) used two kinds of toys chosen to elicit high and low levels of motor activity. She found that children who gave M (human movement) responses on the Rorschach test preferred low-activity toys such as a kaleidoscope, a coloring book, or a puzzle. Children who did not give M responses chose high-activity toys such as a jump rope or a rubber ball, significantly more often. Likewise, Lesser (1962) found that less imaginative children selected toys associated with vigorous motor play, while more imaginative youngsters preferred toys which required little motor activity, but a greater outlay of imagination. Gilmore (1964) studied the toy preferences of anxious versus nonanxious children of 5 to 8, and found that his subjects preferred novel or complex toys to simple ones in a variety of situations.

Much research has been done by Sears (1947) and his students on how children express their feelings of frustration and aggression through play with a doll family in a dollhouse. However, the only study using these materials as a controlled variable was made by Phillips (1945) a student of Sears. She compared the effects upon preschool children's doll play of materials of high realism (miniature, lifelike furniture, and bendable dolls appropriately dressed) with materials of low realism (crudely constructed, blocklike furniture, and sexless stuffed dolls without clothing). Her results showed that her subjects spent significantly more time exploring the high realism materials, but that the low realism materials elicited a significantly greater number of themes in the children's play. "Because of the ambiguity of the pieces, there was relatively more leeway with respect to the kinds of themes which the child appeared to feel free to build [p. 138]."

All of the studies just cited, while not in agreement as to objectives or results, showed the differential effect of various kinds of toys upon children's behavior. Therefore it was decided, in this study, to compare the effects of two degrees of structure upon children's fantasy play. It was hypothesized that minimally structured materials such as blocks, clay, or simple rag dolls, would stimulate children's fantasy more than extremely realistic toys, which left little to the imagination. The effects of such stimulation might be expected to manifest themselves in richer, less reality-bound fantasy productions. Furthermore, a greater variety of fantasy themes might be elicited by minimally structured playthings because the child's responses would be less anchored to specific stimulus situations. A bride doll could only suggest stories about a wedding, while a simple rag doll could be a baby, a witch, or a fairy princess. It was also predicted that children would tire less quickly of playing with simple, un-structured materials which could be adapted to many uses, than with highly structured toys which were obviously limited in function.

To test this hypothesis, two sets of playthings were assembled which were matched in function, but differed as much as possible in degree of structure. For example, a box full of "dress-up" materials of all kinds, which a child could combine into many different costumes, was matched with a selection of ready-made costumes for boys and girls, which were complete in every detail. The two sets of playthings were then presented to two groups of children with different levels of predisposition to fantasy, in order to study the experimental effects.

Fantasy Predisposition as a Variable

Three measures of fantasy-predisposition were selected after a pilot study, each of which is assumed to tap a different level of fantasy life.

1.   *The Barron (1955) Movement Threshold Inkblots.*   This was devised to measure only the M variable and is easy for young children. The first 8 plates were omitted as too difficult, but the remaining 20 were presented to each child on the theory that the earlier human movement was perceived, the greater was the child's predisposition to fantasy.

2.   *Singer's (1961) structured interview.*   This consisted of the four ques-tions which discriminated between high- and low-fantasy children (see Chapter III).

3.   *A drawing test in which each child was asked to draw a picture of "whatever you like to think about."*   The child was then encouraged to make up a story about his drawing, in order to see how imaginatively he responded. Altschuler and Hattwick (1947) have pointed out that children often verbalize more freely while painting, and it was felt that fantasy content would be more freely expressed during this task.

Personality Correlates of High Fantasy Predisposition

From evidence in the literature, it was hypothesized that children with a high predisposition to fantasy (HF) would not only play more productively and longer than children of low fantasy predisposition (LF), but would show certain personality characteristics which would distinguish them from low fantasy children. Hartley *et al.* (1952) and Lieberman (1964) have described the joy and delight manifested in play by children described as spontaneous, original and well-adjusted. Therefore, it was expected that HF children in this study would be rated as showing greater enjoyment in the play sessions than would LF children.

The finding that high fantasy children were able to sit still longer than low fantasy children (Chapter III) led to the hypothesis that HF children would show less motility in play than LF children. This expectation was also substantiated by Riess's (1957) study indicating that highly imaginative children showed greater motor restraint during a waiting period than did less imaginative children. The latter findings are a part of the theory regarding the meaning of the early M response discussed previously.

Another hypothesized characteristic which might be expected of HF children was flexibility when the structure of the situation and the demands upon subjects were suddenly changed. To test this, a flexibility test was devised which involved a sudden interruption of each child's free play; he was then given increasingly structured directions with which he was expected to comply. This situation was designed to test Singer's (1966) assertion that high fantasy is associated with the ability to control impulses and delay gratification. A child interrupted in the midst of free play would need to have such control in order to comply amiably with the demands made upon him. Furthermore, if fantasy is, as Singer states, a creative, cognitive skill, it might be expected to have some of the characteristics that have been associated with creativity, such as divergent thinking (Guilford, 1956); flexibility, originality, and inventiveness (Torrance, 1962); or productivity and uniqueness (Wallach & Kogan, 1965). It was predicted that it would be possible to rate the responses to the flexibility test in terms of divergency or originality of content, as well as conformity to instructions.

Interaction Hypothesis

In addition to predicting the effects of structure degrees in the toys and levels of fantasy predisposition in the subjects of this study, it appeared theoretically possible that these two factors might interact to produce differential results. Children of low fantasy development levels, it was theorized, might need the stimulation of highly structured toys. A model train might elicit a more imaginative story from a low fantasy child than would a row of blocks, though the high fantasy child might be able to use the blocks equally well just by imagining that they formed a train. If this should be the case, it was hypothesized that the use of more or less structured toys would differentially affect fantasy production in children with different levels of predisposition to fantasy. This study was therefore designed so that children of high and low predispositions to fantasy would be exposed to both highly structured and minimally structured playthings. In this way, any significant interaction between the two factors of fantasy predisposition and structure of the toys could be observed.

The Role of Sex Differences

A third independent variable included in the design was the factor of sex. Since previous research reviewed by Kagan in Hoffman and Hoffman (Eds.) (1964, Vol. 1, pp. 137-167) had indicated a positive correlation for girls between the educational level of the family and involvement with male-typed toys and games, it was expected that a sample chosen from upper middle-class homes in which most parents were college graduates would show a similar pattern of interests.

Characteristics of the Sample

Studies of the fantasy play of children in the early grades have been relatively few (Foster, 1930; Green, 1922; Jersild et al., 1933). It was the intent of this study, therefore, to investigate the fantasy of a group of children in the primary school grades.

The findings of Singer et al. (1956) suggest that cultural background, socioeconomic level, intelligence, and verbal facility, ability to control impulses and delay gratification are related to fantasy development. For the present study, therefore, subjects were selected from a relatively homogeneous group of children of above-average intelligence and verbal ability who came from homes of high socioeconomic status. All the children were white and almost all of them were culturally of Anglo-Saxon families. By using such a restricted sample, it was hoped to limit cultural and intellectual differences in tendency toward fantasy such as were found by Singer and McCraven (1962) in a comparison of adult ethnic groups.

The Experimental Procedure

Subjects

The subjects used in this study were chosen from among the 70 children enrolled in the kindergarten, first, and second grades of an exclusive private school in Nassau County, New York. These children were fairly homogeneous as regards above-average intelligence, verbal ability, and socioeconomic status. Almost all their parents were college graduates who expected their children to have the same educational advantages.

The kindergarten, first- and second-grade children were selected for this study because they were verbal enough to describe their fantasies, yet naive enough to react freely in the play situation. Screening tests were administered to all 70 children in these three grades, in order to select groups with high and low predispositions to fantasy. The screening consisted of the following procedures.

1. Barron's (1955) inkblots were presented to each S. Scores were ranked so that the S with the earliest M response received the highest rank, and Ss who never did give M responses received the lowest.

2. The structured interview described in Chapter III was conducted with each child. Answers were scored positively if they tended to indicate a preference for solitary or fantasy activity. A child whose favorite game was football

and who watched television when alone received negative scores, while one who preferred playing Batman or cowboys when alone received positive scores.

3. Each child was asked to draw a picture, and then to tell a story about it. The drawings were judged, not as art work, but as an expression of fantasy. They were rated on a 5-point scale with drawings of something concrete from the child's immediate experience (his dog, his house, etc.) receiving the lowest rating. The highest ratings went to fantasy drawings (ghosts, fairies) or stories such as, "This is a magic tree."

The scores of all three tests were ordered into continuous measures and the sum of the ranked scores for each child was used to compute Kendall's W. After a correction for ties was applied (Siegel, 1956, pp. 233-234) the coefficient of concordance among the measures for boys was significant ($\chi^2 = 54.87$, $df = 31$, $p < .01$). That for girls fell below the level of statistical significance ($\chi^2 = 39.99$, $df = 31$, $p < .20$). The value of W was .59 for boys and .43 for girls. The HF group was then selected from among children ranking in the top half of each list, while the LF group was selected from the bottom half. Both experimental groups included 16 boys and 16 girls, with equal representation from each grade (see Table 1).

TABLE 1

Means and Ranges of Ages and Vocabulary Scores by Grade[a]

	N	Mean age	Age range	Mean vocab. score	Range of vocab. scores
Kindergarten		5.7	4.11-6.2	8.3	4-10
Boys 14					
Girls 12					
First grade		6.7	6.2-7.9[b]	9.6	6-12
Boys 10					
Girls 12					
Second grade		7.5	7.1-8.3	11.0	7-17
Boys 8					
Girls 8					
Total 64					

[a] As of January 1, 1967.
[b] One girl repeating grade.

In order to equate the groups for intelligence, the vocabulary test from the Stanford Binet Intelligence Scale was administered to each child. Since vocabulary scores correlate very highly with IQ's on the complete scale, this test is often used as a quick screening measure of intelligence. Table 1 shows the mean vocabulary score for each grade level. All the means were above the norms (expected or extrapolated) for these three age levels. A t test for the difference between the means of the HF and LF groups showed no significant difference ($t = 1.45$, $df = 31$, $p > .10$) so the groups were demonstrably equated for age, sex, and intelligence as measured by the Binet Vocabulary score.

Materials

Five categories of play materials were selected for this study. Each category included highly structured (HS) toys matched with equivalent materials which were as unstructured as possible (MS or minimally structured).

1. *Paints*   The MS materials consisted of 12- × 18-inch sheets of white drawing paper and five jars of washable water colors. In the HS situation, the same water colors were used to paint washable plastic plaques on which were raised pictures of animals and a clown.

2. *Clay*   Soft, pliable Playdoh in four colors was freely manipulated in the MS situation. In the HS play session, the children had to use plastic molds or cookie cutters in animal forms to shape the Playdoh.

3. *Construction Materials*   In the MS condition, the children were allowed to build whatever they liked out of wooden blocks or cardboard cartons, using wooden door knobs, pipe cleaners, tongue depressors, cardboard, and Scotch tape to construct furniture. A Fisher-Price doll family of five painted wooden knobs was supplied. In the HS situation, the buildings were already constructed and included a service station complete with cars, tools, oil racks, a lift, and plastic servicemen. There was also a fully furnished six-room metal doll house, with a proportionately sized family of five bendable rubber dolls, all realistically dressed.

4. *Dolls*   In the MS situation, there were two rag dolls 12 inches tall, with yarn hair and simple gingham costumes representing male and female. With them were two 6-inch stuffed stocking dolls representing a child and a baby. In the corresponding HS situation, there were two Barbie dolls, one dressed as a bride, and a Ken doll in a dark suit. A plastic case held assorted clothes and accessories for both male and female dolls. There were also a G.I. Joe doll in Army fatigues and a G.I. Joe diver doll in an underwater suit and helmet, with a tiny knife.

5. *Costumes*   A box of "dress-up" materials for the MS situation held lengths of satin and velvet, "junk jewelry," flowered hats, pocketbooks, and a Japanese paper parasol. For the boys there were guns and holsters, a false beard, and various hats and belts as well as a top hat and tails. In the corresponding HS situation, there were specific costumes with accessories: a nurse's outfit and a bride costume with veil and bouquet for girls; an Army uniform and a silvered astronaut suit with space helmet for boys.

Procedure

Each child was taken individually from his classroom by the examiner (E) on four separate occasions. He had two 15-min sessions with each of the two sets of toys in prerandomized order. The playroom was equipped with a tape recorder, a large closet for storing toys, and a one-way vision screen behind which sat a concealed observer (O) recording each child's behavior. Toys for each session were displayed in a constant, prearranged order. As E brought each child into the room, she would point out all the different toys and say, *You may play with anything you choose, but I'd like you to make up a story or put on a play for me.*

The experimenter would then seat herself across the small room from the toys, flick on the tape recorder and stopwatch, and begin taking notes. She was careful to appear attentive and interested, but injected herself into the child's play as little as possible. Some children preferred to talk to her, in which case she gently directed them to the toys. Some were very interested in the tape recorder, in which case she promised a playback if S would tell her a story. Some children moved around the room handling or looking at one toy after another without playing for more than a few seconds with any one of them (described as exploratory behavior). Most children explored for 30 sec to 1 min and then said something like, *Oh, I want to play with the doll house,* and settled down to play with one object. Sometimes they played for the entire session with their first choice (paints and clay were particularly absorbing); more often they would announce, *Now, I'm going to play with . . .* or simply leave one toy and move to another. After the first session, they often came in announcing what they were going to do, and went straight to the objects of their choice. Almost all the children seemed to enjoy the play sessions and many responded voluntarily to the mere presence of a warm, permissive, interested observer who was well known to them by the time the experimental sessions began.

If a child did not respond voluntarily, E would ask periodically, *What's happening? What's going on?* or *Can you tell me a story about it?* Every effort was made to do this as infrequently as possible, but no standardized timing could be worked out, as each child's pattern of activity was so different. Some children ran all over the room, hurling grenades or shooting guns. Some took paints or clay to the small desk provided, and sat down where they could be observed by both observers with no difficulty. Some got down on the floor to play house or build blocks, and talked to themselves so softly that E had to slide the microphone across the floor and sit close behind them in order to catch their words. A few children were self-conscious about being watched, and asked what E was writing, and whether these records would be shown to their mothers or the headmaster. Most seemed to forget about E, or accept her as the audience for their play after the first session; in fact they appeared to enjoy her undivided attention.

Flexibility Test Procedure

At the end of the second session with each set of toys (in other words, after 30 min of free play with either HS or MS playthings), the flexibility test was presented. The experimenter would interrupt whatever the child was doing by giving him a bendable rubber cowboy, 6 inches high, with big feet, a wide belt, and scarf, and a removable red cowboy hat. The instructions were:

Now, I want you to stop what you are playing and do something different. See this funny cowboy? I want you to tell me the most exciting story you can make up about him.

The experimenter would then hand the cowboy to the child and begin to record latency of response and length of time spent in telling a story. The reactions were highly individual. Some children could not adjust to the demand, while others took it in their stride. Four HF children calmly integrated the cowboy into whatever they had been playing before; they put him into the doll house or had him ride a horse cut out of clay.

After the completion of the story, or after one minute of waiting and encouragement, *E* would say:

Now, I want you to tell me a story about this cowboy when he captured a flying horse. Make up the most exciting story you can.

Again the reactions ranged from complete rejection (*I can't. There isn't such a thing as a flying horse, so how can I?*) to fanciful stories lasting as long as 4 min. (Time was recorded in units of 30 sec.) Not only was the timing and content of the story recorded but the emotion shown by the child was rated as accepting or rejecting by the observers. Since the flexibility test was presented twice, and since, due to counterbalancing, this occurred 2 days in succession in half the cases, the second presentation often brought forth remarks such as, *Again?* or *I did that yesterday.* The experimenter ignored these remarks, continuing for 1 min to urge the child to respond. If the child began to repeat the same story he had told before, *E* would say, *See if you can make up a different story this time.*

On the fifth day of the week, or the day after his last play session, each child was asked which of the playthings he had liked the most, and which he had liked the least. He was then presented with a big gaily decorated straw basket filled with prizes, and invited to make a choice. The prizes consisted of 2-oz cans of Playdoh (unstructured material) or brightly colored plastic racing cars, and doll carriages containing a baby doll (highly structured, sex-typed toys.)

Observers and Establishment of Rating Reliability

Two observers, who also acted as judges, took part in this study; both of them were college graduates who had had advanced professional training, but who were unfamiliar with the hypotheses of the study or the groups to which children were assigned.[1]

Data

The main source of data for this study was the children's verbalizations during play, as recorded simultaneously by E and O, and the tape recorder. The recorder was employed after each session to check parts which had been missed because the observers could not keep up with the child, or there was doubt about the meaning. For the most part, there was excellent agreement between the records; very rarely did the human observers disagree. The running records of the two observers were then pooled and typed up as a single protocol, consisting of four play sessions. These protocols were read and scored by E and the O who had been present at that play session. Half of them were also read "blind" by the alternate O in order to establish reliability between the judges.

Dependent Variable 1–Richness of Fantasy

The data on these protocols were scored in a number of ways. To measure the criterion of fantasy richness, three instruments were used:

1. The Transcendence Index developed by Weisskopf (1950) was used to measure the number of imaginary items present in each fantasy production.
2. A 5-point Fantasy Rating Scale to assess the distance from daily reality of the children's productions.
3. A 3-point Organization Rating Scale to assess the degree of organization and plot development in the children's stories, as distinguished from the content of the above.

A description of each of these measures follows:

Transcendence Index: This consisted of a count of the number of imaginary items supplied by the child, as opposed to what was already supplied in a given stimulus situation. Using the HS doll house as an example, no credit was given for identification of the family members, since this was obvious in the appearance of the dolls themselves. If, however, a child volunteered that the father "was going to work in New York City," he was given credit for two imaginary items: (1) going to work, (2) in New York City. Anything said by the dolls or any feelings or activities ascribed to them were scored and summed up.

---

[1] The observers were Mrs. Patricia Lee (1), a speech therapist with a master's degree, and Mrs. Euphemia Bruenner (2), who has had graduate training and experience in teaching art to children. Each is the mother of three children. The writer's daughter Mrs. Elizabeth Mertens (3), a psychology major who had considerable experience in observing children at the nursery school connected with Wellesley College, filled in during vacations and emergencies, and assisted with statistical treatment of the data.

In the MS situation, the observers made every effort to count each detail supplied by the child, whether mentioned by him or not. If he molded a dinosaur out of clay he was given credit for a spiked back, short arms, and big tail as each of these appeared, whether he specifically mentioned them or not. On the other hand, if he cut a horse out of clay with the HS molds, and said it was a horse, he received no credit. If he said it was a horse *walking* in the *forest*, he received 2 points. Any further mention of the *forest* would receive no further credit, as each item was scored only once, so as not to confuse verbal productivity with imagination.

Not all the items that received credit were verbal. Many expressive noises were noted and scored if the observers agreed as to their meaning. Police siren noises contributed to a story of cars crashing, as did the wedding march hummed while playing with the bride doll. One little girl got dressed up in high heels and minced across the room in unmistakable imitation of a woman in a tight skirt. The motions of space-walking by boys in the astronaut costume were extremely expressive.

Fantasy Rating Scale: This was constructed by the three judges to assess the child's ability to deal with the fantastic aspect of make-believe—fairies, witches, life on another planet—as opposed to the reality of the child's everyday experience. The various steps in the rating scale are described as follows:

0 Anything likely to be part of the child's daily experience: e.g., Christmas trees, Indian headdress. Events with a high probability of having been experienced directly such as getting gas, going to the circus.

1 That which exists in reality, but most likely has been experienced only indirectly through conversation, books, or television e.g., knowledge of the solar system, stories of dinosaurs, castles, outer space.

2 That which exists largely in the emotions: silly aggressive fantasies of the television cartoon type: emotional fantasies; fantasies verging on the bizarre; e.g., mother puts the baby in the toilet, hangs him on the clothesline to dry.

3 Fantasy that gives a new twist to familiar realities: e.g., an umbrella is used as an air conditioner; a "junk jewelry" chain becomes a pair of handcuffs.

4 Addition of fantasy details to a reality stimulus: e.g., a snowman is magically able to talk and grants three wishes. The story centers around the real stimulus, but adds fantasy details.

5 Addition of fantasy events to a reality stimulus: e.g., the diver doll becomes a "fantastic hero" who has adventures moving away in time and space from the immediate situation. The fantasied events take precedence over the original stimulus.

Organization Rating Scale: This was a 3-point rating scale designed to assess the degree of organization and plot development in the stories told by the subjects.

0 Series of events, often unrelated, strung together by "and then." Commonplace, stereotyped or rambling plots.

1 Series of at least three events in logical time sequence.

2 Sequence of cause and effect; something happened and as a result something else occurred.

3 Integrated plot with beginning, development, and conclusion.

Dependent Variable 2—Variety

The second criterion, that of variety in the themes suggested by the two types of play materials, was measured in the following way. For each of six categories of toys in each play situation, all the stories told by the children who played with that toy were grouped together and scored as follows:

0 For any idea or theme which occurred more than twice (because each child had two opportunities to use the same theme); e.g., eight children built houses out of blocks, so none received a score.

1 For repetitive items having some unique, imaginative feature: e.g., "George Washington's house" built with blocks.

2 For a response unique in this sample, but not improbable: e.g., a tower built with blocks.

3 For an unusual and imaginative response: e.g., a castle with a moat and drawbridge, built from blocks.

Working independently, two judges then scored all the responses given to each category of toys according to the preceding variety rating scale. The total number of responses was 385. The Pearson product-moment coefficient of correlation between the two sets of judgment was .93. The mean of the scores assigned by the two judges to each response became the score for that particular response. Then each child's responses were added up to comprise his score for a variety of responses in each of the two play situations. The scores ranged from 0 for children who had no original ideas to as high as 8 in one session.

Dependent Variable 3—Time Spent in Play

A third criterion was a measure of the length of time S remained interested in one toy. This was timed by stop watch to 30 sec and recorded in units of play or exploratory behavior. No finer measure could be used because it was not always possible to tell whether a child had actually settled down to play with a specific toy or was just exploring. If he became interested in one toy and played with it for a minute or more his activity was recorded as a unit of play. Thus the records reflected the individual differences between children who briefly handled every toy in the room, and those who looked around for a moment or two and then settled down to play with selected toys.

Personality Variables

Three more dependent variables were assessed by ratings of each child's affect, motility, and concentration in each play situation. Both observers participated with *E* in constructing 5-point rating scales based on studies of nonverbal cues reviewed by Yarrow [in Mussen (Ed.), 1960] and on personal observations. Brief descriptions of the rating scales follow:

Variable 4–Affect Rating Scale   Each child's emotional reaction to the two sets of toys was judged by his expression, his behavior, his remarks showing pleasure or boredom, and his tangential behavior such as looking out of the window or asking to go to the bathroom. The ratings ranged from 1 for uninterested behavior and critical remarks to 5 for eager enjoyment of the toys, shown by laughter, singing, and reluctance to leave the playroom.

Variable 5–Motility Rating Scale   This was designed to assess activity level, speed and vigor of movement, postural and gestural freedom, and speed and tempo of speech. Ratings ranged from 1 for dreamy, apathetic behavior to 5 for hyperactivity shown by jumping, yelling, and throwing toys around the playroom.

Variable 6–Concentration Rating Scale   This was designed to show how quickly the child settled down to play, how deeply absorbed he became, and how much exploratory or tangential behavior he exhibited. Ratings ranged from 1 for brief or little interest in the toys, with many questions to *E* and quick response to irrelevant noises (e.g. the buzz of the electric clock) to 5 for deep absorption in play and extended activity with one toy.

Subsidiary Variables

Other data gathered in this study included the children's post-test toy preferences (Criterion 7), choices of a prize (8), and a count of their choices of sex-typed toys (9). An analysis was also made of fantasy themes which might be considered sex-linked (identified with males or females). These would include domestic themes for girls, and stories of war and violence for boys. These data were used as a measure of Criterion 10.

Dependent Variables 11 and 12–Flexibility Ratings

An additional 5-point rating scale (Criterion 11) was devised to measure the flexibility with which each child responded to the flexibility test. This was given after two sessions with either MS or HS toys. Associated with this was a rating (Criterion 12) of each child's willingness to accept or reject the test instructions. The steps in the flexibility scale are described below:

0 Rejection. The child was unable or unwilling to follow the instructions; e.g., *I don't know any story. I'm sick of this cowboy already.*

1 Description. *He's laughing. He's losing his hat.* The child described and manipulated the cowboy without really telling a story about him. Repetition of the stimulus already given: *He captured a flying horse.* Repetition of a story told previously.

3 An adequate story following the directions given; e.g., cowboys and Indians fighting, cattle rustling, or standard television "good guy versus bad guy" plots.

4 A story following directions, but incorporating original ideas; e.g., the flying horse flew to Alaska or Hawaii.

5 Truly original, unique, and well-developed stories covering a span of time and/or space.

Dependent Variable 13—Global Fantasy Scores

After the experiment was completed, the scores on four measures which best discriminated HF from LF subjects (transcendence, fantasy, variety, and flexibility) were transformed to standard scores and averaged to give each S a global fantasy score. This score was used to compare each child's performance in the experimental situation with a previously secured classroom teacher's 5-point ratings of his imaginativeness as shown in the classroom. In addition, a doctoral candidate in psychology[2] who had no knowledge of the children or of the experiment read through all the protocols and rated each one for the degree of creativity and imagination shown in the child's responses. This rating was done on a grade level basis, using a 5-point scale, and the resulting scores were also correlated with the global fantasy scores described already.

Design

The three factors or independent variables used in the analysis of variance were:

A. Predisposition to fantasy a_1: (High or HF) a_2: (Low or LF)
B. Sex b_1: (Boys) b_2: (Girls)
C. Degree of structure of toys c_1: (High) c_2: (Minimal)

Of the dependent variables listed below, the first six provided evidence for Hypotheses 1 through 3.

1. Richness of fantasy as measured by:
   (a) Transcendence index
   (b) Fantasy rating scale
   (c) Organization rating scale
2. Variety of themes as classified in general categories.
3. Length of time spent in play.

[2] Mrs. Barbara Borden, now Ph.D.

4. Affect as rated by rating scale.
5. Motility as rated by rating scale.
6. Concentration as rated by rating scale.
7. Expressed preference for HS or MS toys (Hypothesis 3 only).
8. Choice of HS or MS prize (Hypothesis 3 only).
9. Choice of sex-typed toy (Hypothesis 4 only).
10. Number of sex-linked themes (Hypothesis 4 only).
11. Flexibility as rated on the basis of the cowboy stories given in response to the flexibility test (Hypothesis 5 only).
12. Affect rating of child's acceptance or rejection of the directions for the flexibility test (Hypothesis 5 only).
13. Global fantasy scores (Hypothesis 2 only).

The experimental design used in the statistical analysis of this data was a $2 \times 2 \times 2$ factorial analysis of variance with repeated measures on each child across levels of C or toy structure (Edwards, 1962, pp. 233ff). Analyses of variance and chi-squares were performed on all data except those collected as evidence for Hypotheses 5 and 6. Here the criterion measures were dichotomous, and chi-square analyses were performed. The required level of significance was set at $p = .05$.

Results

Evaluation of Rater Reliabilities

The reliability of the findings of this study are almost entirely dependent upon high interobserver agreement. Therefore, the three judges who participated spent considerable time in practice, scoring the protocols from the pilot study and from subjects not used in this experiment. The scores given for transcendence were the most subject to variability, since they ranged from 4 to 328, while the other measures consisted of 3- or 5-point rating scales. Accordingly, the transcendence measure was used as a critical test of reliability.

Each girl's protocol was scored by three judges: the experimenter, the observer present at that particular play session, and the alternate observer who scored it "blind." The scores were then ranked and Kendall's coefficient of concordance W was computed and found to be .97, a value significant at well above the .01 level. Each observer's rankings were then correlated separately with those of the experimenter; the resulting correlation coefficients are listed in Table 2. Thereafter, E and O_2 scored the boys' protocols with equally high reliability, indicating that though the minutiae of scoring might differ, the rankings obtained between carefully trained observers were substantially the same.

The ratings of the graduate psychology student who read the protocols "blind" were also correlated with the subjects' global fantasy scores. The positive correlation reported in Table 2 supports the reliability of independent ratings

TABLE 2

Reliability Coefficients for Rating Scales

Instrument	Judges	Correlation Coefficient	Value	p
Transcendence index	E, O_1, O_2	Kendall W	.97	.01
Transcendence index	E, O_1	Spearman ρ	.94	.01
Transcendence index	E, O_2	Spearman ρ	.99	.01
Variety ratings	E, O_3	Pearson r	.93	.01
Flexibility ratings	E, O_3	Pearson r	.97	.01
Creativity ratings	Psychologist,	Pearson r	.59	.01
	global scores	Pearson r	.35	.01
Imagination ratings	Teachers,			
	global scores			

of the same data by a trained person unconnected with the experiment in any way.

Hypothesis 1–Effect of Structure of Playthings

The first hypothesis was designed to test the main effect of the degree of structure of the toys. It stated that *simple, minimally structured play materials would elicit greater richness and variety of fantasy, and longer periods of interest from children engaged in free play than would a related section of highly structured toys.* This was tested by comparing the responses of all Ss to the MS and HS play situations.

The degree of structure in the play situations (Factor C) showed a significant main effect on only two of the measures performed. There was a significant difference ($F = 48.85, df = 60,1, p < .001$) in the *variety of themes* produced, with a far greater variety of themes being elicited by the MS materials than by the HS toys. Thus the hypothesis was partially confirmed, in that all Ss were shown to have produced a greater variety of themes in response to the un-structured toys. Additional significant data, while not previously hypothesized, was found in the analysis of motility ratings. The structure of the playthings (Factor C) had a significant effect on the ratings of motility given in the two play situations ($F = 20.84, df = 60,1, p < .001$). An analysis of the means showed that all Ss displayed greater motility in the HS situation than they did in the MS condition. This was probably due to the action elicited by the cars, the most popular toys in the HS situation.

No other significant effects ascribable to the structure of the playthings appeared in any of the findings. The MS toys did elicit greater richness of fantasy, although the main effect of the playthings was only close to reaching significance ($F = 3.56, df = 60,1, p = <.10$) in the analysis of fantasy ratings. The evidence suggests that with a different sample or a different selection of toys, these effects might have reached statistical significance.

It must be noted here that the dependent variable of time spent on play

(Criterion 3) proved to be useless. Measures of extent of interest in one toy (units of play) and of exploratory behavior both proved to show no significant differences between the experimental groups.

A qualitative impression of the children's play with the two groups of toys was that there was more manipulative play with the HS toys than with the MS play materials. Manipulative play, for the purposes of this study, was defined as that in which a child played consistently with one category of toys for one minute or more, without telling a story or describing this play in any way. It included dressing and undressing the dolls, shooting the guns, or simply handling the clay without making anything. There was a good deal of this play with the cars and service station, which also accounted for much of the motility observed in the HS situation.

The relative popularity of the different categories of toys is shown in Table 3. In the HS situation, the cars were most often chosen, closely followed by the clay molds and then by the plaques for painting. In the MS situation, paints led the field while clay was second in popularity. This indicated that paints and clay, the most plastic materials, were high in popularity both in structured and unstructured form, which undoubtedly contributed to the lack of differentiation between the two play situations.

TABLE 3

Number of Choices of Each Category of Playthings

Category	No. of choices
MS situation	
Blocks	25
Wooden and rag dolls	20
Paints	49
Clay	36
Dress-up materials	34
Pipe cleaners, cotton balls, deflectors	30
HS situation	
Costumes	21
Paints and plaques	33
Doll house	21
Clay and molds	44
Dolls	23
Service station and cars	49

Hypothesis 2–Effects of Fantasy Predisposition

The second hypothesis was concerned with the main effects of the two levels of fantasy predisposition. It stated that *HF children would play at a higher level of fantasy with both MS and HS toys than would LF children.* This hypothesis was tested by the preselection of HF and LF groups. It received strong and clear support from all three measures used to assess the richness of fantasy. The analysis of fantasy ratings showed a significant main effect ($F = 28.36$, $df = 60,1$, $p < .001$) indicating that HF children were able to tell fantasy stories less anchored to everyday reality than were LF children.

The effect of predisposition was also significant in the analysis of transcendence indices ($F = 24.59$, $df = 60,1$, $p < .001$) indicating that HF children were able to include more imaginary details in the stories they told than did LF children.

In the analysis of organization ratings, the effect of predisposition was again significant ($F = 13.85$, $df = 60,1$, $p < .001$) indicating that HF children were able to organize their stories better than LF children. No other main effects were significant on any of the three measures; the evidence pointed strongly to fantasy predisposition as being the most important factor in determining richness of fantasy.

On the second criterion, the variety of themes, the analysis of variance again showed that Factor A (predisposition) had a significant main effect ($F = 29.01$, $df = 60,1$, $p < .001$). A chi-square was performed to analyze the relationships between fantasy levels and concentration ratings. The results indicated that HF children were judged to show high concentration significantly more often than LF children, who more often showed low concentration ($\chi^2 = 12.57$, $df = 1$, $p < .001$). This confirmed Hypothesis 2c, which postulated that *HF children would become more deeply absorbed in their play than would LF children.* High-fantasy children did not, however, receive significantly higher ratings for affect or lower ones for motility as hypothesized.

In summary, the factor of predisposition to fantasy had a main effect on six out of eight criterion measures (see Fig. 1) used to assess fantasy play (including the flexibility rating scale which has not yet been discussed). The importance of predisposition emerged all the more clearly, because of the very small interactions obtained throughout the statistical analyses of the data.

Qualitatively, the differences between HF and LF children were often very noticeable; the observers, who had no knowledge of which group the children belonged to, soon became aware of differences on the basis of one or two play sessions. HF children generally appeared pleased and interested in the playthings, and seemed to be able to fulfill the requirements of the situation with more self-confidence and command of the situation. They did not notice the noise on the playground or in the classroom downstairs, whereas some of the wriggly LF children responded to minimal distractions such as the buzz of the electric clock or the holes in the dollhouse wall where the roof had come unlatched. HF children tended to tell much longer stories, and to do so voluntarily, with less questioning by *E*.

Another interesting tendency seen more often in HF children was to integrate more than one category of toy in their play. Six HF children, as compared with two LF children, were able to do this. One little girl dressed up as Mary Poppins

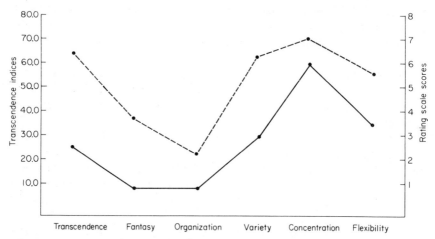

Fig. 1. *Comparison of mean scores for HF (- - -) and LF (——) on six criterion measures. Scores to the right of transcendence refer to rating scale scores.*

and used the rag dolls as the two children whom she took flying through the air. Several of the boys used the cars from the service station for the adventures of the G.I. Joe dolls.

Characteristics such as those previously mentioned suggest that the ability to use fantasy freely is indeed a cognitive skill related to concentration, fluency, spontaneity, and the ability to organize and integrate diverse stimuli.

Hypothesis 3–Effects of Interaction

The third hypothesis was designed to test the effects of interaction between the two degrees of structure and the two levels of predisposition to fantasy. It was postulated that *HF children would show higher levels of fantasy when playing with MS playthings, whereas LF children would respond more productively to HS toys.* This was not borne out by any of the dependent variables already described. There were no statistically significant effects for the A X C interaction; although at the level of near-significance, there were two A X C interactions which will be mentioned. One appeared on the analysis of fantasy ratings ($F = 3.44$, $df = 60,1$, $p = < .10$) and suggested that HF Ss produced higher levels of fantasy in response to unstructured materials than to highly structured toys. For the LF group there was little difference. Also in the analysis of affect there was an A X C interaction closely approaching significance ($F = 3.97$, $df = 60,1$, $p = < .10$) which is graphed in Fig. 2. This shows that while HF children consistently expressed greater enjoyment than LF children; their affect ratings were higher in response to MS playthings, and were somewhat lower in the HS situation. Low fantasy children, on the other hand, showed a

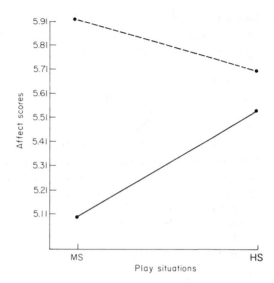

Fig. 2. *Affect means for HF (- - -) and LF (——) groups across levels of structured play.*

lower response to MS materials than to HS toys. These results, if decimal points were rounded, could be said to provide evidence for the hypothesis that *the degree of emotional affect shown by the two experimental groups would be differentially related to the two play situations;* the results were in the expected directions.

The interaction hypothesis also postulated a reverse relationship in regard to motility ratings. It was predicted that *HF children would show less motility in the MS situation than in the HS, while LF children would show less motility in the HS situation.* No support for this was found in the data.

More successful was the test of *differential preferences for HS or MS playthings* after the experiment was completed. Evidence (Criterion 7) was supplied by asking the children with which toys they had most enjoyed playing. The results were significant ($\chi^2 = 10.72$, $df = 1$, $p < .01$) in the expected directions. HF children preferred MS play materials and LF children preferred HS toys. Some children reported preferences for toys from both play situations (e.g., *I liked the blocks and the space suit.*) in which case both preferences were tallied. The evidence supplied by the children's choices of HS or MS prizes (Criterion 8) was, however, inconclusive.

Hypothesis 4–Effects of Sex

The fourth hypothesis was designed to test the effect of sex (Factor B), the third independent variable. It postulated *differences in the fantasy play of boys and girls, particularly in the HS situation,* in which many of the toys were sex-typed. The data showed only two significant main effects of sex. One was found in the analysis of affect ratings ($F = 4.08$, $df = 60,1$, $p < .05$) and suggested that boys, regardless of fantasy predisposition or play structure, show greater overt enjoyment in fantasy play than do girls.

A second significant main effect of sex appeared in the analysis of motility ratings ($F = 4.53$, $df = 60,1$, $p < .05$) graphed in Fig. 3. LF boys, regardless of the play situation, showed greater motility than girls. This did not hold true for the HF children; here there was little difference in the scores, regardless of conditions. This result suggests that the relationship between sex and motility is dependent on the level of fantasy predisposition of the children. *Boys who are less prone to make-believe play are the most active of children.* Compare this finding with the evidence in Chapter II that high fantasy 3- and 4-year-olds were less aggressive in play than low fantasy boys. See also Biblow's findings on aggressive tendencies following frustration for an older group of high and low fantasy children (Chapter V).

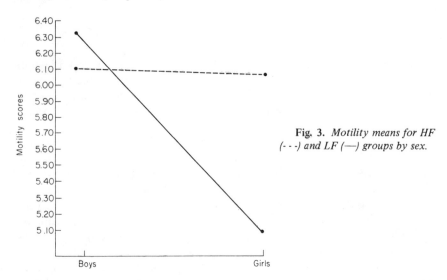

Fig. 3. *Motility means for HF (- - -) and LF (—) groups by sex.*

The B X C interaction was also significant in this analysis ($F = 5.39$, $df = 60,1$, $p < .05$). These results are graphed in Figure 4 and indicate that boys, regardless of other conditions, played at a higher level of motility than did girls, but that motility ratings for both boys and girls increased in the HS situation.

A comparison of the sex-linked fantasy play of boys and girls brought out some interesting facts. There was not as much difference as hypothesized between HS and MS situations. The number of sex-linked themes in the two situations (Criterion 10) were approximately the same (MS, 68; HS, 66). In both cases, the children told roughly twice as many stories that were not sex-linked as those that were. Nor was there any significant difference between boys and girls in the number of sex-linked themes that were produced in either play situation

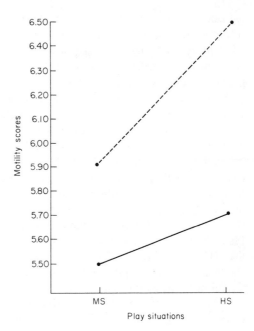

Fig. 4. *Motility means for boys (- - -) and girls (——) at two levels of play.*

($\chi^2 = .66$, $df = 1$, $p < .50$). There was, however a significant difference ($\chi^2 = 5.38$, $df = 1$, $p < .05$) in their willingness to play with toys of the opposite sex (Criterion 9). In the MS situation this occurred rarely, probably because of the nature of the toys. Three boys played with the Fisher-Price dolls, and one girl dressed up as a magician in top hat and tails. But in the HS situation there were 17 girls who played with masculine toys; these were usually the cars in the filling station, which were popular with boys and girls alike. On the other hand, only seven boys played with the doll house, one of whom looked sheepishly at E and remarked, *I'm just fixing this up for the next girl who comes.* In addition, there were many more deprecatory comments from boys than from girls. The latter tended to make inquiries such as, *Is that a G.I. Joe doll?* Boys, on the other hand, made scornful remarks such as, *All girl things—nothing I like!* or *I wouldn't play with the doll house—I'm not that kind of girl!*

Hypothesis 5—Effects of Flexibility Test

The final hypothesis concerned *the ability of children to submit to a sudden interruption in free play and respond to increasingly structured directions.* It was predicted that *HF children would be able to respond more quickly, more willingly, and more productively than LF children to the experimentally imposed flexibility test.* There was no clear pattern in the latency of response, regardless of HF and LF groups; nor did the length of time spent in making up stories seem to vary significantly in any direction. The scores for transcendence and fantasy following each type of play situation were compared to the level of performance immediately preceding the flexibility test, but again no consistent pattern of response was observable.

Two measures, however, showed significant results. One was a measure of affect, rated as showing acceptance or rejection (Criterion 12). Those children who obeyed the instructions without complaining received "acceptance" ratings. Those who refused, whined, or said that they did not know how to follow the instructions, were rated as rejecting them. Chi-square analysis revealed no relationship between the two play situations and the frequency of rejection. It showed, however, a significant difference between LF and HF children in this respect. Each child had two chances to respond to the test instructions; HF children responded positively three times as often as they responded negatively. LF children, on the other hand, responded negatively significantly more often than HF children ($\chi^2 = 17.02$, $df = 3$, $p < .001$). This finding indicates that HF children could accept interruption and change more willingly than LF children, regardless of the level of play being interrupted.

A final measure was that of the flexibility with which the children responded to the flexibility test (Criterion 11). The stories they told in response to the instructions were rated by two judges on the scale previously described. An analysis of variance was performed on these ratings which showed a significant difference in the flexibility of response between HF and LF groups ($F = 23.17$, $df = 60,1$, $p < .001$). An examination of the means showed that HF children received significantly higher ratings than LF children, regardless of sex or structure of play. Thus, as predicted, the HF children showed greater ease and flexibility in coping with increasing demands upon their ability to produce fantasy; they also responded less negatively to the interruption of their play.

Content of Fantasy Productions

This study has been concerned chiefly with the effect of the structure of the toys on children's fantasy productions. The content of the fantasy and the language in which it was expressed can be reviewed only briefly here; another study of these aspects of the data is in preparation. However, the egocentric quality of children's language which has been discussed by Piaget (1932), Werner (1948), and Church (1966), is clearly apparent in many of these records. One child described the "blumpy, plobby" feet on the rubber cowboy. Another spoke of a flying horse that was "mocha troll" (remote-controlled). A second-grader describing the adventures of a "fantastic hero" in the depths of a volcano full of acid and molten lava, remarked that his hero did not get hurt because *he had everything-proof clothes on.*

The content of the children's fantasy is listed by categories in Table 4. Stories of family life—of the day-to-day reality of a child's routine—were by far the

TABLE 4

Content of Children's Fantasy Productions

Content	Girls	Boys
Stories from TV and books	6	5
Family life and domestic situations	32	12
Female activities (shopping, dancing, going to church)	4	0
Animal stories	5	4
Illness or operations	2	1
Traffic accidents and arrest	4	5
Snow and snowmen	5	6
Christmas (trees, decorations, stories of gifts)	7	1
Dinosaurs	2	5
Kings, queens, or princesses	3	1
Food	3	0
Marriage and honeymoon	6	0
Flowers and trees	3	1
Ghosts	2	1
Pirates	0	2
Gangsters, bank robbers	0	3
Monsters (giants, robots)	0	10
Spacemen, planets and flying in space	0	11
Tidal wave	0	1
War	1	2
Shooting and fighting bad guys	0	15
Shooting animals	0	2
Sharks	0	4
Houses or buildings	1	11
Boats and planes	0	3

most common, and ranked high with boys as well as girls. There were many stories of animals, and of Christmas and snow. The last theme may have been seasonal, since the experiment began soon after Christmas and many of the children asked how come Santa Claus had given E all those toys. There was no mention of the witches and bogeymen mentioned in other studies of children's fantasies (Griffiths, 1935; Isaacs, 1933; Markey, 1935), but the monsters and robots of the space age were present, and even a few ghosts.

The boys' most common fantasies were about fighting. *(He frows a hand grenade and it resplodes.)* There were the usual battles among "bad guys," variously called Mexicans (at the Alamo), Japs, Germans, and "the Betman" (Vietnam). Stories of kings and princesses were few; modern TV heroes such as James Bond, the "Invisible Man" and Quick-Draw Dan McGraw seem to have taken precedence. Some of the frequencies are obviously related to the stimulus characteristics of the play situations; the numerous stories of traffic accidents (see also Opie and Opie, 1969 on this theme), and weddings were inspired by the cars and the bride costumes, while the diver doll seemed to suggest stories of sharks. Here and there were stories which seemed to arise out of the inner problems of the child; the descriptions of operations, and sometimes the kinds of houses and buildings were clinically very revealing. One boy who was known by teachers to have been rejected by parents and peers alike told this story:

Wal, this little house is very lonely. He doesn't have any friends. All the other houses say haha, and laugh at him. He doesn't think that's nice. Especially it isn't. So he goes and takes a walk to another place. Then he walked back, and then he went swimming, and that's it.

There were perhaps a dozen stories like this, where the child's fantasy served as an outlet for his inner anxieties. However, out of 385 responses to the playthings, most of the children's responses showed, in greater or lesser degree, the ability to deal freely and flexibly with the events of their daily experience.

Discussion

Structure of the Toys

Careful consideration of the results of this study has led to the conclusion that the effect of the toys was "too little and too late."

By "too little," it is meant that there probably was not enough difference between the two sets of toys. The attempt to match the playthings was undertaken so carefully that, except for the construction versus constructed materials (blocks, etc. versus doll house and service station) the two sets actually were much alike. The interesting point is that paints and clay, whether in structured or unstructured form, were very popular in both situations, underlining the child's need for plastic materials to express his fantasy. Novelty, which in Gilmore's (1964) study, was a factor in the attractiveness of one set of toys, was not a variable here. All of the toys and materials were familiar to these children of affluence, who sometimes stated that they had "better ones at home." The dollhouse, for example, was of the type found in any department store, which, to quote Matterson (1967) leaves "little scope for the imagination and none at all for the elbows [p. 69]." Part of the attractiveness of the toys whose over-realism prompted this study, is due to novelty; children see the latest thing on television and set up a clamor for it. More research is needed to study the effect of novelty versus structure complexity. For present purposes, however, there was so little difference in the responses to the two sets of toys that one must look for sources of constancy rather than sources of variance between groups. These Ss were carefully selected for homogeneity of social, intellectual and economic factors. Added to these were other constant factors: Ss were taken to the same room every day at the same time by the same E who asked the same questions and presented them with playthings very similar to those in their homes or in the kindergarten at school. Possibly the amount of experimental control imposed contributed to the lack of differentiation in the results.

But it is now felt that the effect of structure in the toys was also "too late." The results of this experiment show clearly that by the age of 5, children have a well-developed fantasy predisposition which affects their functioning regardless of sex or circumstances. This will be discussed further later; however, the implication is clear that this type of study should be repeated with preschool subjects in order to see at what age level the structure of toys has an effect on the development of fantasy.

Effects of Sex

As regards fantasy play, the boys and girls in this study appeared to be more alike than they were different. There was a difference in their motor behavior, and emotional response to the toys, with girls taking the quieter, more conforming role. There was also a difference in their choices of toys, but not as much as had been expected from the results of earlier studies. The trend that Kagan foresaw in 1964 for the increased freedom of the middle-class girl to share in boys' activities seems to be increasing, judging by the results of this study. This statement is based not only on playing with the cars, which might be regarded as approaching common ground, but also with the male costumes and weapons, and the G.I. Joe dolls. The general trend is comparable to the findings of Sutton-Smith and Rosenberg (cited in Herron and Sutton-Smith, 1971).

Another interesting effect of sex was that it appeared only on the measures on which fantasy level had no strong effect. This suggests that the influence of predisposition to fantasy was so strong that the other differences which might have been expected to appear were neutralized and only had strength enough to manifest themselves on measures not closely related to fantasy development. All the evidence thus far points to the importance of fantasy development in predisposing children to behave in certain ways, regardless of sex or stimulus characteristics.

Predisposition to Fantasy

What made the difference in the way these children, equally bright and equally privileged, responded to the same situations? Some were constricted and stereotyped; others were original, creative, flexible, and well-integrated. What made the difference?

An attempt was made to examine some of the factors that might have contributed to the fantasy development of the children in this sample, such as nursery school attendance or exposure to television. No significant relationships could be found. Obviously, more research is needed into the environmental and cultural factors that contribute to fantasy development in early childhood.

Fantasy as a Cognitive Skill

The results of this study have clearly shown that high fantasy children are equipped with many of the cognitive skills which contribute to creative functioning. Originality, spontaneity, verbal fluency, free flow of ideas, flexibility in adapting to new situations—all of these factors in one form or another have been described in the research on creativity and divergent thinking. A factor analytic study of fantasy productions might yield factors closely allied to those identified in studies such as Lieberman's (1964) multiple correlation between playfulness and divergent thinking. She feels that the value of identifying such factors as fluency, flexibility, and joyful spontaneity in play, is that they provide "... a clue to a similar ease of functioning when the child is faced with a more structured task that requires flow of ideas and shift of set [p. 102]." It is to this end that longitudinal studies should be directed—to see whether high fantasy children can do better in the tasks ahead of them, such as adjusting to new situations and responding creatively and flexibly to the demands of life, whether in college, camp, military, marital, or vocational situations.

Implications for Early Childhood Education

The implications of this study for parents and nursery school teachers are several. If the structure of toys has any bearing on the development of children's fantasy, it must be most important during the preschool years. Recent research is opening up tremendous new possibilities for teaching very young children. In a review of these findings called "How to Raise a Brighter Child" Beck (1967) gives lists of toys "to trigger the imagination . . . the more simple and less structured, the more creatively they can be used [p. 95]." Matterson (1967), an English nursery school authority, has published a book on how to make or build sturdy, simple toys that will help children develop and grow up "with the imagination to dream dreams and the courage to go out into the world and make them come true [p. 171]." It should be added here that the children's strong preferences for the plastic materials (paints and clay) noted in this research, deserve consideration. Most schools have ample materials and equipment to satisfy this need, but many homes do not. It is the responsibility of parents to recognize the necessity for such creative play, and to cultivate opportunities for its expression.

Another way in which parents may effectively help their children develop fantasy is by acting as models for them (see the chapter by Gottlieb for an experimental study in this area). Parents can play "let's pretend" games and make up stories for their children in a way that encourages them to use their imaginative resources without confusing fantasy and reality. Some of the world's most delightful fantasies, such as "Winnie the Pooh" were written by parents for their children. A mother of two HF subjects in this study described to the writer how her family always looked for a leprechaun on a bend in the path through the woods near their summer home. De Mille (1967), in "Put your Mother on the Ceiling," stresses the importance of parents' playing imaginative games with their children. "People can learn to be intuitive and expressive, flexible and perceptive, and they can do it without giving up reason, communication, purpose, or emotional control . . . It helps to start learning this as a child [p. 26]."

Another source of fantasy models for children could well be developed through television programs such as the Children's Television Workshop. The research begun by Bandura, Ross, and Ross (1961) could be extended to bring before children, adults who could act as models for them in role-playing, or storytelling, or in games of dress-up and make-believe. Surely the avid interest shown by children in television cartoons could be diverted into more creative channels, both literally and figuratively. If toy manufacturers could be persuaded to sponsor such efforts instead of exploiting their childish audiences, a new era in children's creative development might begin.

CHAPTER V

Imaginative Play and
the Control of Aggressive Behavior

Ephraim Biblow

Introduction

The study which follows represents a further step in ascertaining some correlates of the measure of imaginative predisposition. More important, however, is its attempt to demonstrate how observation of play can be used to test the hypotheses generated by contrasting theoretical models in the field of personality. It also points the way toward further research possibilities in the study of the possible effects of television or related popular media upon overt aggressive behavior in children. However repugnant on moral grounds one may find the emphasis on violent action that characterizes much of the movies or television, the actual consequences of such presentations pose a question for scientific investigation. The criteria for scientific evidence and a number of the major issues and researches involved have been reviewed extensively elsewhere (Singer, 1971). The study that follows points the way toward an integration of personality research, the study of play, and an approach to answering a critical social question about the effect of televised aggression on children.

Also of special interest is the measurement of different moods that is carried out in this work. It is increasingly important for psychological theory that the relation of the information-processing capacities and styles of man be related to his emotional make-up. While psychoanalysts and clinical psychologists have generally paid lip service to the importance of "feelings," they have not sought to discriminate the different affects systematically nor built any formal theories around emotion. One of the few theoretical systems that moves boldly into an effort to tie feeling to the rate and complexity of information-processing is that of Silvan Tomkins (1962, 1963). As yet, however, there have been few efforts to elaborate the implications of Tomkins system in operational terms for studies with children. The following study therefore may represent a first effort in that direction as well.

JEROME L. SINGER

Alternative Models of Drive-Reduction and Mood Change in the Control of Aggressive Responses

The Cathartic Theory of Fantasy

It has long been believed that imagination or daydreaming can inhibit the overt expression of violent behavior. The method by which fantasy may operate to reduce aggression has been the subject of much controversy. In accordance with the notion of a fundamental biologically rooted aggressive drive (Freud, 1922; Lorenz, 1966; Storr, 1968) is the cathartic theory which maintains that fantasy operates to lower aggression in a quantitative or drive-reducing manner (Dollard *et al.*, 1939; Feshbach, 1955).

This hydraulic concept of catharsis is based upon the analogy to a liquid held under pressure in a container. As Hendricks has described the process (in Buss, 1961) "additions to the liquid increase pressure on the walls. There are regular channels for drainage. . . . Each increase in the liquid adds pressure for release of the liquid; each time there is drainage, there is at least a temporary decrement in pressure for release [p. 75]." The pressure, in this context, is analogous to aggressive impulses, with the walls of the reservoir representing inhibitions against expressing the aggressive impulses. The overt expression of aggression represents draining of the reservoir; the more drained, the less aggressive drive that remains and thus the less pressure exerted by these impulses seeking release. In Hendrick's terms "the diminution in the tendency to aggress as a consequence of such expression of aggression is called the cathartic effect [p. 75]." Lorenz has similarly described the building up of aggressive pressure as the spontaneous accumulation of some vaguely defined excitation or substance in neural centers, with a quantitative reduction in aggressive excitation occurring spontaneously when accumulation reaches a certain maximal point.

Catharsis theory further stipulates that when the individual engages in fantasized aggression, small quantities of energy are discharged, thus reducing the pressure of the aggressive drive. In Dollard's (1939) terms, involvement in fantasy aggression may serve as a "displacement" providing a harmless "release" for hostile impulses and thus reducing the instigation to overt acts of aggression. This notion that aggressive energy is dissipated to some degree when the individual engages in fantasized aggression stems from Freud's original notion that thought and fantasy discharge small quantities of energy and thus reduce the pressure of the drive (Freud 1958). Experimental support of the catharsis position was offered by Feshbach (1955) who found that insulted college students given an opportunity to engage in aggressive fantasy through TAT story-writing expressed considerably less subsequent anger than those insulted subjects given no fantasy opportunity.

Refutation of the Cathartic Function of Fantasy

The bulk of experimental evidence has, however, cast serious doubt upon the cathartic view of fantasy by demonstrating that there is no reduction or even an actual increase in aggression following an aggressive fantasy opportunity (Berkowitz & Rawlings, 1963; Feshbach, 1956; Mussen & Rutherford, 1961). Feshbach, in his 1956 study, found that play centering upon aggressive thematic material (a record with related story and toys featuring Indians, cowboys, soldiers, or pirates) failed to reduce the aggression of 5- to 8-year-old children in contrast to expectations of catharsis theory. Indeed, the boys originally low in aggressive behavior demonstrated a significant increase in overt classroom hostility after exposure to experimental sessions revolving around these aggressive themes.

In an attempt to make these results consistent with the cathartic hypothesis, Feshbach maintained that in order for fantasy to drain aggressive energy, components of the aggressive drive must first be present or evoked. That is, Feshbach stated that since the children had not been initially aroused to anger, the aggressive play experience could not be used to reduce hostility. Feshbach in fact offered subsequent experimental evidence (1961) demonstrating that only especially angered persons showed a reduction in aggression after viewing a prize fight film. Catharsis theory is seriously weakened by this major qualification that subjects must first be angered if aggressive fantasy material is to have a drive-reducing effect. The catharsis position maintains that there is always some drive energy building periodically in the aggressive reservoir of the individual; thus there should be no need to anger the individual and further add to the reservoir before it can be drained.

Of even greater damage to the catharsis position are experimental findings (Berkowitz & Rawlings, 1963; Mussen & Rutherford, 1961) which have offered evidence that even in the presence of anger, engaging in fantasy does not reduce aggression level. Mussen and Rutherford frustrated first-grade subjects and then presented them with either an aggressive or nonaggressive cartoon or with no fantasy opportunity. Those subjects exposed to the aggressive cartoon evidenced higher final aggression levels as measured by a tendency to pop a balloon than did subjects either allowed no fantasy opportunity or presented with the nonaggressive film. This supported the hypothesis that "viewing violence in a cartoon may actually stimulate or intensify the child's aggression in a subsequent permissive situation [Mussen & Rutherford, 1961, p. 462] " in direct contradiction to a cathartic theory.

Fantasy as a Fundamental Skill

In place of a simplistic, catharsis framework, more recent theoretical conceptions (Hartmann, 1958; Singer, 1966) view fantasy as a general style of the organism—a dimension of human skill or competence available for enhancement and enrichment of life. This approach clearly extends beyond drive reduction, attributing to fantasy a much greater and more variegated role (Singer & Herman, 1954; Singer, Meltzoff, & Goldman, 1952; Singer & Spohn, 1954; Singer et al., 1956).

Specifically, in regard to aggression, it is proposed that the practiced daydreamer can turn to the fantasy realm to work out resolutions of the situations which can arouse anger whereas the low-fantasy individual is more limited to the direct behavioral expression of his aggression.

A large number of studies (Hurwitz, 1954; McCully, 1961; Singer, 1961; Singer et al., 1956) have demonstrated that a significant correlation does exist between high fantasy level and lower levels of overt activity as reflected in motor control, inhibitory capacity, and delaying ability. Most significantly, recent studies (Pytkowicz, Wagner, & Sarason, 1967; Townsend, 1968) have demonstrated that this relationship exists specifically between level of imaginal predisposition and behavioral aggression with the high-fantasy individuals exhibiting the least amount of overt aggressiveness. Townsend studied the Rorschach protocols of 63 boys aged 7 to 12 who had been divided by the staff social worker into high- and low-aggression groupings. It was found that the greater the fantasy level of the child (as measured by the number of human movement responses), the less apt he was to be in the high aggression group.

Pytkowicz et al. (1967) found that subjects who, by self-report, were frequent daydreamers were able to utilize a fantasy experience more effectively for the reduction of hostility than subjects who were infrequent daydreamers. More specifically, the authors found that insulted male college students who were skilled in fantasy usage (as measured by the frequency of daydreaming) utilized either a free daydreaming period or the opportunity to write stories to four TAT cards to reduce their hostility. Subjects generally low in fantasy capacity had no significant reduction in aggression. However, the authors' conclusion that a cathartic reduction of hostility had occurred for the high-fantasy males can be seriously questioned. Since catharsis theory maintains that all individuals will demonstrate a reduction in hostility following a fantasy experience, it is inconsistent to maintain that only individuals skilled in fantasy usage will show this cathartic reduction.

In analyzing the content of the fantasy material used by subjects to reduce aggression, Pytkowicz *et al.* (1967) offered evidence in further refutation of catharsis theory. A logical consequence of a drive-reduction position is that a decrease in aggression can occur only through aggressive fantasy stimuli since it is the aggressive elements within the fantasy material which purge or drain away the aggressive energy of the individual. Pytkowicz *et al.*, however, found that the majority of the *S*s' daydreams were either based upon fairly mundane themes (tests, grades, dating, etc.) or were of a freely imaginative nature (flights into fantasy, imaginative conjectures, fragments of the past or future, etc.). "Most subjects described the period as relaxing or soothing, a few reported it was boring or difficult . . . but no subjects reported hostile or even anxious daydreams [p. 301]." It is thus proposed that the role of fantasy in the reduction of aggression is dependent upon the individual's imaginative skill and not upon the specific thematic content of the fantasy material. That is, the high-fantasy individual can utilize any fantasy experience, aggressive or nonaggressive, to effect a reduction in aggression.

A cathartic, drive-reductive view of fantasy is not consistent with the findings that it is only high-fantasy individuals who can utilize a fantasy experience to reduce aggression and further that any fantasy experience and not solely an aggressive one can be so employed. Instead it is proposed that the fantasy experience operates to change the individual's prevailing aggressive mood or affective state. In this scheme, aggression is viewed, as suggested by Tomkins (1963) and Izard and Tompkins (1966), as an affect rather than as a drive. Izard and Tomkins' (1966) motivational theory of affects suggests that it is the affects or emotions rather than drives which are the basic motivating forces behind human behavior. According to Tomkins:

> Affect is a complex concept that has neurophysical, behavioral, and phenomenological aspects. At the neurophysical level, affect is defined in terms of density of neural firing or stimulation and changes in stimulation. At the level of behavioral or motor expression, affect is primarily facial response and secondarily visceral and bodily response. At the phenomenological level, affect is essentially motivating experience. To activate an affect is to motivate [p. 87].

Tomkins has designated eight innate affects, the three positive ones being interest–excitement, enjoyment–joy, and surprise–startle and the five negative affects consisting of fear–terror, distress–anguish, shame–humiliation, contempt–disgust, and anger–rage. Each affect is an organized set of responses triggered at subcortical centers where specific "programs" for each distinct affect are stored. Tomkins specifically explains the process of affect activation at the physiological level in terms of the density of neural firing or stimulation, i.e., the number of neural firings per unit time. If internal or external sources of neural firing suddenly increase, the individual will startle, or become afraid, or become interested, depending upon the suddenness of stimulation increase. If such sources of neural firing reach and maintain a high, constant level of stimulation, he will respond with distress or anger, depending upon the level of stimulation. If neural firing suddenly decreases, he will laugh or smile with enjoyment, again depending upon the suddenness of decrease of stimulation.

Thus, in order for an affect to be aroused and sustained, it is required that a specific density of neural firing or stimulation be maintained. Applying this affective theory to the area of aggression, Singer (1966) has maintained that fantasy can temporarily provide another stimulus situation for the individual that is less negative and intense than the aggressive situation and may thus relieve some of the prolonged quality of the incoming stimulation. Especially for persons who are skilled daydreamers, that is, for those who can use a fantasy situation most fully, fantasy opportunity after a frustrating experience affords a chance for a shift away from negative affect and leads to a change in mood, thus reducing the final expression of aggression.

A specific study was devised to demonstrate that reduction in aggression following any fantasy activity is effected, for the individual skilled in fantasy usage, through a change in mood. It was hypothesized that:

1. While catharsis theory maintains that all individuals can utilize aggressive fantasy to reduce their behavioral aggression, it is proposed that only high-fantasy individuals can effectively reduce aggression through fantasy.

2. While catharsis theory maintains that only aggressive fantasy can be used to reduce aggression, it is hypothesized that the high-fantasy individual can utilize any fantasy experience, aggressive or nonaggressive, to reduce hostility.

3. While catharsis theory maintains that aggression is hydraulically drained away or purged from the individual through a quantitative lessening of his aggressive drive, it is hypothesized that the high-fantasy individual uses fantasy to change his prevailing affective state or mood from an angry one to a new and distinct mood.

Experiment

Subjects

Thirty high- and 30 low-fantasy subjects were selected from a group of 130 white, middle-class, fifth-grade children with IQ scores in the 90 through 120 range. All were between 9.5 and 10.5 years old. Fantasy level was determined upon the basis of the score for movement (M) responses to twenty selected cards of the Holtzman Inkblot Test (Holtzman *et al.*, 1961) combined with the score received on the "Just-Suppose" task (Torrance, 1966). The M score was employed on the basis of evidence (discussed in Chapter III) indicating that perception of movement on inkblots is significantly correlated with the individual's general imaginative predisposition (Page, 1957; Singer & Herman, 1954; Singer *et al.*, 1956).

The "Just-Suppose" task assesses imaginative level or divergent production by presenting four improbable and unusual situations with the subject required to list the possible consequences. For example, the first "Just-Suppose" situation states, "Just suppose clouds had strings attached to them which would hang down to the earth. What would happen?" Fantasy level was determined by the number of appropriate responses given, by the originality of responses, and by shifts in focus from one response to the next. High scores on this task have been found to be significantly correlated with teacher and peer nominations of imaginativeness (Torrance & Arsan, 1960). In addition, Gottlieb (1968) obtained significant correlations between the "Just-Suppose" task, the Holtzman M response, and a third measure reflecting subjects' preference for imaginative rather than motoric activities (see Chapter VII).

The two tests of fantasy were group-administered to classes of 25 to 30 children. The 30 male and 30 female Ss eventually selected were those who had received the highest and lowest composite fantasy scores. Subjects were divided into groups of four with each group composed of a high-fantasy male, a high-fantasy female, a low-fantasy male, and a low-fantasy female. Each group underwent a separate experimental session with five groups placed in an *aggressive film* condition, five groups in a *nonaggressive film* condition, and five groups in a *nonfantasy* condition.

Procedure

Phase One—Frustration Period   In the 6.5-min frustration phase, each group of four children was required to complete a construction activity in which interlocking wooden pieces and plastic disks are assembled to form objects. Four easily constructed model objects were presented, and each child was made responsible for copying one of the models. The children were informed that the group completing construction in the shortest time span would receive expensive prizes which were prominently displayed in the room. Two older sixth-grade children were introduced to the group as helpers who would aid the children if they needed assistance. The children were asked to engage in this activity under the pretext that the experimenter would soon be in charge of a new recreation center and that he was interested in the children's reactions to some proposed toys and games.

While the experimenter and an observer unfamiliar with the hypotheses pretended to busy themselves with paper work, the older youngsters deliberately prevented the younger children from completing the task, interspersing their interference with a set of remarks found to be effective in eliciting aggression.

During the final 2.5 min of this frustration condition, the experimenter and observer each rated two children on two scales. First, for a period of 2 min, subjects were rated on an Initial Aggression Scale (See Appendix) where they received a score from 0 to 4, depending upon the degree of aggression shown, for each of eight consecutive 15-sec intervals. Interrater reliability for this scale was found to be .93.

During the final 30 sec of the frustration condition, subjects were rated on a Mood Checklist (see Appendix) where they received a score ranging from 1 to 5 in each of eight mood areas depending upon the presence and intensity of the mood in their behavior. This mood scale was grounded theoretically in Tomkins' (1962) theory of affects and Nowlis' (1965) experimental findings of mood factors. As mentioned earlier, Tomkins has posited the existence of eight major affects and significantly six of these are equivalent to major mood dimensions found by Nowlis in a factor-analytic study of 130 mood adjectives describing an individual's attitudes and feelings. The six mood dimensions common to both Tomkins' and Nowlis' work and taken as major dimensions of the Mood Checklist are aggression or anger, anxiety or fear, surgency or excitement, elation or joy, sadness or distress, and guilt or shame. In addition, a seventh factor of contempt–disgust derived solely from Tomkins' theory and an eighth dimension of fatigue–sluggishness based upon Nowlis' findings were also included in the Mood Checklist, since they seemed particularly relevant to the mood which might arise in children in either a frustration or fantasy situation.

Phase Two–Experimental Condition   Immediately following the frustration activity, each of five experimental groups was presented with an aggressive film, five groups with a nonaggressive film, and five groups with a nonfantasy activity. The children were told that these films or tasks were being presented to occupy them while the experimenter and observer readied some other toys which they wanted the children to consider for inclusion in the recreation center. The aggressive film entitled *The Enemies,* written specifically for this study, consisted of a tape-recorded story and accompanying slides depicting verbal and physical arguments among several children. The nonaggressive film also consisted of a tape recording and accompanying slides, but was based upon *The Adventures of Chitty Chitty Bang Bang* by Ian Fleming. Both films were found in pilot work to be of great interest and enjoyment to children of this age.

The nonfantasy activity consisted of a series of three tasks, each comprising seven problems and a sample; specifically (1) adding together five one-digit numbers, (2) computing the total amount of money represented by a picture of seven coins, and (3) placing a series of six numbers in ascending order. The tasks were presented through slide projections at a rate found to be of sufficient duration for the children to complete the problem satisfactorily, but which allowed as little free time as possible which could be utilized for fantasy activity. In order for this task to be as absorbing as possible, the stimuli were prepared in an interesting visual form with, for example, the numbers to be added incorporated in unusual geometric designs.

Phase Three–Play Period   Immediately following presentation of the film or tasks, the group of subjects was placed in a play situation where aggressive

Fig. 1. *Nonaggressive film.*

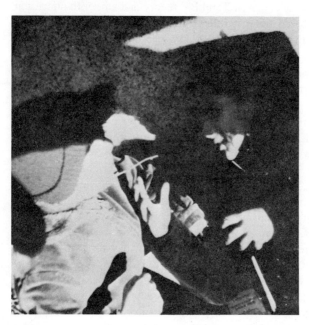

Fig. 2. *Aggressive film.*

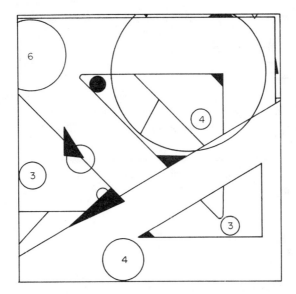

Fig. 3. *Nonfantasy film.*

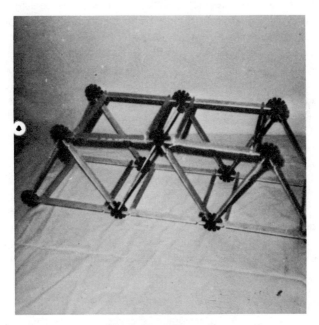

Fig. 4. *Frustration task.*

and nonaggressive toys were available. Subjects spent 10 min in spontaneous play activity. Their behavior was again rated by the experimenter and the observer. The first 4 min were divided into 30-sec intervals during each of which the subject received a score from 0 to 4 on a Final Aggression Scale (see Appendix) measuring their aggressive behavior, physical or verbal, directed toward another child, toward a toy, or toward the self. The observers were then allotted 2 min in which to rate the children again on the Mood Checklist. Finally, the last 4 min of the play period were again divided into 30-sec intervals and an aggression score was noted for each child during each interval. There was a total of 16 intervals in the play period during which the child's aggressive behavior was rated. (For details of mood and aggression scoring see Appendix at the end of this volume.)

Results

Analysis of Data

Overt or behavioral aggression scores were obtained at two points during the experiment. First, an initial aggression score was recorded during the final minutes of the frustration period for each subject. Second, the subject was rated on the Final Aggression Scale during the play situation. Aggression in each instance was rated from 0 to 4 for each of the eight intervals in the Initial Aggression Scale and for each of the sixteen intervals in the Final Aggression Scale. The mean score obtained for each subject for both initial and final aggression levels was taken as the dependent variable. The data thus consisted of 120 scores; specifically, an initial (Stage 1) and a final (Stage 2) aggression score for each of the 10 Ss in each of the six treatment groupings (i.e., high-fantasy–aggressive-film; high-fantasy–nonaggressive-film; high-fantasy–no-film; low-fantasy–aggressive-film; low-fantasy–nonaggressive film; and low-fantasy–no-film groupings).

A 2 X 3 X 2 trend analysis of variance was applied to these data. The three factors considered were fantasy (high and low levels), films (aggressive, nonaggressive, or nonfantasy), and stages (initial and final aggression levels). Furthermore, in order to determine specifically which group or groups had undergone significant changes in overt aggression from initial to final scores and to ascertain if differences existed among the six groups either among their mean initial scores or among their mean final scores, a Duncan's New Multiple Range Test was applied to the data.

A similar procedure to that used to analyze the behavioral aggression scores was employed for the data consisting of the initial and final mood scores. For each of the eight mood dimensions under consideration, a separate analysis of variance was applied to the initial and final scores. The dependent variable for each of the eight analyses of variance consisted of the mood score, ranging from

1 to 5, assigned to each subject during the frustration period and the score, again from 1 to 5, achieved by the subject during the play activity. For each mood or affective state rated by the Mood Checklist, a $2 \times 3 \times 2$ trend analysis of variance was employed. The factors considered for each analysis were fantasy (high and low levels), films (aggressive, nonaggressive, or nonfantasy), and stages (initial and final mood levels). Again following each analysis of variance, a Duncan's New Multiple Range Test was applied to the data to determine the precise nature of the differences between the experimental groups.

Analysis of the data was also undertaken to determine if any differences existed between the sexes for behavioral aggressiveness. A $2 \times 3 \times 2$ analysis of variance on the dependent variable of initial aggression scores was applied to the data to determine if any differences were present between the boys' and girls' aggression levels during the frustration period. The factors considered were fantasy (high and low levels), films (aggressive, nonaggressive, or nonfantasy) and sex. A $2 \times 3 \times 2$ analysis of variance was also applied to the final aggression scores with the same three factors considered to determine if there were differential effects for sex upon behavioral aggression after exposure to the fantasy or nonfantasy experience.

General Results

The analysis of variance of behavioral aggression scores (see Table 1) revealed that of the three factors under consideration, there were significant main effects for fantasy and for stages as well as a significant Fantasy $\times$ Films $\times$ Stages interaction. The Duncan's New Multiple Range Test applied to these data (see Table 2) revealed significant *decreases* from initial to final levels of behavioral aggression for high-fantasy Ss presented with the aggressive and with the non-aggressive films. The high-fantasy Ss given no fantasy opportunity and all low-fantasy Ss evidenced no significant changes in behavioral aggression.

The eight analyses of variance for each of the mood dimensions under consideration revealed in all cases a significant main effect for fantasy. The results of the Duncan's New Multiple Range Tests applied to the data for each mood dimension are summarized in Table 3. The significant mood changes consisted of decreases in *angry–annoyed* scores for high-fantasy subjects presented with the aggressive and nonaggressive films, and increases in *sad–down-hearted* and *ashamed–contrite* mood scores for high-fantasy–aggressive-film Ss and in *elated–pleased* scores for the high-fantasy–nonaggressive-film group. For the high-fantasy–no-film Ss, and for all low-fantasy Ss, there were no significant changes in any of the eight affective states.

The analysis of variance undertaken to evaluate sex differences revealed that the main effect for sex was not significant for either the dependent variable of initial aggression scores or for final aggression scores. That is, there were no differences between the sexes in overt aggression during either the frustration or play periods.

TABLE 1

Analysis of Variance of Overt Aggression Scores

Source of variation	Sum of squares	df	Mean square	F
A: Fantasy	54.74	1	54.74	184.94**
B: Films	.93	2	.47	1.57
A × B: Fantasy × Films	1.81	2	.91	3.06
Error (a)	16.01	54	.30	
C: Stages	2.14	1	2.14	12.53**
A × C: Fantasy × stages	5.65	1	5.65	33.06**
B × C: Films × stages	.98	2	.49	2.87
A × B × C: Fantasy × films × stages	1.47	2	.74	4.31*
Error (b)	9.23	54	.17	
Total	92.96	119		

*Significant at the .05 level.
**Significant at the .005 level.

TABLE 2

Summary of the Duncan's New Multiple Range Test Applied to the Differences between the Treatment Means of the Overt Aggression Scores

Group	Prescore	Postscore	Significance of difference
High-fantasy–aggressive film	1.80	.80	Sig.*
High-fantasy–nonaggressive film	1.77	.85	Sig.*
High-fantasy–no film	1.82	1.63	n.s.
Low-fantasy–aggressive film	2.71	3.11	n.s.
Low-fantasy–nonaggressive film	2.74	2.71	n.s.
Low-fantasy–no film	2.68	2.81	n.s.

*α = .05

TABLE 3

Summary of the Results of the Duncan's New Multiple Range Tests Applied to the Initial and Final Scores for Each of the Eight Mood Variables

Mood	Group	Prescore	Postscore	Significance of difference
Angry- annoyed	High-fantasy—agg-film	2.6	1.6	Sig.*
	High-fantasy—nonagg-film	2.7	1.8	Sig.*
	High-fantasy—no-film	2.7	2.5	n.s.
	Low-fantasy—agg-film	3.4	4.0	n.s.
	Low fantasy—nonagg-film	3.7	3.8	n.s.
	Low-fantasy—no-film	3.6	3.7	n.s.
Fearful- tense	High-fantasy—agg-film	1.6	2.1	n.s.
	High-fantasy—nonagg-film	1.8	1.2	n.s.
	High-fantasy—no-film	1.7	1.6	n.s.
	Low-fantasy—agg-film	1.2	1.1	n.s.
	Low-fantasy—nonagg-film	1.1	1.1	n.s.
	Low-fantasy—no-film	1.0	1.5	n.s.
Lively- excited	High-fantasy—agg-film	1.2	1.7	n.s.
	High-fantasy—nonagg-film	1.2	1.5	n.s.
	High-fantasy—no-film	1.5	1.5	n.s.
	Low-fantasy—agg-film	1.7	2.3	n.s.
	Low-fantasy—nonagg-film	1.5	2.0	n.s.
	Low-fantasy—no-film	1.8	2.1	n.s.
Elated- pleased	High-fantasy—agg-film	1.2	1.3	n.s.
	High-fantasy—nonagg-film	1.2	2.4	Sig.*
	High-fantasy—no-film	1.4	1.8	n.s.
	Low-fantasy—agg-film	1.3	1.2	n.s.
	Low-fantasy—nonagg-film	1.2	1.4	n.s.
	Low-fantasy—no-film	1.3	1.2	n.s.
Sad- down- hearted	High-fantasy—agg-film	2.5	3.2	Sig.*
	High-fantasy—nonagg-film	2.4	1.7	n.s.
	High-fantasy—no-film	2.1	1.9	n.s.
	Low-fantasy—agg-film	1.3	1.2	n.s.
	Low-fantasy—nonagg-film	1.0	1.1	n.s.
	Low-fantasy—no-film	1.1	1.5	n.s.
Ashamed- contrite	High-fantasy—agg-film	2.2	3.1	Sig.*
	High-fantasy—nonagg-film	2.4	1.6	Sig.*
	High-fantasy—no-film	2.1	2.0	n.s.
	Low-fantasy—agg-film	1.1	1.1	n.s.
	Low-fantasy—nonagg-film	1.4	1.2	n.s.
	Low-fantasy—no-film	1.1	1.3	n.s.

*$\alpha = .05$.

Table 3 *(Continued)*

Mood	Group	Prescore	Postscore	Significance of difference
Contemptu-	High-fantasy—agg-film	1.9	1.6	n.s.
ous-	High-fantasy—nonagg-film	2.2	1.4	n.s.
disgusted	High-fantasy—no-film	1.8	1.7	n.s.
	Low-fantasy—agg-film	3.3	3.6	n.s.
	Low-fantasy—nonagg-film	3.7	3.2	n.s.
	Low-fantasy—no-film	3.5	3.7	n.s.
Fatigued-	High-fantasy—agg-film	1.9	2.3	n.s.
sluggish	High-fantasy—nonagg-film	1.7	1.4	n.s.
	High-fantasy—no-film	2.0	1.6	n.s.
	Low-fantasy—agg-film	1.0	1.0	n.s.
	Low-fantasy—nonagg-film	1.1	1.2	n.s.
	Low-fantasy—no-film	1.1	1.0	n.s.

Evaluation of the Hypotheses

The first hypothesis maintaining that not all individuals but only those of high-fantasy predisposition can effectively reduce aggression through fantasy was supported by the data. High-fantasy subjects presented with either the aggressive or nonaggressive film evidenced significant decreases in behavioral aggression mean scores from initial to final conditions as revealed in the Duncan's New Multiple Range Test. The high-fantasy subjects in the aggressive-film group obtained scores which decreased from a mean of 1.80 during the frustration period to a mean of .80 during the play period with all ten subjects achieving decreasing scores. The mean scores of subjects in the high-fantasy–nonaggressive film group showed a reduction from an initial level of 1.77 to a final mean score of .85 with all ten of these subjects displaying decreasing levels of behavioral aggression.

In contrast, the low-fantasy subjects presented with the aggressive or nonaggressive film manifested no reduction in overt aggression, with the low-fantasy-aggressive-film group demonstrating an increase (not statistically significant) in aggression scores from 2.71 during the frustration period to 3.11 during the play session. All ten subjects in this group had scores which *increased* after exposure to the aggressive film. Subjects in the low-fantasy–nonaggressive-film group evidenced no significant change in overt aggression having obtained an initial mean score of 2.75 and a final mean score of 2.71 with four subjects achieving increasing scores, five achieving decreasing scores, and one remaining at the same level of overt aggression.

The second hypothesis stating that high-fantasy individuals can utilize any fantasy experience, aggressive or nonaggressive, was also supported by the data. As already mentioned, the mean aggression scores of subjects in the high-fantasy–aggressive-film group decreased from 1.80 to .80 while high-fantasy Ss in the nonaggressive-film group evidenced a reduction from 1.77 to .85. In order to ascertain if the reductions in overt aggression were the same for these two groups, i.e., after exposure to either the aggressive or nonaggressive film, a t test was applied to the data. Results indicated that the decrease in aggression shown by high-fantasy–aggressive-film Ss was not significantly different from the reduction manifested by Ss in the high-fantasy–nonaggressive-film group. The results thus support the contention that high-fantasy Ss are able to utilize either an aggressive or nonaggressive fantasy opportunity to lower their overt aggression level.

The third hypothesis maintaining that fantasy is used by the individual with high imaginal predisposition to change his prevailing affective state or mood from an angry one to a new and distinct mood was also supported by the data. The high-fantasy–aggressive-film Ss demonstrated a significant decrease in *angry–annoyed* mood (2.6 to 1.6 with eight Ss manifesting reduced scores and two showing no change in this mood area) accompanied by significant increases in the *sad–downhearted* mood (2.5 to 3.2 with six Ss increasing and four remaining at the same level) and in the *ashamed–contrite* mood (2.2 to 3.1 with nine Ss increasing and one remaining the same). For high-fantasy Ss in the nonaggressive-film group, there was a significant decrease in *angry–annoyed* scores from an initial mean level of 2.7 to a final mean level of 1.8 with eight Ss evidencing decreases and two remaining at the same level of anger. For these Ss, there was as well a significant increase in the *elated–pleased* mood (1.2 to 2.4 with nine Ss achieving increasing scores while one remained the same) and a significant decrease in *ashamed–contrite* scores (2.4 to 1.6 with eight Ss decreasing and two remaining at the same level).

Thus, high-fantasy Ss in the aggressive-film group changed their mood away from an angry one to one characterized by increased *sad–downhearted* and *ashamed–contrite* aspects while those high-fantasy Ss exposed to the nonaggressive film changed their mood away from an angry one to one of greater elation. To demonstrate that the mood change was a result of the exposure to the fantasy experience, it is noted that control high-fantasy Ss, i.e., those given no fantasy experience, demonstrated no significant changes in any of the eight mood dimensions. All low-fantasy Ss, who had demonstrated no reduction in behavioral aggression after the aggressive film, nonaggressive film or nonfantasy task, also revealed no significant changes in any of the affective areas.

Evaluation of General Differences between High- and Low-Fantasy Subjects

Analysis of all data strongly confirmed the existence of significant differences between high- and low-fantasy Ss both in behavioral aggression and in all mood states. In the analysis of variance of overt aggression scores and in seven of the analyses of variance of mood scores, the main effect for fantasy was significant at the .005 level and in the eighth mood analysis of variance at the .05 level. During the frustration period, the behavioral aggression scores of the high-fantasy Ss were significantly lower than those of their low-fantasy counterparts, indicating that under the same frustration conditions high-fantasy children displayed significantly less overt aggressiveness. However, even while less aggressive at the initial stage, high-fantasy Ss presented with the aggressive or nonaggressive film evidenced a significant reduction in behavioral aggression while low-fantasy Ss demonstrated no decreases.

Further striking differences between the high- and low-fantasy youngsters were revealed in the evaluation of mood scores. During the frustration period, the high-fantasy Ss showed significantly less *excitement* and *contempt* and more *fear, sadness, contrition,* and *fatigue* than did the low-fantasy Ss. After viewing the aggressive film, the high-fantasy Ss manifested significant increases in the *sad–downhearted* and *ashamed–contrite* moods and increases approaching significance in *fearful–tense* and *fatigued–sluggish* scores while the low-fantasy–aggressive-film group evidenced no change in any of these dimensions. Furthermore, the high-fantasy Ss showed a decrease, although nonsignificant, in the *contemptuous–disgusted* mood while the low-fantasy Ss manifested a nonsignificant increase in this mood score after exposure to the aggressive film. Finally, as previously mentioned, the high-fantasy–aggressive-film group showed a significant decrease in the *angry–annoyed* mood while low-fantasy Ss actually increased, although nonsignificantly, in their anger after exposure to the aggressive film.

For the two groups who were presented with the nonaggressive film, high-fantasy Ss decreased significantly in *ashamed–contrite* mood and nonsignificantly in *fearful–tense, sad–downhearted* and *fatigued–sluggish* states while the low-fantasy Ss remained the same in these mood areas. In addition, there was a significant increase in *elated–pleased* mood for the high-fantasy Ss, but no change in this mood for the low-fantasy group. Finally, the high-fantasy Ss significantly decreased in *angry–annoyed* mood after viewing the nonaggressive film while the low-fantasy children evidenced no change in this mood.

Conclusions

Refutation of Catharsis Theory

The results of this study offer strong refutation of the cathartic, drive model of aggression reduction. It was found that only the angered high-fantasy Ss and not the frustrated low-fantasy children were able to utilize a fantasy experience to reduce their aggression and further that exposure to either aggressive or nonaggressive fantasy material was effective in reducing aggression for the high-fantasy Ss. The finding that the low-fantasy Ss evidenced not a decrease, but a trend toward an increase in aggression following exposure to the aggressive film is in direct contrast to the hydraulic notion that all individuals will evidence reduced hostility following an aggressive fantasy experience. The present results are consistent with a body of literature (Feshbach, 1956; Mussen & Rutherford, 1961) demonstrating that no reduction or an actual increase in aggression occurs following an aggressive fantasy opportunity for at least some children.

Furthermore, the finding that the high-fantasy children utilized either the aggressive or nonaggressive fantasy experience to achieve similar significant reductions in aggression refutes the catharsis hypothesis that it is specifically the drive-related aggressive elements within the fantasy situation which are utilized to drain away aggressiveness. This indication that the individual with well-developed imaginal skills can employ any type of fantasy experience to reduce his aggressiveness is in accord with the experimental findings for young adults already mentioned (Pytkowicz *et al.*, 1967).

Refutation of a cathartic position is in accord with the theoretical belief that aggression is perhaps best not regarded as a basic drive with a given quantum of energy to be reduced by catharsis. By contrast, one can look to a position such as that presented in Tomkins' theory.

Tomkins conceives of each affect as an organized set of responses triggered at subcortical centers where specific "programs" for each distinct affect are stored. In order for an affect to be aroused and sustained, it is required that a specific density of neural firing or stimulation be maintained. Specifically, the affect of anger requires a high, constant level of neural stimulation in order to be activated and sustained. Applying this affective theory to the area of aggression, Singer (1966) has maintained that fantasy can temporarily provide another stimulus situation for the individual that is less negative and intense and may thus relieve some of the prolonged quality of the incoming stimulation. Singer believes that, especially for persons who are skilled daydreamers, fantasy opportunity after a frustrating experience affords a chance for relief from negative affect and leads to a change in mood, thus reducing the final expression of aggression. The results of the present study indicating shifts in mood state from anger to shame and sadness after exposure to the aggressive film and from anger to elation after viewing the nonaggressive film are thus consistent with the theory that fantasy operates to effect mood change.

Consistent with Tomkins' affect theory and with the results of the present study is the view that fantasy has a much greater and more variegated role than that dictated by drive-reduction theory, specifically that of generating, main-taining and modifying diverse mood patterns. The breadth and ramifications of this theoretical model of fantasy operation are more clearly demonstrated when, for example, juxtaposed with Berkowitz's (1958, 1962, 1964), guilt theory of aggression inhibition. Berkowitz maintained that the strong arousal of socially disapproved behavior, such as aggression, serves to elicit fairly strong restraints against the display of the prohibited actions. Thus, Berkowitz believes that there is no reduction in feelings of aggression as a result of fantasy, but rather that fantasy may produce guilt leading the individual to inhibit any overt expression of his felt aggression. While the current findings that the high-fantasy–aggressive-film subjects showed behavioral implications of guilt through increased *sad–downhearted* and *ashamed–contrite* mood scores seem perhaps similar to Berkowitz's position, it must be noted that high-fantasy–nonaggressive-film subjects showed significant reductions as well in aggression without any manifestation of increased guilt. In fact, these children demonstrated instead a significant increase in the *elated–pleased* mood dimension. The wide scope of mood theory, while not negating Berkowitz's guilt-inhibition hypothesis, relegates it to a subsidiary position as only one possible result of fantasy exposure. The results of the present study suggest that the individual skilled in fantasy usage may respond to a fantasy situation with guilt, but that he has as well a wide range of other moods which may be activated by the fantasy experience.

Implications of Fantasy Predisposition

The experimental finding that low-fantasy Ss evidenced no reduction in behavioral aggression and no significant change away from an *angry–annoyed* mood after exposure to either the aggressive or nonaggressive fantasy material reveals the significance of fantasy skill for the individual. That is, the low-fantasy Ss seemed to make very little use of their vicarious fantasy opportunities to alter their aggressive feelings, with the only trend toward change occurring in the nonsignificant increase in *angry–annoyed* mood scores following presentation of the aggressive film. This increase might possibly be traced to the fact that these angered children were further stimulated by the aggressive film, but were less able to deal with this arousal through fantasy means and thus expressed anger more overtly during the play situation.

Response to Frustration   During the initial period of anger arousal as well as during the play session, significant differences emerged between the high- and low-fantasy Ss. In response to frustration, the high-fantasy youngsters seemed to internalize the anger they felt toward the frustrator during the construction task to a much greater degree than did those youngsters less skilled in fantasy usage. Not only did the high-fantasy children manifest less overt aggression than their low-fantasy counterparts, but they also evidenced a greater degree of anxiety (*fearful–tense* mood scale) and guilt (*sad–downhearted* and *ashamed–contrite* mood scales). The existence of a relationship between high fantasy tendency and anxiety has in fact been noted in the literature (Singer & Rowe, 1962; Singer & Schonbar, 1961); that is, it has been proposed that internally aware and sensitive individuals are more in touch with their fears and doubts as well as with their pleasant thoughts thus creating more guilt and anxiety in them. In Singer's (1966) terms, "the penalty of self-awareness and introspection is the direct confrontation of anxiety [p. 142]."

Play Behavior—Direct Observations of Fantasy and Sex Differences

The differences between high- and low-fantasy children as well as between the sexes are strongly revealed in their manner of play. During the play session, notes were taken regarding the nature of each child's play with the various toys and with the other children in his group. In general, the play activities and especially the aggressive play of all the children reflected the presence of the two adult observers, although efforts were made by the latter to be as unobtrusive as possible by seating themselves in a distant corner of a large room and by feigning absorption in paper work. Despite these efforts, the behavior of the children was constrained and modulated since the expression of aggression in its various forms is defended against in most psychosocial contexts (Berkowitz, 1958; 1962). This modulation was evidenced in the Final Aggression Scale and on the Mood Checklist where scores generally clustered in the lower ranges. The aggression which was expressed largely tended to be of verbal or symbolic nature rather than a direct physical expression of aggression toward another child or an overt destructive act toward a toy. The aggressor would often verbally deride another child's creation, would choose to play with a more aggressive toy, or would create something of aggressive, symbolic significance such as a gun out of clay.

The absence of sex differences in the expression of aggression, surprising in light of the large body of evidence pointing to much greater inhibition of aggression for girls than for boys (Jersild & Markey, 1935; Sears, 1951) can perhaps be explained by the fact that aggression was predominantly verbal (critical remarks or jeering) rather than physical with an absence of more extreme aggressive responses. Thus it appeared that the subdued manner of the children contributed largely to the absence of sex differences.

Despite the modulated nature of the play of all subjects, there were marked differences between high- and low-fantasy children in the specific manner in which the various toys were utilized and in the amount of time spent with a toy. Tabulated accounts of Ss' time spent with each activity indicated that the low-fantasy youngsters were more prone to play with a toy for a shorter time period and thus to play with a greater total number of toys during the 10-min play period than were the high-fantasy children. In addition, on the basis of general observational notes, it appeared that the low-fantasy child was more motorically oriented, less creative in his play, and more direct in his approach to play materials and in his expression of aggression than the high-fantasy youngster. To illustrate these different patterns of play behavior and to provide a more complete picture of the play activities of all the subjects, a composite picture of a group of four children and a running account of their play activities follows. While the spectrum of play behavior was broad and varied, there were certain patterns typical of the high- or low-fantasy child which seemed to pervade the play activities so that a hypothetical group can be reconstructed.

The four children, a high- and low-fantasy boy and a high- and low-fantasy girl, had just witnessed the aggressive film and had then been immediately exposed to the play activities. While all four children initially appeared hesitant and inhibited, the girls, who were first attracted to the doll play, seemed even more restrained and slower than the boys to become immersed in play, with their behavior having a self-conscious tone. Perhaps the nature of doll play which tends to be more private and personal in its verbal aspects contributed to this hesitancy with each girl possibly fearful of being overheard by the boys, by the adults, and indeed by the other girl.

The boys both initially chose to play with the action-oriented and potentially aggressive game "Fort Apache" which consists of a metal fort and plastic horses, cowboys, Indians, and pieces of military equipment including a cannon and bullets. Although the two boys were attracted to the same toy, as were the girls, there was initially little interaction, but rather parallel play in evidence for both sexes. The children seemed to choose the same toy primarily to be near one another since they were uncertain of the nature of the setting, and not solely out of a desire to play together.

Although they played with the same toy, the two boys each saw different aspects or features of the activity which intrigued them and thus each approach to the toy was quite different. The low-fantasy boy evidenced a more immediate and direct involvement with the "Fort Apache" game, appearing to take the initiative in making contact, i.e., shooting the gun, picking up soldiers and placing them on horses, and commenting *These bullets really go. . . . Watch me blast these guys.*

The high-fantasy boy at first seemed to be less active and appeared to be listening and watching rather than being directly involved with the game. However, he gradually became more directly engaged in the play, but rather than manipulating the pieces in the same fashion as his low-fantasy playmate, he arranged the soldiers in a planned manner with the Indians on one side of the fort and the soldiers on the other, placing some of the men in strategic spots. He seemed to be mainly involved in arranging the figures rather than in actually staging a fight between sides.

The low-fantasy boy, on the other hand, positioned only several men and then tried to shoot them with the cannon, seemingly unconcerned with the broader fort situation. At this time, there was little direct interaction between the boys, but there was some verbal interchange while each was engaged in his separate play, e.g., *Hey let me have some of those Indians . . . . Give me more bullets.*

As time progressed, more direct interaction in play became evident as the low-fantasy boy began to shoot at his playmate's soldiers saying, *Ha, ha, got him,* and to upset his companion's planned layout commenting *The Indians are wiped out again.* The high-fantasy boy would reply, *Come on, cut it out . . . . What are you doing, stupid?* in an annoyed tone of voice; he would rarely knock down the other boy's soldiers or try to restrain his companion physically, but would limit himself to verbal rebuke. The play ended with the low-fantasy boy appearing to lose interest and walking away to another activity while the high-fantasy child remained and continued to arrange the soldiers. At this point, the need of the children to be together was not so apparent as they adjusted to the situation.

During the initial minutes of play, the girls were occupied with the dolls and doll house and while they interacted more than the boys there was still largely parallel play in evidence. For the low-fantasy girl, there was little obvious representational play or organization with little use of the doll house and no evident development of a nonverbal story or specific theme. She confined herself mainly to dressing and undressing the dolls and was more self-conscious and verbally inhibited than the boys, occasionally commenting, *Oh this is cute.* There were also occasional aggressive comments derogating the doll or its clothing, e.g., *I don't like this, it's ugly.* The high-fantasy girl was more representational and while there was no overt verbal development of a story, fantasy play could be inferred. She would place the dolls in the doll house, around the kitchen table or in their beds, dressing them obviously with a specific activity in mind, thus lending an air of purposefulness to her activity. There was no evidence of interaction between the girls through use of the dolls and no common story theme was developed, even on a nonverbal level about the dolls. The low-fantasy girl was in general more abusive in her handling of the dolls and showed less patience, often tugging and pulling at the clothes. The aggression which was expressed between the girls took the form of scornful comments about the other's doll or of being possessive and unwilling to share. The low-fantasy girl would occasionally annoy her playmate, pestering her and becoming a nuisance and mockingly saying, *What are you doing? . . . Why did you put her there?*

When the low-fantasy boy left the "Fort Apache" activity, he was then attracted to the clay. He made very simple objects, rolling the clay out and forming a snake and an ashtray and evidencing no complexity in design. Of importance was the manner in which he handled the clay, slapping it and pounding it on the table and showing an absence of finer manipulation. He made several objects then destroyed them and created new ones. After several minutes, the high-fantasy boy joined him and after kneading the clay for several moments spent much time in the creation of one object—a figure with distorted facial features which he then altered to a monster-like creature with grotesque additions.

The low-fantasy boy continued to pay less attention to finer details and to engage in more coarse manipulation of the clay, often leaving objects in a rough state. During this play, there was much criticism of the other's work, e.g., *Blech, what's that supposed to be? . . . That looks creepy. . . . Can't you make any-*

thing? There were also one or two instances of physical interference where the low-fantasy boy grabbed his playmate's creation, squeezing and flattening the clay and commenting, *Why don't you make the nose this way?* His playmate expressed annoyance, but did not physically retaliate.

After several minutes, the girls joined the clay activity. The low-fantasy boy then remarked, *I had enough of this* and left to play with the "Targetland" game. The girls then seemed to imitate the high-fantasy boy and also began making figures, but the low-fantasy girl did not seem to enjoy this activity and commented, *This isn't too much fun.* Observing the "Targetland" game, she left the clay activity and joined the low-fantasy boy. The high-fantasy children remained playing with the clay for the remainder of the session, mainly in solitary play and with no physical interference, but with remarks frequently made belittling the other child's creative attempts.

The low-fantasy youngsters, in play with "Targetland," showed much active competition, not actually keeping score, but matching shots. There was a very hurried quality in shooting at the targets and much action with the children running to retrieve the darts and loudly stating, *Hey watch this . . . . Can you do this?* There were many sarcastic remarks made about the other's shooting performance such as, *You couldn't hit it from two inches away.* The children evidenced much movement, attempting to retrieve the darts by running to the target and snatching them and then shooting with great force.

In general, then, the low-fantasy child was more action-oriented and exhibited less of a symbolic approach to play. For all of the children, however, there was generally a low-keyed, modulated expression of affect with aggression expressed predominantly in verbal form. There were, however, several more extreme examples of aggression, especially demonstrated by some of the low-fantasy children who had been exposed to the aggressive film. For example, these children would push or shove their playmate away to retrieve darts in play with "Targetland" or would show more physical destruction of their playmate's arrangement in play with "Fort Apache." There were also instances in which the children would throw clay at one another or around the room. When such extremes of physical aggression were apparent, they were largely caused by the boys. It appears that it is only because there were so few extremes of aggressive behavior that there was failure to obtain significant differences between the sexes.

Theoretical and Practical Implications

The results of this study cast tentative doubt upon the popular view that violence on television and in the movies is harmful to children. It would appear from the present results that in some cases, i.e., for high-fantasy youngsters, the effect might even be beneficial, since viewing an aggressive film was found to decrease overt aggressive behavior for these children skilled in fantasy usage.

Violent television or movie films may provide an opportunity for these children to modify angry feelings. However, it must be noted that the opposite effect might be expected when low-fantasy youngsters view violence; their aggression may indeed increase since these children cannot deal with their aggressive feelings on a fantasy level and instead are prone to act upon them. The crucial element, then, seems to be not the film itself, but the fantasy level of the child, with the same film having beneficial or destructive results depending upon the youngster's ability to utilize the aggressive elements of the film on a fantasy level. Future research, in considering the effects of filmed violence, could also study as well other factors as they interact with fantasy level in affecting reaction to the viewed aggression. Specifically, it would be interesting to investigate the effects of individual differences including defensive patterns and conscience development, familial attitudes toward aggression, and ethnic and socioeconomic factors, and the interactions of these factors with fantasy predisposition.

The belief that reaction to filmed aggression is dependent upon the individual's ability to operate on a fantasy level and not upon the specific content of the film could perhaps find an analogy in the individual's ability to appreciate humor, and particularly aggressive or hostile humor. In fact, the notion that aggressive humor operates for all individuals to facilitate emotional catharsis and release of tension has been under much recent attack. This notion was based largely on Freud's hypothesis that hostile wit or humor (humor of a derogatory nature or dealing with themes of suffering or destruction) is a disguised attack with the individual deriving gratification from this expression of aggression. The humorous form conceals the destructive motives of the humorist and so reduces inhibitions against the expression of aggression in both the joke-teller and the audience. Freud further maintained that the audience recognizes the humorist's invitation to join in the assault, and thus enjoyment of hostile humor is a form of aggression and should be capable of providing a cathartic reduction in further expressions of aggression.

However, previous research has refuted the cathartic theory of humor by demonstrating that neutral humor is as effective as hostile wit in reducing aggressive motivation. This is in direct contradiction to the cathartic notion that it is the expression of aggression inherent only in hostile humor which leads to a reduction in subsequent aggressive expression. Dworkin and Efron (1967) compared hostile humor, neutral humor, and a control recording in their effects on aroused subjects. It was found that both the hostile and the neutral humor reduced aggressive motivation as measured by a Mood Checklist. "While hostile humor may have reduced the aggressive impulses by a cathartic process and the neutral humor by some other process, the absence of a correlation between 'funniness' ratings of the hostile humor and amount of aggression reduction makes this a questionable interpretation [Singer, 1968, p. 3]." Singer also found that for aroused subjects, both hostile and neutral humor were aggression- and tension-reducing as measured by a Mood Checklist. It would be interesting for future research to investigate the correlation between fantasy predisposition and appreciation of hostile humor to determine if, as in the case of filmed aggression, reduction of aggression is dependent upon the fantasy skill of the individual and not upon the specific content of the joke.

In conclusion, the results of the study are in accord with an affect theory of aggression rather than the traditional hydraulic or drive conception. High-fantasy Ss shown the aggressive or nonaggressive film evidenced significant decreases in behavioral aggression scores following the fantasy activity. The similarity of the reduction following either film supports the position that high-fantasy Ss can utilize any fantasy opportunity to lower their overt aggression and thus refutes the cathartic notion that only aggressive fantasy can effect this reduction. All low-fantasy Ss showed no decrease in aggression with children in the low-fantasy–aggression-film category manifesting an actual, although nonsignificant, increase in aggression scores, with these findings refuting the cathartic position that all individuals can utilize fantasy to reduce aggression. The theory that the individual undergoes a mood change received support from the findings that high-fantasy–aggressive-film Ss evidenced a significant decrease in *angry–annoyed* mood scores and significant increases in *sad–downhearted* and *ashamed–contrite* moods. High-fantasy–nonaggressive-film Ss manifested a significant increase in *elated–pleased* mood and significant reductions in *angry–annoyed, ashamed–contrite* and *contemptuous–disgusted* dimensions. All low-fantasy Ss evidenced no significant changes away from their prevailing *angry–annoyed* mood. High-fantasy control Ss allowed no fantasy opportunity, revealed no reduction in aggression and no mood change. Results also indicated no significant differences between males and females in aggression level during either the frustration or play period.

Refutation of a cathartic position is in accord with the theoretical belief that aggression is not a drive, but rather may be viewed as the mood or affect of anger. In accord with Tomkins' position that the affect of anger requires a high, constant level of neural stimulation to be sustained, it is maintained that fantasy provides another stimulus situation for the individual that is less negative and intense and thus relieves some of the prolonged quality of the incoming stimulation. This relief from negative affect brought about by the fantasy situation leads to a change in mood, thus reducing the final expression of aggression.

The differences between high- and low-fantasy children as well as between the sexes were clearly revealed in their manner of play. The low-fantasy child, as observed during play, presented himself as more motorically oriented, revealing much action and little thought in play activities. The high-fantasy child in contrast was more highly structured and creative and tended to be verbally rather than physically aggressive.

CHAPTER VI

Increasing the Imaginative Play of Urban Disadvantaged Kindergarten Children through Systematic Training

Joan T. Freyberg

Introduction

As yet, we have little information of a systematic nature on cultural and socioeconomic class differences in make-believe play. The anthropological findings reported in Whiting (1963) suggest that children show striking differences in the degree of make-believe play in four different cultures. Smilansky's (1968) highly original study also indicates that children from differing socioeconomic levels in Israel reflect a marked difference in what she calls sociodramatic play. Eifermann's (1971) data from Israel also point up cultural differences in patterns and age of symbolic play. It remains to be seen whether the conditions of poverty, such as overcrowding and lack of systematic parental modeling opportunities and encouragement, have the same effect on children in other urban cultures.

From our own research in the series of studies presented in this volume, only one comparison is possible. The data for comparably aged upper-middle-class children from Dr. Pulaski's investigation (Chapter IV) and the lower SES group in the following study by Dr. Freyberg are available. Keeping in mind that the ratings of spontaneous play occurred with different raters and in very different settings, the results do seem in line with those of Smilansky (1968). The middle-class children's mean for fantasy play using a somewhat more strict criterion of make-believe was 2.23, while that for the poor ghetto-school kindergarteners was 1.74 using a more liberal scale. These data are suggestive at best and clearly we need very careful comparative data if we are to make broader generalizations in this area. Perhaps more important than merely establishing differences between social classes in fantasy is the importance of teasing out the factors that make the differences in producing more or less make-believe in children's play. We also need to be able to show whether special types of school or classroom conditions can produce increases in spontaneous resort to socio-dramatic play. Such research can have important educational and clinical implications.

JEROME L. SINGER

Theoretical Models of Imaginative Play

The importance of enhancing a child's ability to engage in imaginative play seems implicit in the view of fantasy as a constructive and useful cognitive skill, in contrast to the older Freudian drive-reduction notion. The child specialists of the Freudian school (Anna Freud, 1937; Greenacre, 1959; Klein, 1960) view the play behavior of children as cathartic and communicative and make use of play as a major therapeutic tool with children. Erikson (1940), who is closer to the ego psychologists, considers play as an infantile way of thinking over difficult experiences and restoring a sense of mastery. It is clear that Erikson stresses the coping rather than the drive-reducing aspects of symbolic play. He also speaks of the pleasure derived from the sense of coping and mastery involved in the imaginative role-play behavior of young children in which they try out new experiences and relive old experiences.

Piaget, in contrast with the psychoanalysts, links symbolic play with general intellectual growth. He considers fantasies and imaginative play of children as necessary to their cognitive development toward operational thought. Like Erikson, Piaget refers to the joy which comes to the child through self-assertion or efficacy in symbolic play. Piaget notes the adaptive aspect of symbolic play in that it develops, fixes, and retains new abilities, as well as its compensatory aspect, that it "improves upon reality" to render it more agreeable. Piaget, as well as White and Schachtel (see Chapter II), points to the need for the opportunity and freedom (from anxiety or grossly unmet needs) to play in order to achieve higher cognitive development. These authors have emphasized that manifestations of exploratory and creative play are most likely to be found among children whose biological and most elemental needs are reasonably well gratified and whose anxiety is kept to a minimum. Piaget and others have stressed that richness and variation in the child's environment tends to enrichment of his inner experience as the child incorporates the world around him into his existing schemata.

There is some evidence that modeling effects exist in the development of fantasy and imaginative behavior in children. As cited in Chapter III, children who are high in fantasy predisposition (middle-class children 6 to 9 years old) reported more association between themselves and their parents than children low in fantasy predisposition. This suggests a relationship between fantasy ability and identification with one or both parents. From this study, Singer suggests that an important environmental factor in the development of fantasy predisposition may be the opportunity for regular contact with at least one parent whose actions and speech patterns are available for imitation. Bandura and Walters (1963) have emphasized the important influence of the parent as a model for children to use in the development of their fantasy and make-believe activities. Thus, children who grow up with parents who represent models of aggressive, impulsive, or distrustful behaviors are probably less likely to engage in fantasy.

Singer (1966) also suggests the importance of the attitude of the parents and the subculture group toward imagination as playing a significant role in fantasy development in a particular individual. Since language ability plays an important role in fantasy and imaginative behavior, the modeling concept has significant implications in terms of the verbal abilities of the parents whom children will tend to imitate in their speech development. The modeling concept implies that middle-class children, whose parents are educated, verbal, generally more tolerant of imaginativeness, and have more time to spend with their children, will be more likely than lower-class children to learn to fantasize and play imaginatively. The importance of modeling in the development of symbolic thought has also been stressed by El'Konin (1966) in a review of the Soviet psychologists' view of imaginative growth.

Explanations such as those involving information-processing models seem to fit the data concerning imaginative play and are more parsimonious than psychodynamic explanations. This cognitive model implies that the development of fantasy predisposition has to do with the balance an individual develops between attention to inner and outer experience. The model invokes the idea of an information-processing channel with limited capacity. Tomkins (1962) emphasizes human efforts to amplify and seek out stimulation and he views personality as a two-way communication between individual and environment. He suggests that affect is involved in the development of the image or fantasy that governs purposive behavior. The organism uses the feedback about the discrepancy between the present state and the image to activate the affect system which is motivational and cue-producing.

As evidence begins to mount that fantasy and imaginativeness can be a useful, cognitive skill, some thought has been given to the idea of cognitive training. If one looks at fantasy disposition no longer in Freudian drive-reduction terms, but rather from the vantage point of information-processing models, there does seem to be scope for modification, especially at early ages. Researchers in the area of creativity have sought ways to increase imaginativeness in children as a way of enhancing their cognitive functioning (Getzels & Jackson, 1962; Guilford, 1967; Torrance, 1966; Tayler, 1964; Wallach & Kogan, 1965). DeMille (1967) developed methods of exercising children's imagination, which he found improved with practice. Marshall and Hahn (1967), Smilansky (1968) and the present investigator have successfully engaged in training imaginative play in young children and observed gains associated with cognitive development.

The Possible Value of Imaginative Play

In reviewing some of the studies in which training of imaginative play was involved, it appears that increased pretend play was associated with other gains. Marshall and Hahn (1967), who trained middle-class children in role-playing and imaginative behavior, found that they were successful in increasing the frequency of such behavior. After training, the Ss also engaged in significantly more associative behavior with peers. These investigators viewed imaginative play as a vehicle to enhance the social development of young children. Smilansky (1968) trained middle- and lower-class Israeli children to play more imaginatively, with the intention of helping them to integrate more easily into real-life patterns of their immediate environment by imitation of it in their play. Smilansky found that increased role-playing behavior resulted in more positive affect, less fighting and hyperactive behavior, use of more parts of speech, and more verbal communication.

The study described here was carried out at about the same time as those of Marshall and Hahn and Smilansky. Lower-class 5-year-olds were successfully trained to play more imaginatively. The enhanced fantasy play proved also to be associated with greater verbal communication, longer and more complex sentence usage, more sensitive responding to the cues of other children, more apparent spontaneity, more creative use of play material, more inventiveness and originality, more labeling, and increased attention span. There were also considerably more positive expressions of emotion in the trained than in the untrained group.

This latter finding is important in light of Tomkins' speculations on the motivational and cue-producing functions of affect. For lower-class children like the subjects of this investigation, positive affect in relation to classroom activities may serve an important function in breaking down negative attitudes about school frequently held in ghetto areas. Another finding in this investigation was that children who were hyperactive and who engaged in endless, ungratifying motoric behavior or fighting were able to learn to play more imaginatively and to delay immediate responsiveness to outer stimulation. The ability to engage in imaginative play implied more organization, more delay of immediate gratification, and more reflectiveness before taking action.

Imaginative play, as Erikson has written, can reduce anxiety by enhancing a child's sense of mastery over the unknown, about new and unfamiliar roles and relationships. There were many examples of children experimenting with unfamiliar roles and relationships in this and the Smilansky study. Therefore, it would seem that imaginative play gives the child a way of reducing his sense of inadequacy, a way of improving on reality when reality is unpleasant (as in long waits), and a way of amusing himself and delaying responsiveness when that is appropriate. In a situation where a child must delay gratification or inhibit natural motor tendencies (a common occurrence in the school setting), it is likely that an imaginative child would have greater ability to make the time pass more pleasurably. The less imaginative child, without fantasy resources, might have to resort to physical contact with his environment even when this is inappropriate or unrewarding.

It should be noted that the very nature of make-believe behavior requires the unfolding of longer sequences of activity than most other kinds of play because it is built around plots and themes (Singer, 1966). These are inherently more complex schemata than many other behavior types and involve retention of material to be shifted from short-term memory. This is in marked contrast to kaleidoscopic or motoric play, which is more dependent on the external environment and kinesthetic cues. It would seem that engaging in activities that in themselves involve more organization and longer and more complex schemata would be facilitating to cognitive development. The role-playing involved in imaginative play also lends itself to more verbal communication and increased vocabulary, as well as spontaneity, inventiveness, and practice in responding to the cues of others.

Socioeconomic and Cultural Class Factors

There is some evidence from studies using projective techniques suggesting differences between lower- and middle-class fantasy behavior. Korchin, Mitchell, and Meltzoff (1950) reported that their middle-class Ss produced significantly longer fantasy stories than did lower socioeconomic class Ss. No differences between Negro and white Ss emerged when social class was controlled. Downing, Edgar, Harris, Kornberg, and Storm (1965) and Ames and August (1966) found Negro lower-class elementary school children less productive, less accurate, and less imaginative in their response to the Rorschach inkblots than white children of comparable age, intelligence, and socioeconomic levels. Stainbrook and Siegel (1944) found that Negro high school students gave fewer responses of any kind on the Rorschach than white students, particularly those kinds of responses associated with fantasy predisposition (M responses). Megargee (1966), on the other hand, found no significant differences between white and Negro lower-class juvenile delinquent males on 69 TAT variables, nor on seven variables of the Rosenszweig Picture Frustration Test, when the subjects were matched for mental age. The only significant differences he found were on the Holtzman inkblot test: the white Ss gave more popular and the Negro Ss more anatomy responses. The Downing *et al.* and Ames and August studies suggest both cultural and socio-economic differences in fantasy predisposition, but admittedly the evidence is only suggestive.

Researchers in the preschool project conducted by Dr. Burton L. White at the Harvard School of Education (Pines, 1969) found that middle-class children engage in role-playing behavior five times more frequently than lower-class children of the same age. These researchers, who visited the children's homes for intensive observation, found that children with interested, involved mothers spend about one-fifth of their time in make-believe and pretending activities and that children of overworked and overwhelmed mothers (usually lower-class mothers), who do not have much time to interact with their children, almost never engage in such activities.

Marshall and Hahn (1967) matched three groups of middle-class children for age and sex and, after a period of observation, trained one of the groups in role-playing or pretend behavior, assisted one group in puzzle play, and gave no training whatsoever to the third group. The experimental group displayed increased role-playing behavior as part of regular play following training, as well as increased associative play. In this study, the researchers found all children engaging in some pretend play before training, and found improvement in all children in the experimental group after training. These findings agree with other studies involving middle-class children, i.e., most middle-class children engage in pretend behavior within a wide range of frequency, and with training most will engage in it more frequently.

In the first phase of the Smilansky study, five field workers observed 36 classes of 35 to 40 pupils (18 middle-class and 18 disadvantaged classes of Israeli children) and recorded their observations of the children's play. In contrast, in the study described in this chapter, however, the children were not systematically observed. Instead, five centers of interest in the classroom were identified: block corner, hospital corner, house corner, doll corner, and playground, and ten examples of play were recorded for each of these centers for an unspecified period of time per observation. Smilansky found that the middle-class children engaged in more role-playing activity than the disadvantaged children, with and without play equipment. The themes of play were similar, but the middle-class children displayed more diversity and variety of roles than the disadvantaged children. Most of the latter engaged in desultory manipulation of toys and play equipment or in repetitive use of miniature adult objects in imitation of adult use, but without any attempt to enact an adult role. It was also found that the middle-class children spoke more than the disadvantaged, used more vocabulary words, longer and more complex sentences, more parts of speech, and did more labeling of objects. The pretraining play of most Ss in this investigator's study was also found to involve mostly manipulation of toys and repetitive, stereotyped activities with play equipment. It was found that, prior to training, these lower-class children engaged in very little verbal communication with one another, made minimal use of words in their play, and seemed to do very little labeling or talking about their play activities. Both Smilansky and this investigator found a high degree of aggression, "bossiness," hyperactivity, and over-excitement, as well as extreme passivity, among the disadvantaged children. In both studies, this kind of behavior diminished following training in imaginative play.

Deutsch (1964a), who has worked extensively with children from lower-class homes, speculates that crowded conditions and few toys or even household objects with which to play result in stimulus deprivation in many such children. Metfessel (personal communication) found that lower-class children studied at the Center for the Study of the Education of Disadvantaged Youth were frequently underdeveloped in the use of symbols and concepts existing apart from concrete objects. He found that lower-class parents were much less accepting of imaginary playmates than middle-class parents. Lower-class parents were inclined to look upon imaginativeness as lying and inclined to punish it when they observed it. He found that lower-class children need to see the concrete and immediate implications of what they are doing, which brings them into conflict with the school situation where delay of gratification is often essential for learning.

Riessman (1964) cautions, however, that we not overlook the differences among lower-class children as well as the cognitive strengths they do possess. He makes the point that lower-class life is not necessarily less varied and stimulating than middle-class life and that it often takes a good deal of ingenuity to survive conditions of severe poverty. There often may be better verbal ability among lower-class children in *out-of-school* situations, in circumstances that do not converge with school values and emphases. He found poor children particularly verbal in role-playing situations out of school. Riessman concedes that deficiencies do exist among lower-class children in formal language and in cognitive functioning, but he places emphasis on the great differences he has found between the formal language required at school and public language; lower-class children appear to be much better at the latter than the former.

John (1963) also stresses the differences in cognitive functioning among lower-class children, but points out a tendency for lower-class families to place less reliance upon language as a means of communication and of cognitive exploration. She attributes much of this to the noise and interference that comes with the overcrowding of many lower-class homes. Brown (1964) also found that lower-class children generally perform less well than middle-class children on tests of verbal power, but not on measures of verbal output. He suggests that this finding be further explored to assess the specific cognitive strengths and weaknesses of lower-class children.

A study by Deutsch (1964c) found that, when the IQ was held constant, differences in speech quality based on variety of verbal output were not significant between lower- and middle-class children. Some investigators (Davidson & Greenberg, 1967) specifically avoid equating for IQ because they feel that this equates only for abilities measured on standard IQ tests and may obscure other abilities that aid cognitive functioning or that could be built upon with special training methods. Deutsch (1964b,c) points out that lower-class children tend to score within a fairly broad range on tests of cognitive functioning, a fact that is often obscured in a literature that emphasizes average differences rather than degree of group overlap.

Deutsch has placed more emphasis on identifying lower-class youngsters who are deficient in cognitive skills, assessing their specific strengths (which may be obscured by traditional tests), and on finding innovative methods of building upon their strengths. He points to evidence that, even in the most economically deprived areas, where school retardation rates are highest, there are children who show considerable school success. There are considerable variations in the home environments of children in ghetto areas, and it cannot be assumed that a so-called "underprivileged" area possesses homogeneous characteristics. Ausubel and Ausubel (1963) argue that there is sufficient consistency of experience for lower-class urban children to speak of such experience as having some deleterious effect on these children's cognitive functioning. While the statistical difference between lower- and middle-class children is generally acknowledged, there is a more recent trend toward building on the specific strengths of the lower-class child; the current focus seems to be on isolating the factors associated with the subgroups within the lower class that do relatively well in contrast to those that do relatively poorly in their cognitive functioning.

If the evidence suggests that middle-class children play more imaginatively than lower-class children, there is a great need for more definitive data. No studies have directly and systematically compared lower- and middle-class children matched for age, sex, IQ, and quality of schooling. Such direct comparisons would have to be based on long-term, systematic observations carried out by a team of observers. Once sufficient long-term data are gathered, we can begin to make judgments on the consistency of children's play. As it is now, there is a chance that behavior samples in the quoted studies may not be totally representative. Lower-class children should perhaps be observed away from school, in which authority figures may be inhibitory. Use of paraprofessionals from the community may be essential in determining whether differences in verbal and cognitive style mask abilities among lower-class children when observed by middle-class persons.

There are unresolved issues around the training of children in imaginative play, since no follow-up studies have been done to determine whether gains can be maintained. No standardized tests have been given to children after training to determine whether gains in ability to play imaginatively are significantly associated with cognitive gains. Uniformity of training is methodologically necessary if statistical results are sought, but once we know more about the components of imaginative play, more individualized training may be most effective and parsimonious. In experimental studies, it is necessary to equate groups for intelligence, but it may be that IQ scores derived from traditional tests mask other abilities that relate to imaginativeness. Because of their heavy reliance on middle-class-oriented tasks, traditional tests may not accurately assess the intelligence of lower-class children. Instruments must be developed for the measurement of intelligence that do not rely so heavily upon verbal skills, so that we may gain more understanding of the relationships among imaginativeness, intelligence, and verbal ability in lower- as well as middle-class children.

Training Poor Children in Imaginative Play

The specific hypotheses of the study were as follows:

1. Lower-class kindergarten children who receive training in imaginative play will play more imaginatively than a group of children who do not receive such training.

2. Lower-class kindergarten children who receive training in imaginative play will show more positive affect during play than a group of children who do not receive the training.

3. Lower-class kindergarten children who receive training in imaginative play will play with a higher degree of concentration than a group of children who do not receive the training.

4. Children designated as "high" in imaginative play predisposition will be rated higher in imaginativeness, affect, and concentration after training than children designated as "low" fantasizers.

5. Parents of children with high-imaginative-play predisposition will report more time spent with the child, more playful and imaginative interactions with him, and more encouraging and tolerant attitudes toward imaginativeness than parents of children with low-fantasy predisposition.

The rationale for the second hypothesis is derived from Piaget and Erikson, both of whom speak of the pleasure in coping and mastery through imaginative play, as well as of "improving on reality" through pretense. Hartley *et al.* (1952) and Lieberman (1965) both have described the joy and delight of children engaging in spontaneous and original play. In Chapter III we mentioned that children who are high daydreamers were able to tolerate waiting, possibly because of their pleasurable fantasy activity. The hypothesis that the experimental group will, after training, be more absorbed and concentrate more in their play receives support from the findings cited in Chapter III relating fantasy ability and inhibition of motility. The hypothesis that children with "high" imaginative predisposition will improve more than those "low" in fantasy tendency was derived from the observation that the lower-class subjects of this study engaged in very little imaginative play before training. It was speculated that those children who engaged in no imaginative play whatsoever represented that hard-core subgroup referred to by Deutsch (1964b,c) who are resistant to remedial training. The final hypothesis is derived from the findings cited in Chapter III and those of Davidson and Greenberg (1967) in relation to possible predisposing conditions for the development of fantasy ability.

Measuring Fantasy Predisposition

For the purpose of determining the imaginative-play predisposition of the subjects, each child was seen individually by the investigator. The four following questions, which comprise Singer's Imaginative Play Interview, were posed: (1) *What do you like to play best? What is your favorite game?* (2) *What do you like to do best when you're alone?* (3) *Do you ever have pictures in your head when you're awake?* (4) *Have you ever had a make-believe friend or playmate?*

Following the interview, the investigator administered the Barron Movement Threshold Inkblot Test to each child. This test consists of a graduated series of 28 inkblots in which it is progressively easier to see human movement (M). Each child was told that he or she would be shown some pictures and the investigator wanted to know what they looked like. Each response was recorded until the child saw human movement on two consecutive cards. The score on this test was the number of the card on which a child first gave M responses.

A third measure of imaginative predisposition was derived from teachers' ratings of imaginativeness based on 3 months of observation of the child's spontaneous play. The teachers rated each child on a 5-point scale of imaginativeness developed by the investigator and carefully explained to the teachers involved. Before actual rating, teachers were asked to rate a few observations in the presence of the investigator to determine if their ratings agreed essentially with hers. Each child was thereby given a score between 1 and 5 on these teachers' ratings of imaginativeness.

Eighty-five children were tested initially in this phase of the study. On each of these measures—interview, Barron Inkblot Test, and teacher's ratings—each child was placed in the "high" or "low" group depending on whether he fell above or below the mean of this group on this particular measure. A child's overall fantasy predisposition score was high if he was above the group mean on two of the three measures and low if he was below the group mean on two of the three measures. For 79 of the children there was complete agreement of all three measures. That is, a child classified with a high-imaginative-play disposition from the interview also scored above the group mean on production of movement responses and in the teachers' ratings. From the six remaining children in whose records there was some discrepancy, a girl with low fantasy scores on only two out of three measures was randomly assigned to one of the groups. The remaining five children were not included in the study, although they went through all procedures so as to avoid any implication of their being rejected.

Subjects

The final group consisted of 80 5-year-olds who were in four kindergarten classes at a Special Services public elementary school in New York City. The head of the household for all 80 Ss was either on welfare or engaged in unskilled labor. No parent of these children had completed more than 8 years of schooling. Seventy-seven percent of the fathers were living at home; the remaining 23% were either absent or dead. Eight percent of the families were welfare recipients. All children spoke English. Children were assigned at random to the experimental and control groups. Each of these groups contained equal numbers of boys and girls and equal numbers of high- and low-fantasy children. The vocabulary subtest of the Stanford Binet Test was given each child to obtain an estimate of verbal intelligence. The mean IQ for the control and for the experimental group was computed to ascertain that no significant difference in IQ existed between the two groups. The mean mental age for the experimental group was 5.35 and that for the control group 5.36, an obviously nonsignificant difference.

Observations of Spontaneous Play

In order to be able to compare the play behavior of the children before and after training, their free-play activities were systematically observed by two independent observers. Each child was observed for six 5-min pretraining protocols and twelve posttraining segments. The behavior was recorded in minute detail, including physical movements, facial expressions, social interchanges, play equipment used, all verbalizations, and tone of voice. The observers were present in the classrooms on separate days, so that they were never recording the same class simultaneously. Children were randomly chosen for observation sequences in the hope that this would result in obtaining protocols representative of the child's usual patterns of play. The observers did, however, record three segments of behavior from the first half of the 45-min playtime for each child and three segments during the second half, in case fatigue, boredom, or other factors were operating differentially during the different time segments of the play period. During free-play time, children were free to do as they pleased and to play with whatever they wished. There was a doll house and a block corner, art supplies, and all manner of games, puzzles, and play equipment available.

Before undertaking the actual observations, the two observers practiced recording the behavior of the same children, and these protocols were shown to several outside psychologists who agreed on the high degree of similarity.

When all protocols were obtained for each child, his name was removed from the record sheets and a code number substituted, so that his identity would be unknown when the protocols were rated. The protocols were rated by three separate persons: the two observers and a third person who was unfamiliar with any details of the study. Before the actual rating, the three raters discussed the criteria and the investigator provided examples for each point in the rating scales from some pilot observations. The independent ratings were then compared and found to be in high agreement. Once the reliability was established, the protocol of each child was rated separately by the three raters on 5-point scales of imaginativeness, affect, and concentration (see the Appendix for descriptions of these scales). These scales were developed by the investigator but based on those used by Pulaski (see Chapter IV). Kendall Coefficients of Concordance were obtained on the three dimensions for pre- and posttraining protocols and found to be high and significant. They ranged from .85 to .89. Therefore, it seemed justified to give each child a pre- and a posttraining score in imaginativeness, affect, and concentration by averaging the ratings across the three raters. The ratings were also analyzed on the basis of separate scores for each of the protocols provided by the two observers. Separate Pearson Product-Moment Correlations were computed for pre- and posttraining imaginativeness, affect, and concentration between the two sets of ratings. These correlations were all in the high .90s and obviously significant. They lead to the conclusion that the observers did not elicit differential patterns of behavior and, in addition, were objective recorders of readily identifiable samples of behavior.

Imaginative Training Procedures

Following the first set of observations, the investigator gave eight 20-min training sessions to small groups of four experimental-group children at a time. They were taken to a separate room where they found an assortment of fabrics spread on a large table along with pipe cleaners, clay, Playdoh, blocks, Tinkertoy sets, and a wide variety of wooden shapes. During each of the eight sessions, the investigator introduced a separate theme (based on the children's interests) and began to enact small plots in which pipe-cleaner people were made to talk and engage in make-believe roles, using the play equipment imaginatively as props. Verbalizations were made by the investigator in different tones of voice for the different characters of the story plot. Sounds of sirens, wind, water, etc. were simulated. Children were encouraged to adopt a role, using play equipment of their own choosing and to engage in verbalizations as though they were one of the characters in the story. Each child was given the opportunity to participate in each story plot. There were four themes, each used twice in the eight sessions: (1) the story of a boat and sailors caught in a storm; (2) a family situation around the dinner table; (3) a classroom situation with interaction between teacher and pupils; and (4) a magic genie situation in which all manner of disappearing acts and tricks were performed. At the very beginning, the investigator had to participate heavily and prod the children to join. However, once the idea caught on with the group, the investigator was largely excluded and the plots took all kinds of spontaneous, original, and sometimes surprising turns.

The Control Task

The children in the control group were also taken to a separate room in groups of four for eight 20-min sessions. These sessions were devoted to helping the children assemble jigsaw puzzles and construct Tinkertoy structures. The investigator made friendly conversation with the children, helping each one either build a replica of a structure pictured on the Tinkertoy box or put together a puzzle of his choice. The children showed interest in the toys and seemed to enjoy their sense of mastery. There was a warm and pleasant interaction between children and investigator. Their productions were generously praised. The emphasis was on providing a balancing experience of warmth and interest and training in a game of mastery.

Analysis of the Data

After the Ss' pre- and posttraining scores were computed, three separate analyses of covariance were performed for imaginativeness, affect, and concentration to determine whether the training sessions had a significant effect in increasing the imaginativeness of play, the positive affect displayed during play, and the degree of concentration exhibited in play. It was also possible to determine by these two-way analyses of covariance whether the high-fantasy group improved more than the low-fantasy group as predicted. The analyses of covariance were used in order to eliminate the variance due to individual differences on the pretraining scores in determining the effects of training. The small differences between the boys' and girls' scores did not seem to necessitate separate analyses by sex.

Interview with Parents

To gather data in relation to the fifth hypothesis, the investigator conducted interviews with the parents of six children with scores in the low-fantasy-predisposition distribution and with parents of six children with high-fantasy predisposition. Each interview was about 45 min long and took place in the child's home. Information was sought on the following points: ordinal position of child; number of people in family in how many rooms; number of children and how closely spaced; presence or absence of a father; occupational and educational level of parents; whether mother worked in child's preschool period; amount of time spent doing things with child; kinds of activities engaged in with child; kinds of games child usually plays at home; attitude of parents toward imaginativeness; person in family to whom child is closest; and a general assessment of parent's overall concern for child.

Results of Training

The major results of the study are presented in Tables 1-4. As the major result of eight 20-min training sessions over a period of 1 month, the experimental group improved significantly in the imaginativeness of their play, as well as in the expression of positive affect and in the degree of concentration shown in their play. The control group remained unchanged. That these changes in the experimental group were not quickly dissipated is attested to by the fact that the greater imaginativeness continued consistently during the 2 months of post-training observations.

The existence of the control group with which the investigator engaged in some structured activities, along with friendly conversation, would seem to rule

TABLE 1

Phi Coefficients between Fantasy Measures

	Experimental sample	Source population
Barron test–Play interview	.98*	.89*
Barron test–Teacher's ratings	.98*	.90*
Barron test–IQ	.08	.06
Play interview–Teacher's ratings	.99*	.92*
Teacher's ratings–IQ	.08	.07
Play interview–IQ	.08	.08
Overall fantasy–Imaginative play (pretraining)	.81*	.82*

*Significant at the .01 level

TABLE 2

Intercorrelations between the 12 Variables of the Study

	Pre-imag.	Pre-aff.	Pre-con.	Post-imag.	Post-aff.	Post-con.	Fantasy	Sex	Mental age	Barron[a]	Teacher's ratings	Inter-view
Preimagination	1.00	.97	.96	.76	.72	.73	.81	.17	.22	-.79	.80	.81
Preaffect	.97	1.00	.96	.76	.72	.72	.80	.16	.26	-.78	.76	.78
Preconcentration	.97	.95	1.00	.72	.68	.69	.77	.21	.18	-.73	.75	.76
Postimagination	.76	.75	.72	1.00	.98	.98	.61	.13	.21	-.61	.65	.64
Postaffect	.72	.72	.68	.98	1.00	.98	.56	.16	.24	-.56	.62	.61
Postconcentration	.73	.73	.69	.98	.98	1.00	.57	.14	.22	-.57	.62	.62
Fantasy	.82	.80	.77	.61	.56	.57	1.00	.01	.15	-.88	.87	.87
Sex	.17	.16	.21	.13	.17	.14	.01	1.00	.15	-.02	.13	.13
Mental age	.22	.26	.18	.21	.24	.22	.15	.15	1.00	-.22	.16	.21
Barron test[a]	-.79	-.78	-.73	-.61	-.56	-.57	-.88	-.02	-.22	1.00	-.78	-.81
Teacher's ratings	.80	.76	.75	.64	.62	.62	.87	.13	.16	-.78	1.00	.92
Imaginative play interview	.81	.78	.76	.64	.61	.62	.87	.13	.21	-.81	.93	1.00

[a] All the Barron correlations are negative, since in contrast to the other measures, a low score on the Barron is related to high fantasy and a high score to low fantasy.

TABLE 3

Means and Standard Deviations for Imaginativeness, Affect, and Concentration

	Experimental group (N = 40)		Control group (N = 40)		Combined (N = 80)	
	Mean	SD	Mean	SD	Mean	SD
Pretraining						
Imaginativeness	1.80	.84	1.68	.84	1.74	.84
Affect	1.91	.77	1.77	.76	1.84	.76
Concentration	1.73	.66	1.68	.69	1.70	.68
Posttraining						
Imaginativeness	3.03	1.45	1.72	1.34	2.38	1.40
Affect	3.09	1.32	1.90	1.20	2.50	1.26
Concentration	3.15	1.44	1.87	1.33	2.51	1.38

TABLE 4

Number of Subjects Improving, Remaining the Same, or Declining with Training

	High fantasy			Low fantasy		
Group	Improved	Same	Declined	Improved	Same	Declined
Imaginativeness						
Experimental	18	2	0	13	2	5
Control	14	4	2	0	13	7
Affect						
Experimental	16	1	3	16	2	2
Control	12	3	5	13	4	3
Concentration						
Experimental	18	2	0	14	1	5
Control	16	2	2	15	3	2

out the factors of warmth, interest, and more individual attention as causes of the experimental group's improvement. The fact that the trained children played more imaginatively in the presence of the observer who was not the investigator would seem to indicate that the children had learned new skills as a result of training that they were able to apply in different situations, and that they were not simply imitating the investigator's behavior in a simple, direct way when she was present to serve as a cue.

The question may be asked, "How could these significant changes in the children's play behavior be brought about with only 2 hours and 40 min of training?" The answer must certainly be that the children had the potential for more varied and complex play than they were displaying. What appears to have been lacking were the specific play techniques or skills to actualize their potential, perhaps due to lack of instruction or the lack of adult models after whom they could fashion their imaginative play. This seems to indicate that despite limitations in experience, some verbal deficiencies, crowded living conditions, overburdened mothers, and other similar factors thought to be associated with lower fantasy predisposition, most of these children were able to learn quickly to engage in role-playing and more imaginative play. As Smilansky (1968) points out, perhaps there are certain behaviors that must be learned by means of adult intervention at particular points in a child's development. This training by imitation of models may happen more as a matter of course with middle-class children because of the value placed on the advice of childcare books in the middle-class home, the presence of fewer children, earlier reading experiences, as well as the middle-class mother's perception of her role in training the child.

Despite these rapid changes in play obtained in this study, there is evidence of a persisting limitation of certain cognitive skills among these lower-class children. The low-fantasy group, after training, did not attain the level of imaginative play of the middle-class group studied by Pulaski. The posttraining behavior of the experimental group in this study included more verbal communication, longer and more complex sentences, more sensitive responding to the cues of others, more spontaneity, more creativity, more labeling, more discriminating use of language, and increased attention span. To the extent, therefore, that this improvement is maintained, it can be hoped that these children will function at a higher level than the control subjects in their first-grade work.

In summary, it can be stated that modeling effects and direct teaching by adults can be very effective at certain points in children's development, by serving as a catalyst to develop skills that are basically within the resources of the child. These modeling and teaching effects can result in marked changes in the child's functioning despite some long-term lacks in experiential background and cognitive development. The significant improvement in positive affect and concentration should also be strong assets for the lower-class child in his efforts to adjust to and learn in the middle-class-oriented school.

Imaginative Play Predisposition (High versus Low Fantasy)

In relation to interaction effects, it was found that the high-fantasy group improved significantly more than the low-fantasy group with training in imaginativeness and concentration, but not in positive affect. The low-fantasy group improved significantly in all three dependent variables, but not as much as the high group (except in positive affect), nor did as many low-fantasy children improve as high-fantasy children. Tables 5–7 indicate some of the results for high- and low-fantasy groups.

TABLE 5

Number of Subjects by Sex Improving, Remaining the Same, and Declining after Training

	High fantasy			Low fantasy		
Group	Improved	Same	Declined	Improved	Same	Declined
Imaginativeness						
Experimental						
Boys	9	1	0	7	1	2
Girls	9	1	0	6	1	3
Control						
Boys	6	4	0	0	6	4
Girls	8	0	2	0	7	3
Affect						
Experimental						
Boys	7	1	2	8	1	1
Girls	9	0	1	8	1	1
Control						
Boys	5	1	4	5	3	2
Girls	7	2	1	8	1	1
Concentration						
Experimental						
Boys	8	2	0	8	0	2
Girls	10	0	0	6	1	3
Control						
Boys	9	0	1	9	1	0
Girls	7	2	1	6	2	2

TABLE 6

Mean Scores of the High- and Low-Fantasy Groups

	High fantasy			Low fantasy		
	Pre	Post	N	Pre	Post	N
Imaginativeness						
Experimental	2.53	4.02	20	1.06	2.04	20
Control	2.31	2.46	20	1.05	1.03	20
Affect						
Experimental	2.58	3.93	20	1.24	2.26	20
Control	2.33	2.49	20	1.21	1.32	20
Concentration						
Experimental	2.28	4.12	20	1.17	2.18	20
Control	2.17	2.46	20	1.18	1.27	20

TABLE 7

Mean Scores for Boys and Girls

	Boys (N = 40)		Girls (N = 40)	
	Pre	Post	Pre	Post
Imaginativeness	1.59	2.20	1.88	2.57
Affect	1.72	2.29	1.96	2.71
Concentration	1.56	2.32	1.85	2.69

From these data, it seems likely that the high group of this study is similar to the low groups of middle-class subjects and the low group represents that subgroup of lower-class children who are particularly deficient in cognitive skills and who are very resistant to remediation.

The high intercorrelation between the measures of imaginativeness and concentration suggest that they may be a unitary dimension and that by its very nature imaginative play requires longer drawn-out sequences of behavior. The similar interaction effects for imaginativeness and concentration support this idea. While affect also correlated significantly with imaginativeness and concentration, the interaction effects were different. The experimental group played with more positive affect after training, but this was equally true for both high- and low-fantasy groups. Despite the fact that the high-fantasy group played with more imaginativeness and concentration than the low-fantasy children after training, both groups improved equally in the degree of positive affect with which they played.

It seems very likely that a cause-and-effect relationship exists between imaginative role-playing behavior and positive affect. Anyone watching a child playing out a role and making believe can sense and plainly see his joy at trying out new experiences and having others relate to him in that role and at reliving old experiences in play that were pleasurable. The overriding lack of positive emotionality in the majority of the children prior to training assured that any change could only be in an upward direction. The joy in their new skills was great, independent of degree of improvement in imaginative play.

Prior to training, the low-fantasy children were either extremely apathetic and passive, often staring at other children playing, or extremely hyperactive, engaging in desultory manipulation of play equipment or in overexcited running and fighting behavior. The high-fantasy children prior to training engaged in fleeting bits of imaginative play revolving mainly around repetitive and stereotyped themes of eating, driving, and family illness. The children from the low-fantasy group who did play more imaginatively following training were able to engage in some pretend episodes, but did not sustain them long or elaborate them. They were not very original in the use of play equipment. There was not much verbalization as part of a role. On the contrary, the high-fantasy group, following training, played imaginatively with much consistency and with highly organized plots. The themes were often quite imaginative and transcended the area of the children's immediate experiences. The high-fantasy children became extremely absorbed in their roles, using simulated voices and maintaining the roles even when others attempted to relate to them outside the roles. Play equipment was used creatively and there was greater use of complex sentences, more labeling, and more attention to detail. They were more responsive to each other and obviously enjoying themselves.

Familial Determinants–The Interviews

It was primarily to determine some familial characteristics associated with the high- and low-fantasy predispositions that the interviews with the 12 parents were carried out (see Table 8). Ordinal birth position differentiated the groups, with high-fantasy children more often being the oldest or only child. The low-fantasy children were often the middle child (see Chapter III). This suggests that, even if only for a short time, the high-fantasy child had more of his parents' at-home time and attention. The high-fantasy group also was found to have many fewer siblings and more living space at home than the low-fantasy group. This also suggests that the high-fantasy child had more of his parents' time and more chance for quiet and privacy. It was also found that the parents of the high-fantasy group had more years of education than the parents of the contrasting group, indicating that the former probably were perhaps a bit better able to use language as a means of communication and cognitive exploration.

The high-fantasy-group parents also proved upon inquiry to be more tolerant and encouraging of imaginativeness in their children than low-fantasy-group parents. More high-fantasy-group mothers worked part time during the child's preschool years than low-fantasy-group mothers. The latter, while physically present more than high-fantasy-group mothers, were apparently too preoccupied with their other children to play with the child or to serve as a model for imaginative-type behavior. The high-fantasy child (according to mother's report) was more often closer to his mother than the low-fantasy child, who did not seem to have any particular pattern of familial closeness (see Chapter III). This reported closeness to the mother on the part of the high-fantasy child would suggest that this identification facilitated imitation of the behavior of mothers who were found to be somewhat educated, encouraging of imaginative-type activities, and willing to engage in such activities with the child. These data support the notion of limited-channel capacity expounded by Tomkins and

TABLE 8

Results of Interviews with Twelve Parents

High fantasy ($N = 6$)	Low fantasy ($N = 6$)
1. *Ordinal position* 4 oldest or only children 1 youngest child 1 middle child	1. *Ordinal position* 4 middle children 2 oldest children
2. *Person/room ratio* 4/3; 4/3; 5/4; 4/3; 5/4; 3/3 Overall ratio = 25/20 = *1.25*	2. *Person/room ratio* 5/4; 9/4½; 7/4½; 9/4½; 11/5; 5/3 Overall ratio = 46/25½ = *1.80*
3. *Number of children* 3; 2; 3; 2; 3; 1 Mean = 2.33 children	3. *Number of children* 3; 7; 5; 7; 9; 3 Mean = 5.66 children
4. *Father's presence or absence* 5 present, 1 absent	4. *Father's presence or absence* 6 present, but 1 nearly always at sea
5. *Educational and occupational level of parents* all parents unskilled workers 5 sets of parents finished elementary school 1 set: father—8th grade; mother—5th grade	5. *Educational and occupational level of parents* all parents unskilled workers no parents finished elementary school fifth grade was highest grade completed
6. *Mother's occupation in child's preschool years* 3 mothers worked part time 1 mother worked full time 1 mother did not work 1 mother abandoned family	6. *Mother's occupation in child's preschool years* no mothers worked during child's preschool years
7, 8. *Amount and kind of interaction between parents and child* 2 parents reported no time spent with child in any activities 4 parents reported very little time spent with child, with occasional reading, storytelling, and guessing games	7, 8. *Amount and kind of interaction between parents and child* 3 parents reported no time at all spent with TV watching together 3 parents reported no time at all spent with child
9. *Child's usual play activity* all 6 parents reported some pretend activity, like playing house, school, or dectectives	9. *Child's usual play activity* 2 parents reported they did not know what child's usual activity was 2 parents reported TV watching 2 parents reported child usually helps with housework

TABLE 8 *(Continued)*

High fantasy ($N = 6$)	Low fantasy ($N = 6$)
10. *Attitude of parent toward imaginativeness* all 6 parents expressed some positive attitude	10. *Attitude of parent toward imaginativeness* 2 parents could not express any attitude 4 parents expressed negative attitudes
11. *Person to whom child is closest* 3 to mother 1 to grandmother (mother substitute) 1 to older sister 1 to no one in particular	11. *Person to whom child is closest* 1 to mother 1 to father 1 to older sister 1 to brothers and sisters 2 to no one in particular
12. *Interest and concern of parent for child as judged by interviewer* 4 parents judged as highly interested in and concerned about the child, much awareness of his individuality 2 parents judged to have minimal interest in and concern for child because of own problems	12. *Interest and concern of parent for child as judged by interviewer* all 6 parents judged to be only minimally interested in and concerned for child because of own problems

Singer. If a child grows up as a middle child in a large family of siblings in a few rooms, it would seem less likely for him to have developed the capacity to attend to his inner stimulation to the same extent as a firstborn, only, or middle-class child.

The most striking differences between the high and low groups were in number of children in the family, education of parents, usual play activity of the child, and attitude of parent toward imaginativeness. The fifth hypothesis, that parents of children with high-fantasy predisposition would spend more time with their child, have more playful and imaginative interactions with him and more encouraging and tolerant attitudes toward imaginativeness than parents of low-fantasy children, was supported, except for the factor of more time spent with the child.

Some Implications

It would seem reasonable to conclude from these findings that the dimension of fantasy predisposition is a stable, consistent one that can be measured reliably in a number of ways that are highly correlated with each other: a projective technique, an interview about play preferences, and by teachers' ratings of imaginativeness based upon their relatively long-term observations. Fantasy predisposition is unrelated to verbal IQ (as found in this study), but is related to ratings of imaginative play. This lends support to the assumption that fantasy represents a dimension of divergent production or associational fluidity independent of intelligence. Pretraining scores for imaginativeness of play based on observations of children's play correlated .81 with the fantasy rating derived from the Barron inkblots, play interview, and teacher's ratings. In summary, it was found that fantasy predisposition in young children is independent of sex and intelligence, highly related to play that is characterized by pretense, role-playing, positive affect, and concentration, and that it can be measured reliably by a variety of instruments that tap somewhat different behavioral manifestations.

The significant statistical results attest to the finding that the experimental group improved more than the control group in imaginativeness, positive affect, and concentration. However, these statistical findings do not give any inkling of the rich clinical data in the actual behavioral protocols. A major finding was that there was very little imaginative play among the children prior to training. There was very little role-playing or elaboration of themes; seldom was a pretend situation concerned with themes not in the child's direct experience. Following training, there was more and qualitatively different imaginative play. There was much more organization in the pretend situations, which often involved themes not part of the daily life of the child—trips to the moon, visits to the hairdresser, hospital operations, boat rides to Africa, etc.

Another striking difference that was observed in the posttraining imaginative play was the greater use of role-playing with changed voices. There was also simulation of different sounds, which was totally missing in the pretraining period. The use of toys and other play equipment involved a considerable amount of originality, whereas previously there was little use of toys that was not obviously suggested by the objects themselves. There was a great increase in dialogue following training; previously there were mostly fleeting comments tacked onto otherwise unimaginative play. Conversations were longer, more complex, and sustained over longer periods of play. There was much more labeling, attention to detail, and names of small items woven into the pretend themes. The trained children were more absorbed in their play and would often resist interruption. Their great enjoyment of the role-playing and pretending was obvious to all.

Some Examples

Two short case histories will illustrate the dramatic changes from the pretraining to the posttraining period.

J. was a forlorn little girl who would sit in the corner of the room during free-play time, sucking her thumb and staring dully into the room. When the training sessions began, she was reluctant and fearful about leaving the room with the investigator. However, she was very responsive to the individual attention she received in the sessions. She participated in all the training sessions, although with much hesitancy in the beginning. In the second session, she began to engage in role-playing and even began to smile and laugh. When the investigator entered the classroom, *J.* would smile and run over asking to play games with her. In free-play time shortly thereafter, *J.* was seen role-playing with increasing frequency, although she never was very original in her themes or in her use of play equipment. She smiled often in her play, talked to the other children much more, and stopped sucking her thumb. *J.*'s marked change was instrumental in gaining greater cooperation for this study from the teachers who previously had made considerable but unsuccessful effort to involve this child in activities with her classmates.

D. was one of a set of triplets—all girls—in the same kindergarten class. Before training she nearly always sat with her two sisters, as blank-faced and detached as they were. The three seldom smiled or spoke, but would color together or build with construction toys in a very uninvolved, unsustained manner. *D.* became a member of the experimental group and her two sisters were in the control group. Following training, *D.* was usually found in the housekeeping corner playing house with several other girls, role-playing and smiling as she spoke in adultlike tones. Her two sisters remained as before, passively and unsmilingly manipulating toys in a desultory, uninvolved manner. One of the other sisters asked the investigator why she had played "better games" with *D.* than with her.

Once *D.* was pretending to be sitting on a park bench, wearing high heels and a big floppy lady's hat, rocking her baby in the carriage, when her two sisters came over to her and asked her to come sit with them. *Can't you see I'm trying to get my baby to sleep? Don't talk so loud, D.* said to them with great seriousness, never stepping out of her role. The two sisters shrugged, looked puzzled, and walked off to resume their usual activities. The training resulted in *D.* separating herself from her sisters to engage in imaginative play with other children who regularly played in that manner.

Implications for Further Research

The practical implications of this study are that interventions such as those described herein can serve to enhance cognitive development of young children, as well as to increase their positive affective experiences, in a relatively short time. These methods are more economical and far reaching than one-to-one methods based on deficit models, since they can be incorporated into the curriculum of the regular nursery and kindergarten classes. The training sessions can be related to the children's particular interests and experiences. Discussions and other enrichment experiences may be coordinated with the training in imaginative play, as Smilansky did so effectively. It would seem that the findings of this study are especially relevant for psychologists and others who work in the urban ghettos, attempting to find ways to enhance the cognitive skills of the disadvantaged child. Traditional approaches of remediation in specific areas of academic functioning may exacerbate one of the major difficulties of the disadvantaged child, that of conceptual integration of experience. It is here suggested that training of some fantasy ability is important for such children precisely because it provides the means by which greater conceptual integration of experience is possible.

In order to assess the long-term consequences of enhancing imaginative play, it will be imperative to follow up children who were successfully trained to evaluate their subsequent academic performance in comparison with children who were not so trained. This assessment of academic achievement should be carried out at certain and regular intervals by means of grades, teachers' ratings, and by standardized achievement tests. Only in this way can we ascertain whether there are cognitive benefits from enhanced fantasy ability and how lasting these gains may be.

The development of more discriminating rating instruments (employing more scale units) and the breakdown of imaginative play into components for which subscales may be developed would seem to offer the possibility of increasing our understanding of the complexities of this kind of play. Then methods can be developed for the individual play needs of each child where performance on components is not even. More comparative studies between lower- and middle-class children using subscales for different components of imaginative play might elucidate the special strengths of the lower-class child upon which to build. It is possible that the lower-class child's strengths in some components of make-believe may be masked by the use of overall scales of imagination. A possibility of this kind is suggested in some of Eifermann's (1971) findings.

In order to increase our understanding of the construct of fantasy predisposition and its relationships with other personality dimensions, it would be useful to conduct studies in which we try to relate measures of fantasy to measures of other personality dimensions about which we have some knowledge. For instance, it would be enlightening to have a better understanding of the relationship between fantasy predisposition and creativity, as both seem to encompass the elements of originality and the ability to attend to and manipulate mental images. Lieberman (1965) suggests that spontaneous and original playfulness may be used to predict cognitive style and creativity, defined as divergent thinking. It is clear, however, that high-fantasy persons are not always creative in the sense of productivity. The relationship can be investigated by determining whether persons high on fantasy measures (Barron Inkblot Test, Rorschach *M,* etc.) are also high on standardized tests of creativity (Guilford Test Battery, Torrance Creativity Test, etc.). It may be that fantasy is related to some components of creativity but not others. Guilford has identified five traits of creativity: fluency of thinking, flexibility, originality, elaboration, and ability to see problems in novel ways. In several studies, high-fantasy children have been observed to be creative and original in their use of play equipment and in story-telling. It may be that a person high in fantasy predisposition may be high in some, but possibly not all, of the components Guilford defines as creativity. If children's academic careers are followed throughout their school years, many correlates of high- and low-fantasy ability may be defined. Proceeding in this manner, we can increase our understanding of the construct of fantasy predis-position, its operation, and its relation to other personality variables, and thus develop a nomological network of psychological theory as it relates to this area of human functioning.

CHAPTER VII

Modeling Effects upon Fantasy

Sybil Gottlieb

Introduction

So far, we have emphasized studies that deal with relatively young children and their imaginative play. Somewhere between ages 6 or 7 and 12 we generally see a decrease in overt manifestations of make-believe play. Of course, as noted in some previous anecdotes that reach into the early teens, some imaginative or socio-dramatic play continues as in the case of boys playing sports-oriented board games. We do see some more socially-sanctioned persistence of make-believe in the dramatic performances, spontaneous or rehearsed, that young adolescents manifest. I recall how a friend and I used to entertain the younger children in our apartment house by making up Sherlock Homes playlets. Since my friend resembled Sherlock and also owned a deer stalker's cap, he played the detective and I was left with more dubious roles such as Dr. Watson, Professor Moriarty, and the Hound of the Baskervilles.

Persistence of make-believe play that calls on the exercise of imagery can also be observed in playing party games. Charades or Pantomime are examples of instances where the effort to communicate a book title or a proverb to one's teammates often calls upon considerable skill in simulating make-believe situations and in evoking imagery. While the art of mime itself is no longer widely practiced in Western civilization, the continued appreciation of an actor like Charlie Chaplin reflects the fascination of the audience with the simulation of events not actually present to the naked eye. Greatest of the mimes today is undoubtedly Marcel Marceau, who uses in an almost magical fashion the anticipation imagery and memory imagery of the audience to convey, without any props, the whole life of a man or a prisoner in a cage.

With the apparent, gradual disappearance of most overt symbolic play, then, does it follow that make-believe also fades from our experience? Piaget, Freud, Lewin, and Werner, among other authorities on human development, have proposed that symbolic play activities become internalized in the form of "images in the mind," "implicit interior monologues," daydreams and fantasies. While most clinical investigators also assume this to be the case (Schaefer, 1969) conclusive evidence of how internalization occurs is lacking. We need to understand the mechanisms and situational factors which produce this change in our communicative repertoire. Klinger (1971) has argued cogently that the symbolic play and dreams of children are continuous with the spontaneous (daydream) or elicited fantasies (story-telling) of adolescents and adults.

The study which follows carries us from our emphasis upon make-believe games to elicited fantasy in children aged 11 through 14. The issue raised is one that cannot settle the difficult question of internalization, but it does move us a step closer to understanding how change in fantasy patterns may occur. As in Freyberg's demonstration that make-believe play tendencies can be modified, Gottlieb points toward at least one mechanism—the imitation of an adult model—which can influence the type of fantasy behavior and degree of imaginativeness manifested by an older child. Her study also examines our measures of imaginative or fantasy predisposition with older samples and provides some data on the content of early adolescent or late puberty fantasies.

JEROME L. SINGER

Origins of Fantasy

Modern psychoanalytic theory has been more explicit than Freud in acknowledging the constructive function of imagination. Kris (1951), by introducing the concept, "regression in the service of the ego," refers to a regression which occurs under the control of the more mature or highly differentiated personality structure—reality. This concept enables psychoanalytic theory to explain the apparent contradiction implied in viewing imagination as simultaneously representing a mature and an infantile process. Here, imaginative thought involves the conscious control of the primary process; there is a volitional stepping in and pulling back.

Although he moves within traditional psychoanalytic theory, Erikson's views (1963) of imagination go beyond those of Freud. He sees play and imagination as ways of working out problems, defeats, frustrations; imagination is seen as a catharsis or release of tension; it is also seen as a method used in training to postpone, to cope with premature emotional expression, with suppressed and expressed impulses. Early in life it is action-bent; it is played out in the most primitive sense in that it includes the body and objects close at hand. Erikson labels this early stage, the Autosphere. The Autosphere is extended to the Microsphere, where small objects are used in the creation of a miniature world; there is an extension and intensification of the mode of expression of an organ or organ system. Later, the child's imaginative play utilizes life-sized objects as background for thought, that is, he uses the Macrosphere. Finally, the child no longer needs to execute his thoughts overtly. Covert actions form the basis for thought and more elaborate make-believe sequences are possible. Whole scenes can be played, compressed both in space and in time.

Thus, imaginative behavior is not an intermission from life or a discharge of energy, it is a continuation of life and an expression of development on a sign level. It demonstrates the interplay between development and fantasy and the influence of external and internal factors as it unfolds. It represents differentiation, articulation; it is a midpoint between the extremes of infantile perceptualization, sensualism, action, and realism characterized by the concrete, the immediate.

The concern for differentiation of fantasy from the perceptual and the concrete has been expressed by both Lewin (1951) and Werner (1957). Both authors view the young child's cognitive structure as limited with a corresponding paucity of fantasy life. The richness and elaborateness of the fantasies of adolescents point to the manifestation of their cognitive maturity, their ability to recombine events in novel ways, the utilization of thought. These extremes, as well as Erikson's developmental sequence, suggest that there is a cognitive skill of imagination (Singer, 1966) and that it follows the same processes and structures underlying coding, storing, checking of information as well as organ systems' maturation.

The implication here is that imagination requires stimulation from the environment, peer contact, parental approval and contact, and adequate time and space, in order to flourish. Essentially, these are factors associated with learning in general, and social learning in particular. If this is so, then one way children might learn fantasy behavior is through the observation of models.

Modeling and Social Learning

What is meant by "modeling"? Bandura and Walters (1963) describe it as a tendency to reproduce the actions, attitudes or emotional responses exhibited by live or pictorial and verbal models. They delineate three effects: (1) an *imitative* effect, consisting of a relatively precise mimicry pattern, directly aping the behavior of the model in an identical form; (2) a *disinhibitory* effect, which awakens responses already in the observer. They may not match precisely those made by the model, but contain individual variation; the threshold is lowered for some class of response; and (3) an *eliciting* effect, in which the model's behavior interacts with the predisposition of the observer, bringing previously unassociated ideas into contiguity, thereby "releasing" or facilitating the behavior.

The potential for imitative learning is broad and includes a wide variety of conflicting data. Sheffield (1966) and Bandura (1965a) have taken the position that such learning occurs in one trial and contiguity alone can produce it, although Bandura adds the requirement of verbalization of the matching responses. More recently (Klinger, 1967) demonstrated that at least with young adults, modeling effects can be independent of verbal contents, visually perceived aspects of the model's expressive behavior having an impact in their own right. Similarly, the role of reinforcement appears unnecessary for acquisition (Bandura & McDonald, 1963), serving merely to motivate the observer to attend and providing the cue that imitation of the model is permissible. Copying cannot be produced on the basis of reward alone nor can we explain its occurrence in free play, when there is the least likelihood of reward.

Mowrer (1960b) explains imitation through a conditioning concept whereby the observer imitates someone being rewarded without being rewarded himself, because he experiences some of the model's behavior. The theory depends upon the arousal of hope and fear in anticipation; it could be described as "sympathetic" behavior. Yet it is incomplete, since it does not explain the behavior of a prison inmate who imitates the guard who bullies him the most. Only those associated with pleasurable experiences should be imitated. This behaviorist framework evoking cognitive constructs such as "satisfaction," "mediation," "secondary reinforcement" vis à vis modeling, are not very useful, for it is difficult to state with certainty which construct clearly applies.

Many of the difficulties in the study of imitative learning seem to be related to lack of standardization of experimental manipulations and dependent measures rather than to controversy over reinforcement, learning versus performance issues, and hypothetical constructs. Admittedly, antecedent conditions are the most difficult factors to control; findings are easily confounded by covert responses. However, unification of basic procedures would do much to compare findings and arrive at sound understanding of the processes involved.

A parsimonious approach is offered by Singer (1966), who conceives of modeling as a two-part system: first is the selection of others as models; second is the adherence to the values, ideas, behaviors assumed to be mastered by those selected, presumably to recapture positive affects, prestige, power, and competence. In this manner, adults influence children's imaginative behavior, probably beginning with infancy when parents, relatives, or grandparents wave rattles, sing songs, or play peek-a-boo. After age 1, play is decidedly imitative; the youngster enjoys doing whatever those he is dependent upon are doing. This is the foundation upon which later imaginative behavior is built.

A useful link between modeling and imaginative behavior is provided by Piaget's (1932, 1955) concepts of assimilation and accommodation. There is assumption that symbolic and make-believe play contribute to the development of representational thinking; it is pure assimilation, repeating and organizing thinking in terms of images and symbols already mastered. On the other hand, imitation is accommodation to external reality, an adjustment made to the external world. Intellectual development is related to the active waxing and waning and interchange between assimilating and accommodating and culminates in equilibrium. For Piaget, both symbolic and make-believe play as well as imitation are part of normal development and go through similar stages of maturation.

Piaget (1955) implies that imaginative behavior has no essential role in *providing structures for* intellectual development, whereas imitation does; in adolescence, it becomes a balanced subordinate process of cognition. It appears likely that imagination is not displaced by realism with age, but rather imagination becomes more elaborate and complex with age. It manipulates symbols to create new conceptual domains. Divergent thinking, originality, flexibility, all require more than simple copies of external reality. Nevertheless, both imitation and fantasy are the prerequisites for the development of cognitive skill. There is an evolution of accommodation and assimilation so that imitation may start as a photocopy of reality and later only approximate reality. Similarly, assimilation in the realm of imagination may begin with active play and bloom, with maturity, into symbolic thought.

Not only is there a developmental sequence in physical, intellectual, and emotional life, there is also a similar sequence in modeling; there are different models for each age group. The young child would be likely to select adult models such as parents and teachers; the adolescent, with his broader transactions with the world, might choose among peers, heroes, film, and television characters. Furthermore, imitation follows sequences other than model choice. Forms vary from stage to stage. Infants can imitate actions from their own behavioral repertoire; later they can imitate all kinds of movements, even with a delay between their actions and those of the model. Subsequently, patterns rather than direct mimicry can be noted and finally accurate reproductions and innovations occur. Thus, social learning follows a design in which the observer finds his own level in relation to the model and this is dependent on the developmental sequence.

Methods for Studying Fantasy

Although experimental studies have contributed to an understanding of conditions under which modeling takes place, the studies tell us little about whether or not imaginative behaviors can be learned in this manner. The study of these behaviors calls for procedures that are ambiguous, susceptible to disguised purposes, are related to fantasy or unconscious material, and are capable of measuring cognitive or personality dimensions at the same time. The projective techniques seem to provide both the quantification—the well-standardized method of content analysis—and qualification—the exploration of fantasy processes.

An approach to thematic apperception techniques (TAT) has been to score the responses to pictures for creativity, or "transcendence" (Weisskopf, 1950), which is the ability to include elements which go beyond what is actually presented. These elements include, among others, characters, objects, time elements, atmosphere, etc., and represent deviations from observation per se; they are independent of what is shown in the picture and appear to denote an imaginative ability. The additions to the stimulus are the imaginative creation of future and past events, rather than the "what" and "how" of other measures. They are the thoughts and feelings in fantasy rather than perception and sensation.

Although little experimental work has been done using the Transcendence Index, the existing literature reveals its reliability and validity (Singer & Herman, 1954; Singer et al., 1956). These studies support the notion of a common factor of introspection or introversion in Rorschach M, FM, M threshold and the Transcendence Index. Another factor, motor inhibition and planfulness, was also uncovered; these were measured by fantasy behavior and perception of Rorschach M. The high loadings on both motor inhibition and introspection suggest that Weisskopf's measure is appropriate for scoring imaginative response and that it is a reliable measure of fantasy.

Suitable quantitative data for measurement of imaginative characteristics can be obtained from another projective technique, the Holtzman Inkblots (1963). Like the Rorschach (1942), the Holtzman utilizes association to the stimulus, the relation of the association to the characteristics of the stimulus, and the structure of the association to determine imagination and personality style. The movement response (M) in particular is seen as reflecting inhibited overt motility and imaginative tendencies, regardless of the nature of content (Singer, 1960; Piotrowski, 1960). It is associated with interpersonal awareness and inner life (King, 1960), as well as productive imagination and creative ability (Roe, 1952). These findings coincide closely with the empirical findings reported by Holtzman et al. (1961) resulting from the standardization studies performed in connection with the development of his inkblot technique, referring to the implications in the human movement projection of a capacity for fantasy and creativity.

Unlike the Rorschach, Holtzman M is scored wherever movement or potential for movement is projected onto the blot material, regardless of the source of the movement, be it inanimate, animal or human. Furthermore, research use is enhanced by the limitation of one response to each of 45 cards, providing possibilities for division of the set into pre- and postcomparisons. Recently, Lerner (1966) used this technique to indicate that dream-deprived subjects produced more M on the following day than did controls.

It appears, then, within the theories of fantasy projection, both Rorschach (and Holtzman) and TAT-type research findings yield information suggesting bipolar inclinations toward the imaginary. At one pole, there are those persons with inclinations to accept inner stimuli, to daydream, to plan for the future, to postpone impulses. At the opposite pole are those who tend to respond to external stimuli, to act on impulses, to express emotions directly, to engage in motoric activity.

The Experiment

Hypotheses

There seems, then, a general consensus among theorists that imaginative ability can be viewed as an expression of a high level of personality organization. However, many questions are unexplored. Model-mediated aggression has been shown to occur with the use of films (Singer, 1971), but would imaginative behavior be modeled? Would observers exposed to films interpreted by models in imaginative, though benign, nonaggressive ways produce similar fantasies? Would such motives as aggression or achievement persist? Under such circumstances, when do adults become less effective as models? Are there personality differences in the tendency to model fantasy? These questions suggest that the presentation of fantasy and realistic models and the observation of responses to such models is an important area for exploration. In addition to modeling impacts, such factors as age and predisposition must also be included in the exploration. Contents too, should reflect imagination as a cognitive skill, revealing differential development.

It is therefore offered as the basic hypothesis of this study that children who observe a model behaving in imaginative ways will tend to reproduce this behavior even when there is no direct reinforcement for it. Exposure to the model will either disinhibit or elicit the desired behavior. Eliciting effects will be expressed in terms of interactions of the modeling conditions and predisposition to imaginativeness.

Specifically, the following hypotheses were examined in this study:

1. *Modeling Effects*

Children who observe a model interpreting ambiguous material will tend to reproduce this behavior even when they are not directly reinforced for it. Modeling behaviors will produce shifts in observers in accordance with experimental conditions. The subjects will imitate the model directly or they will express eliciting or disinhibitory effects.

2. *Imaginative Predisposition Effects*

(a) Children who show a moderate imaginative tendency (moderates) will produce precise, imitative responses to the model because they are most likely to be responsive to external stimulation.

(b) High imaginative children will show evidence of greater differentiation in their internal personality organization than moderates or lows, obtaining higher scores on response measures.

(c) Low fantasy predisposition children's responses to the stimulus will be relatively concrete, cliché-ridden, unsophisticated and lacking in explication, as evaluated by response measurements.

(d) Highs and lows will display disinhibitory and/or eliciting effects rather than imitative effects. Highs' responses will contain originals of already-organized fantasy response tendencies without regard to the model or in interaction with the model. Lows' responses will be sparse and constricted, with little regard to the model or in interaction with the model. These anticipations are based on assumptions that highs' and lows' propensities are sufficiently stable and powerful to overcome the effects of the model, or when appropriate, to interact with the model.

3. *Age Effects* Consistent with the assumption that fantasy is an adaptive, cognitive skill differentially developed, responses of junior high school children will be expected to show greater analysis and structuring than those of elementary school children.

(a) Elementary school children's fantasies will have contents that describe actions through the use of adventure stories with a team or group. Junior high age fantasies will be concerned with opposite-sex romances, vocational planning, and achievement.

(b) Junior high school children should be more likely to engage in fantasy than elementary school children because fantasy expression is assumed to be an adaptive cognitive skill, differentially developed.

4. *Interaction Effects* Interaction between imaginative predisposition and modeling is expressed in eliciting effects. Responses latent in the observer will be released by exposure to the model; modeling becomes a cue which acts together with the observer's previously developed disposition.

(a) Moderates will not show interaction and will respond to the model in terms of main effects only.

(b) Highs and lows will display eliciting effects, the influence of the model interacting with internal forces.

In summary, hypotheses were generated in terms of modeling, predispositional, and age effects. They were tested in terms of a 3 × 3 factorial design for each group as shown in Table 1.

Selection of Subjects

The strategy of this investigation involved selection of subjects, evaluation for their predisposition to imaginativeness and exposure to an experimental situation wherein a model behaved realistically, imaginatively, or in a neutral manner.

TABLE 1

Factorial Design for Both Elementary and Junior High School Children of High, Moderate, and Low Imag-Predisp under Fantasy, Realistic, and Neutral Modeling[a]

Modeling	Fantasy			Realistic			Neutral		
Imag-predisp	High	Mod.	Low	High	Mod.	Low	High	Mod.	Low
N Elementary age	28	28	28	28	28	28	28	28	28
N Junior high age	19	19	19	19	19	19	19	19	19

[a] These represent adjusted N's. In distributing subjects into the 18 categories, there was an overloading of 27 Elementary and 15 Junior High Moderates; they were randomly eliminated.

The subjects (N = 410) were chosen from two age groups: (a) elementary school children aged 10.5 to 12; (b) junior high school children aged 12.5 to 14. All were of average intelligence (mean IQ = 115.4) and there were no systematic or significant differences among them after their distribution into experimental modeling conditions or in accordance with their assignment to high, moderate, or low groups on predisposition to imaginativeness.

All subjects were evaluated for predisposition to imaginativeness (imag-predisp) as follows:

Within each age group, subjects were divided into tercile rankings of high, moderate, and low imag-predisp using the Holtzman Inkblot Test, movement determinant (Holtzman, 1963), "Just Suppose" (Torrance, 1966), and an Activity Preference Scale constructed by the experimenter. A further division was established if subjects fell into the same tercile in at least two out of three tests so that three levels of imag-predisp could be established. When this was not possible, where subjects were low, moderate, and high in each test, they were placed in the moderate imag-predisp category. Intercorrelations among the three measures were significant at the .01 level of confidence, and highs, moderates, and lows differed very significantly from one another with regard to imag-predisp on each of the three measures used.

Imag-predisp was established through the use of Holtzman Inkblot Test, Form A, "Just Suppose" and the Activity Preference Scale, as follows:

1. *Holtzman Inkblot Test, Form A* Subjects were administered half of Form A of the Holtzman Inkblot Test within the "home room" grouping. Twenty-two color slides were projected onto a standard 4½- X 6-foot grainless screen in an adequately darkened room, using a Kodak Carousel projector. Administration was varied with alternate classes between odd and even-numbered slides, to eliminate the possibility that one set might elicit more movement responses than the other. Answer sheets were provided, labeled "Designs," on which the following verbal instructions were written as a heading:

You will be shown a series of designs, each of which will be projected on the screen before you for one minute or so. Using your imagination, write down a description of the first thing the design looks like or reminds you of. Include in your description what about the design is important in making it look the way it does and whether you use a part or the whole design.

None of these designs has been drawn to look like anything in particular. No two people see exactly the same things. There are no right or wrong answers.

The instructions were paraphrased and subjects were asked for any questions they might have about the procedure.

The first three designs were each exposed for 120 sec; the next three for 100 sec; the next three for 90 sec; and the remainder were each exposed for 75 sec, in accordance with Holtzman's technique (1963).

The records were scored for movement in accordance with the scoring guide accompanying the test. Wherever the scoring of a response was not adequately covered in the guide or the intention of the subject was unclear, it was evaluated by an independent scorer, experienced in the use of the test. The scorer was given no information with regard to the identity of the subject and had no more than a vague idea of the nature of the study. Hence, it was assumed that the judgment was relatively unbiased, the final decision being made between the scorer and the experimenter.

Movement scores for both elementary and junior high school children were normally distributed, (elementary mean = 6.69, junior high mean = 7.08) and differences among the highs, moderates and lows were significant at .001 level.

2. *Torrance "Just Suppose"* Two to three days after administration of the Holtzman, Torrance's "Just Suppose" was presented. Test forms labeled "Just Suppose," and containing the verbal instructions indicated were distributed together with the following information:

I think you will have a lot of fun doing this activity. This will give you a chance to think up new ideas. It calls for all of the imagination and thinking ability you have. So I hope you will put on your best thinking caps and that you will enjoy yourselves.

You will now be given an improbable situation—one that will probably never happen. You will have to JUST SUPPOSE that it has happened. This will give you a chance to use your imagination to think out all of the other exciting things that would happen IF this situation were to come true.

Just suppose that the situation described were to happen. Then think of all of the other things that would happen because of it. In other words, what would your ideas be? Make as many guesses as you can.

The specific situations employed were, for example:

Just suppose clouds had strings attached to them which would hang down to earth. List your ideas and guesses.

When you finish the first page, go on to the second and continue until you complete each JUST SUPPOSE.

If you will look at the board, I have sketched what I think No. 1 and No. 2 might look like. Go ahead.

The test was scored in accordance with the Torrance Scoring Guide, as follows:

Fluency

The fluency score of the Just Suppose task was determined by counting the number of different consequences or possibilities listed. No credit was given for inappropriate and irrelevant responses or responses that described conditions that already exist or have no direct relevance to the situation to be examined. Occasionally, respondents listed within one sentence a number of difference consequences or ideas; under this circumstance, multiple scoring was made.

Flexibility

A score of 1 was given for each change or shift in attitude or focus. There was no credit given when there was no change in focus, no mental leap from one approach or concept to another, but merely a continuation within the same frame of reference.

Originality

Originality was judged primarily by the rarity of the response generally in accordance with Torrance's samples as well as in accordance with this sample. Obvious responses, populars, which required little or no mental leap, were not considered original, despite rarity. A list of both common, unoriginal and original responses is included in the appendix. Responses not included in this list and which were remote from the obvious received two credits. Those designated "original" on the list received one credit.

Scoring was performed by the experimenter and three graduate psychology students, specially trained by their professor in these techniques as part of an advanced seminar in testing. Mean Pearson product-moment coefficients between experimenter and student scoring with two transformations are: fluency,

0.99; flexibility, 0.94; originality, 0.91. These findings indicate that acceptance of the Torrance Scoring Guide as a basis for judgment assures reliable correlation with special training and that experimenter judgment can be admitted.

The distribution of these scores approached a normal one, which is consistent with the finding of previous researchers (elementary mean = 20.55; junior high mean = 37.15) for four "Just Suppose" tasks.

3. *Activity Preferences (Ideational versus Motor)* This test was administered within the "home room" immediately following the completion of the previous task. The following instructions were delivered verbally to the class after they had settled down:

> *On the sheet before you are pairs of activities. I would like you to look at each pair and decide which one you prefer. Please underline the ONE activity of each pair you prefer in general, NOT taking the frequency or the availability of the activity into consideration. To make this experiment valid, it is absolutely necessary not to omit any pair, even if it is difficult to make a choice. Don't forget, be sure to underline one activity of each pair.*

In this two-category task, a score was obtained which indicated how often the item for ideational interests was chosen. Those who scored in the first tercile were designated highs, those in the second tercile were moderates, and those in the third tercile were lows.

The distribution of these scores approached normal, the younger group obtaining a mean of 16.57 and the older group a mean of 12.85. In contrast to the previous tasks, the younger children obtained higher ideational scores than older children. It appeared that the youngest tended to choose activities that rely on an adult for their execution whereas the oldest group rejected such choices, contributing to the high score of the former. As such, it may be that ideational interests develop out of dependency needs which may dissipate with age.

The Experimental Modeling Procedures

Seven to ten days after the imag-predisp measures were obtained, modeling procedures were initiated. This time gap was necessary to permit scoring and distribution of subjects into their appropriate tercile ranks. Each grade level was completed before initial testing was begun with other grades within the same school building to forestall discussion of the experiment.

Six subjects, three boys and three girls, high, moderate, and low in imag-predisp, were tested together under one of the three modeling conditions. This heterogeneous group was told that some interesting short films would be shown. The first of these, Film "A," was a 16 mm sound color film by Norman McLaren called "Short and Suite" and required 4 min, 47 sec for viewing. Titles and credits were deleted, leaving unexposed film and a "count-down" to permit the children to settle down. The film was projected onto a 4½- X 6-foot grainless screen with a Graflex 16 mm projector in an adequately darkened room. The projector was an unusually fine one, relatively insensitive to light, casting a clear, bright image onto the screen at all times. Upon completion, the female experimenter served as model and interpreted it in one of the ways expressed below:

Realistic (To all age groups):

> *This is a film made by Norman McLaren, a Canadian film artist, who put moving patterns of color and light to the feeling and rhythms of music written by the famous musician, Eldon Rathburn, for a well-known jazz group. The film was made without a camera by the artist drawing and coloring directly on the narrow ribbon of film with pen and ink. Different themes, different instruments, different movements are interpreted by line and color variations and motion. It won an award at the International Film Festival, Venice, Italy. Now let's see another one.*

Neutral (To all age groups):

> *That was an interesting film, wasn't it? None of it is meant to look like anything in particular and I am sure that all of you have different ideas as to what it is all about. But now, let's see another one.*

Fantasy (elementary school):

> *Once there was a little monkey who lived in a beautiful jungle full of flowers and birds. This monkey was different from the other monkeys because he could fly. Although he loved to fly with the pretty colored birds, he was lonely. None of the other monkeys would play with him because he could fly and they couldn't. One day, flying high over the jungle, he saw hunters collecting animals for a zoo. He rushed to the other monkeys and flew them all to safety. From that time on he was never lonely and all the other monkeys made him their friend. Now let's see another one.*

Fantasy (junior high school):

> *Bill and Jane were skin diving while on vacation in Bermuda. They enjoyed themselves looking at the beautiful coral, underwater plants and jewel-colored fishes. They entered the mouth of a cave, partially obscured by boulders. Before their eyes lay the remains of the sunken*

island of Nada, said to have disappeared hundreds of years ago. Their discovery made them famous and scientists from all over the world came to study there. Now let's see another one.

Upon completion of the modeling condition, Film "B," "A Phantasy," by Norman McLaren was shown with these instructions:

What do you think this film was all about? I'm sure all of you have different ideas and I'd like you to write them down now. Remember, no two people will have seen exactly the same things. There are no right or wrong answers. Just write down your feelings of what this film is all about.

Subjects were given as much time as they required to write their interpretations. They were dismissed with the admonition to refrain from discussion of the film until the study was complete. Another group of six from the same classroom was taken immediately thereafter until all subjects were exposed to the films under various conditions.

Scoring of the Students' Stories

Interpretations of Film "B" were scored as follows to provide evidence for the dependent variables listed below:

1. *Richness of Fantasy* was measured by (a) *Weisskopf's Transcendence Index* (1950), which provided a composite score indicating how far the subject is capable of going when he departs from the stimulus using eleven different attributes; (b) a five-point *Level of Fantasy Classification* scale designed to assess fantasy quality or distance from concrete experience. Ratings range from no response to elaborate interpretations of feeling states and complete story plots.
2. *Content analysis* of the general themes of the written responses was carried out. The stories were classified according to *action, adventure, romance, sex,* and *achievement.*

Every response had been typed and numbered beforehand so that the experimenter and two judges had no knowledge of either the imag-predisp classification or experimental condition from which a respondent was drawn. The tasks were performed independently and interjudge agreements were adequate.

Results

A 3 × 3 factorial analysis of variance was used in this study. The three factors were: predisposition to imaginativeness, modeling condition, and age.

Scheffé's test, a fairly conservative one, was used for statistical analysis because there are 9 and 18 cells in the design and mutually independent comparisons are mathematically impossible. Although all comparisons were planned beforehand, F' rather than F was the appropriate value and larger differences are required for significance. Scheffé suggests taking an α of .10 rather than .05 when using this test and this procedure was followed when appropriate.

Modeling behaviors were expected to produce shifts in observer responses in accordance with experimental conditions, so that children had the opportunity to imitate directly or to approximate fairly closely the expression of the mode. Differences in means among fantasy, realistic, and neutral conditions occurred as predicted for both groups; however, modeling effects were much more powerful among elementary school children than among the junior high group and the latter group failed to reveal the modeling effects in the fantasy versus realistic condition as measured by the Transcendence Index. These results appear in Table 2 which summarizes the analyses of variance.

Both Transcendence and Level of Fantasy Classification measures were used to discriminate whether the obtained modeling effects were disinhibitory effects. If this were the case, then subjects would follow the model's conceptual framework rather than imitate directly or in a parrot-like fashion. For this reason, the Level of Fantasy Classification was used to ascertain if the concept, "Story," with all of its ramifications, was the example followed. This was indeed the case, although the effect was less powerful with the junior high school children, leading to the conclusion that older children are somewhat less susceptible to the influence of adult models than are younger children. The indications are quite clear that the modeling effect was not one merely of inducing the children to repeat the remarks of the model in a rote fashion. Instead, the model's influence was to allow a response that followed the same general category, neutral or fantasy.

Hypotheses related to questions of predisposition to imaginativeness yielded more complex results. The first of these stated that children who obtained a

TABLE 2

Influence of Modeling on Fantasy: Summary of Analysis of Variance for Elementary and Junior High School Children

Source	Model characteristics: fantasy versus realistic		Model characteristics: fantasy versus neutral	
	F'	p	F'	p
Transcendence Index				
Elementary school	29.93	.01	33.39	.01
Junior high school	11.22	n.s.	16.43	.05
Level of Fantasy Classification				
Elementary school	72.93	.01	59.39	.01
Junior high school	14.95	.10	24.18	.01

moderate score for imag-predisp would be ambivalently and anxiously motivated toward imitation and would produce a precise, imitative response to the model, influenced by their desire for approval. Direct imitation was almost unobservable in the population studied, only 20 children out of 410 revealing this phenomenon. Statistical analysis was not performed, the hypothesis being rejected outright.

The second hypothesis, predicting that high and low imag-predisp children would respond largely in terms of their personality attributes failed to be supported in the younger group, and the hypothesis must be rejected. However, junior high school children's scores support the hypothesis partially, although differences between highs and moderates failed to achieve a satisfactory level of significance. Comparing highs and lows, however, indicates that junior high school children's imag-predisp does influence scores on the Transcendence Index ($F' = 28.04$, $p < .01$) and those high in imag-predisp showed greater evidence of complexity, abstraction, and organization than those low in this dimension ($F' = 14.00$, $p < .10$); hence personality rather than modeling influences are present here. Findings appear in Table 3. There appears to be support for the notion that, at least for older children, highs' and lows' propensities are sufficiently stable and powerful to overcome the effects of the model.

In general, for the older children, the effect previously noted appears to be disinhibitory in nature rather than directly imitative, and junior high school children reveal their fantasy predisposition regardless of the modeling condition. Elementary school children, on the other hand, appear to show less uncrystalized imag-predisp, for they seem to be more submerged in the modeling condition.

Hypotheses dealing with age were well supported, all surpassing the .01 level of significance. Table 4 summarizes the findings that willingness to entertain the imaginary or to express fantasy is indeed an adaptive, cognitive skill differentially developed.

Finally, it was predicted that the contents of elementary school children's fantasies would describe actions through the use of adventure stories with a team or group, and that these would differ from junior high school children's fantasies, which would be concerned with opposite-sex romances, vocational planning and achievement. This hypothesis is clearly supported by the data which appear in Table 5. A positive association exists between age and contents with a probability of only about .005 in a distribution with 2 df. Sex differences are not significant for either age group.

It appears that imaginative behavior increases with age and as such, it can be concluded that it is a skill that develops with differentiation, that there are age trends in ability to engage in fantasy and in the content of fantasy as well.

Hypotheses concerned with eliciting effects were not supported by the data. Modeling operated independently of both imag-predisp and age; age was inde-

TABLE 3

Influence of Predisposition to Imaginativeness: Summary of Analyses of Variance for Elementary and Junior High School Children

Source	High versus moderate		High versus low	
	F'	p	F'	p
Transcendence Index				
Elementary school	n.s.		n.s.	
Junior high school	13.68	.10	28.04	.01
Level of Fantasy Classification				
Elementary school	n.s.		n.s.	
Junior high school	n.s.		14.00	.10

TABLE 4

Influence of Age on Imaginative Behavior: Summary of Analyses of Variance for Modeling Responses

	Transcendence Index			Level of Fantasy		
	F'		p	F'		p
Junior high school versus elementary school	8.28	$<$	.011	5.78	$<$	.01

TABLE 5

Content Analysis of Responses According to Sex, Number of Responses of Junior High and Elementary Age in Three Categories: Action or Adventure; Romance, Sex, Achievement; None or Ambiguous

Responses	Junior high		Elementary		Total		Grand Total
	Boys	Girls	Boys	Girls	Boys	Girls	
Action or adventure	29	21	67	48	96	69	165
Romance, sex, achievement	35	40	30	39	65	79	144
None	20	16	31	28	51	44	95
	84	77	128	115	212	192	404

χ^2 differences between age: 11.40 sig. at .005 level
χ^2 differences between sex: 2.61 n.s. junior high
χ^2 differences between sex: 2.80 n.s. elementary

pendent of imag-predisp. Eliciting effects would be evident when modeling interacts with the other main effects; with these unreliable interactions, the responses
can only be labelled, "disinhibitory," the awakening of responses already in the
observer.

Having considered the impacts of model-mediated imaginativeness, a number
of additional findings will be considered now; they are concerned with (1) sex
differences in response measures, with (2) verbal expressiveness in relation to
imagination and with (3) response length.

1. It appeared desirable to investigate sex differences in response measures
(Level of Fantasy Classification and Transcendence Index) because the model-
experimenter was female. However, statistical analysis revealed that the sex of
the model did not influence boys and girls differently for either measure.

2. Scales of the type used in this study are open to criticisms that response
biases of one sort or another can occur. One might be in terms of verbal expressiveness. Is imaginativeness being measured or merely verbal skill, the ability to
give extended fluent verbal accounts?

In order to show that the experimental conditions rather than fluency
accounted for verbal expressiveness, count was made of the number of words in
responses. There were 90 elementary and 90 junior high protocols selected by
consulting a table of random numbers to shorten the task. Table 6 shows the
effects of modeling on response length. Elementary school children use more
words in the fantasy condition than in the realistic or neutral conditions.

TABLE 6

*Summary of Analyses of Variance Showing Effects of Experimental
Condition on Response Length*

Group	Condition	df	F'	p
Elementary	Fantasy versus realistic	1	5.04	.10
	Fantasy versus neutral	1	11.47	.01
Junior high	Fantasy versus realistic	1	< 1.00	n.s.
	Fantasy versus neutral	1	< 1.00	n.s.

Junior high subjects do not follow this pattern, the word count revealing no
significant differences among the modeling conditions.

It appears that a word count might be a useful predictor of stimulus-bound
versus stimulus-free for elementary school children only. That is, when young
children depart from literal, realistic interpretations, they tend to use more
words for self-expression. This does not appear to hold for older children, where
the extensiveness of their verbal accounts was not influenced by experimental
conditions.

In order to examine this question further, another analysis was deemed important. Transcendence Index is a measure which, in part, is dependent upon verbal fluency for a high score. On the other hand, Level of Fantasy Classification depends less on fluency and more on organization of thought; a high score can be obtained with relatively few transcendences. Positive correlations between the two measures for the two age groups are .55 and .57 ($p < .01$). Such high agreement suggests that verbal expressiveness per se is not responsible for high scores and that there is a strong relationship between imaginative and cognitive expression.

3. An examination of modeling procedures might lead to the conclusion that there is a relationship between the number of words used by the experimenter and the number of words produced by the subjects. Are the effects produced, the result of modeling conditions or are they the result of imitation of stimulus length? However, this is far from likely. First, it does not seem possible that the length of the experimenter's remarks could be internalized and retained in memory with an intervening time of 10 min. What could be retained would be a general impression of how the model behaved, but scarcely response length. Furthermore, response length may be a function of age rather than other factors, with older children producing more words than younger children in all conditions. Table 7 summarizes the average number of words each group produced in response to the stimulus.

TABLE 7

Average Number of Words of Ninety Randomly Selected Elementary School and Junior High School Children in Response to Movie "B"

	Fantasy		Realistic		Neutral	
	Mean	SD	Mean	SD	Mean	SD
Elementary children	44.7	18.6	31.4	25.0	24.9	13.7
Junior high children	63.3	36.1	67.8	36.0	55.5	25.7

In summary, results of this study appear to support the notion that imaginative behavior can be influenced through modeling, although modeling effects are stronger among elementary than among junior high school children. For the latter, imaginative predispositions influence responses to the film whereas such predispositions have less clear-cut impact on the story-telling of younger children.

Some Examples

Aside from the quantitative findings, the qualitative responses must interest the reader, and typical stories created by the children follow:

A 10-year-old fourth-grade girl, exposed to the fantasy model, responded,

Once there was a church and the people of the church wanted to make it beautiful. So they took yards of ribbon; they used two of them to decorate. They decorated the rocks too. A butterfly came along and pushed the other yard of ribbon into the sky. And the balls of ribbon did a dance in the sky, fell to earth and made a beautiful tree.

An eighth grader, under the same condition, wrote,

It's John Brown running for his life. He had just blown up five enemy bridges all by himself. The Germans were after him with tanks, planes, and dogs. John fled into the forest, not an ordinary forest, but one filled with many legends. There were animals and a hideous monster who was believed to be a descendent of the two-million-year-old Tyranasaurous Rex. He was never heard from again.

Another child, high in imag-predisp, created this story,

I think the film was about a boy and a girl who love each other. The boy has many friends and they persuade him to run for office. He wins and he slowly forgets the girl he knew when he was poor. Slowly he becomes more and more powerful and forgets completely about the girl, who still loves him. He then builds a huge castle with more and more lands. He becomes a king. Soon after, a revolution comes and he is captured and about to be killed. When the poor girl hears of this, she plots and rescues him. Poor and powerless, he realizes he loves her and so they walk into the sunset. Oh? I forgot to say that when he becomes rich and famous, he goes with a girl, not because he loves her but for her money. At the end, however, he leaves this woman to go back to his real love.

A fourth-grade boy, exposed to the realistic model, responded:

Colors running into each other forming a picture.

Two eighth graders; responses were not dissimilar:

Designs and patterns moving to the rhythm and beat of the music. It created a pleasant mood, like traveling far away, then being brought home again.

The film had smooth movement to it and sea objects. It included coral, rocks of varying sizes and designs.

A fourth-grade girl, under neutral conditions, wrote:

1. Atoms   2. Different colors.

An eighth-grade girl, under the same conditions, produced the following:

It's a sadder film than the other—as expressed in the kind of music used. It is more mellow—more use of circular shaped forms rather than the angles perceived in the first movie.

A seventh-grade girl, low in imag-predisp, in the presence of the neutral model, said:

The film dealt with balls dancing around each other. The movement of the balls was set to music. It did not impress me. It made me feel sleepy. The tone of the music did nothing but make me sleepy.

Generally, there was a consistent tendency for the children exposed to the fantasy model to produce longer responses, more imaginative records and more clever or original responses than those in the realistic or neutral condition. Thus children, particularly young children, can perform imaginatively if they are exposed to models who behave in such a manner. In all grades there was a strong pull to the interpretive level as well as transcendence of time, space, persons under this condition. Following the model, the children related stories with a complete plot, described feelings and emotions.

Just as modeling influenced the children's writing, imag-predisp affected it as well. The following productions emerged more as a consequence of personality variables rather than as a consequence of experimental manipulation:

A seventh-grade boy, moderate in imag-predisp, wrote:

Plants growing, making seeds, the seeds growing. Mother Nature. Birds and butterflies. One bird was killed.

Two seventh-grade girls, low in imag-predisp, responded:

Hi ya! I thought the second part of the film was very boring. It had dull colors and the music was practically the same throughout the second part. I have no idea what the film was about. Sorry!

The balls are drops of water in the atmosphere which fall to the ground again.

A sixth grader wrote:

Sea, men, bird, the body, cemetery, garden, colors.

Finally, here are some examples of those high in imag-predisp:

The film is about the troubles of six creatures who live in A. The time is 10 eons after World War III and A. is now situated 2 miles under the Hudson. The creatures live on music, which has taken the place of light as a source of energy for life. They lead a very happy life except for the bird who visits them sometimes. The bird hates music, for it needs light in order to live. Whenever the sun shines this bird flies around, singing and soaring, interrupting the music of the ground creatures. They are always trying to kill the bird and finally they do. The sun goes away, leaving the creatures to their music.

Once there was a lonely person. He never played with his friends because they didn't like him. He watched all his friends play all day long. They would make beautiful trees come out of the ground and flowers, too. He was lonely because he was odd. He just sat and watched. One day, when he was watching, he felt something strange. All of a sudden he was just like his friends. He would play and play. From then on he lived happily ever after.

Some new forms of life take a journey throughout space. They have a relaxed, soft trip and land on a new planet, a barren one. They make it a living planet, one with a great variety of strange and beautiful people. But this new life is not too different from earth's, at least how it should be. Actually, life is not at all like that now but how feelings might be. The birds flying might symbolize freedom, there is a sense of death and love as well (birds were kissing). There is also a feeling of the seasons, Winter, Spring, Summer and Fall. This might also reflect human feelings of sadness, death and happiness.

These data support the notion that imag-predisp, particularly among the older students, emerges despite the experimental condition. The same conclusion cannot be drawn about elementary school children, whose imag-predisp seemed to be masked in the experimental condition.

Content analysis revealed unique differences between the various age groups and reflected developmental interests. Examples of elementary school action and adventure responses follow:

The film was about seven boys who are bored and wanted to do something exciting. One day, a fairy sent the boys into space, so far away they couldn't see or feel the sun. Then they got separated and wandered away. Later on, six of them found each other. About five days later they found the seventh one and the fairy took them back to earth.

I thought the film was about invaders from another planet, who are coming to make more of their people. After they made more people, they invaded the planet. After that, they would go to another and invade that too. Until they found a planet to stay. It was a very colorful film and good.

Title: The Night Dancers. This looked like to me a film about certain little creatures that are produced by a certain object and dance all night until they fall down and sleep.

Examples of junior high responses with themes of romance, sex, and achievement follow:

I think that this movie was about a couple who went to a party. This party started late in the afternoon and ended around midnight. At the party there was a lot of drinking and eating. On the way home the couple was killed.

The film seemed to be the inside of the mind of a person trying to escape from the problems of life. He kept moving outward but was enclosed again. He was finally subdued and died.

I thought that was all about Creation. First there was life, then the sea, the planets, the sun, animals, trees and flowers. Then there was death. The flowers and stone were at a cemetery where someone had died.

I think it is about the evolution of man. In the beginning he builds a glorious civilization. Then it crumbles. The bird symbolizes the evil of man. In the middle, man was trying to rebuild his civilization. Then the bird, Evil, again took hold. But then man destroyed Evil. In the end, he had a glorious height of civilization, higher than ever before.

At the beginning, everything is still, like it was according to religion. Then two figures come together and start a boom. Like in the bible, Adam and Eve come together and start mankind. After several, possibly six generations (the six balls), new things start . . . with the intermingling of families.

Two pearls of sweat in space fertilize the desert and multiply. They play "Time," they play "Space" and turn into witches and beauties. They become thoughts that someone had in the night that grow and bloom and become a fantastic new idea that will become somebody's new discovery.

These qualitative differences emphasize, not only higher levels of expression from the older children, but also the projection of internal fantasies appropriate to the conflicts of adolescence. It appears then that imaginative behavior not only increases with age, but also reveals internal conflicts, wishes, aspirations when an analysis of contents is made.

Some Conclusions and Speculations

With regard to modeling of fantasy, there is clear support for the notion that expression of fantasy is enhanced for young children by exposure to an adult model. This is consistent with previous experimental demonstrations of the effectiveness of models in altering children's behavior (Bandura *et al*., 1961; Klinger, 1969). However, very little direct imitation was noted. Rather, the children reflected the important cognitive strides they have made from earlier levels by their present capability of regulation by schemata rather than by simple pictorial representations. This is consistent with the theory that in early forms of modeling the child reacts at the same time or in the same place as the presented content. Later, there are delays or deferments. Such delays presuppose a regulation by some kind of internal model, to which the model must enter as a discriminating cue; in this way, the response varies in a manner that becomes more and more autonomous with experience. In other words, the increased differentiation of context of execution from the context of presentation implies an increasing ability to transform patterns of observed behavior into personal symbols. Thus, the modeling in this study must be defined as "disinhibiting" rather than the direct imitation illustrated by Bandura's subjects.

It can be argued that the use of schemata is a source of pleasure in its own right, providing the "reward" inherent in this experiment. The children appeared to be trying to order the stimulus in spite of its ambiguity, attentive to every available cue that might lead them to such ordering. By "matching" the model to existing schemata, performance was facilitated as well as rewarded, thereby permitting the "disinhibitory effect" evoked in the fantasy or realistic condition.

When such cues were not accessible or when the model did not provide an opportunity to make discriminations, as in the neutral condition, another picture emerged. Under this circumstance, the children appeared confused by the model's "interpretation" of the film, finding it difficult to know what was expected of them. Their responses reflected this confusion in their concreteness; many of the observers resorted to previously-learned behaviors connected to the model (e.g., "Just Suppose" instructions) and listed a series of objects in response to the film. The neutral condition, then, did not provide any structure or landmarks for the children, preventing them from utilizing their own resources such as defenses or inner fantasies, evoking some confusion and fragmentation of response.

This lends support to the notion that exposure to imaginative models enhances imaginative behavior; that exposure to training in realism or the absence of clarification of demands leads to factualism and usefulness in the socialization process.

As Schachtel (1959) has formulated it, there are pressures on the developing child to accept the codes and views of society in explicit and implicit ways. Some parents and teachers foster explorative curiosity, independence, and imaginative behavior *implicitly* by their own divergence, openness to experience, and enthusiasm for the less conventional aspects of life. Other adults are models of studiousness, conformity and convergent thinking. In some respects, the experimenter may have provided a microcosm of such a learning situation, "disinhibiting" either the imaginative or conservative components of the children.

When the imaginative component of the children was cued or called forth by the model, this was the "self" they revealed; when the realistic component was stimulated, they responded in kind; the neutral model, on the other hand, presented no distinctive cues and the children rushed to the safety of the conventional and the conservative.

It appears then that imaginative behavior was an emergent phenomenon, resulting from the cueing or modeling of such behavior so that observers demonstrated that aspect of self. Modeling effects were most powerful among children of elementary school age, superseding their predispositional tendencies.

These predispositional tendencies are not to be overlooked, for they provide avenues for further speculation. As noted beforehand, moderates in imag-predisp did not engage in direct imitation, contrary to hypothesis. It could be conceived that moderates are less responsive to outer and inner promptings than highs, yet less cut off from internal stimulation than lows thereby establishing a midpoint represented by the defense of repression. For this group, it may be that the highly ambiguous stimulus set off anxiety-producing cues leading to a narrowing of response, a diminished utilization of adaptive introjects "out there." Their low responsiveness could be a maladaptive way of handling strong stimuli, or a reflection of "binding" of ideas.

Responses that were imaginative as well as complex, sophisticated, explicated, and developed were characteristic of junior high students high in imag-predisp. This was not the case for the younger group, whose responsiveness was generally dictated by the model rather than their imaginative predispositions. The adolescent children tended to structure the task in their own terms rather than the model's. Highs were willing to express divergent modes of thinking without sacrificing organization; the demonstrated a depth and intensity of affect that was absent among their peers. Lows seemed bound to literalness and detail, the fancifulness, playfulness and story-telling aspects of highs' productions being noticeably absent in the former.

It appeared that feelings and emotions depended upon cognitive awareness of

a stimulus and that cognitive skill is the prerequisite for rich, imaginative response. Fantasy requires a two-way path between affect and ideation; this ability
lies within the adolescent observer rather than within the stimulus or the model.

In general, the findings support the notion of dynamic and structural differences between elementary and junior high school children. Younger children
appeared responsive to demands of the external world; adolescents' behavior was
internally determined to a larger degree. Internal conflicts seemed to be related
to a growing awareness of sexual development, moral commitments, future goals
of living and adult role possibilities.

The study suggests that, in the continuum of development, each child deals
with his own responsiveness to his environment and to inner experiences as well.
Which experience takes precedence over the other is a function of the stage in
development. Hopefully, the integration and interaction between the two will
come with maturity and the balance between external and internal will free the
child to express the power within.

Some Practical Implications

The outcomes of this study have important implications for research, for
education and for psychotherapy as well. Because this study was conducted by a
female experimenter with middle-class children, the findings must be limited to
the model-observers described; yet questions relating to broader issues must be
raised.

Insofar as novel, situational variables are concerned, this model undoubtedly
was able to achieve the greatest attention from the observers. With the exception
of the fourth grade, all elementary school children had male teachers. It would
be worthwhile to replicate the study using a male model or generally comparing
responses between groups whose teachers are the same or opposite sex from the
model.

Of equal importance is model's age. Would junior high school children be
more likely to respond to peers as models rather than adults? What would be the
influence of models of varying power within the school? Would a different
setting affect behavior? In view of our knowledge and speculations about peer
group influence about authority in general, an investigation of this sort should
be made.

Socioeconomic status should also be studied within this context, with particular emphasis on differing contents of fantasies within various subcultural
groups. In one study (Singer & McCraven, 1961), Negro and Jewish groups
showed the highest daydream frequencies and Anglo-Saxons the lowest. The
exposure to models might alter this pattern and much might depend upon the
age, sex, color, and status of the model.

Teachers too, often appear to be unaware of their roles as models of imaginative behavior. The experimenter noted classroom differences in responsiveness to

measures of imag-predisp and speculated that climate in the classroom affected this variable. It would be interesting to observe and evaluate teachers beforehand, to see which teachers permit and encourage their children to manipulate, play with ideas, and to engage in divergent thinking. How would this variable affect responsiveness to the stimuli used in this study?

More work deserves to be done with individual differences as well. Clinical work with highly disturbed individuals suggests that the extremes in predisposition to imaginativeness are unlikely to be influenced by models. If this is so, perhaps repeated exposure will prove more effective, serving to direct imaginative behavior into adaptive channels.

Finally, it would be well to examine the impacts of modeling after some time interval. It is important to ascertain if the effects are one-performance effects or whether the influence of the models is more durable.

Implications for therapy and education in general are manifold and the observations of such transactions are the true beginnings of this study.

It is in the therapeutic encounter that modeling and imagination are vividly demonstrated. The patient, in a dependent relationship with the therapist, learns to behave in certain prescribed ways through the observation of the model, or therapist. In subtle ways, the patient adopts the values and behaviors of the therapist, learning to attend to the same internal cues as the therapist. Therapeutic work with adolescents might prove more rewarding and successful than it now is if dichtomized dyads were established. Two patients, one constricted and the other highly imaginative, might meet together with the therapist, who would make appropriate interventions and interpretations. In this way, both patients would develop in the direction of the internal-external attentiveness to feelings, thoughts, and emotions.

Further, therapy based on modeling techniques may be capable of shaping prosocial responses. Thus, seriously disturbed children might receive training or demonstrations of how to cope with tasks of varying degrees of difficulty for them. Experimenter-therapists might discuss problems in a demonstration with the patient, jointly reaching decisions concerning the appropriateness of the social response made. In this way, the goal of therapy, be it to interpret reality or encourage fantasy, can be reached with greater efficiency and effectiveness than with the traditional "insight" methods.

Not only therapists, but teachers, parents, community and culture play large roles as models. Procedures and programs must be designed to evaluate this aspect of learning as well. Questions of homogeneous and heterogeneous groups in the classroom should be raised and perhaps some divisions could be made on the basis of imaginativeness—particularly among adolescents. If, indeed, adolescents are likely to learn this skill from peers, then positive, productive interaction should occur from heterogeneous groupings.

Finally, the level of imaginative thought attained by children of various ages may inform us where they are developmentally and at which point we must start to take them forward. Thus, if 12-year-old children are behaving imaginatively on an imitative level, the teacher might use her own behavior and demonstration of imaginativeness to encourage the children's growth. The evaluation of changes from direct imitation to greater self-expression could be a measure of growth and enable teachers to have a multifaceted view of their pupils.

It appears important to support and encourage imaginative behavior in the general population and in the schools. Trends in early training in realism, which are so marked in recent years, may have to be reversed. If imaginative behavior is related to environmental effects or to training rather than to internal systems or "talent," then education has an important role in the promotion of this behavior. As yet it is not clear as to how to educate for such an ability. If, indeed, modeling plays an important role, then adults must start early in life by demonstrating to their children that such behaviors are desirable and acceptable. The culture at large must reward and encourage as well, orienting its members towards examples of them. These examples should demonstrate that openness and imaginativeness are desirable qualities, valued by all members of the community, and intrinsically valuable as well.

CHAPTER VIII

Some Theoretical Implications

A Cognitive-Affective Model of the Origins of Make-Believe

Attempting to formulate a particular systematic approach to make-believe play and its relation more generally to personality and cognition is a formidable task. At almost every step, we must move away from available evidence because as the reader must know by now there is so little formal research that can be of use in this specific area. There is also something very humbling about making an attempt at theory construction in a field like this when the realization confronts one that there is perhaps so little to add to what Piaget wrote on this subject as early as 1926 (the original date of *Language and Thought*) or more recently in 1962 (Piaget, 1932, 1962). The long shadow of Freud must also be noted. He opened up so many vistas for theory in this area as early as 1907 or even in his *Interpretation of Dreams* of 1900. More recent elaborations of the pyschoanalytic model regarding play presented by Peller (1959), Erikson (1963), and especially Ekstein (1966) are also impressive. For that matter, it is hard to find much on the subject of play that was not already foreshadowed by Groos and his writings at the turn of the century (Groos, 1901).

If there is to be anything novel in the approach of play and imaginative predisposition which will be proposed, it will be the emphasis on a careful examination of actual empirical data that has not been available to previous theorists. It will pay greater attention to the nature of the information processing task of the growing child especially to the interrelationships between information processing and personality. In the past, the theorists on play have tended to use the notions of imagery in a somewhat loose fashion and did not have available to them the increased information on imaginative responses now beginning to emerge from the work of such men as Paivio (1970) and Rohwer (1970). Indeed Piaget himself has only completed his first careful study of imagery in 1966 (Piaget & Inhelder, 1971). The presentation which follows will be particularly close to the recent positions of Millar (1968), Klinger (1971), and Smilansky (1968). These investigators have all tried to cast the nature of symbolic play into a form compatible with the emphasis on information processing and feedback systems in organizing experiences that now seem the most useful for psychological theory construction.

Tomkins' Cognitive-Affective Theory

A very special feature of the position outlined here is its relationship to the model of personality as a manifestation of the subtle interrelations of man's cognitive and affective subsystems which has been proposed by Silvan Tomkins (1962, 1963). Tomkins' theory has special importance because it attempts in a more specific fashion than any other current theory, to spell out how man's different emotions are in effect closely related to the rate and complexity of his information processing tasks. It also serves to indicate how important the affect system is in man as a motivational basis for behavior. A system such as Tomkins' is especially intriguing because it provides us with some basis for approaching the close relationships between the emotions a child shows while playing and the intellective tasks involved in his play.

Although the great writers on play from Groos through Freud and Piaget have all made incidental observations concerning the joy that children manifest while engaging in make-believe games, these authors do not really work the emotional component directly into the structure of their theoretical positions as regards fantasy play. To the extent that make-believe games are dependent in part on the child's developing use of imagery, one can search the literature on imagery itself for some effort to tie this function in with emotionality. But again one looks in vain. The very careful attempt on the part of Piaget and Inhelder (1971), while impressive, is focused largely on the child's imagination of movements and physical shapes with very little emphasis on the spontaneous productions of these responses during play. The work of Rohwer (1970), Paivio (1970), and Reese (1970a-c) focuses more on the use of imagery in verbal learning tasks. None of the recent imagery studies calls attention to the strong emotion often associated with the occurrence of imagery and make-believe play nor to the fact that so much imagery relates to the reproduction of interactions or anticipation of encounters with other people in the child's environment. In this sense, Freud's early speculation that thought and imagery were related to the child's attempt to hallucinate the image of the mother or of the absent breast when it became hungry has perhaps greater relevance despite its untestable nature.

The power of the theory proposed by Tomkins and supported more recently by experimental work such as that of Ekman *et al.* (1971) and Izard (1971) is that it gives a central role to human contacts and especially the human face as the seat of the emotions and major stimulus source, particularly for the young infant. Much of what Piaget calls reproductive and anticipatory imagery (Piaget & Inhelder, 1971), for example, in very young children may well be built around the face of the mother or the movements of adults in the immediate environment of the child even more than they are upon the physical structures of objects in the environment. In this sense, the cognitive-affective theory has the advantage of using the important structural hypotheses developed by Piaget and many other theorists of a cognitive persuasion without abandoning many of the important insights on human interaction and the socialization process generated initially by Freud and elaborated most effectively by clinicians such as Harry Stack Sullivan (1953).

In moving ahead with our effort at a theoretical construction, it will be necessary to review somewhat briefly some of the propositions of Tomkins' theory. A concise formulation of Tomkins' position is presented in a fine summary by Izard and Tomkins (1966) and no attempt will be made to provide a thorough review of this complex position.

In approaching a theoretical model such as that of Tomkins, one must also keep in mind that so much of psychological and psychiatric theorizing in the past has hinged upon notions of there being a limited number of fundamental drives originating biologically that push people toward specific goals and that form the basis for satisfaction or positive and negative reinforcements. The drive-reduction models which have largely dominated our interpretations as socialization are contrasted with what might be called a cognitive-developmental model (Zigler & Child, 1969). The latter position places greater emphasis upon the intellective aspects of human behavior and their fundamental nature in organizing human experience and indeed perhaps in generating directional tendencies which we describe as motives. A cognitive-developmental position also emphasizes the fact that certain capacities are available at various points of child development that are less available earlier or later as a function of the inherent constitutional structure of the child. The socialization experiences, that is, the interaction with family and peers, must be viewed as influencing the child only through the medium of its current capacity for information processing. Such a position should be contrasted with the various learning and modeling positions which emphasize primarily the acquisition of responses through need satisfaction sequences or imitative behavior on the part of children. It also contrasts with the extension of the Freudian systems by Erikson (1963) which emphasizes an overlay of fundamental developmental contents such as basic trust and autonomy built on the earlier structures of orality, anality, and phallic conflict.

Izard and Tomkins (1966) propose that personality be viewed as a complex organization of five interacting systems. These are the *homeostatic, drive, affect, cognitive,* and *motor* systems of which the first two are primarily related to biological maintenance, reproduction and regulation of the body while the latter three are more important for social interaction and the higher human functions. They propose that the affect system be viewed as the primary motivational system, in contrast with the earlier views that the drive system was the basis for motivation, and that the cognitive systems be regarded primarily as a communication system while the motor system is, of course, related to direct action. While all of the subsystems may dominate the personality at any given time, a central assumption of this position is that it is the affect system which is the primary motivating structure. Of course there are circumstances where the homeostatic system (as in the case of a gross disturbance in metabolism) may completely determine a personality process. Certainly under great states of deficit such as hunger, thirst, or, to a lesser extent, sexual deprivation, the drive states may become dominant. Most of the really critical aspects of human behavior can be traced to the latter three systems with the particular importance of the human emotions as providing the motivating information that will determine a particular personality direction.

Affect is viewed by the authors as

> a complex concept that has neuro-physical, behavioral, and phenomenological aspects. At the neuro-physical level, affect is defined in terms of density of neural firing or stimulation and changes in stimulation. At the level of behavioral or motor expression, affect is primarily facial response and secondarily visceral and bodily response. At the phenomenological level, affect is essentially motivating experience. To activate an affect is to motivate. When neural firing via innate programs produces affective (facial, bodily, visceral) responses and the feedback from these responses is transformed into conscious form, affect is both a motivating and a cue-producing experience. Phenomenologically, positive affect has inherent characteristics that tend to enhance one's well-being and to instigate an approach toward and constructive relations with the object, while negative affect tends to be sensed as noxious and difficult to tolerate and to instigate avoidance of and/or nonconstructive relations with the object [Izard & Tomkins, 1966, p. 87].

Tomkins (1962) has attempted to delineate a specific set of eight human emotions which have presumably been "wired" into us as a result of natural selection in evolution. Animals are likely to have a somewhat less complex emotional structure, but they too presumably have a limited and differentiated affect system. A critical feature of Tomkins' view of affect is that the emotions are aroused by the very task of processing information from the environment or from the memory system of the organism.

A most intriguing, but as yet speculative feature of Tomkins' theory, is his attempt to relate the specific affects to the density of neural firing of the brain or in effect the complexity of stimulation that must be handled by the organism. There are three general ways in which affect can be aroused. These involve an increase in stimulation, a decrease in stimulation and the level of stimulation maintained over a time period. Three classes of emotions are guaranteed by this system. For example, when there is a relatively sharp increase in stimulation which comes in at fairly rapid rates, the emotions experienced will be surprise, fear, or interest. When stimulation maintains a fairly steady level differing only in the degree of neural firing level, then the emotions of distress or anger are likely to be activated. Finally, when there is a decrease in stimulation from a previously relatively high level, there follows the affect of enjoyment.

> With respect to density of neural firing or stimulation, then, the human being is equipped with affective arousal for every major contingency. If internal or external sources of neural firing suddenly increase he will startle, or become afraid, or become interested, depending on the suddenness of increased stimulation. If internal or external sources of neural firing reach and maintain a high, constant level of stimulation he will respond with distress or anger, depending on the level of stimulation. If internal or external sources of neural firing decrease he will probably laugh or smile with enjoyment, depending on the suddenness of decrease of stimulation .. stated another way, such a set of mechanisms guarantees sensitivity to whatever is new, to whatever continues for any extended period of time, and to whatever is ceasing to happen, in that order [Izard & Tomkins, 1966, p. 88].

Particular emphasis in this theory is placed on the fact that behaviorally the affects are primarily facial responses such as the smile and the weeping reaction or the cry of distress or anger. An important place is given to the feedback effects of one's own spontaneous reactions to incoming stimulation which then trigger memories of earlier reactions along this line and may then generate a "program" of specific responses that have been associated with the evocation of emotion. In addition, since the face is, in effect, structured so as to permit fairly limited muscular manifestation of each of the emotions (Izard, 1971; Ekman *et al.*, 1971), we learn to pay careful attention to the faces of others as clues to whether we are likely to evoke anger or a smile and also for indications of lack of interest. Tomkins (1962) proposed that there are eight innate affects each linked to a specific set of facial reactions. There are three positive affects; interest–excitement, enjoyment–joy, and surprise–startle. Each of these has a characteristic facial expression. There are five negative affects; distress–anguish (weeping), fear–terror, shame–humiliation, contempt–disgust, and anger–rage. The ability to describe these emotions on the basis of facial expression has recently been supported both within our culture and across very different cultures in the world by the work of Ekman *et al.* (1971) and Izard (1971).

While the theory is far too complex to go into in greater detail at this point, it places emphasis on the role of memory, feedback of affective responses and matching them with material from the long-term memory system, and anticipatory images based upon not merely expectations of events, but of their associated affects. Man is viewed in this system as an image-making creature constantly trying to organize his experiences into schemata or structures which can be effectively stored in a long-term memory system and which can be used to help in rapidly deciphering incoming stimulation so that the organism does not startle or become overwhelmed by the mass of new material. In effect then this notion is one in keeping with many other current views in the cognitive realm such as those of Miller, Galanter, and Pribram (1960).

We shall deal a little more with image construction and its central role for describing human behavior somewhat later in this chapter. What is important for our purposes now is to note that Tomkins' cognitive-affective system does provide a basis for examining the interaction of emotion and information processing in a fashion that goes beyond the emphasis of Piaget who has treated affective experiences only in a very limited fashion (Pulaski, 1971).

The Origins of Imagery

The human's capacity for storage of information is truly astounding. Recent work has suggested that a great range of objects can be recognized after only one viewing sometime later by the simple method of recognition. This includes objects that have not even been part of the regular experience of the subject in the past. While one cannot prove that these objects are stored as pictures, there seems little question that most people can readily call to mind a tremendous range of reasonably well-reproduced scenes from their past as well as to a lesser extent sounds and smells or tastes. Extensive reviews in McKellar (1957), Richardson (1969), and Segal (1971) amply document our current knowledge of imagery. An important development within the past 5 years has been the emergence of an impressive amount of literature indicating that imagery can play a significant role in early learning processes in children. Especially important contributions in this area have been made by Paivio (1970), Reese (1970a-c), Rohwer (1970).

Paivio, for example, cites research which suggests that children as well as adolescents who score higher in imagery ability on various measures turn out to be superior in learning situations which involve both pictorial and verbal materials. At least in some instances they also are better at the recall of incidental components of a complex situation than children low in imagery ability (Paivio, 1970).

Reese (1970a-c) beginning as a fairly strict behaviorist, has been forced by examination of a series of studies as well as his own work, towards a model that has more of the cognitive-developmental features in relation to imagery. He proposes that images play a key role in certain types of learning, that they are stored in the brain and are modified both by repetition and also by a natural sequence of development so that they move in the direction of what Piaget has called "figurative conceptions." These are more general classifications of images in a coding system that includes a variety of images which can be independantly called forth as required. Verbal input and output systems and imagery can be modified by task demands or predispositional set and by conditioning. Rohwer (1967, 1970) has perhaps carried out the most extensive studies of imagery and paired-associate learning in children. He writes,

> . . . it seems to me that the available data converge in suggesting that mental imagery is one of the processes whereby children represent and store information. It also seems to me, however, that a preference for a capacity to make effective use of visual representation and storage develops later than is the case for verbal modes of representing and storing information. This interpretation of both the item-property data and the elaboration data runs counter to the usual claim that pictorial forms of representation develop earlier than verbal. . . . Language is a coherent, well-organized system; imagery is not. The capacity for utilizing well-organized systems is easier to acquire than the capacity for using more *ad hoc* means of controlling one's own behavior, or of storing and representing information. Accordingly, the ability to use linguistic or verbal means for storing and preserving information emerges earlier mentally than the ability to use visual or imagery processes for accomplishing the same ends [Rohwer, 1970, p. 401].[1]

Rohwer's extremely interesting work on comparison of lower and middle class children, aged five through eight, lead him to conclude that the high socioeconomic status children were slightly, but significantly better than low SES children in their learning ability (which involved both verbal and imagery methods) with the exception of the one method where both the picture and the names of objects are presented simultaneously. He proposed that the reason for this discrepancy was dependent on the degree to which individually-initiated conceptual activity is required by the child. Thus, when a child merely hears the names of objects, he must supply an image of them or when he sees the pictures he must supply their verbal labels. In the case of sentences, again either an action image or (if shown a picture) a verbal label must be supplied. If on the other hand the child is presented with a picture and hears the name of the object depicted, he need not supply anything further on his own. Rohwer suggests that the difference between the social classes lies in the fact that the middle class children have learned to elaborate upon what they have been presented while this particular set has not been built in sufficiently for the poor children. Rohwer (1970) makes the following two proposals for instruction techniques:

> . . . given a choice the stimulus or cue for some desired response should be concrete rather than abstract, and pictorial rather than verbal. Whenever possible, items to be associated should be presented in some kind of meaningful linguistic context rather than as isolated terms and, especially for older children, the items

[1] This and the quote on the next page are copyright 1970 by the American Psychological Association and Reproduced by permission.

should be depicted in some kind of spatial relation, or involved in some kind of meaningful action.

The second class of recommendations has to do with the kinds of activities children should be taught to engage in so as to increase their own powers of learning. In brief, they should be taught the use of both verbal and visual kinds of elaborative activities. ... the child cannot always count upon the world to offer up information in optimal ways; therefore, he should be equipped to transform information himself into a form that renders it maximally renderable [Rohwer, 1970, p. 402].

While there remains a great deal of work to be done in elaborating the details of the function of imagery in great variety of learning situations, it seems increasingly clear that these so-called covert mediational responses are a critical part of the child's behavioral repertory. There is undoubtedly controversy as to how important the role of the verbal dimension is with Bruner (1966) arguing that iconic or pictorial imagery takes precedence over verbal skills and Rohwer questioning this on the basis of his recent data. It seems likely that for most practical situations there is a complex interaction between representation in the brain of materials stored according to sensory modality and also materials stored in terms of a summarizing verbal label. Currently, investigators are inclined to feel that there is an especially important change in the period from about six through eight when the child shows a greater trend toward what Piaget and Inhelder (1971) call anticipatory imagery as contrasted with simple reproductive imagery and what Bruner *et al.* (1966) refer to as development of verbal symbolic methods or modes of thinking. It is intriguing to speculate on the possibility that these changes in imagery are also occurring at the time that the child begins to limit overt verbal expression of his make-believe games in favor of apparent internalization and also a time when there is a more general increase in motor control on the one hand and the increase in imaginative responses on the Rorschach test (Singer, 1960).

I have taken a long detour in the discussion of cognitive-affect theory and recent work on imagery in order to set the stage for the following discussion of the early function and origin of make-believe play and its role in cognition and personality development. The following proposals do not represent by any means a contribution to the very complex problem of what images are in the brain or how they are stored. It is proposed that make-believe play represents one of the important ways in which children practice imagery and rehearse a variety of elaborate skills both imaginal and verbal and in addition develop a learning set which prepares them for later and, in many cases, more effective use of imagery in the learning process.

The Beginnings of Make-Believe Play

Affect and the Accommodation-Assimilation Sequence

In his famous speculation on the origin of thought, Freud proposed that the beginnings of this process occurred when the child, aroused to hunger in the absence of the mother, hallucinated the image of the breast or the mother and found this partially satisfying. Freud went on to develop his notion of the origins of the ego and of the fundamental delaying capacity of the child and of later synthetic processes in thinking, out of this ability to temporarily delay gratification by the use of a hallucinated image of the absent gratifier (Freud, 1959; Rapaport, 1960). This highly speculative model is essentially a deficiency hypothesis. It persisted for many years as a major proposal about the nature of thought, as Rapaport's elaboration of it in his attempt to integrate systematically all of psychoanalytic theory as recently as 1960 suggested. As already noted, the emphasis on the adaptive role of certain cognitive functions to which Hartmann (1958) called attention, led to serious questioning on the part of psychoanalysts as to whether all of the ego functions needed to be derived from deprivation or conflict situations.

More recently, in his remarkable study of fantasy play in therapy with the extremely disturbed, Ekstein (1966) has proposed that to depend completely on frustration as the only way to get from purely need-oriented behavior to "secondary process thought" or "reality adapted thought and action" is not sufficient. Ekstein chooses to follow Freud's use of the mother–child nursing experience as a model, but points out that after the child has been sufficiently gratified and his hunger as well as sucking need is largely satiated, the child then actually begins to play with the nipple. "He pushes the nipple out, searches for it again, takes it back, until finally he either falls asleep, or the mother breaks up the game and the play [Ekstein, 1966, p. 291]."

Continuing this vein of speculation, Ekstein (1966) proposes that this nipple play permits the child to weave fantasies, a form of trial thinking in an effort to revive the gratifying past.

> Since the baby cannot recall in thoughts, he recalls in the act . . we conceptualize, therefore, the "after play" with the nipple as a recounting of his blessings as it were, through a play repetition of the earlier rooting, sucking, and pushing out of the nipple . . . this play can also be conceptualized as an adaptive device, as serving him as a preparation for next time to prepare for the future through repetition, and thus reinforces the means-end relationship between past pleasures and future work. Rather than speaking now about the compulsion to repeat we speak about rhythmic, spontaneous repetition in which, instead of a compulsion to repeat, which is its pathological equivalent, the baby's afterplay turned into adaptive behavior [p. 293].

Ekstein goes on also to relate this rhythmic repetition to the so-called functional pleasure in play early identified by Karl Bühler (1930). Curiously, Ekstein at this point does not seem to call attention to the similarity of this position with Piaget's emphasis on the accommodation-assimilation cycle in children's behavior.

I have cited Ekstein here particularly to emphasize that even if one starts from a more classical Freudian position, one cannot avoid recognizing that the apparent origin of play seems to go beyond the view of a response to a deprivation condition. At the same time, by hewing so close to Freud's emphasis on the satisfaction of the hunger drive, Ekstein perhaps does not give sufficient generality to the process of the origin of play.

By contrast, there seems to be ample evidence from the many observations of Piaget and other investigators which suggests that an attempt to imitate actions earlier engaged in or observed in others as well as the need to manipulate objects and to explore the novel in the environment, seem intrinsically given in the child. These actions need not be narrowly related to specific satisfaction of oral needs. Indeed, Piaget's data strongly suggest that early in the child's life moving stimuli in front hold just as much fascination. The child attempts to manipulate such stimuli with the consequent evocation of positive affect when the object is moved or touched. Such reactions seem far removed from the type of hunger drive model that Ekstein has presented. White (1959) and Schachtel (1959) have both called attention to the fact that, if anything, the occurrence of a strong drive serves primarily to inhibit exploratory behavior. Once a drive such as thirst or hunger is satisfied, it is possible for the child to engage more extensively in curious exploration of his environment and to practice competence skills.

Tomkins proposes four functions of affect: maximizing positive affect, minimizing negative affect, as well as expressing affect as fully as possible and yet at the same time learning to control affect expression. We can guess that some of the child's exploration involves the somewhat cautious manipulation of environment to yield a moderately increasing rate of complexity of stimulation which evokes the positive affect of interest or surprise. If the situation leads to too great an increase in novelty, the child will startle and become afraid. If some degree of control can be maintained so that new material being explored is presented in small enough doses, the child will experience positive affect. As he becomes increasingly familiar with the material, there follows a decline in the gradient of unassimilable material and the consequent experience of joy and smiling.

This position is demonstrated with Harlow's well-known movies of the baby monkeys clinging to their cloth mothers at the appearance of a mechanical bug. After the first leap of terror from the field onto the cloth figure, after a while, the monkey gazes at this strange object and begins to detach itself from the cloth mother. It makes approach movements toward the object until, as it gets closer, the loud clicking noise and complex appearance of the object yield a startle response and the monkey leaps back up onto the surrogate mother. Yet again the animal makes approach responses suggesting that in moderate fashion, there is a search for novel stimulation as a fundamental positive experience.

One can also interpret the accommodation–assimilation cycle that Piaget has described so effectively from this perspective. The child is confronted with novel situations and attempts to imitate them directly sometimes or to manipulate them when they are present. When the objects are no longer present (the objects may include physical aspects of the environment or aspects of parental behavior) the child still seems to have some memory of them or attempts to reconstruct the circumstances, but within a very limited schematic capacity. This creates what, to the adult, looks like bizarre or curious behavior, as described in an earlier chapter. For the child, however, it represents an interesting and novel environment. In effect, the very effort at assimilation that characterizes a child's behavior creates in its own right new sequences and stimulus patterns. So long as these new assimilations are not excessively complex, they keep the child interested and evoke positive affects of interest and surprise as well. With repetition, the child experiences the affect of joy as the material is assimilated into established schemata and the complexity of the material is drastically reduced.

In the preverbal stage, we currently have little clear evidence that the child does make any extensive use of images as such. It would certainly appear that there is some imagery capacity that serves as the initial storage basis for the attempt to assimilate previously imitated words, phrases, movements into the current schemata of the child, playing by himself in a crib or on the floor. Certainly some early instances of this are evident in the child's imitation of certain sounds that may occasionally precede the capacity for extended verbalization. Thus a child may learn to imitate the sound of a truck or a bell and show signs of incorporating this in play even though there is still relatively little overt verbalization. It is quite possible, however, that Rohwer's observation is correct and verbal skills may actually precede imagery skills or at least they may be more or less concomitant in development. I propose that it is possible that storage of material takes a dual form increasingly with both images specific to the sensory modalities being stored independently in an imagery specific system in the brain while, at the same time, a verbal or linguistic coding system comes into play increasingly as a more efficient summary and more easily retrieved coding system for the sensory experiences. Eventually, the adolescent or young adult may make optimal use of the more abstract language coding system for quick retrieval of most information. This verbally coded retrieval is less functional for certain kinds of situations where complex detail is required or where it is desirable to evoke not only the details of the event, but the associated affective reactions. In other words, it is likely that the storage of the affect surrounding certain perceptions takes place primarily in the specific modality while the linguistic label is "filed" separately in the brain. This separation may account for the occasional cliché nature of so many of our adult responses (Schachtel, 1959). This also may reflect the appeal that poetry, with its evocation of full imagery and complex detail, has in producing a stronger emotional reaction than merely stating the same point in words (Singer, 1970).

What is being proposed then is a relationship between information processing and positive and negative affects which accounts for the child's efforts to move from accommodation to assimilation and for the pleasure that the child takes in assimilating novel material into its schemata and in actually repeating the material so that the novelty drops eventually. This activity does not lead specifically to make-believe, but is also in evidence in games of mastery or later on in games with rules. A particular aspect having to do with make-believe play does, however, involve the increased use of the capacity for image formation as a fundamental cognitive skill.

The Stream of Thought as a Stimulus Field

Let us consider the possibility that the very nature of the operation of the brain requires a constant recoding and rehearsal of stored material. That is, the brain is not an organ that stores things in a certain place where they lie inactive. Instead, it is a system that involves constant activity and a replaying of the literally millions of images and verbal coding labels that have been experienced and stored. This seemingly tonic or continuous aspect of brain function is manifest in nocturnal sleep when we become aware of a great deal of mental activity. The more recent work on sleep stages makes it clear that while the most vivid and expressive dream material emerges during the so-called Stage 1-EEG— Rapid Eye Movement periods (REMs), there is ample evidence that thought content can be evoked by awakening subjects during other stages of sleep. The difference in reporting content may, in various sleep stages, conceivably be a function not only of the cycle of sleep itself, but of its effects on the ability to verbalize and to recall immediately preceding events.

The continuous brain activity provides an internal stimulus environment (Singer, 1966). Klinger (1971) has proposed this be called a respondent as contrasted with an operant system of stimulation which provides an alternative to the processing of material from the external environment. Under most circumstances, the organism must learn to process primarily the material from the external environment in order to survive. If we were to pay more attention to the ongoing processing of our brain in the normal course of our daily routine, we would find ourselves bumping into objects and passing by acquaintances without greeting them or risking our very lives by inattentiveness and failure to plan ahead our appropriate motor sequences. William James's notion of the stream of thought can be seen as representing a very fundamental part of the way the body functions, but one which we must learn to ignore a good deal of the time in order to maneuver safely in our physical environment.

The limited schemata of the young child, both for organizing and differentiating the external environment, may be viewed against this background of ongoing processing of already stored material. The assimilation process then appears in part as a direct response to ongoing internal stimulation as well as an attempt to rehearse material recently acquired through imitation or attempted accommodation to the adult world. As a matter of fact, it may not be an easy task for the child to determine which stimuli are basically internal in the form of reproductive imagery and snatches of past conversations that have been stored and which are the external stimuli currently in the immediate environment. Kohlberg (1966) has beautifully teased out the manner by which children determine that their dreams are not actual events, but are products of their own inner activity. Indeed, he has done an intriguing cross-cultural study in a society where the adults genuinely believe that dreams are manifestations of reality and must be viewed as externally derived messages. The children first go through a phase of learning quite on their own that dreams are inner manifestations and then once having reached this point at about age 12, they begin to adopt the adult-influenced cultural stereotype.

If the brain's activity is relatively continuous and we are almost constantly confronted with the possibility of becoming aware of this activity in the form of images and remembered phrases, smells or feels, we must undoubtedly develop protective mechanisms for "gating out" this irrelevant stimulation in the course of ordinary motor activity. This situation is not too different from what is required of us in order not to notice our noses and to be able to ignore the many gurglings, twitchings and other spontaneous activities of the machinery of our own bodies. In fact, recently there has been considerable attention to the degree to which we have ignored, on occasion at our own peril, many of the kinds of kinesthetic feedbacks that characterize much of our muscular and autonomic activity.

Storage and Replay

Two major principles may be operative in determining what contents do come to mind on a regular basis and which of these are stored more effectively than others. In addition, these principles may suggest how a particular set is acquired toward the development of imagery or attention to internal experience as a cognitive skill. Klinger (1971) has emphasized that the content of children's play or dreams reflects basically the "current concerns" of the child's daily life, in contrast with the earlier psychoanalytic emphasis on infantile instinctual gratification. A similar position has been taken by Breger (1967) who has argued that the content of dreams reflects the urgent, immediate unfinished business and momentary problems facing the individual in his life situation. I would broaden this position somewhat by arguing that it is likely that *as we store new material, we label it as more or less relevant to particular urgent issues* in our lives. In a sense, we "ticket it" for replay as part of a more general "plan" or what might be called by Piaget a "figurative conception." This means that when in the course of the ongoing busy work of the brain, we confront this material again, already in part in association with other urgent schemata, we are likely to attend more carefully to it and replay it at least briefly within our short term memory system. This rehearsal increases both the instrumental possibility of its recall and also the likelihood of its becoming linked with other schemata and in addition coded under an even more general classification. The sheer probability is increased that this material will be presented again at a point when our attention to the external world is sufficiently fluid so that we can take notice of it.

Our second principle involves the construct of a *set* toward attention to inner activities which may be acquired to some extent through actual experience or modeling or encouragement by adults. This orientation to internal processing suggests why certain people are more likely to be aware of dreams, daydreams, fantasies, and indeed are more capable of using this material as part of their general behavioral repertory (Singer, 1966). The set toward processing ongoing internal material and replaying it on the screen of consciousness may represent a general personality trait in the sense that a person appears to be a highly introspective person aware of all kinds of nuances of his own memories and examining perenially the subtleties of previous experiences à la Marcel Proust. On the other hand, one's set may be fairly specific, oriented primarily towards searching out material related to urgent current concerns, to the needs of a particular task whether it be creative or simply relevant to one's chores or business activities. It can be an outgrowth of a particular specialized experience as in the case of a person undergoing psychoanalysis constantly reexamining his own thoughts or behavior to the annoyance of his friends.

The importance of these two principles, *current unfinished business* and the *set* toward *processing* and *reprocessing,* is that we need not accept the ongoing activity of the brain as merely an epiphenomenon. Instead, the person whose set is toward awareness of internal activity by the very fact of increased replaying of certain memories increases the likelihood of their recurrence or sharpens them and organizes increasingly more complex categories and retrieval and coding names. In addition, the novelty of this experience and the joy of reducing some of its novelty by linkage to earlier material creates a positive, affective environment (Singer, 1970). A special problem is posed for this notion, however, by the concept of recurrent obsessional thoughts and attitudes of tortured self-concern which characterize certain neurotics or which are the consequence of traumatic experiences. Obsessional ruminations may reflect instances either where the person has already a well established learning set toward processing internal material, but is at the same time someone who has been subjected to great humiliation. As a result, he primarily finds himself replaying negative experiences. Traumatic replays may also occur in someone whose learning skills at reprocessing internal material were not well established, but who has been subjected to terrifying experiences which must be replayed just to assimilate them eventually into some kind of schema.

The Child's Replay and Set to Inner Processing

Let us again consider the situation of the very young child. A glance at some of the protocols of the 3- and 4-year-old children in the studies of make-believe play previously cited make it clear that their ongoing activity involves a rapid sequence of motor interactions with the environment as well as snatches of conversation from past stories or television shows. They show a direct response to the immediate play objects. These objects can quickly be transmuted, at least for some children more than for others, into representations drawn from long-term memory and bearing only minimal resemblance to the actual form of the plaything at hand.

The child thus confronts an environment which consists in part of memory material as well as the material directly presented to the senses. The very young child may make no clear distinction between these two sources of stimulation interweaving them seemingly in a random fashion. Gradually, the combinations of the momentary concerns and problems of the child as well as the predispositional set which the child is already beginning to acquire toward make-believe in imagery, may begin to assert themselves.

Depending on the amount of external stimulation available and its complexity or danger, as well as pressure from parental figures, the child is almost inevitably pulled toward "reality," that is, toward paying more attention to immediate demands and situations that confront it directly. Where there are many other children around who constantly intrude on the child's privacy, they may demand direct reactions to their interventions, sometimes in self-defense or sometimes by their sheer presence as novel stimuli. In order for the child to develop a greater awareness and skill at attending to the material from his long-term memory system, he must have some degree of privacy and period of uninterrupted opportunity to enjoy this inner realm. The likelihood is that it takes some time to improve the quality of imagery and to make the story lines and complexity of material become more coherent so that on reprocessing they run off more naturally and are less demanding of the child. In this sense, the skill of developing imagery involves a consistent opportunity for some practice.

Even the most extroverted kind of persons still do have dreams which involve relatively vivid imagery. The fact remains, however, that many of them do not remember as many dreams and indeed the reports of dreams based on actual interruptions during the night show a tremendous range in degree of vividness and imaginativeness. Thus Foulkes (1966) and his co-workers were able to demonstrate that persons already oriented toward greater imaginative behavior and more introspectively inclined as well as emotionally well balanced showed dreaming immediately at the onset of sleep of a relatively vivid type while persons less oriented toward inner activity tended to show their most vivid dreaming only relatively later in the course of the sleep cycle and particularly during the EEG Stage 1 — REM periods well along in the morning.

Rohwer (1970) suggests that both middle and lower socioeconomic status children have the capacity for imagery, but that the former have more of a set towards elaborating the imagery material for further learning purposes. Young children who are given the "advantages" of a middle-class upbringing with its attendant opportunities for privacy and for a controlled interaction with adult models around subjects such as verbal skills and make-believe are more likely to develop skill in the elaborative use of imagery. The data from Freyberg's chapter and the study of Smilansky (1967) also indicate somewhat lower tendencies for make-believe play on the part of poor children. These differences between socioeconomic classes may reflect variations in a set toward increased processing of internally generated material which has, as a consequence, the development of an increased skill in rapid processing of such material and is also elaborating on this material for later use in appropriate cognitive situations. In addition, one must keep in mind that there are important differences in the type of input provided the children in different classes. Where children are surrounded by many aspects of fictional material or stimuli relating to far away events and places, there is a greater likelihood of incorporating this material into complex play sequences and therefore organizing a much more differentiated set of schemata which can call these up and make the solitary play of the child intrinsically more interesting.

Conditions Conducive to Image-Formation and the Set to Reprocessing in Children

The child's world of make-believe can be viewed as the combination of the ongoing activity of the brain which is endlessly processing and reprocessing stored material with a special set toward attending to this material. This set or predisposition can be enhanced by a variety of circumstances. These circumstances include:

1. An opportunity for privacy and for practice in a relatively protected setting where the external environment is reasonably redundant so that greater attention can be focused on internal activity. Naturally, such a situation exists also at the time of preparation for sleep and during sleep itself.

2. Availability of a variety of materials in the form of stories told, books, and playthings which increase the likelihood that the material presented to the child in the course of the reprocessing activity or in the course of a set toward elaboration of this material will be interesting and sufficiently novel so that the child will experience positive affect while playing make-believe games.

3. Freedom from interference by peers or adults who make demands for immediate motor or perceptual reactions. The development of imagery requires the unfolding of relatively longer sequences which inevitably will compete for "channel space" with the processing of the new material from the external environment. Therefore, the unfolding of make-believe sequences must require some time and the practicing of imagery must also involve relative freedom from competing external demands on the sensory motor apparatus.

4. The availability of adult models or older peers who encourage make-believe activity and provide examples of how this is done or provide basic story material which can be incorporated in privacy into the child's limited schemata.

5. Cultural acceptance of privacy and make-believe activities as a reasonably worthwhile form of play. We have noted earlier that King Louis XIII as a young boy was given great freedom in playing with his dolls and toy soldiers. Somewhere around the age of 6 or 7 these were taken away from him and he was required to learn the more extroverted skills of riding and fencing. Specific family groups and the broader cultures in which they are embedded differ widely in the milieu they establish for the acceptance of make-believe activity on the part of the child. To the extent that the family does not significantly impede the child's spontaneous make-believe play or shame and mock the child in the course of it, the likelihood is that the child will go even further in developing this skill. Indeed there are cultures in which such activities are particularly encouraged.

As a child grows a little older, there is not only an increased richness and depth in the material used in make-believe, but it also becomes possible for it to use this activity as a means of dealing with conflict situations. In an extreme form as in the case of the child Tommy, the "space child" described by Ekstein (1966), the likelihood is of a withdrawal from many social interactions and a heightened emphasis on make-believe play and imagery. This may have the negative effect of reducing the opportunity the child has for learning effective means of social give and take. On the other hand, in some situations, considerable solitariness may lead to an extremely valuable heightening of imagery capacities and creative tendencies. Isolation can bring on a serious imbalance between the tendency to engage in make-believe and the necessity for acquiring social skills. These skills include an awareness of humorous interplay between peers, the ability to tease and be teased, the ability to be empathic in intimate relationships. The introverted young adult in later life may have to redress this imbalance through some form of psychotherapy or important personal relearning experience. Many of our therapeutic endeavors with disturbed persons often involve two contrasting aims—to help some people make up for failures in effective use of imagery and fantasy and introspective skills or to help others who have already developed their inner skills but who now must acquire the capacity for warmth, intimacy, and social ease.

In summary, the position taken is that make-believe play can be best viewed as a normal outgrowth of the fundamental information processing activity of the child. Such cognitive activity involves not only the external environment, but also requires the child to attend to the brain's processing of long term memory material. Such stimulation provides a novel and affectively positive environment for the child. With increasing age and complexity of material processed, the child learns to ignore some of the internally generated material, but may develop specific or general sets toward attending to this material or taking the time to elaborate on it under conditions of relative privacy. Particular urgent current problems determine, in part, which materials have a greater probability of recurring and becoming the focal point of the play behavior of the child. At the same time, the very act of engaging in make-believe play under most circumstances represents an opportunity for the child to develop a novel and stimulating environment and also to develop its competence in the area of image construction and the verbal coding skills related to make-believe situations. The complex interplay of visual or auditory imagery that makes up so much of make-believe play with the verbal coding that goes on at the same time increases the likelihood that the child will develop a set toward effective use of both verbal and imagery materials for subsequent learning experiences. In this sense, make-believe play represents not simply a natural development at a certain stage of the child's growth, but also has the potential for development of a series of cognitive skills that can be ultimately part of the older child's effective behavioral repertory. The child who has begun to develop this set toward elaboration of imagery and verbal materials into novel settings can find greater interest even in toys that are nonspecific (see Chapter IV). Such a child can deal with situations that may arouse anger or can use vicarious fantasy more effectively to change its mood from anger to enjoyment (see Chapter V). The predisposition to fantasy may lead to a greater ability to deal with periods of isolation or privacy and to generate longer attention sequences (see Chapter III).

The Later Course of Make-Believe Play and Fantasy

So far, I have been stressing the earliest manifestations of make-believe play and its relationship to the imagery and verbal stimulation of the child. No one doubts that gradually the overt manisfetations of make-believe begin to drop out in children. This seems especially true in the periods from ages 6 to 8. At the same time, careful incidental observations of children in *privacy* suggest that on such occasions there is still a continuation of overt verbalization of make-believe games. As I noted earlier in referring to the peer-supported sports make-believe play of boys, it is quite likely that many young people would happily continue make-believe in a relatively open fashion were it not that most societies frown rather strongly on this.

If make-believe play is forced to go "underground," what actually does take place? This is indeed very difficult to establish. A fascinating program of research might be developed on the question of just how much of the make-believe that young children exhibit, gradually takes the form of subvocalization and later becomes a kind of interior monologue and how much of it is incorporated as imagery and daydreaming. Certainly, we have many indications that daydreaming is at a peak during adolescence (Singer, 1966). Quite possibly there is little change in the internal experience and imagery. Instead, there may simply be a dropping out of accompanying outspoken verbalization. If ongoing processing of memory material is continuous, then the critical factor is not so much the occurrence or nonoccurrence of internally generated material from the long-term memory system, but rather the direction of attention and the degree to which there is a set in the child toward transferring internally generated material to focal consciousness.

At the most general level, what would appear to be happening is that the child is confronted more and more by social demands requiring what Piaget called "socialized" rather than "egocentric" speech. It learns to run off speech sequences more rapidly at a subvocal level and also to carry on a greater degree of coding and classification by means of linguistic abstractions which are certainly the most powerful systems of coding in the human repertory. Such miniaturization of vocal sequences and greater use of verbal abstraction seem to come about in the normal course of development.

The individual differences in fantasy predisposition emerge along a continuum of attention to the inner processes and sets toward "playing" with them. In this sense, some children at the extreme may very well avoid as much as possible any further attempt to verbalize subvocally about their make-believe attitudes and to concentrate as much as possible on dealing directly with the sense data in their immediate environment. These children would fall into the category of what Broadbent (1958) has called the *short samplers*. That is to say, they react to a stimulus by matching it against a very limited sample of materials from the long-term memory systems and relatively quickly make an overt response or move on to the next stimulus sequence. At the other extreme are children who, for various reasons, are oriented toward increasing or maintaining the phasic level of their processing of internally generated material. They would fall into the general grouping of *long samplers*. The incoming material presented to them is then matched against a complex array of material from long-term memory and the result is the revival of more imagery and fantasies before an overt response is likely to emerge. The long samplers are likely to be somewhat slower in overt motor or verbal response. They should produce more complex images and schemata which in turn they review in their short-term memory systems with the likelihood that even more complex material gets stored.

If the reader will look back at the differences between the high and low imaginative predisposition adolescents in the Gottlieb chapter, he will see at once rather striking differences in the complexity of material produced to a simple request to tell about the abstract movie shown. We know that the differences cannot be attributed to general intelligence nor indeed simply to fluency of verbal output, but rather to an orientation toward processing complex material. Obviously, this tendency is also related to the skill in divergent production or associational fluency that has been mentioned earlier in the references to the work of Guilford (1967) and Wallach (1971). Libby (1970) has reported data which support the hypothesis that adolescents capable of producing more "remote" or original associations have more variable reaction times than poor "remote associaters." The remote associaters do seem to direct more attention "inward," hence they are slower in many cases to make an overt rapid response.

Differences between children in the long and short sampling orientation, for example, may show up later as personality styles. The most obvious general personality trait is the introversion-extraversion continuum which has always fascinated personality theorists, but has never been adequately clarified. Similarly, the major classifications of neurotic style, the obsessional and the hysterical, represent two manifestations of the same cognitive orientation. The obsessional personality is clearly a long sampler endlessly examining the interconnections between long-term memories and material newly presented to the senses. The hysterical personality spends relatively little time in matching new material against a complex array of long-term memories, but rather plunges actively into verbal and social interchanges that are generally of a relatively cliché and mundane quality. This last maneuver successfully avoids confronting in any detail the great personal difficulty of one's life, but at the same time has certain direct social value. The long sampling obsessional, on the other hand, is racked by indecision and by slowness of response which frequently is not functional in particular social or intimate situations. Clearly, these patterns may also be related to other well-established cognitive styles such as Witkin's cognitive differentiation or field-dependence, field-independence which will be reviewed in more detail later.

Reality and Fantasy

In addition to the inhibition of vocalization and the emphasis on reprocessing as part of what happens in the transition from childhood to adolescence, still another controlling factor on the role of make-believe would appear to be the element of realism. Reality is not easy to define and indeed some of the great French students of imaginal processes and play, Bachélard (1964) and Chateau (1967) have argued that the inner experience is a critical part of the human's reality and the distinction between external stimulation and internal stimulation is not to be judged along that dimension. Probably it would be better to talk in terms of the realistic possibilities that exist in a person's life space.

The very young child has only a limited concept of what is and is not possible in the manipulation of symbols and in terms of his own future actions or behaviors. He has no way of knowing that he is not likely ever to be a cowboy, or even a fireman or policeman. He thus has a greater range of materials to play around with in terms of potential role taking. The shift that Gottlieb reports from adventurous fantasy to romantic and achievement fantasy occurring in the elementary and junior high school age groups in her study reflects in part the gradual narrowing of the possibilities of action for the young person. The fact that love and romance are more prominent in the fantasy of the early adolescents is obviously a cultural and perhaps secondarily a biological phenomenon but the shift also to *achievement* reflects the cultural awareness that adult roles beckon in the near future.

The great *range* of adolescent fantasy reflects the fact that for most adolescents many things are still possible that are soon precluded forever for them by the time they reach the ages of 21 or 22. Following high school or college, the likelihood of unusual romantic adventures or very high levels of achievement have already been ruled out for most young people. Their internal make-believe therefore focuses more and more upon the immediate possibilities of their life situations. The work on daydreams of normal young and middle-aged adults certainly suggests that most adult fantasies are closely related to reality and to what happens next summer or what other kinds of jobs or ways of making a living one might find (Singer & McCraven, 1961). If one's make-believe inner world remains too far-ranging after this period, one is likely to be confronted again and again with failure experiences or potential failures. The consequence is a generally negative affective tone as part of one's inner life or presumably the gradual refusal to turn attention upon inner activity. For the indefatigable daydreamer who has not clearly delineated the inner realm as one of play, something to enjoy, but not necessarily to take *fully* seriously, engaging in actions that may be self-defeating is a likelihood. Such an outcome was beautifully depicted in Flaubert's famous novel of *Madame Bovary,* which introduced into France the term *le Bovarysme,* meaning a tendency toward romantic daydreaming.

When there is a relatively clear delineation between what is fantasy and reality in a person's life, engaging in extensive daydreaming may be quite pleasurable. The factor analytic studies carried out on adult daydreaming suggest again and again a dimension of positive vivid daydreaming which is characteristic of normal individuals and which seems to involve a great deal of enjoyment of fantasy without, however, any necessarily neurotic consequences (Singer & Antrobus, 1972). The delineation of reality itself in young children may in part depend upon the capacity to engage in make-believe play. By the ages of three or four most children, if they are directly questioned, seem quite clear as to the fact that the games in which they are engaging are make-believe. There is even the likelihood that fantasy as part of the overall play situation helps the child establish the difference between what is direct sensory material and material from long-term memory. There are various suggestions in the research literature that persons more experienced in daydreaming can distinguish more effectively between their own illusions and actual externally derived sensory events (Segal, 1971). It is quite possible that the opportunity to provide oneself with feedback about one's experiences, which is a form of long sampling, helps to clarify the meaning of these experiences and puts them into perspective.

Cast into the format of a make-believe play game, even wishes and fantasies of a child become circumscribed; they take on an interest and value in themselves and yet are at the same time differentiated from direct action. Ultimately, the child may find outlets for expressing the same make-believe tendencies in a story or drawing which again carefully delineates another source of stimulation and interest quite clearly separated from direct action. This point is especially important not only because of its role in the separation of reality from fantasy, but also because it may be an important aspect of the way in which the child develops increased control over overt behavioral tendencies.

Earlier work by this author and others had suggested that the inhibition of overt movement led to increased "movements in the mind's eye" as exemplified by Rorschach Human Movement Response (Singer, 1955, 1968). One need not, however, go to the lengths of assuming some internal shift of energy in order to understand this process. Perhaps what happens is best described in information processing and affective terms as an increased cognitive repertory and concomitantly an increased range of affective possibilities in a given situation. From this standpoint, then, the child who has a greater range of alternatives in play is less likely to erupt into impulsive action that may have negative consequences for itself or others when provoked to anger or frustrated or interfered with in some fashion. By contrast, an unimaginative child left alone for an extended period may engage in a great deal of physical manipulation of the environment. The adults may come back to find the place turned upside down with bad consequences perhaps both for the child and the adults later on. If the child can find some small playthings or manipulanda which can serve as the basis for an extended make-believe game that is absorbing and interesting, there is relatively little likelihood of overt disruption. The make-believe games of a child, therefore, provide interesting novel environments that may have social value as well as value in terms of increased learning of imagery and development of divergent production skills.

Aggression and Fantasy

Turning further to the control of aggression or violence, we can see some additional possibilities for the view of make-believe being proposed here. Consider again the findings in Biblow's chapter. The young children who are frustrated by having an older child interfere with their construction and problem-solving activities were clearly aroused to anger. For those children who already had, as part of their general tendency, an inclination toward long processing or imaginative predisposition, the level of anger reached was lower to start with. Perhaps this was because they began to see other possibilities in the situation. In addition, given an opportunity to observe fantasy in television either aggressive or nonaggressive in content, they found themselves able to respond emotionally to these in ways that reduced the likelihood of subsequent, overt aggressive behavior.

For example, shown the aggressive material on television, the fighting scene, the more imaginatively predisposed children seemed to feel somewhat more saddened and perhaps self-incriminating as if they began to examine their own previously aroused angry feelings in relation to the violence on the screen. The other highly imaginative children, who had no aggressive content shown to them, but a rather pleasant and humorous scene from *Chitty Chitty Bang-Bang,* were able apparently to empathize with the scene and experience considerable enjoyment and positive affect with the consequence that their level of subsequent behavior was reduced by comparison with the control subjects. Those children low in imaginative predisposition first of all were aroused to a somewhat high level of anger by the frustration, perhaps because they could not fit into any broader panorama and could only respond specifically in terms of an interference by others with a specific goal. The introduction of the vicarious fantasy material on the television screen did not modify significantly their negative moods. If anything, the aggressive story seemed somewhat to increase their anger and the likelihood of subsequent aggression. These children, less varied and complex in their orientation towards make-believe, seemed less capable of using the fantasy medium as an alternative for dealing with their aroused emotions and for varying the kind of overt behavior manifested.

Klinger (1971), reviewing a great deal of the literature on fantasy as measured by TAT responses, is led to the conclusion that persons with a great deal of experience in aggressive fantasy are more likely to express complex aggressive material in qualified forms on TAT responses, but less likely to express this behavior overtly. By contrast, children or adults with little experience in dealing through fantasy forms with anger, may express the aggression in a direct and unqualified form on a TAT. They also are more likely to engage quite directly in overt aggressive behavior. Thus, it would appear as if for the former group there is an inverse relationship between the expression of overt anger or aggression and fantasy, while for the latter there is a direct relationship, the greater the amount of aggression expressed in story-telling activity, the greater the likelihood of direct attacking behavior.

A key role may be played here by the degree of self-awareness shown by the individual. As Klinger (1971) has noted, "The thematic content of an individual's fantasies seems more closely related to his self-concept than to his overt behavior, and he may indeed base his self-concept partly on what he knows of his fantasies [p. 335]." Many young adults and children who are aware of many temptations toward aggression, but who also had either in fantasy or to some extent in reality, the experience of being punished or threatened with punishment for such behavior, may present considerable *fantasy* aggression without actually attacking anyone. Persons who have not been introspective and examined fully all of the consequences of aggressive behavior, may, if presented with opportunities to tell stories under conditions of provocation, show considerable aggressive fantasy material unqualified by guilt or anxiety. They also may explode quite naturally into direct aggression.

Make-Believe and the Self-System

The relationship between make-believe play and the development of self-attitudes, self-concept, and a differentiated self-system has yet to be explored and is a most inviting area for future research. Freud proposed that the origin of the *ego* occurred in the combination of delay and fantasy (Singer, 1955). The usefulness of the concept of an ego as a specific subsystem of personality is at this point very questionable. There does seem to be, however, considerable basis for studying the notion of self-system, that is to say, a set of attitudes that people carry about themselves which may vary in consistency and also in positive or negative associated affect. While it is not clearly demonstrable that these self-attitudes strongly govern overt behavior, they are an important part of the general experience of people and can scarcely be ignored (Gergen, 1971).

It seems very likely that one consequence of make-believe play for the child is an increasingly differentiated self-concept or awareness of self. In effect, by practicing a variety of make-believe selves and roles, a child gradually differentiates himself out from the field around him and sees many options within himself that are not automatically called for by the external situation. In putting it in this form, I do not mean to say that a child makes this kind of conscious decision or can even grasp the type of concept I have just suggested. Rather, it seems likely that the child begins to get some sense of "what I am compared to many other kinds of things that are possible." This delaying quality of long sampling associated with make-believe efforts helps establish a distinction between an I-sense in the child and the feeling of direct responsiveness to a variety of external stimuli. At the very least, one can conceive of the likelihood that the child who has had a good deal of experience in a variety of play situations, including make-believe, can see parts of himself in all of these situations and may begin to organize his experience around the notion that he is a complex person. By contrast, the child who is less differentiated both in the variety of games generally as well as in the make-believe area is likely to have only a limited set of responses which he considers to be his "true" self. The less differentiated self-concept may be a rather gross, somewhat nonfunctional pattern of response in many situations. Indeed, as I have tried to show, there is such a tremendous range of ongoing inner processing of memories and incidents from the past that in effect the less differentiated self-system is short-changing the true range of possibilities and the true complexities of a given individual. The short sampling, "reality-oriented" youngster may be effective motorically and may win esteem by athletic skills or speed of reactions. He may also underestimate the range of possibilities for imagery that exists within himself and overlook the range of alternative qualities that may be a part of his overall personality structure.

Make-believe play also opens the possibility for a greater range of trial selves and for tentative imagined excursions into the future which ultimately become the basis for effective planning. A great neurologist, Kurt Goldstein (1940), proposed that one of the highest of human capacities was the adoption of an "attitude toward the possible." In effect, make-believe play represents the beginnings of such an attitude. As make-believe becomes more complex and enriched by increased personal experiences in overt behavior as well as increased vicarious experiences by reading and popular media, multiple potentialities of human behavior flourish as a domain at the grasp of the individual.

Richardson (1969) has presented evidence that imagined practice can indeed increase overt proficiency for example, in gymnastic tasks. Where situations are more social and less dependent on very specific motor and kinesthetic cues, the likelihood is even greater that imaginary practice can be beneficial. At the very least, it can suggest the dangers in certain situations and lead to more inhibited behavior which may be especially valuable under a variety of circumstances. On the other hand, it may also indicate novel possibilities that would not ordinarily be expected in the situation. This is one of the major functional advantages of the higher processes of divergent thinking.

The seemingly trivial make-believe play of the child grows essentially out of the very nature of the child's cognitive experience. It follows the assimilation and accommodation cycles and involves the seeking of moderate levels of increasing stimulation or reducing such moderate levels of stimulation to produce an experience of joy. It may portend, therefore, enormously important later consequences for development. This is not to say that make-believe play specifically serves that function. Rather, the capacity to generate imagery and to practice imagery and the associated verbal skills of elaboration are simply fundamental capacities with which most human beings are "wired" and which they can develop to varying degrees depending on external circumstances and learning opportunities. Our brain is busily producing images or at least trans-forming them into some form of the neurochemical and electrophysiological terms most of the time. We must learn to ignore much of the "noise" generated by this activity, but we can also learn to use it to particularly great effect.

Imaginative Play Predisposition and Personality

So far, we have been emphasizing the more general nature of imaginative play and its origins in the assimilation accommodation process, the development of imagery and verbal capacities and the relation of all this to the affects associated with information processing tasks. Let us now particularize this material in relation to the development of specific trends toward greater or lesser predisposi-tion to imaginative play as a dimension of personality. It is a task for future research, stimulated hopefully by this book, to determine some of the more extensive ramifications of imaginative play predisposition within personality structure in normal and pathological forms of development. Our efforts thus far have succeeded in demonstrating that a combination of interview and Rorschach measures produces a reasonably satisfactory estimate of spontaneous make-believe play or fantasy tendencies in children and adolescents.

What follows is largely speculation, a kind of educated guess about the possibilities of the origin of imaginative predisposition filtered through personal recollections, direct observations of children's play, as well as available clinical literature and, finally, the kinds of formal research presented in earlier chapters. Any attempt is in effect the creation of a kind of myth or scientific metaphor which necessarily goes beyond available information. It is hoped, however, that such a myth can have the psychological value of stimulating others to look more sharply at the early play behavior of children in a systematic way and to begin to note similarities and differences from this model. This may then lead to more effective further research exploration in this area.

Constitutional Factors and Early Styles of Imagery, Exploration, and Information-Processing

Today it is no longer possible to deny the likelihood that children are born with important differences in motility and exploratory activity as well as in intensity of reaction to stress which persist through infancy and may well play a role in later personality development. Some of these constitutional factors may lead to varying degrees of exploration of the immediate environment and the possibility of differential acquisition of schemata which in the course of the accommodation-assimilation process generate different degrees of long-term memory activity. If a child lies passively in the crib and does not manipulate the environment or explore it, he may not significantly discriminate what is available there. Such passivity may yield a more global pattern of response at least for a while until stimulation from the adult encourages greater activity.

The work of Escalona (1968) does indeed suggest that some children are not very active from birth. If no adult interacts with them, by 6 months they will show a retardation in certain motor skills when compared with another group of infants who are actively manipulative of the environment irrespective of adult interest. The more passive child will suffer when there is no adult attempt to play little games, smile, tease, and generally do the silly things adults do with babies. Such lack of outside stimulation will seriously limit the child's tendency to explore the physical world. Such a child may not learn to enjoy the interaction of accommodation to the outside world with the assimilation of the material into a novel, internal environment when left to its own devices. The more passive child who does experience stimulation by adults may, once encouraged, because of its quieter nature, engage more extensively in private assimilation than the more active child. The latter's motor skills are generally less dependent on adult interaction. Therefore, the initially active child seems less likely to attempt to assimilate the *parent's* movements and actions into its own schemata.

In a sense, the difference described by Escalona already suggests the beginnings of a kind of introvert–extravert style. The more active child may constantly be seeking new environmental stimulation, interested primarily in the objects of the environment or in short-term processes. The more passive child, if stimulated by adults, may spend more time in private moments assimilating memory material rather than actively exploring each new physical environment. This contrast, of course, is highly speculative, but it does point a way in which constitutional factors can begin very early to influence the development of an imaginative tendency.

Still another area that may be constitutionally based has to do with the *imagery* capacity of different children. We have only relatively limited amount of data on individual differences in imagery at early ages, but there do seem to be indications that very young children are already quite variable in this respect on various imagery measures. These imagery differences are also reflected in some differential learning skills (Paivio, 1970). The dramatic phenomenon of imagery known as *eidetic imagery* in which children show the capacity for looking at objects and almost developing the vividness of photograph in their capacity to describe the object shortly afterwards has been subject of considerable controversy and question by various writers.

In the 1920s and 1930s, the Jaensch brothers in Germany made much of the personality differences between *eidetikers* and other children as part of their racially oriented theories of personality structure. More recently, Haber and Haber (1964) have carried out important studies of a large number of children to test for the occurrence of eidetic imagery with a view to understanding the implication of this phenomenon for perception more generally. These investigators, using very ingenious methods for evaluating the ability of the children to reproduce images found a very small percentage of children who qualify as genuinely eidetic imagers. Even more careful examination in a subsequent study (Leask, Haber, & Haber, 1968) made it clear that perhaps only a very tiny percentage of a large school age group qualified by any reasonable definition as truly eidetic. Doob (1966), in a survey across cultures of the indications of eidetic imagery, found that anywhere from 0 to about 20% of children in different cultures were described as eidetic imagers. Of course he was not in position to provide the kind of extremely careful tests carried out by Haber and Haber.

Therefore, it seems unlikely that sheer differences of a very gross nature in imagery capacity are evident in most children. It is even questionable that eidetic imagery has any necessarily significant role in make-believe play. For example, Hebb (1968) has brought together evidence suggesting that extremely vivid imagery of this type in quite young children would be an argument for some brain dysfunction since at least from Hebb's theoretical point of view of central nervous system processing, an important element in storage of images would be the spread of the image into other coding systems beside the simple direct reproductions. A child whose imagery was so pictorial was very likely not capable of also coding the image in an abstract form.

It remains possible, however, that some moderate capacity for discriminating imagery in the various sense modalities may play a role in the predisposition to make-believe play. Provided that the imagery is not too vivid, the child with a moderate degree of clarity in restoration of scenes or auditory images has some greater likelihood of being able to enjoy these in privacy and of using them more effectively. Other cognitive style differences in early childhood may also play a role in setting up conditions fostering later development of imaginative games.

An important cognitive dimension that has been extensively studied by Kagan (1966) has been the dimension of *reflection-impulsivity*. This dimension refers to the speed with which children make decisions about responses in problem-solving tasks or the degree to which they move rapidly from one toy to another or show other aspects of long and short sampling (Broadbent, 1958). Such a style also seems to have a genetic or constitutional component. For example, Scarr (1966) conducted a study of identical and fraternal twin girls between the ages of 6 and 10. A measure of short or long response times in a play situation involving some ambiguity yielded evidence that there was a very *high* correlation in the tendency to delay response for the monozygotic twins while the correlation obtained for fraternal twins was much lower. A similar finding was reported by Reppucci (cited in Kagan & Kogan, 1970, p. 1319) who found that the one-egg twins who were observed during free-play as early as 8 months of age showed consistent tendencies either to play for longer periods with individual toys or to show a great fluctuation in their play during the period of observation. This suggests that the tendency for persistence, contrasted with rapid shifting from one plaything to another, may again be associated with a constitutional factor.

A rather intriguing study of free-play behavior involving children aged 2½ was carried out by Pederson and Wender (1968). The children who persisted for longer periods of time in playing with specific toys as against those who shifted a great deal were then also studied 4 years later through administration of the Wechsler Intelligence Scale for Children. The children who had demonstrated a slow tempo of shift turned out to do better on those scales in the intelligence test that required some delay of response in order to yield the most adequate score. Additional evidence (Reppucci, 1968, 1970) indicates that 2-year-old boys who showed long periods of attention in a particular activity in contrast to those who showed very short duration involvements also were found to have had a slower tempo of play at 8 months and at 27 months. There was even evidence that as early as 4 months old, boys who were extremely slow in tempo change in play turned out to be slow also in habituating in their attention to achromatic faces which were shown to them (Kagan & Kogan, 1970, p. 1318).

It is not necessary to review the very extensive work by Kagan and his associates on the reflective-impulsive dimension to see that it bears some possible relationship to the development of imaginative predisposition in children. If constitutional factors are implicated in speed of decision processes and in some type of short and long sampling tendencies in children, at least some portion of the variance attributed to individual differences in imaginative predisposition is now explicable. Some children from the very beginning take more time in surveying stimuli, are inclined to play more extensively with a given stimulus, or take longer in reviewing the related images and associations in connection with an object before providing an overt response. These long-sampling tendencies conform to what we know about the behavior of persons given to fantasy and make-believe from a great variety of the Rorschach studies already cited as well as studies such as those by Siipola and Taylor (1952) with Rorschach-like instruments. Maddi (1965) also reported work which suggests that those subjects who sat quietly for longer periods of time subsequently produced more imaginative or novel responses to thematic apperception test pictures. This result is similar to a number of findings also reported by Singer (1960) in connection with waiting room behavior of schizophrenics who produce more human movement responses on the Rorschach test. The study by Riess (1957) may also be noted here since it indicates that children who produce more Rorschach human movement responses are inclined to sit more quietly during a waiting period.

In summary, we have no definitive evidence at this point that can link the tendency of make-believe play to specific patterns of genetic or constitutional variation. At the same time, it is hard to avoid the conclusion that, at the very least, cognitive processing dimensions such as reflection–impulsivity or tendency for some type of long and short sampling seems to be evident extremely early in babies. These seem to have at least some constitutional aspect as measured by twin studies. It is quite likely that such early styles are indeed implicated in the subsequent emergence of make-believe play predisposition.

Early Learning through Modeling and Parent–Child Interaction

The Role of a Stable Mother Figure

There is general agreement that the cognitive development of the child follows some pattern roughly similar to that proposed by Bruner *et al.* (1966). The child's initial contacts with the environment are primarily at the physical and sensory-motor level, only later at the level of imagery (Bruner's Ikonic Stage), and finally at the abstract or symbolic level. There are differences among theorists as to the degree to which learning experiences play a role in influencing how rapidly each of these stages may emerge (Berlyne, 1970).

The controversy of whether the developmental stages emerge more or less inevitably or are strongly modifiable by specific learning experiences need not concern us in detail at this point. This shift from the more overtly verbal to increased reliance on imagery takes place partly as a function of the growing brain development of the child. It is also extremely likely that specific types of interaction can speed up the emergence of certain patterns.

Undoubtedly the role of the mother or some one individual closely associated with the child at an early age is crucial in development of aspects of imagery and fantasy. Even if one rejects the single-minded hunger model proposed by Freud (and made the basis for the psychoanalytic theory of motivation by Rapaport), one must recognize that the interaction with an adult early in life must certainly play a critical role in the development of a variety of ultimately internalized processes. It would be too much of a detour from our present intent to examine all of the important implications for mental health and socialization as well as development of positive or negative affective orientations dependent upon the kinds of rapid reinforcement available from the mother as well as her emotional reactions to the child. There is at least some reason to believe that children who are not responded to or stimulated by adults in infancy suffer subsequent negative consequences whether in the learning of motor skills or in the development of a general depressive state. What is clear is that adults do initiate play with children. They bend over children and tickle them. They say "goo-goo!" or other nonsensical phrases. They smile a great deal and laugh and generally make all kinds of noises that are geared to evoke some kind of response from the child.

Needless to say, the parent figures also frequently show very negative affect to the infant, close up. A mother who bitterly resents having to care for her child will undoubtedly make angry remarks and reveal facially negative affect which will eventually become apparent to an older baby. Incidents of gross physical assault on young infants are becoming increasingly studied and are obviously more widespread than had been appreciated. Parents also may indicate disgust at having to care physically for the child, changing their diapers, cleaning their faces after feeding, or having to hear persistent whimpering. There may actually be instances of gross ignorance by adults concerning the degree to which the child is capable of engaging in directly motivated acts. I have observed situations where infants in arms were struck by parents who blamed them because the child's rather random motility injured another girl or another member of the family or pulled off the glasses of one of the grandparents.

In view of this extensive interaction with adults, it seems very likely that an important element that goes ultimately into the development of make-believe play will be the degree to which the parent is available regularly as a model on a sufficiently consistent basis so that the child will begin to attempt to reproduce the words and behavior when alone. This seems especially likely to occur when the parent's behavior is positive and associated with smiling and positive affect as well as with actual gratification of physical needs. The degree to which the parent also encourages little vocal and motor games with the child or presents the child with simple toys or rattles may also stimulate subsequent independent play of this kind on the part of the child as part of the accommodation-assimilation cycle. This cycle may be regarded as an outcome of the child's seeking to enhance positive affect through establishment of a moderately novel environment or through reducing the strangeness of isolation by producing familiar images and the consequent experience of the affect of joy.

The emphasis so far has been on the important role of a parent in generating subsequent accommodation and assimilation. This emphasis reflects perhaps the author's experience as a clinical psychologist and psychoanalyst. Certainly the psychoanalytically oriented investigators from Freud through Ekstein have also focused on the importance of early mother–child contact as part of the way in which fantasy and play develop. This kind of emphasis on early experience is also critical in attempts to develop theories of internalization (Schafer, 1968) and object representation (Blatt, 1972). Sullivan's (1953) emphasis on the empathic interaction between mother and child is another example of the clinician's focus on this dimension. At the same time, Piaget gives more attention to the child's contact with the physical environment.

A most intriguing study by Feffer and Gourevitch (1960) indicates the tendency of a child toward what Piaget has called "centering" even in the interpersonal sphere. The child's difficulty in shifting away from the immediate situation toward an alternative possibility of an object can be shown to occur not only for physical objects as Piaget had emphasized, but also for role-taking orientations. For this clever study, the authors had very young children tell stories about one of three characters in a picture. They were then required to tell stories from the standpoint of each of the other characters, thereby necessitating a shift of their point of reference. Feffer and Gourevitch in fact found that defective centering could also be demonstrated in this *interpersonal* realm. Decentering may occur later in the child's cognitive development than *physical* decentering. One might wonder if this is indeed the case from the standpoint of the clinician's experience that it is the interpersonal dimension that is perhaps earlier more critical for the child than the relation to the physical world. This remains an intriguing opportunity for more extensive research.

It is very likely that some mothers or parents in general may engage in a greater number of make-believe or peek-a-boo games at the very earliest age with their children. They may also quickly communicate a positive affect with the child associated with finding hidden objects or with various games that emphasize at least some element of imagery. They may play games such as "This Little Piggy Goes to Market" with the toes and fingers of the children thus introducing into a simple manipulative game some beginning elements that call for imagery or make-believe.

Of course if the mother never leaves the child alone, the likelihood that the child can engage in any extensive assimilative process is reduced considerably. A somewhat attentive and even Oedipus-complex-provoking mother may have an important part in the generating of closeness, internalization, and identification on the part of the child. The excessively "smothering" mother, however, simply does not leave the child alone long enough for it to practice sequences of independent play. This creates an excessive dependence on the mother that precludes the likelihood of an imaginative development of any scope. Some clinical evidence in support of this hypothesis in individual cases of children who have had difficulties in the development of imaginative play and who show a poverty of make-believe in their spontaneous behavior has been reported by Fineman (1960). If the mother is, however, sufficiently self-confident and not excessively tied up with the child, she can go about her chores or attend to other children and leave the child alone in crib or playpen for relatively long periods of time. This then permits at least some degree of practice and internalization of memories of the mother's activity. In this sense, one might say that a moderate or intermittent reinforcement by the mother may establish conditions in which there is greater resistance to extinction. The child may seek to recapture the mother's memory and to replay some of the interactions with her as part of making the solitary environment more interesting.

A special feature in the development of fantasy may also be the degree to which there is *one* clearly defined and unique figure in the child's life. The importance of this central figure of great stability, a benign and loving mother, has been emphasized in much of the analytic literature. These reports are based on extensive case studies which suggest that lacking such a warm benign figure there is greater likelihood for the development of an early sense of mistrust and insecurity. The stability of the "object," a curious term indeed for a warm loving mother, but one which unfortunately persists throughout psychoanalytic literature, is emphasized by clinicians as diverse as Freud, Sullivan, Fairbairn, and Erikson. The latter builds much of his notion of the early development of basic trust around this view of the maternal role. More recently, Blatt (1972) carried out a somewhat speculative analysis of the role which both parents, particularly the mother, play in helping the child to establish the boundaries between reality and unreality. He notes that the

> . . . repeated appearance, disappearance and reappearance of a consistent need-gratifying object also facilitates the child's developing a memory of the object, including consistent mental representations and verbal signifiers for the object, which persists even when the object is unavailable . . . the repeated sequences of frustration-gratification by a consistent object enables the child to distinguish the actual object from his memory and mental representations of the object. The child comes to know that there is a difference between the actual object and the mental representation and he comes to know that the "idea of the object is inside while the object itself is outside" (Schaefer, 1969). These differentiations between self and

non-self, between an object and the mental representations of the object, and between inside and outside are critical development steps in the evolving capacity for reality testing [p. 13].

Blatt places his emphasis upon the importance of close contact with the mother and yet the separation from mother as establishing a basic sense of boundaries in the subsequent imaginal representations of self and of others. He makes an impressive case for the fact that a great deal of the dilemma that the schizophrenic patient faces in social perception has to do with his inability in establishing boundaries. Blatt adduces a great deal of data on attention difficulty and psychological test studies of the apperceptive and fantasy behavior of schizophrenics to support this boundary difficulty.

One need not accept all of the complex armchair speculations about the intrapsychic nature of internalization and the layering of various identification and incorporation patterns (Schaefer, 1969) to recognize the fact that a good deal of the child's early experience will involve attempts to rehearse experiences engaged in with the mother or with some other surrogate mother or guardian. Therefore, it seems especially important to understand that a closeness to one stable figure may become the basis for a later extended fantasy development. This hypothesis suggested that adults who showed a great deal of daydreaming tendency (based on self-report) would also show greater closeness to their mothers than to their fathers. This relationship was modestly substantiated in a number of studies (Singer, 1966). In the case of our study of the children aged 6 to 9, the data did not make it specifically the mother, but rather the focusing on one adult as a preferred one in the family which was critical. This opens the possibility for much more extended research on the question of identification and role-playing as related to imaginative predisposition development.

Parental Encouragement and Modeling

Whether or not one can demonstrate that the mother or a specific close adult plays the key role in internalization that we have been discussing, it certainly seems possible to demonstrate the importance of the role of the adult figure in generating other aspects of imaginative play through example and imitation if not indeed instruction. Beginning with peek-a-boo and hide-and-seek games, a mother may progress to little songs and stories associated with feeding the child. Clever mothers will have the child open its mouth on the cue word which indicates that "the bird is going to fly into the nest" at which point they pop in the cereal. During the early 1930s, the cartoonist and writer, Milton Gross, published an extremely humorous group of stories, all of them presumably versions of famous American legends and poems as told by a dialect-speaking Jewish mother to her small child as an inducement to "have another spoonful of farina, dollink!"

Stories like *The Three Bears* or *Little Red Riding Hood* become regular bedtime rituals for many families. One can of course explore these studies in terms of their symbolic and psychodynamic meaning, and this has been extensively attempted by the psychoanalysts. Our focus here is rather upon the introduction of the make-believe and the way in which it generates assimilative efforts on the part of the child in an attempt to integrate the story line with the limited schemata available. As a consequence of this effort, there are some rather quaint and curious variations on the story that emerge when the child is overheard talking to itself in bed or replaying the scene in its crib.

A lovely little book, *Winnie the Pooh*, exemplifies some of the best elements of a fantasy tale that continues to be popular with children. Part of this may be because it contains within it some fine insights on early childhood experience of a Piagetian type. For example, Christopher Robin, the boy whose make-believe playmate is Winnie the Pooh the teddy bear, speaks of Winnie as living in the woods under the name of "Winnie ther Pooh." The term "under the name of" is in actuality a rather abstract notion from an adult standpoint, referring to the use of an alias or of a special name. It involves a *decentering* to some extent from the actual terminology in order to understand, from an adult's standpoint, the meaning of the phrase "under the name of." Christopher Robin simplifies this by simply having Winnie live in a house with a sign above the door saying "Winnie ther Pooh" so that the bear lives literally under the name of "Winnie ther Pooh."

In another scene in the book, the important role of fantasy in helping to distinguish reality from fantasy is amusingly depicted. Winnie the Pooh, in an effort to disguise himself from the bees and steal their honey, borrows a blue balloon from Christopher Robin and floats aloft near the honey tree. He asks Christopher Robin if he is invisible since he has purposely chosen a blue balloon to blend in with the sky. Christopher Robin, however, explains to him again and again that he still looks like a brown bear hanging on to a blue balloon.

Stories of this type undoubtedly generate additional efforts on the part of the child to assimilate some of the peculiarities of this behavior into his limited schemata. I recall having heard this particular story read on a number of occasions. Eventually, I learned to read it and found that I had some strange notions as to what animals such as Eeyore the donkey or Piglet looked like.

A special area for study involves the frequent use of animals in human-like roles for the entertainment of children in stories or television or movie cartoons. Since we are not focusing in this volume on symbolic meaning and the content of fantasy to any degree, it would take us too far afield to explore all of the possibilities for the inner life of children of symbolic animals. At the purely cognitive level, however, it seems very likely that the many varied forms in the animal world make the animals intrinsically interesting and novel to children. At the same time, the children are much more limited in their capacity to envision a greater complexity and variety of animal interactions since they have so little experience with them. Instead, they rely on assimilating the varied shapes and forms of animals into their limited schemata of human interactions, the relationships they observe between their parents and themselves, or their parents and the other children in the family. Again, the parents perpetuate and foster many of these tendencies. They repeat the stories they heard as children and by their own enthusiastic participation in the make-believe story or game associated with these creatures encourage their children to experience the same affective reactions.

Other Models and Assimilation-Practice

Of course it is not necessarily the parents alone who provide imaginative stimulation. It is entirely possible that this role will be taken by grandparents, other relatives, or older siblings taking on various child-care functions. Literature is replete with accounts of old servants, grandmothers, or ancient sea captains who hold children spellbound with their story telling or recounting of ancient legends. In Arab countries, story telling persists and may account for the high level of fantasy play among Arab children reported by Eifermann (1971). Indeed the cultural significance of story tellers has only recently begun to fade in Western civilization. Until the advent of television, there was a widespread reliance upon various forms of public story telling in the 1920s and 1930s on radio and before that on the various lecture circuits or Chatauqua platforms. A recent revival has been the Hal Holbrook portrayal of Mark Twain who was, needless to say, a great story teller at the turn of the century.

An important concomitant of exposure to story telling or other similar instances of make-believe or even historical accounts by adults is the opportunity on the part of the child for private play. If the child is living under circumstances where there is constant interruption of make-believe efforts at assimilating the recently heard novel material, the likelihood of developing the skill at integrating the new materials into the current schemata of the child will be lessened. If anything, children tend to interfere greatly with each other's concentration. Even the little examples we have quoted earlier indicate how many interruptions there are in make-believe sequences that prevent fully carrying out a particular story line. This is the reason in part why one might expect only or first born children to show somewhat more tendency toward make-believe play or daydreaming.

Of course older siblings may sometimes organize fantasy games with younger children as actors. Except for the status of being the only child, however, there is nothing intrinsically special about birth order that should produce greater make-believe tendencies. Rather, it seems to be a question of the psychological situation in which the child finds itself. Thus a third or fourth born child relatively widely spaced from older children may experience much of the same kind of privacy necessary and indeed may even be encouraged in make-believe play by the example of the older siblings (Sutton-Smith & Rosenberg, 1967) who are old enough again not to interfere directly with the privacy of the younger sibling. Direct observations of family life in extremely poor, urban households indicates that even under crowded conditions, children will often crawl or walk away into a corner and strive for some privacy (Herbert Nechin, personal communication).

In effect then, closeness with one parent under circumstances which foster opportunities for imitation and identification and which at the same time provide opportunities for privacy and practice of make-believe play should lead to a greater predisposition on the part of the children. This certainly seems to have been the case in the findings based on self-reports of the children of our earlier study with the 6- to 9-year-olds and also in Dr. Freyberg's report of the interviews with the mothers of the high- and low-fantasy children of kindergarten age. Freyberg's finding, though obtained with a relatively small sample, is all the more important because the groups were so close in socioeconomic status, educational level, and other variables. An important influence seemed to be the parents' tolerance and interest in imaginative play on the part of the children. The fact of the small, but significant difference in education suggests at the very least some greater degree of awareness and striving toward providing the children with an enhanced education opportunity.

The role of other children has not been stressed much up until now, except in the likelihood that they can actually interfere with the development of high fantasy predisposition. We have really very little knowledge on this point from formal research. It is certainly likely that when two or three children who are interested in make-believe games come together they can enhance this potentiality mutually and find great enjoyment in extended fantasy play. Such an instance is evidenced in the story of Tom Sawyer where Tom's leadership is critical in fostering the imaginative play of his small group of friends.

Often enough, however, the child who early shows a strong tendency toward make-believe play may become irritated and distressed by the fact that other children are not as interested. They may interrupt the fantasy game in order to run off after some other children or to start swinging on a tree trunk or spinning a garbage pail or to get into a mock fight. Such instances may, in individual cases, lead the more imaginative child to withdraw from social contact in frustration and to find that he prefers solitary play. The consequence of this withdrawal may be social introversion. Where there is additional encouragement of this pattern by parents who say that it is best for the child not to play with the other children who are just "riff-raff," a much more extensive introverted phase may develop. Occasionally, one can observe the fostering of great intellectual or creative tendencies in the child, but often there is some penalty in the form of loneliness and failure of development of normal social skills.

Again, there is no clear evidence, but it seems highly likely from observation that make-believe games do have intrinsic interest and excitement even for early adolescents and certainly for children between 9 and 12. What seems to be necessary is for some leadership to be shown on the part of one or two more imaginative youngsters and also for circumstances to be such that these games can be carried out in relative privacy without the likelihood of teasing by other children, parents, or teenagers. Gradually, this type of play may merge into more formal kinds of sociodramatic play with actual playing out of scenes from movies or television shows or romantic scenes from magazine stories. Incidental exposure to situations of this kind can of course further strengthen the imaginative predisposition of younger children.

Some Effects of Culture and Popular Media

At a broader cultural level, various aspects of group exposure may play a significant role in minimizing or heightening the likelihood of imaginative play predisposition. We have already mentioned the significance of books and reading materials as part of the parent–child interaction. It is my own hunch, but not demonstrable to any extent, that the extensive exposure of children in the 1930s to early 1950s to radio stories increased the imaginative tendencies of certain children. Of course, it is possible that the ones already predisposed toward fantasy were the most avid auditors of the old radio plays such as "Buck Rogers," "Chandu the Magician," "Jack Armstrong," or "Inner Sanctum." It seems very likely that the attempt to reconstruct through imagery the events taking place on radio stories may have had a beneficial effect in increasing the range and scope of imagery capacity for a large number of children. This seems less to be the case for television which provides an *external* substitute for the imagery and which may keep the child attuned to the set. If, however, there are periods when the child is alone without observing the television set, the complex material presented may provide a stimulating source of make-believe material. This content undoubtedly does increase the likelihood of development of greater differentiated fantasy play as a result of attempted assimilation of the material.

It seems quite possible that television has played a significant role in increasing the opportunity for development of make-believe play and fantasy potentialities in poor children growing up in crowded homes where parents are less interested in or knowledgeable about storytelling and the fostering of a variety of make-believe sets. Television may have enhanced the children's interest in far off countries and strange groups of people, and this may serve as an initial stimulus for fantasy development. What may then interfere is that children in truly poverty circumstances often have relatively little privacy for make-believe play and may therefore resort simply to watching whatever is on the television set in a quasi-hypnotic fashion. We need considerable research to evaluate whether such possibilities for differential affectiveness of the television medium exist. Work by Stein *et al.* (1972) has emphasized possible "prosocial" and noxious effects of television on very young children.

Imaginative Play Predisposition as a Personality Trait

We have attempted to describe how differential tendencies toward imaginative play may develop; let us now consider some of the personality and cognitive correlates and consequences that may be generated by high and low degrees of fantasy play predisposition. In talking of high and low imaginative play predispositions, we are not speaking of *types* in the more traditional sense, but rather of children who score at somewhat contrasting ends of a continuous distribution. It seems likely that all children play at least to some extent at make-believe, but there are great variations in the frequency and consistency with which given children play in this fashion. We are concerned for the moment with the children who are moderately high to moderately low in imaginative play predisposition. That is, we are interested in dealing with what might be called the differences that occur within still a normal range of functioning. We shall deal later with the question of those children who are at the extremes in fantasy play predisposition and who may show pathological manifestations of the presence or lack of make-believe play.

As indicated earlier, we have as yet no clear evidence as to whether the tendency toward make-believe play is just one facet of a more general cognitive style such as field dependence–independence or reflection–impulsivity. For the moment therefore, we shall not address that question, but focus specifically on the effects of a relatively high degree of symbolic play as part of the child's behavioral repertoire. One consequence of an interest in make-believe play may be that the child has available an opportunity to control his physical environment under conditions in which it is not demanding of rapid motor responses.

Waiting Behavior, Isolation, and Frustration Tolerance

In situations of waiting, relative isolation, or where there has been a moderate degree of negative stimulation (such as the arousal to anger in the Biblow study), the high-fantasy child has available resources that can moderate this impact of the environment without the child having to interact in a committed fashion with the objects or people in the milieu. That is, the high-fantasy child can, relatively speaking, create his own private play world using a few toys, if they are available, and (as Pulaski's study clearly shows) using those toys in a flexible fashion, so as to gain maximum variety from the structure of the playthings themselves. In this sense, the high-fantasy child may appear to the outsider as relatively calm, capable of positive affect and enjoyment, and "a good child."

By contrast, the child who has had little development of his make-believe play tendencies will find a situation that requires patient waiting, one in which he becomes aroused to some anger or moves toward a state of some degree of frustration or deprivation. A situation of social isolation may become extremely difficult for such a child. Lacking a set toward the development of make-believe games or a sufficient repertoire of already established themes, he may have to engage in active exploration of the environment. This physical exploration may result in some damage to the physical environment and possible disruption of the activities of adults, who are presumably engaged in some important work that prevents them from attending to the child's needs. Situations vary considerably, but it is conceivable that what may be genuine and effective exploratory behavior for the low-fantasy short-sampling child in one case may, under other circumstances, emerge as a maladaptive disruptiveness and tendency to be "nagging" or interrupting of adults. When it is important that children "be seen and not heard," the make-believe play capacity of the high-fantasy child will stand him in good stead while the low-fantasy child may end up in some trouble.

This notion can be carried a step further in relation to reactions to frustration. If we adopt Tomkins' position that the persistence over a long time of unassimilable stimulation yields the affect of anger, we can explore the consequences for high- and low-fantasy children. In a situation in which the child is confronted by a frustration or an aggressive act which yields a high persisting level of what Tomkins would call *density of neural firing* (Tomkins, 1962), the imaginatively predisposed child may be able to shift his set away from repeated attention in imagery to the frustrating circumstance or to the potentially distressing event. By engaging in some make-believe game related or unrelated to the impending event or to the past frustration, for the moment he may simply change his mood. This shift may reduce the likelihood for aggressive behavior which would be disruptive and might lead to more severe consequences for himself. The child with limited capacity for make-believe play put in a situation of this sort will find himself primarily concentrating over and over again on the source of frustration. This persisting focus of attention with the consequence of continuing high density of neural firing and the evocation of anger yields a likely consequence of some type of aggressive reaction. The study by Biblow certainly affords at least some indications in support of this position.

Even if the high-fantasy child cannot completely eliminate evidences of frustration or the distress he may at least reduce the overall level of incoming stimulation by his shift to more familiar materials in the form of fantasy play. This reduction in the *level* of persisting density of neural firing leads to mild *sadness* and *distress* as against a continuing experience of *anger*. It is hard to say that distress and sadness are "better" experiences than anger. In many instances where there is little practical recourse to affect the delay or frustration, the experience of sadness may have less likelihood of evoking an act that triggers off others' *counteractions.* An angry overt set may yield detrimental consequences to the child even more than initial frustrating circumstances.

Related to this aspect of sadness is the finding in Biblow's study that the high-fantasy children exposed, after frustration, to an aggressive film, showed a shift from anger toward sadness or distress. A similar result in some respects was also noted for adults in the study by Pytkowitz, Wagner, and Sarason (1967). These investigators found that high-fantasy young adults aroused to anger and then exposed to an opportunity to engage in fantasy showed a greater turning inward of their anger and an increase in self-incrimination. These data suggest the possibility that an important consequence of imaginative predisposition or daydreaming tendency is a heightened tendency toward introspection and self-examination in connection with the external events that do occur.

Make-Believe Play and the Ego or Self-System

There may be a relationship of fantasy predisposition to the emergence of an ego or self-structure as part of the overall assimilative process. The fact of engaging in make-believe may help the child gain some distance between itself and the external environment, make a sharper differentiation between "what I do and play" and "what is out there." A manifestation of this trend in association with make-believe may be the fact that scales of manifest anxiety and other indicators of heightened self-awareness do seem to be associated with make-believe play in children (Sutton-Smith & Rosenberg, 1960; Singer, 1966; Schonbar, 1965; Wallach, 1970).

The notion of a consistent sense of "I" and "Who I am" and "What I do" is of course central to the general area of personality theory. It remains a question as to whether one's experience about oneself has significant consequences for overt behavior, something denied by more radical objective behaviorists. Nevertheless, as a distinctive quality of experience it certainly seems intrinsic in personality development. Engaging in make-believe play, by the very fact of its quality of shifting roles, that is, shifting between direct response to reality and the introduction of elements drawn essentially from long-term memory, coupled with the necessary distinctions between the toys played with and the objects imagined, all may begin to create a more differentiated sense of separation between self and environment.

As Piaget has noted, the very definition of symbolic play hinges on the child's ability to tell the difference between the cloth being put to sleep as a game and the real cloth. In some sense, the high-fantasy child within reasonable limits may be practicing a more acute differentiation of self and environment and may develop a heightened sense of self. In its more extreme forms, such a tendency could become self-consciousness and be evident in undue sensitivity or excessive introspection. Under most circumstances, self-awareness may have simply the value of enhancing effective distinctions between what comes from inside oneself in the way of fantasies and images and what is provided by the physical environment.

A variety of studies of discrimination between images and external signals or between self-generated responses and leakages of external stimuli in sensory-deprivation studies also suggest that persons initially experienced in fantasy and daydreaming or "tolerance for unreal experiences" are better able to distinguish between their own thoughts rather than to react as if they are hallucinating (Segal, 1971; Singer, 1966).

The child experienced and actively disposed toward make-believe play may also begin to develop a greater complexity in his use of stimuli. In a clinical study, Frankenstein (1962) argued that fantasy is best regarded as an important facet in the development of abstract thought. He stresses that the child through fantasy also is freed from a "concretistic attitude towards the world" and that "fantasy not only leads to the permanent discovery of a new relation ... [it] also creates the experience of values, because every connotation which has been imagined transcends in its value the object to which it is related [p. 15]."

This view of make-believe play as part of the cognitive skill development of the child can also be seen as useful in the acquisition of new behavior patterns and in other forms of social learning. The extensive work of Bandura and various colleagues on the importance of modeling in social learning has placed increased emphasis upon the symbolic modeling or covert mediational processing that takes place in the child (Bandura, 1971). Gerst (1971) in an ingenious study with young adults, was able to show that they could acquire information about a complex set of movements equally effective by either concise labeling which took the form of what Piaget might call a figurative conception or a high-order image or by vivid imagery itself. Both of these methods were clearly superior to merely trying to recall a detailed verbal account of each of the complex acts observed.

In situations where concise labeling or actual open rehearsal of observed behaviors is not practical, the *internal* rehearsal of behavior sequences has been shown to increase retention in formal experiments (Bandura, 1971; Michael & Maccoby, 1961). It seems likely that the high-fantasy child has developed a set toward utilizing more of what goes on in adult behavior for subsequent covert rehearsal and make-believe play and this almost certainly will lead to an increased sensitivity to some of the adult behavior patterns. In this sense, it represents a basis for later planning of social behavior.

By turning so much of what he observes into fantasy play situations, the high-imaginative-predisposition child may also sharpen his tendency to use various elements of the culture. So much of what has to go on in learning in the classroom or in the enjoyment of popular media or artistic activities also requires some degree of suspension of belief or the adoption of a playful attitude. In this sense, the high-fantasy child may be increasing his openness to using a greater variety of contents from the environment and also may be prepared more quickly to adapt to the structure of classroom teaching by example and by the narration of teachers.

Smilansky (1968) has formulated a long list of generalizations which reflect how *sociodramatic* play of children (which includes make-believe games in groups) influences the creativity, intellectual growth, and social skills of the child. Among these generalizations are the following:

1. Creating new combinations out of experiences.
2. Selectivity and intellectual discipline.
3. Discrimination of the central features of a role sequence.
4. Heightened concentration.
5. Enhanced self-awareness and self-control.
6. Self-discipline within the role context (e.g., a child playing a special role in the game may inhibit crying if he hurts himself because the character in the game would not ordinarily permit weeping under those circumstances).
7. The acquisition of flexibility and empathy toward others.
8. Development of an intrinsic set of standards.
9. Acquisition of a sense of creativity and capacity to control personal responses.
10. Development of cooperative skills since make-believe play games in groups require effective give and take.
11. Awareness of the potential use of the environment for planning and other play situations.
12. Increased sensitivity to alternative role possibilities so that the notion of a father need not be just one's own father, but may include many kinds of behavior that grow out of the game.
13. Increased capacity for development of abstract thought by learning first to substitute the image for overt action and then later a verbal coding system for both the action and the image.
14. Heightened capacity for generalization.
15. A set toward vicarious learning and greater use of modeling (Smilansky, 1968, pp. 13-15).

Smilansky writes:

> It is our contention . . . that the more a child engages in sociodramatic play the readier he is to participate in the "school game" . . . .
> In conclusion we can state that the child participating in the sociodramatic play profits at the same time by being actor, observer, and interacter. As an acter he is motivated to utilize his resources and create, but within limiting framework of the role and theme he learns intellectual discipline and self-control.

She goes on to emphasize the importance of empathic development and tolerance and a heightened sense of reality that are part of the overall process. The more elaborate practice of mimicry, gesticulation and various controlled motor activities as well as a more differentiated use of language also are part of this experience drawn from the sociodramatic play (Smilansky, 1968, p. 16).

By contrast with the elaborate advantages set forth here for the development of at least a moderately high degree of make-believe play predisposition in the child and the personality and cognitive implications noted, the child who shows very limited or relative lack of development of make-believe skills may emerge as somewhat handicapped in a variety of situations such as schooling that require a good deal of verbal emphasis, or social situations that require considerable self-control and the ability to restrain oneself during periods of waiting. This does not mean, however, that the child who is relatively low in his resort to make-believe play would necessarily develop in a pathological direction. There are many other kinds of social skills that one acquires in interaction with peers and in the course of learning the disciplines of games with rules or athletic games which enhance self-esteem and help to provide heightened self-awareness under specific circumstances. The studies present here make it clear that within normal children, the differences between high and low fantasy, while they are perhaps statistically significant, are not really tremendous nor are the children in the low-fantasy group apparently handicapped either in overall intellectual develop-ment or in the more gross kinds of social skills. At the same time, it is clear from the specific studies that the availability of make-believe as a resource increases the capacity of the child to enjoy solitary play and to deal somewhat more effectively with aroused anger or to show other aspects of self-control. Some indications that children with *very limited* fantasy tendencies may develop problems of impulsivity, antisocial behavior, or susceptibility to delinquency have been presented in studies by Meichenbaum (1971) and Spivak and Levine (1964).

To some extent, the presentation and speculation about the personality of children differing in predisposition to make-believe play and some of the conse-quences of this difference has been essentially general without a great deal of attention paid to different age levels. It would be possible to elaborate the speculation for each major sequence of age development to some extent that would move us beyond the purpose of this volume. The major intent of this presentation is as a stimulant to further research and theoretical examinations of the issue of make-believe play.

We are quite frankly not yet in a position to make any kind of definitive statement about the significance of imaginative play predispositions at differing ages and also about how this tendency becomes a part of the subsequent daydream pattern of the adolescent and young adult. If anything, our research on daydreaming patterns (Singer & Antrobus, 1963, 1972) makes it all too clear that there are a number of different dimensions of fantasy in the adult. Fairly consistently, one can detect patterns which include a positive accepting attitude toward daydreaming as one dimension. A second grouping involves a tendency

to have considerable amount of daydreaming associated with guilt and obsessional rumination and self-doubt. A third dimension reveals daydreaming linked
to considerable anxiety and difficulty in controlling one's thought without any
richness of content. It seems very likely that at various points in development
the tendency toward high fantasy predisposition intersects with other complex
developmental experiences and personality styles or defense developments and
specific traumatic social or learning experiences.

Make-Believe and Specific Personality Traits

Let us speculate further on some of the possible ways in which the development of imaginative predisposition may relate to broader personality variables.
We have argued that initial development of make-believe play tendencies in any
consistent degree hinges on identification with at least one stable parent figure
and also with opportunities for privacy and practice of this prior to involvement
in more sociodramatic activities with other children. It would seem unlikely that
a high degree of imaginative predisposition would develop in a child growing up
in circumstances of extreme disorganization in the household or under circumstances where there was not at least the foundation of relationship of what
Erikson (1963) calls "basic trust" between mother and child. This does not
preclude the possibility that a dependent child or an overprotected only child or
first-born might not develop imaginative play capacities and remain closely
attached to a parent. At the same time, it is likely that under such circumstances
the use of the make-believe skills will gradually take the form of an increasing
escapist tendency or isolation from social activity and a marked social as well as
thinking introversion pattern may emerge.

Sometimes the parents' own needs may play a role in producing a highly
introverted and socially isolated child whose major resource is make-believe play.
This is the case frequently when a parent has some "hidden agenda" which calls
for the child to remain in perpetual association. This might be the case where a
mother feels no relationship to her husband or is widowed or isolated in other
ways and sees the son or daughter as her long-time companion. In such an
instance, it is entirely possible that the child will be encouraged in fantasy
activities and make-believe, provided with stories and a wealth of toys for private
play, frequently under the guise of this being the most suitable thing for such a
brilliant child or that the neighbors are "beneath one." In these instances it
seems very likely that a somewhat more pathological trend in fantasy play may
develop with, however, the possibility that the social isolation may later be made
up for in part by a change in the child's circumstances or some independent
struggle for freedom from the mother. Emergence from such a situation may
leave the child somewhat behind socially, but able to be aware and trying to
make up the gap without necessarily losing the skill in ideational fluency that
has been developed. Occasional biographical accounts of the lives of famous

writers or artists suggest some situations of this type as having occurred. The biographical note by Auden (1965) certainly hints at some such pattern.

In a sense, what is suggested is that the development of imaginal skills may often be associated with a strongly developed Oedipus complex in the more traditional Freudian usage of the term. It is not implied here that the Oedipus stage is an inevitable one in all human development. If anything, it seems more likely that it is the outcome of specific parental orientations rather than something which each child brings to his developmental experience.

The affective tone that prevails in a family setting may also determine in part how the skill of ideational fluency, which a child is developing out of the high imaginative play predisposition encouraged by a given family, may be expressed. For example, there may be a family setting in which the greatest emphasis is upon control of emotionality and upon limitations of exuberance and positive affect. Such a family may employ a kind of cynical approach or use humiliation and contempt as a means of discipline. The child exposed to these situations who is at the same time imaginatively predisposed or encouraged along these lines by the parents may develop a fantasy pattern that is more characterized by obsessional rumination, guilt, and fantasies of achievement as well as great concern about fear of failure. Children encouraged to express positive affect or exposed to a good deal of laughter and humor on the part of parental figures may find that fantasy takes on a much more positive affective tone and is associated with considerable playfulness and fanciful make-believe. The data from the factor analysis of a variety of daydreaming scales developed in our broader research project (Singer & Antrobus, 1972) suggest that it is possible that a person highly developed and given to a good deal of daydreaming may show extreme obsessional rumination, feelings of guilt, as well as heroic fantasies, daydreams of failure and achievement, and a more generally tortured inner life. At the other extreme, one finds persons quite accepting of their daydreaming activities, showing considerably more positive affect and vividness of visual and auditory images as characteristics of their daydreaming. These two poles may represent also the kind of distinction between the "left" and "right" polarities or negative versus positive affective polarities described by Tomkins (1965).

Make-Believe and Creativity

If we consider high fantasy predisposition in relation to creativity, we see at once certain obvious similarities. These have been pointed out by Wallach (1970). It seems likely that for the range of intelligence above the normal level, the tendency to engage in daydreaming is largely a function of a separate divergent thinking or ideational fluency factor. On the other hand, one must make a distinction between daydreaming, make-believe as one dimension and a general creative or ideational fluency which may be reflected in quite a different realm and may not call as much for the type of make-believe which we have emphasized. Skill in mathematical creativity, originality in the design of engines or in dealing with fiscal aspects of the environment need not coincide with the kind of experience in make-believe play that we have discussed. We do know from the studies of Helson (1965) and Schaefer (1969) that there are indications that young people who have been designated as creative particularly in artistic areas turn out to have had more imaginative play activity or daydreaming as children at least on the basis of their own recollections.

Obviously, this whole area merits considerable further research that attempts to tease out the special differences that may occur in make-believe play or in other types of play between children whose associational fluidity is expressed in interpersonal and social-role-type games as against those children whose associational fluidity and even their make-believe may take a form more oriented around physical environment objects. We wonder to what extent the development of an attitude to be creative may be fostered initially by the same sets of early emphasis on make-believe or fantasy or symbolic play. Later exposure to different kinds of parental models, some more involved with manipulation of the physical environment in actuality or symbolically and others more oriented toward ideational or interpersonal realms, may lead children to rather different types of creative orientations.

It is quite possible that make-believe predisposition in children with its linkage to reflective style and long sampling may develop a child who is playful (Lieberman, 1965) but at the same time not as grossly physically active as the child or young adolescent low in imaginative predisposition. This same general style may be reflected also in tastes in types of playthings as already noted. The imaginatively predisposed child may prefer both toys and other types of playthings including reading materials that allow scope for reflection and for introduction of make-believe aspects or for imaginative activities. Such a child may be somewhat less interested in games with rules or gambling games where the focus is on speed of reaction and speed of decision.

It should be clear, however, that imaginative predisposition does not preclude the development of skills in a great variety of areas including athletic skills, skills in areas such as artistic work, sewing, and cooking. It would be a serious error to overemphasize imaginative predisposition as a fundamental dimension or skill overlooking the many complex kinds of possibilities to which a child is exposed. The high fantasy child may be somewhat more inclined towards a creative set and perhaps less toward being a producer or performer in ways that involve extensive manipulative activities. However, certainly it is possible that life experiences will set up situations in which both types of activity are possible.

For example, a child who is talented musically may spend a considerable amount of time practicing and, by the very nature of the atmosphere built around his being a talented musician at an early age, he may be encouraged to lead a much more secluded or socially isolated life. Hence he might have greater opportunity to develop fantasy activities and make-believe fantasies, very likely built around music. Such a child might become both a skilled musician and a creative composer of music.

The development of considerable skill in a specific activity, however, does not always mean great complexity of fantasy life in other areas. A case in point may be deduced from the newspaper accounts of the great American chess player, Bobby Fischer. Without knowing actual details of his life, other than from what is presented in the press, it would appear that he is obviously spending a tremendous amount of time engaging in internal fantasy activity built around chess and the actual working out of chess matches in his mind. This seems to have been the case since he was at least 10 years old. Newspaper descriptions do not report him as engaging in much extensive rumination about many other things. He seems to have narrowed his life down in terms of range of interests to a remarkable degree. The single-mindedness of his focus on chess is reported as being one of his major assets as a competitive player.

Make-believe play predisposition and fantasy tendencies in later life are much more usually set within a broader and more complex personality orientation. In that sense, these dispositions may contribute to a greater range of personal enjoyment, defense against anxiety and fear, or creativity in a range of social situations as well as in some occupational or artistic development. The essential point is that if we regard make-believe play and its subsequent development as an "as if" attitude or capacity for fantasy and daydreaming *as a skill* rather than as the outcome of some conflict, we can see this skill as being available within the personality repertory for a great variety of functions. Just as any skill can be used to avoid areas of conflict with other persons, socially beneficial purposes, or self-advancement as well as for destructive purposes, so too the skill in fantasizing may be put into the service of a great range of human desires.

It seems likely that more harm is done by attempts to discourage development of imaginative predisposition in children or by what is more likely the simple failure to encourage it in any systematic way as part of the growing child's behavioral repertory. This point has been made most cogently by Smilansky (1968) in her comparison of disadvantaged and educationally advantaged children in Israel. It remains to be seen whether her very strong stand in favor of building sociodramatic play into the curriculum of nursery and kindergarten is supportable by subsequent research. Nevertheless, it seems more reasonable that this direction be taken rather than that we continue to emphasize the defensive or conflict expressing aspects of make-believe play in children, an emphasis which has grown out of the popularity of individual case histories in which play therapy was involved.

Even famous clinical cases such as *Tommy the Space-Child* (Ekstein, 1966) or the adolescent girl in *I Never Promised You a Rose Garden* (Green, 1964) who are presented as having wild fantasy lives, may be viewed somewhat differently from this perspective. It may be possible to regard their ultimate recovery and capacity to live reasonably normal lives and to find expressions for themselves in society because of the strengths they brought into therapy in the area of imaginativeness. Tommy emerges as a space scientist and Hannah as a fine writer. Their capacity for make-believe in their childhood and adolescence which found expression in extremely bizarre fantasies did not really impede the therapeutic course. If anything, by providing much material that the therapist could use and establishing a playful atmosphere that could be incorporated into the therapy, it increased the therapist's interest in the patient and the likelihood that some type of effective communication would be established. Therefore, this make-believe skill also leaves a patient, once some of the distressing conflicts have been worked out, with an ability that can later be used in a more socially effective fashion.

CHAPTER IX

Some Practical Implications of Make-Believe Play

Implications for Child Rearing

By moving well beyond the very limited data in this field to the discussion of some practical implications, one risks misleading the reader who is not sophisticated about the limitations of methodology in psychology. At the same time I believe that important new directions in research come about only as we confront the practical implications of many of our theoretical notions in psychology. For example, while Piaget's work has been important in generating theoretical notions about child development, much of his work still requires far more extensive empirical tests than have been carried out either by himself or even in the flurry of activity in recent years by experimentally oriented investigators. At the same time the serious effort to apply concepts such as his to actual educational procedures may force upon both the educators and educational researchers or learning theorists a confrontation between novel and original concepts of development and practical questions of teaching in learning. The likelihood is that newer and more significant approaches to research will be generated and that more systematic teaching methods may also emerge.

This faith underlines my attempt in this final chapter to indicate some of the practical possibilities growing out of our exploration of the work on imaginative play in children and also out of my personal experience in attempting to do this research, in observing children and in collaborating with others in my research at various points.

The exposure to this problem has forced me to feel that more consistent attention ought to be paid by parents to the spontaneous play behavior of their children and indeed to establishing models of make-believe play and introducing make-believe materials for the children's use. Importance of a close and continuing relationship between the child and the mother cannot be stressed enough. This relationship should be one in which the mother recognizes the desirability of a playful approach to the child with a certain amount of smiling and peek-a-boo activities.

The Origins of Frightening or Aggressive Fantasies

A distinction needs to be made between playful games and little storytelling activities such as those designed to get the child to open its mouth and eat the cereal and more extended teasing which often characterizes the behavior of adults toward children. I have observed on the whole a marked decline in extended teasing activities of younger children at least by young adults and older children in recent years. It certainly was true that a regular part of much of the adult and older child interplay with very young children led to many kinds of frightening playful activity or teasing. Threats to put little girls in the closet or to throw little babies into the toilet and flush them down, "pulling off" an ear or nose in simulated fashion and then seeming to display it by rapid tricks of finger movement are things that were very commonly a part of adult–child interaction and may still be in many segments of society. These undoubtedly evoke tremendous fears in children some of which may later become basis for the make-believe kinds of games described so well by the Opies (1969) in their discussion of dramatic play.

Freud attempted to revise his theory after finding that many hysterical symptoms could not be traced directly to early childhood trauma. He went to the other extreme in suggesting that much of the child's fantasies about castration fears and the Oedipal situations were relatively inborn and biologically rooted so that they inevitably emerged at some point with or without adult intervention. There is probably good reason to believe that adults' teasing behavior and their playful or even direct threats play much more of a role in what becomes the more frightening, mysterious or dark side of children's fantasy play activities. It is my belief that adults very often show poor judgment about the things they say to children at early ages or about the kinds of threats they make or the kinds of angry conversations between adults which they permit children to overhear. I believe it is *this* material which the child then attempts to assimilate in grossly exaggerated or distorted form into his narrow range of schemata. These assimilations lay the basis for the many kinds of frightening images which do occur in children's play as well as for the kind of aggressive quality that make-believe often has and which then becomes a part of ongoing children's play in groups. Naturally to the extent that the child can elaborate and extend on these distortions in make-believe games, the degree of fear associated with the material may be reduced by its increased familiarity and its further assimilation into make-believe settings. It can then be seen as a part of an unreal world. It is the child, who after exposure to this frightening material does not have the subsequent opportunity for extended rehearsal and elaboration, who may become more frightened or more likely to act directly on aggressive suggestions made by parents.

Positive Aspects of Parental Interaction

The opportunity to play make-believe games or to hear stories from the mother or the father or some parent surrogate on a consistent basis may also help the child perceive interaction between parent and child as a pleasant exchange—as something to be looked forward to—and also may open the child toward acceptance of other kinds of make-believe activities or instruction which are inevitably a part of the educational process in a broader sense. It may also prepare the child more readily to seek out additional storytelling outlets in the form of reading materials.

Still another advantage of fanciful modeling by adults is that it establishes the basis for the child approaching the play situation with other children in a more positive and constructive manner. As adults we tend to overlook the degree to which children confronted with each other at very young ages simply do not have sufficient behavioral responses in their repertory to make the interaction meaningful. In this sense it often becomes a function of chance as to whether a contact between two children may turn into a painful experience for one or both and may lead to conflict or to the development of fears of further social interchange. Merely plunking two toddlers down next to each other will not necessarily do either one of them any good. If, however, one or both have already had some experience in make-believe play or in different types of organized games they may find that they can sit quietly next to each other, each engaging in his own game, or occasionally begin to exchange games in a reasonably satisfactory fashion.

A mother should be especially sensitive to her child's play style. Her child may be oriented already toward fairly extended play, whether this is as simple as lining up dolls next to each other in a neat fashion on the table or putting out a set of teacups in an orderly fashion as if preparing for a meal or building a rather elaborate block fortress. If such a child is left in a situation with another child who has no experience of this kind and who is likely to be disruptive of the game, even with the best of intentions, the mother should be prepared to intervene in some useful fashion. She may either teach the new child to play the game or help her own child to find some other area to play where the game will be less disrupted. Naturally some give and take is important in development, and the child must be prepared to accept some frustration in its attempt to play make-believe games. It seems silly, however, to expose the child consistently to frustration in this area if one wants the make-believe play to continue at all.

As suggested earlier, children also need content as part of their make-believe play games and, in general, the richer content available the more kinds of assimilative activities will go on and the more novel and interesting the child's private environment becomes during a free-play situation. Our observations of the play of very young children suggest that they are frequently at a loss for how to amuse themselves or how to find novelty in given situations and that under those circumstances they frequently become distressed and cling to adults. It would therefore seem valuable for the child to be exposed as much as possible not only to the possibilities of make-believe play but also to a variety of interesting content which can become the basis for make-believe games. This kind of content of course comes from stories, picture books, and television.

Television Viewing

What stance should the mother take toward the popular media, such as television? There has been a great deal of heat generated by the concern over appropriate television material not to mention the kinds of reading material to which children are exposed. Obviously one of the major questions has to do with the extent to which exposure to television materials generates aggressive tendencies in children or excessive anxieties or sexual arousal. I have elsewhere reviewed extensively the literature up until 1970 or 1971 on the question of the relation of television and movies to overt aggressive behavior (Singer, 1971a). While no simple conclusions can be drawn on the basis of our current knowledge it does seem unlikely that one can say that all kinds of aggressive materials expressed in fiction on television are necessarily harmful to children. Indeed it is hard to see how many complex and interesting stories could be told via the popular media without involving some degree of conflict between characters and even adventurous rescues and the possibility of violence.

A great deal would appear to depend on the parents' preparation of the child for the television viewing experience. For one thing, *moderate* exposure to television under fairly definite parental control of viewing time should be of value to the child. It enriches the scope of content to which the child is exposed and increases the likelihood of his acquiring a vocabulary and greater range of imagery. Provided that the child does not sit in front of the television at all times during his waking life he will in private moments alone or with other children play out some of the materials seen on television and work this into enjoyable make-believe play situations. In a number of instances our 3- and 4-year-old subjects in the nursery school showed effective use of story material taken from television in playing games which seem to give them great enjoyment during free-play periods.

If television material is clearly identifiable as make-believe it will prove less frightening and certainly less provocative of overt aggressive behavior in the children. This hypothesis is suggested by several research survey findings and by more recent unpublished work still in progress by Dr. Seymour Feshbach of the University of California at Los Angeles. Thus, characters on television who are clearly perceived as make-believe (such as cowboys, knights in armor, and pirates) and who are easily labeled as such from their dress by the children and who also can be further identified as such by the parents viewing along with the children, will become the basis for extensive make-believe play of a very fruitful kind. There may be relatively little generalization of the negative content to the immediate day-to-day experience of the child. On the other hand, scenes involving direct conflict between other young children, scenes of knife fighting between adolescents, conflict between parents or robbery scenes taking place in settings almost identical to those in which the children themselves live would appear especially dangerous and frightening and possibly also provocative of overt aggressive behavior. If there is to be some kind of overt censorship or at least self-censorship on the part of public media then it should be over content that is relatively readily generalizable, frightening, and aggressive material. To ban stories based on jousting between ancient knights seems quite far-fetched indeed, however.

A special point must be made in connection with television depictions of violence in news broadcasts or documentaries. An alert parent might take the precaution of maintaining some control over this type of material as available to relatively young children.

Scenes of soldiers being shot in Vietnam, of the execution of prisoners, or of orphan children following either war or natural disaster ought to be kept from children of relatively early ages. We have as yet very little formal evidence on the impact of news coverage and documentary materials but again Dr. Feshbach's research suggests that material presented as *true* will be more provocative of overt imitation than material perceived as fiction.

A special word needs also to be said about material that might fall somewhat on the borderline between the grossly fictional and realistic. Not long ago there was a popular series on television called "Dark Shadows." This story was sometimes cast in modern dress and sometimes in nineteenth century costume—a costume style which has, along with longer hair, rapidly become relatively undistinguishable from present day dress. This afternoon series was replete with weird happenings: ghosts, vampires literally sucking blood from the necks of attractive girls, Zombies, hands reaching up from within graves, people becoming werewolves at the full of the moon, etc. This type of material while holding fascination for adolescents and obviously attracting a large national audience seemed likely to be unassimilable and extremely frightening to children below the ages of 12 or 13.

Here again is a situation in which great parental concern is required. The same kind of concern seems necessary in exposing children to other types of horror movies which hold their popularity on television particularly for adolescents. The point is that adolescents have already developed a sufficiently differentiated set of schemata so that while they may be momentarily caught up in a story and terribly frightened, that fright merges on a positively rising gradient of surprise and novelty and is very quickly integrated and related to their well-established knowledge of what is real and unreal. This is less likely to be the case for young children for whom such scenes become then the basis for later nightmares, night terrors, and phobic reactions. This is all the more likely to be true for those children who have little experience with make-believe play and therefore little opportunity to take these frightening scenes and work them into the story lines of ongoing fantasy play activities.

Children already oriented toward make-believe will be able to take better advantage of what is presented on television not only to increase their make-believe activities but also as part of the enjoyment of the show and the reduction of high tension levels. This notion is exemplified in the findings reported in the chapter by Biblow. Pending further research in this area, the data may serve as a basis for encouragement of at least moderate degrees of fantasy play, recognizing the interaction between this predisposition and the positive advantages of television viewing.

Toys and the Play Setting

In connection with the early experience of the child let us now consider some of the implications of imaginative play in connection with the use of various toys. The value of some relatively simple playthings of a manipulative and colorful nature for even the youngest infant in the crib has been discussed at length by various writers on the early sensory experience of the child. Piaget long ago called attention to the significant role of objects in the immediate environment of the infant which served to focus attention and also to yield some gross attempts at manipulation. Such objects as blankets or furry animals are early adopted by most children in late infancy and later toddler stages as companions, being dragged around from room to room or being sought anxiously if they are missing at bedtime. Much of the initial significance of these objects seems to be related to their tactile qualities. This issue has been extensively studied in the famous research by Harlow (1958) on the cloth mothers for baby monkeys.

Very soon, however, in the case of the human child the security blanket or fuzzy Teddy begin to be treated not simply as comfortable objects to hold but also as somewhat living companions. Human feelings or attitudes are often attributed to them relatively early. Some of these manifestations represent the child's inability to separate its own affective experiences from those of the objects and this results in what Werner has termed the "physiognomic" response.

We can see the beginnings of make-believe in the transition from the use of the fur cloth merely as a tactile comforter through its use as a make-believe companion or as a plaything that can be "put to sleep" (Gilmore, 1966). in this way the child becomes aware of certain shapes or positions of the object. These shapes now take on some similarities to facial expressions or body postures associated with affects. With the boundary difficulty that the child already has to start with (Blatt & Ritzler, 1972), it is a natural next step to attribute life to the object.

Thus a cloth bent over in an odd shape may be recognized by the child as similar to its own position when weeping or when frustrated. The teddy bear with its head bent over its legs may also be perceived as in a sad position by the child. This combination of the physical structure and the readiness of the child to attribute its own feelings to the object heightens the sense of its being alive. Indeed at this point, then, if it is alive for the child it becomes available as a playmate or companion and the beginnings of make-believe are undoubtedly discernable at this point. This same physiognomic attribution process so evident in the young child has of course become a part of our esthetic experience. We describe a particular tree as "a weeping willow" and this is not hard for most people to imagine as they gaze at the drooping foliage of this lovely bit of flora which so resembles the shape of a saddened human being and conveys the tears coming down one's cheeks. Poets talk of their hearts "dancing with the daffodils" and this "pathetic fallacy" is central to many of our famous poems and literary masterpieces.

In the beginning, therefore, the child requires relatively little of a complex nature in order to be stimulated toward the development of make-believe uses for objects such as fluffy bears or little pillows. They soon become somewhat animated and the basis for some communication between the child and the objects especially at nap times and bedtime. One can in these circumstances overhear little conversations on the part of the child set down to nap which often enough take place between the child and the teddy bear or the security blanket. Here is the conversation of a child aged 1½ (this child seems somewhat precocious):

> *Go grandma and buy a pretty doll grandma for me under the bed for me to play the piano . . . Get up cling-ling-ling. Grandma comes up the steps. Oh Oh Ah Ah Ah lying on the floor all tied up no cap on Theodosia [the doll] lie on the bed, bring yellow sheep to Theodosia run, tap tap tap for Lena. Strawberries, Grandma, wolf lie on bed. Go to sleep darling Theodosia you are my dearest; everybody is fast asleep. . . . A cat came in here, momma caught it, it had feet and black boots on–short cap, band on it. Poppa ran, the sky–grandma gone– grandpa resting–* [Groos, 1901, p. 138].

For the young child a few little playthings like the security blankets or the teddy bears and other relatively simple and manipulative objects which are not easily broken or too complex and specific in their functions quickly become things that are parts of the comfortable simple world the child builds around its rituals of eating and sleeping. Soon the very process of going to sleep is frequently not possible unless the playthings are present to relieve the loneliness of that period of lights out and darkness. For the next few years one can see the infant becoming the toddler and small child clinging to certain limited objects in order to ensure a sense of companionship and similarity in confronting the frightening "nowhere" of the sleep period, night after night. Eventually, however, the child moves to a stage where there may be some embarrassment about the persistence of this ritual particularly under circumstances where the child must sleep in strange homes at a relatively advanced age.

The power of this need for companionship and security should not be lost upon us, however. Even though the child does give up the security blanket (sometimes reduced to just a little square of cloth carried around in the play purse of a little girl), society does afford outlets later in life for the recurrence of this pattern. One need only look around at the rooms of teenage girls or at college dormitories where one is sure to find a great collection of stuffed animals in various sizes and shapes, depending on affluence. The pleasures of the marital bed for both women and men go far beyond the actual sexual satisfactions and erotic stimulation to reflect a great deal of the quality of security and closeness to a companion that we see early manifested in the bedtime rituals of children.

The availability of at least some toys at a relatively early age should undoubtedly enhance the likelihood of make-believe play for the young child by providing additional complex stimuli which can be part of the assimilation process when the child is alone. Obviously toys that involve some resemblance to living objects are especially helpful since they require less of a great leap of the child and have an immediate attraction for it. At the same time it seems generally the case that the favorite toys of young children are not excessively specific in their function. It was this kind of observation that prompted the suggestions leading to the research by Dr. Pulaski described in an earlier chapter. The toys that are clung to most and last the longest for children of toddler and preschool age tend to be dolls or stuffed animals.

Sometimes oddly shaped tree branches will become favorite outdoor playthings and be given names and used for periods of time. In writing this section I recalled an experience long forgotten in which a small rounded stick partially red in color whose original function I have not been able to recall became a regular companion of mine in solitary play and was guarded by me zealously with my other toys during middle childhood. It served as a knife or sword in adventure games and occasionally was given human characteristics in other games which I can only dimly remember at this point. I recently encountered a lad of 13 walking along the road in our neighborhood with a somewhat odd-shaped twig which he identified for me as "Terry." He said this quite humorously and yet it was at the same time obvious from our conversation that he still enjoyed the chance to indulge in a bit of fantasy that this twig was a kind of make-believe companion.

Once children reach the age of at least 2 or 2½, the toys that they are given tend to take on somewhat more realistic shapes. Thus boys receive toy automobiles, airplanes, boats, or various make-believe soldiers of tin or plastic. Girls are more likely to receive dolls of various types and cooking utensils or household furniture. Clearly the sex typing and role development associated with make-believe is established very early and fostered very much by the type of plaything provided the child.

This question of the development of sex role through the make-believe play fostered in the very shape of the toys provided boys and girls from the ages of 2 on is really worth quite an extended treatment and runs beyond the scope of what can be attempted here. If one could find a group of girls brought up strictly on boys' toys without opportunities to play with household objects or to have a variety of dolls, it would be interesting to see whether they develop the "maternal instinct" which is so characteristic of girls' play.

There is probably a subtle and curvilinear relationship between the degree of realism of a toy and its usefulness in stimulating imaginative behavior on the part of the child. One might surmise that a toy that is very well-delineated, colorful and immediately suggests its function to a young child would have a strong attraction. At the same time the very specificity of its function should ultimately limit the later uses of the toy once the particular game has lost its excitement and the child seeks to develop other types of play situations. Similarly, one might surmise that the availability of some fairly specific toys would encourage make-believe play on the part of the children and therefore that children with somewhat greater number of toys more or less specific in nature would be inclined toward a greater degree of sociodramatic play.

The fundamental research resolving many of these questions still remains to be done. In the study by Pulaski, it is clear that the children engage in a greater variety of make-believe games when confronted by a room in which the playthings are all minimally structured. That is to say, when there are no very strict functions of the toys that are available to them, the children make up more different kinds of make-believe play games at least in the case of solitary play as studied in this investigation. Pulaski's study also makes it clear that a most unusual, if highly specific toy with a great many components has a strong appeal to both boys and girls and stimulates a considerable amount of make-believe play. This is the case for the toy garage in her study. In would be interesting to trace the "natural history" of playthings of this type to see over a period of time how long they continue to attract the play behavior of children and to stimulate extended make-believe games. Part of the attraction of the toy garage in Pulaski's study was the fact that it lent itself to a certain amount of motor activity as well. The children could move cars up and down the ramp and out of the garage. Would they have continued to play with this in an imaginative way for weeks or months to come if this were one of a relatively limited number of toys available?

We know, of course, that certain toys do have long-standing values and do engender considerable make-believe play for children over many months or indeed years. Doll houses (usually for affluent girls) even though fairly specific in their function, are nevertheless set up in such a way that a great variety of make-believe themes can be enacted in relation to the structure. Toy castles or forts or airports lend themselves similarly to a fairly extended life in the sense that many different kinds of games can be enacted around the central structure. At the same time, even without such definite geographical functions, a set of Playskool blocks of various simple wooden geometric shapes for many children may turn out to be the most long lasting of all playthings. They are not easily broken. Even if a few are lost the basic block structure permits many different constructions. They lend themselves to games of pure construction, but also can become part, along with dolls and toy soldiers or toy cars or airplanes, of almost any kind of extended make-believe play activity. It is my guess that such relatively nonspecific and flexible toys lend themselves best of all to long-term use and can stimulate make-believe play if mixed with fairly specific playthings such as dolls and other human-like objects. Some basic awareness of this is reflected in the regular use in nursery schools and day care centers of the doll corner and the block corner which generally attract boys and girls differentially although it is likely that this sex difference is less obvious in the earlier years.

It is intriguing that a recent movement in outdoor architecture has led to the development of many new approaches to playgrounds for children. Architects such as David Gates of San Francisco and Richard Dattner of New York have begun with the assumption that public play areas for children should stimulate imaginative play. They are experimenting with a variety of specific and non-specific formats designed to be conducive to imaginative play. Dattner, for example, has built an "ancient play garden" with an Egyptian motif complete with sand and water, forts, and obelisks that will stand outside the Egyptian temple at New York's Metropolitan Museum of Art. As soon as possible one ought to start systematic observations of the play of children in such a setting to see if it is happier, more imaginative, and more varied as the architect assumes!

A special aspect in the choice of toys has to do with concern about the use of warlike or violent implements. Some of the questions raised in this connection are broadly philosophical or ethical and cannot easily be answered simply from the standpoint of psychological research. For example, there might be the question as to whether any society, if it is genuinely peace loving, ought to make available warlike toys or games as part of its instructional role in the play development of children. We simply do not know at this point whether exposure to games of a warlike or violent nature in the make-believe category do indeed foster later tendencies toward warlike development in adults.

There have been protests by groups of parents against the use of and sale of toys involving implements of war such as bazookas or hand grenades or quite recently against the sale of toys which involved weird torture (a pendulum such as used by Poe in his famous tale) or guillotine-like instruments of execution. Elaborate mechanical monsters of various kinds are generally for sale and these, too, have been denounced by parent groups. While a peace loving and esthetically oriented person might be repulsed by such toys, it is still a question for empirical tests whether they have any especially negative effect upon children either in the way of promoting sadistic tendencies or creating fears and night terrors.

It is my impression that monster toys have an initial attraction for children, but that they do not yield any extensive make-believe play for several reasons. First, their very specificity leads their value to be exhausted after the child has played with them just a few times. Second, their construction, with heavy reliance on complex mechanical structure, leads them to break sometimes within minutes after they are used and so they simply become heaps of tin lying around on the child's toy shelf. It appears that the continued sale and popularity of these items is largely a function of their attraction for vulgar and tasteless relatives who purchase them for children. Their purchase is also sustained by television commercials which give the children the impression that the toys are much larger and much more realistic and effective as playthings than they turn out to be in practice.

Whether children are stimulated toward aggressiveness by playing with toy soldiers or toy weapons of various types is not easily answered at this point. It is obvious that games involving competition and war are very much central to the play behavior of most children in Western civilization. After all, our most peaceful yet intellectual games such as chess are also built around the war model. We simply do not know how many of the children who grew up playing elaborate battle games with toy soldiers emerged as military leaders or statesmen eager to set great armies in motion. Certainly the likelihood is that the vast majority of children who play such games never go on to overt destructive or aggressive behavior. It is hard to separate the whole question of sex role from the type of make-believe toy employed and so we cannot be sure that giving dolls to girls and toy soldiers to boys inevitably fosters their subsequent differences in aggressive behavior.

The fact that so much of our history and legendry is built around conflict and war, adventurous exploration, etc., means that the kinds of story material generally available to children and generally attracting their interest will involve some degree of make-believe violence. It is my own hunch at this point that the enjoyment of a great variety of make-believe often enough involving war or conflict is perhaps less significant in the later development of aggression in man than is the exposure of the child to direct models of violence in the behavior of parents, of older siblings or in early direct training in violent behavior which is part of our "frontier heritage."

More specifically, it is one thing to give children make-believe soldiers, *toy* rifles or *toy* forts. Many children, however, who are very young, are provided with *real* rifles and other actual destructive weapons such as bows and arrows or hunting knives and are taught from an early age to hunt and to practice their marksmanship. I would feel safer with a lot of children in the neighborhood actually playing make-believe war games with toy soldiers or even clambering around rocks and shooting at each other with toy guns than to have a 6- or 7-year-old shooting a small .22 caliber rifle at a target in the next yard. We need much more research on these questions, but pending this, I propose that make-believe play represents an important alternative and step away from overt aggressive tendencies, while the direct training of children in the use of weapons may play a much more significant role in the violence that has been so characteristic of our nation.

Implications for Childhood Education and Day Care Centers

It appears that the United States may be moving into an era of much greater concern for the welfare of its children than has ever before been the case. Despite the belief that Americans indulge the younger generations through great freedom, varieties of playthings, and minimal early physical labor, there is evidence that there has been great neglect of children in our society. The recent Head Start program turned up thousands of cases of serious physical disability because of its requirement that medical examination be provided for its participants. Quite apart from extensive evidence of nutritional defects and infant or child mortality rates in this country being well above those of other somewhat less affluent European nations, there are also indications that attention to child care in the form of extensive training both of child-care workers and parents for their own child-care roles have been seriously neglected for large segments of the American population. The new legislation now moving through Congress toward the establishment of child-care centers and the training of increased child-care workers may signal a new step ahead in American society in this respect in the coming years.

The increased likelihood that a fairly high percentage of children will be attending some type of day care center for working mothers either in community, neighborhood, housing projects, or on many university campuses should make it increasingly possible for us to observe the spontaneous play of children and to understand much more about the nature of child development than has been the case in the past. In addition, we should be in a better position to begin some types of improved training for children built right into their early play experiences that can make up some of the psychological deficits characteristic of children from a severely impoverished background or that can generally enhance the cognitive capacities and affective development of all children.

In this connection, the value of early exposure to sociodramatic play would seem specially useful. I have earlier summarized some of the very effective arguments proposed by Smilansky (1968) in favor of a program of sociodramatic play as part of the nursery school curriculum. These need not be repeated again, but the point should be emphasized that make-believe games can be taught and can become an important part of the child's repertory for a variety of cognitive functions. As Freyberg's study demonstrated, the children who were taught make-believe game plays in only "six sessions" showed a striking increase in their enjoyment of their play and in their capacity for imaginative productions in their play. Smilansky's emphasis is also upon the social learning aspects of make-believe play and its advantages to the child in preparing it not only for enjoying it in interaction with peers, but also for more effective use of regular classroom teaching experiences.

One of the questions that might be raised here is how much should the child's development be a function of its freedom to engage in spontaneous play and how much of the early childhood care should involve some more systematic training in make-believe games. We lack formal data on this point, again something that begs for research. In my own opinion, children can benefit greatly from opportunities for modeling and some initial formal structure in the development of make-believe play. That is, children do not automatically learn how to play even though a certain amount of make-believe develops from the intrinsic nature of childhood growth. Children can be seen as frequently interfering with each other's ability to concentrate and to generate extended sequences of make-believe. In this sense, early exposure to a variety of interesting themes and games provided by the teachers can help the children to play out sequences either uninterrupted by others or, what is more likely, to develop more mutually satisfying extended sequences of play.

Watching children play in both middle-class and lower socioeconomic group nurseries has suggested that at least some of the time what passes for creative activities, presenting the children with paints or bead stringing, is often enough not terribly interesting to the child and somewhat wasteful of its time. It would seem quite likely that more attention to the organization of make-believe games and some help for the children in learning to play these by themselves or in small groups with others would be more effective in establishing an atmosphere that has a greater degree of excitement and positive affect than the somewhat aimless and random behavior that one does observe among nursery school children.

I believe there is a mystique that complete freedom generates the best in children. As far as I can see, this is essentially some type of wish or myth held by many liberal individuals. It seems more likely that the child's capacity toward creativeness requires at least some degree of stimulation and formal structure to allow it to move beyond the limitations of the limited number of schemata available to any given child. In this sense, the adult can maximize the interaction of accommodation and assimilation patterns producing much greater rich and differentiated cognitive and affective structure.

If one is to put such a policy into effect, then clearly one must also begin some more extensive training of the child care workers, many of whom are likely to be of only limited educational levels and lacking themselves in some of the childhood experiences of sociodramatic play. These workers as well as many kindergarten and nursery school teachers more formally educated, probably can benefit from specific training in how to develop increased skills at make-believe in their children. Naturally the use of storytelling is extremely effective as well as reading of stories of a simple type. But the actual modeling of make-believe games may prove even more effective since very young children have limited attention spans especially in groups and cannot listen for very long periods either to stories or to material being read to them. The active involvement of teachers who are teacher's aides in some forms of carefully thought out make-believe games may provide an increased basis for the children's later use of these games and for the development on the part of the children of a series or repertoire of make-believe play situations.

A similar kind of attention may be necessary even for mothers who are caring for their own children at home or for women who undertake care of a group of small children in their own residences. Indeed, the day care program can never really be large enough to involve all children in our society and most likely improved child services will require small baby-sitting operations on the part of individual women and also training of the average housewife for more effective care of her own children in her own home. Psychologists may make a very useful contribution in the form of consultation services to mothers or child guardians in their own homes by training them also for make-believe play modeling. This calls not only for the development of adult training procedures, but also for the development of a whole set of materials that can serve as the basis for enhancing the imagery and sociodramatic play skills of the children. The methods developed by Freyberg and discussed in the Appendix represent only the barest beginning in this direction.

A whole series of unusually clever techniques has been developed by de Mille (1967), the son of the famous movie director, who has sought to establish the conditions for effective development of divergent production and desire for play. His book builds up a set of principles such as "For every imaginary event that is difficult to imagine because it contradicts the rules of reality there is a lesser similar event that will present little or no difficulty [p. 35]."

Thus, a child who has difficulty imagining a table or chair floating around could be encouraged to imagine a balloon doing so. deMille goes on to provide a series of very specific games built around different areas which extremely young children can be taught with the help of careful modeling by the parents along the lines laid out earlier in the book. There are, for instance, the games relating to mother. One begins by encouraging the child to imagine that mother is standing right there (pointing) and then attributing various characteristics to mother, describing the clothes she is wearing, changing her clothing around, having her move around the room, putting her in different places in the house and then going so far as to imagine her walking through a jungle or actually up on the ceiling. The games range from Mother and Father through Jumbly, School, Helping, Captive, Hungry, Breathing, Squeeze, Baby, Ouch, Bed, and many others.

Much more extensive formal research on these games is necessary to examine whether they do indeed generate spontaneous make-believe play and also have the effect of enhancing imagery as deMille believes they should. There is clearly a whole avenue of applied research as well as work of theoretical interest that can be generated in an attempt to train people for the use of these make-believe games and also in developing a whole series of additional make-believe situations. It would be particularly valuable to carry out an experiment or a group of experiments which would employ specially designed imagery or make-believe games to see if the children's capacity for imagery as measured by various eidetic techniques such as those developed by the Habers or the kind of elaboration skills as described by Rowher could be systematically enhanced.

In fact, it would be worth checking on the possibility of whether a specific kind of imagery training would be more effective than a more general kind of make-believe game opportunity. The advantages of very specific training might be in their immediate impact for the elaborative capacities of the child in formal tasks such as paired-associated learning. On the other hand, it is possible that make-believe games of an especially enjoyable nature would lead to more spontaneous play and hence practicing of elaborative skills by the children than very specific training procedures. These are questions that beg for empirical study.

Implications for Later Childhood Education

While we have focused thus far on the very young child and his development of sociodramatic skills, the value of make-believe kinds of activities for the older child might also be noted. Again many of the same arguments advanced by Smilansky continued to apply. The suggestions from the work of Gottlieb as well as my own observations and conversations with children between the ages of 9 and 13 indicate that there is a considerable continuing interest in make-believe activities and fantasy games which is largely suppressed.

A number of children have told me that they "sort of" wistfully wish that they had companions who would be willing to indulge more extensively in make-believe games of any continued nature. Occasionally I have observed children given the small impetus of leadership by camp counsellors or by interested adults who organized some type of imaginative play game, often enough something of a make-believe war or cops and robbers variety which led to a fairly extended group game participated in with much enjoyment by the children. Once I saw a group of children splashing about somewhat idly in the snow. An adult and an older boy organized them into the development of a make-believe fort and Eskimo village which they set about constructing reasonably well from the snow. This led them into a game involving combat between Eskimos and explorers which, while mixed in with a good deal of rough-housing and snowball throwing, at the same time included a number of elements of make-believe. The children in this case included boys and girls between the ages of 9 and 11.

If the present suppression of overt make-believe play in children from school age on could be reversed and sociodramatic tendencies put to effective use, school itself might become more interesting. Naturally many teachers recognize the value of some type of sociodramatic activities in a regular classroom through the use of playlets which are extremely successful. These have been found especially worthwhile for children from lower socioeconomic backgrounds for whom the excitement in being part of a dramatic production seems especially novel and morale building. The use of less formal make-believe settings as part of the instructional procedure with children improvising skits about content material being studied in the classroom, undoubtedly will enhance their interest and the positive affect associated with school, but also will help generate greater elaborative skills in communication as well. It remains to be seen whether such training can generalize to the children's independent activities, but this seems like a good possibility.

I believe an important part of what such make-believe training can do for school age children is to help them develop their capacities for planning or some of the other kinds of advantages of make-believe thought. There are many situations as noted earlier where a child must wait quietly on a line or in a waiting room or must remain relatively unobtrusive in the company of adults in the course of some such situation as a long train ride. To the extent that some degree of make-believe play is a part of this child's repertory, he may be able to tolerate the long delay more effectively by internalizing the fantasy game, by drawing on paper, or by adopting a kind of make-believe attitude in relation to the events that are taking place. The critical feature is that the make-believe play situation represents an alternative response to intruding upon the life space of the adults at a point where there is likely to be a reprimand or some other negative reaction that will set in motion a series of unpleasant interactions. If he does disturb the adults, the child may label himself as a bad boy or relate to the adults in some negative fashion. He may begin to be perceived in general as a "trouble maker." Some skill at make-believe can therefore be used to control one's own behavior and also to provide some solace in situations that are boring or frustrating.

The writer Alphonse Daudet has described an experience when he was 13 years old and traveling on a boat with a group of soldiers. He entertained himself by imagining that he was an important person in this group and enhanced his status considerably in his own mind by this technique (Groos, 1901, p. 142). I recall a series of fantasies that occurred at various times when I was 7 or 8 or at the most 9 and the class would be lined up during a long waiting period or on a fire drill or perhaps walking from one part of a building to another through long corridors and up and down steps. I would develop a daydream that I was really not one of the regular students, but instead a secret intelligence agent in disguise, ferreting out a mystery. In fact, that fantasy recurred when I was a lowly Private in the Army in basic training during World War II, marching endlessly through a Texas wilderness. (It is curious indeed that I did actually end up as a Special Agent in Intelligence.)

The great enjoyment that children take in storytelling cannot be over-emphasized. Extremely effective teachers often will find that they can communicate about a subject very well if they can bring in an actual personal narrative or tell an incident about a relative or friend that bears on the content of the didactic material.

An important feature of sociodramatic play that goes beyond its value in maintaining subject matter interest and in developing cognitive skills lies in the area of social skills. It can initiate the children into techniques such as *role reversal* in developing empathy and as a means of resolving conflicts and setting up bases for agreement. By now there is an extensive literature on the various psychodramatic methods developed originally by Moreno (1947) and various followers of Kurt Lewin in the small group approaches (McGrath & Altman, 1966) for dealing with organizational and interpersonal difficulties. Certain aspects of make-believe play could be employed with children in training them for methods such as role reversal. In the course of examining a particular situation, the children might be asked to take the opponent's viewpoint and play the part of the opponent in a spontaneous game. This forces upon the child a consideration of alternatives and provides a basis for later use of imaginative skills in comparable conflict situations.

A review by Johnson (1971) spells out a number of practical values that have been demonstrated for role reversal in the case of a fairly cooperative effort at problem solution by small groups. It seems likely that training in role reversal can have comparable value for relatively young children so that they can begin to use their "as if" skills in resolving a variety of difficulties that might arise between them. Set in a context of make-believe play for fairly young children, training in such skills as role reversal should not at all be difficult for a good teacher. The enjoyment of make-believe can be channeled into focusing his attention upon a useful skill.

The role of empathy as a means of controlling aggressive tendencies is obviously related to the role reversal method. Feshbach and Feshbach (1969) found that boys aged 6 to 7 who scored higher on a measure of empathy also showed less likelihood of overt aggressive behavior. Empathic and sociodramatic or fantasy techniques for the development of inhibition or self-control of aggressive or antisocial acts have also been described by Staub (1971). The use of modeling techniques as well as psychodramatic training in empathy has also been successfuly employed with delinquent boys by Sarason and Ganzer (1969).

The effectiveness of storytelling as a device for holding the attention of young people who are perhaps not geared toward intellectual activities has been touchingly exemplified in a fine story by J.D. Salinger. It is about a youth worker who regularly holds his group of tough city kids entranced with his elaborate tales of make-believe. He ends the story sequence in a most frustrating way for the children when he suffers a setback in love.

Goethe, in his autobiography, described his own youthful efforts at story telling.

> It greatly rejoiced the other children when I was the hero of my own story. They were delighted to know that such wonderful things could befall one of their playfellows . . . although they actually knew about what happened to me in reality and how I spent my days. Still I had to choose the scenes of those adventures which if not in another world at least took place far away and yet talk as if the events had taken place today or yesterday [Groos, 1901, p. 143].

Goethe's examples indicate that there is a certain attraction about having the adventures take place for someone with whom the children could identify although they were quite in touch with reality and knew very well that he was around in their company most of the time and could not really have such adventures.

Reading this account reminded me of some experience I had at the age of 7 or 8. (I can date this quite precisely because of the location of my family's residence at that time.) I had seen some Tarzan of the Apes serial episodes in the movies and had been given some of the Tarzan books by a cousin. I read them avidly and began to recount the stories to the children I met in the new neighborhood into which we had just moved. Soon I would have a fairly regular nightly crowd around for my stories and shortly afterward was given the nickname of Tarzan which scarcely fit my rather skinny shape and noncombative style at that time. It seemed, however, important for the children to use this term for me as an identification and perhaps also to give the stories some greater sense of reality much as Goethe's chums did.

We can go beyond the strictly anecdotal level in describing this process for there has recently appeared a series of investigations directed by Meichenbaum (1971a,b) and Meichenbaum and Goodman (1971) which examine more systematically the value of a form of make-believe training in the reduction of fear and development of self control in children and young adults. Following on the modeling principles of Bandura in the social learning situation, Meichenbaum (1971b) was able to show that even young women frightened by snakes could learn to overcome this phobia when they were exposed to televised female models who engaged in various coping and mastery behaviors and also *verbalized out loud* about their own experiences and coping attitudes. This identification process seems especially interesting for use as part of the educational process by teachers for a variety of situations perhaps not quite as dramatic as the phobic situation itself.

Still another study by Meichenbaum (1971a) was carried out with children of ages 7 to 9 who were listed as having behavioral problems such as hyperactivity and poor self-control. These children were exposed to a modeling and cognitive training situation which involved some element of empathy with the model, but also involved training in self-verbalization. In other words, the children were encouraged to talk to themselves as a means of providing themselves with feedback about their own performance. Gradually there occurred what might be called an internalization of language and an increasingly covert verbalization. An example of this was the following:

> *O. K. what is it I have to do. You want me to copy the pictures with the different lines. I have to go slow and be careful. O. K., draw the line down, go down good; then to right that's it; down some more and to the left. Good, I'm doing fine so far. Remember go slow. Now back up again. . . . that's O. K. just erase the line carefully . . . good . . . finished I did it* [Meichenbaum & Goodman, 1971, p. 117].

A series of studies by Meichenbaum (1971b) has made it clear that a number of forms of emotional disturbance can be affected by training subjects to verbalize both overtly and covertly their experiences and negative and positive attitudes in connection with the acts they are trying to control. Meichenbaum's data suggest that such control can be initiated by self-verbalization. If we carry this a step further, we can see that make-believe play games are one form of training the child for a variety of self-verbalizations at first overt and later internal which can help greatly in behavior control. Here, the teacher's use of psychodramatic and make-believe play with older children begins to be a bridge between the educational and psychotherapeutic enterprises. Examples of clinical use of fantasy and story telling techniques are provided by Winnicott (1971) and Gardner. (1971).

Implications of Make-Believe Play for Psychotherapy

An examination in any depth of the relationship of fantasy play and symbolic activity in children to psychotherapy would really merit an entire volume. The exciting possibilities of observing ongoing child's play and integrating it into an effort at personality modification were early recognized by practitioners such as David Levy, Melanie Klein, Frederick Allen, Anna Freud, and many others. The literature on treatment of children is replete with detailed accounts of the play of specific children at consultation centers and clinics or hospitals. Some of these cases are unusually well written and sensitively presented and have almost become a part of our cultural heritage. Cases such as Virginia Axline's "Dibs" or Rudolph Ekstein's "Tommy" give us an insight into the play and fantasies of individual children that are rare indeed and very moving in their own way. At the same time, we have by contrast surprisingly little intensive exploration of the play of children who are not so grossly disturbed as to come to the attention of clinicians. In fact, it is not very clear how much of the fascinating fantasy behavior shown by the children such as those so well described by Ekstein (1966) are a function of the psychopathology of the child or are perhaps reflections of the special talents of these children which make them more interesting subjects for psychotherapeutic intervention and also for subsequent reporting in the literature.

It seems quite possible that make-believe ought best to be viewed as a special characteristic of normal development and as a cognitive-affective skill available for the child's use under conditions based on constitutional factors, level of cognitive development, and special experiences with adults or peers. From this standpoint then, we can see that many of the disturbances of children often attributed to the bad effects of fantasy are rather the consequences of difficulties in relationship, attention, or identification. For some children, these problems are dealt with through elaborate make-believe or fantasy techniques; for others they are expressed directly in physical or gross psychological symptoms such as phobias; and for others they are expressed directly in actions which may be disruptive, antisocial or grossly self-defeating. In surveying a number of case reports in the literature of children or early adolescents, I have been led to the conclusion that those cases where there were extremely bizarre fantasies as part of the initial description of the problems of the patient often came from children who seemed generally gifted intellectually or who reflected the cultural atmosphere of their homes and who also showed a rather positive outcome after therapy.

One of the schizophrenic girls described by Ekstein (1966) had an elaborate fantasy life of being married. She showed a great deal of bizarre behavior built around repetitive playing of a single love song on a record player. She kept her room in a fashion which suggested that she was indeed married and that certain of the objects in her room were associated with her lover. With extended and very intensive psychoanalytic treatment, this young girl worked through very complex feelings, some of them involving a deep religious confusion and identification with Christ. Her gifted imaginative quality served as an entreé for the therapist who was able to use her accounts of various romantic novels or legends as a means of interchange. Through these he communicated his support of her struggle without having to be too direct and pressing the issue by demanding that she give up unrealistic fantasies. The outcome of the case suggests that the young woman developed ultimately into an imaginative and flexible adult and that her early gifts had indeed served her in good stead.

A similar case can be made for the woman who wrote the beautiful *I Never Promised You a Rose Garden*. Again the initial bizarre fantasy presented by this adolescent patient during hospitalization eventually became the basis for communication between therapist and patient and finally lost its seeming power. The patient gave up her psychotic symptoms, but she did not lose her own gift of imagination, a talent that has been subsequently proven in her authorship of fine short stories and novels.

In examining the nature of psychotherapeutic work through play, Ekstein (1966) proposes that "The space child might tempt us to put such a view about reconstruction into an extreme formulation; the psychotherapeutic process consists of the exchange of one childhood myth for another [p. 335]." Ekstein goes on to elaborate this viewpoint by indicating that the patient has, in an attempt to make some understanding of his past, formulated a myth about desertion and parental neglect which, while having slight justification, was largely a distortion. As a consequence of the therapeutic interaction, the young person is now prepared to reconstruct his view of the past into one which offers "a healthier rationale for living [p. 335]." Ekstein further asserts that ". . . even psychotic-like attempts of reconstruction are functional fantasies which justify present behavior and adjustment. Reconstruction is considered here as an ego function, and demonstrates that memory is not an isolated faculty but has its specific functional task within the psychic apparatus [p. 335]."

According to this view, Tommy's fantasy of a time machine in which he explored different previous lives and cultures was not merely a manifestation of his unconscious conflicts or of past trauma, but also represented a serious attempt to organize and deal with his conflicts.

> We saw in this fantasy an attempt by the patient to demonstrate also how he had been trying to master these conflicts and what ego facilities he had in order to cope with them. The fluidity of the fantasy and the changing use he made of it were an indication of the process that took place during therapy [Ekstein, 1966, p. 336].

Whatever the original actual basis of the boy Tommy's disturbance (and the true causality can never be ascertained even in a case as well-worked out as this one) the fact remains that his use of make-believe and fantasy about space and time travel represent significant efforts on his part to organize his chaotic experience and to give it at least some kind of direction. The fantasy also provided a communication system which the therapist could grasp. In this sense, a child with high imaginative predisposition such as Tommy may often be *more accessible* for therapeutic intervention than a child who has not elaborated a verbal system or capacity for expressing his imagery in play form and whose grossly disturbed behavior may be expressed largely in compulsive acts or unverbalizable fears.

A thoughtful, clinical paper by Fineman (1962) describes a group of children seen for play therapy in which the imaginative predisposition of the child appears to play a key role in whether or not a positive therapeutic outcome is possible. Seven children are described of whom four are capable of very little imaginative play and three would be classified by our measurement system as imaginatively predisposed. Here is a description of a child in play therapy who is characterized by extreme anxiety and involved in an active struggle over toilet training with his mother. By no means a hyperactive child, this boy could sit fairly quietly carrying out such activities as bead stringing and block building of a very stereotyped kind always with his mother's supervision. The following session at approximately age 3 gives an example of his behavior in the playroom:

> Benno takes the girl doll, gives it to the interviewer, says "Cah-Cah" and puts the doll tentatively on the toilet. Benno then takes out another doll, but immediately puts it back into the toy cabinet. Benno picks up the cowboy doll and pretends to take his gun away. Says, "Give me guns. Give me two guns," as he pulls at the gun. He disrupts abruptly, goes into the waiting room and wonders where his mother is. He says to her, "Come watch me." Mother refuses and stays in the waiting room. Benno returns, puts all the dolls back in the toy cabinet, then takes all dolls out again. He puts the father doll on the toilet, saying "Man make Cah-Cah." Then anxiously "Hold him, he might fall." Then the interviewer asks him about this. Benno ignores her and walks over to the crayons. He carries crayons and paper out into the hall, and comes back to a chair near the door—brings crayons and paper to the table, removes all the crayons, picks up a hammer and pegboard and brings them to the table. A few moments later, in the same session, following another interruption when he went to the waiting room and again asked his mother to come in, which she again refused, he returns to the playroom, looks at the dolls, puts them all in the cupboard and shuts the door. As the session continues he involves himself in very meticulously lining up the crayons in the box and the pegs on the table and does not return to the play with the dolls and the doll furniture [Fineman, 1962, p. 174].

In this instance we see perhaps the budding of an obsessional neurotic of the type who eventually may become a most pedantic or bureaucratic person obsessed with petty details and lacking any likelihood of any imagination. At the very least, however, we can assert that this child presents serious problems to the therapist since it is difficult to establish a rapport around which either interpretation or exchange of feeling can develop.

By contrast here is an excerpt from a child who is described as having much greater tendency toward imaginative play at home and also in the therapy session. He had been brought to therapy because of a sibling rivalry problem. He was only 2 years, 9 months old, but already had two younger siblings.

> Gerald goes to the toy box and takes one of the animals to the slide. He says his bunny is at home. Then says, "It's bad." Interviewer questions why. Gerald says "It hit a man." He then throws the bunny on to the slide. He then gets a doll and leaves it in the interviewer's lap, gently sings it to sleep. He takes the bunny away from the slide and puts it in a box with a cover. He then takes the doll, holds it up so that its eyes open, then puts it down with the eyes shut, and brings it and shows it to the interviewer. He picks up the doll and cuddles it, then puts it on a small chair. He sits next to the doll and puts his arm around its shoulders, looks at the interviewer and says, "Martin's at home." [Martin is his next younger sibling.] He then puts the doll down on the small chair again in sleeping position, lifts it up, and says in a loud voice to the doll, "Wake up." [Fineman, 1962, p. 177].

In summarizing her experiences with these children Fineman writes:

> As was noted previously, children seem to fall into two groups—those who used imaginary play early and those who were never able to develop such play to any great extent.... This has been a consistent trend. [After following the children for well over a year] ... we have seen that Carl, Benno and Esther have not shown any appreciable increase in the use of imaginary play, even during later developmental stages and with the conflict inherent to these stages.... Gerald and Ellen have continued to sustain this type of play and to utilize it successfuly as a means of working through conflictual periods and external traumatic events. The earlier anxieties and conflicts have been mastered to a greater extent, and this seems to have left them free to cope more successfully with later developmental stages. It should be added here that a feature of the use of such play has been the fact that these children are capable of relinquishing it when they are called upon to do so, and begin to be able to define the boundaries between imaginary play and the often contradictory elements of external reality. In these children the intrusion of the real world into the imaginary one seems fraught with less conflict, and there is less recourse to regressive attempts aimed at maintaining fantasy world which would jeopardize the eventual acceptance of the reality principle [p. 179].

The children lacking in imaginative play by contrast continue to remain at a more infantile level, constantly striving to reestablish directly with their mothers some type of gratifying relationship and at the same time remain blocked in carrying out any kind of symbolic play activities.

An important aspect of Dr. Fineman's paper is her alertness to the contribution of the mothers in the development of make-believe games in the children. She calls attention to the fact that despite considerable variations in personality structure among the various mothers, the mothers of the more imaginative children all seemed to tolerate and encourage make-believe play to some degree whereas those of the low-fantasy children all seemed to have conflicts and/or difficulties in their own capacities for imagination and in their use of this in relation to the children. She notes "It is not clear whether actual participation of the mother in [imaginary] play is necessary, but this is not as vital to its development as are the acceptance and approval on the part of the mother [p. 180]." This report of the maternal role seems quite similar in its import to the findings based on an interview with mothers of poor children reported by Dr. Freyberg in her chapter.

It seems likely therefore that if we take the position that symbolic play or fantasy has distinct advantages in the therapeutic process, we might wonder whether it would not pay for therapists to institute somewhat more systematic efforts at training children to engage in make-believe play as part of their therapeutic armamentarium. One kind of approach is cited above in the reference to the work of Meichenbaum (1971a). There are isolated case studies in which children have been encouraged to tell stories and given at least some help through modeling in how to do this (Staub, 1971). There are also some examples in the literature of the use of continuous story telling techniques with delinquent adolescents as a means of giving them an alternative fantasy outlet rather than encouraging their "acting out" tendencies. What I am suggesting is that perhaps child therapists might pay even closer attention to the process of fantasy play itself from a structural as well as from a content standpoint and see if they can find means for systematically enhancing it in children. Games such as those suggested by de Mille (1967) or some of the methods developed by Freyberg or Smilansky also seem applicable.

I do not mean to minimize what has already been accomplished in this respect. Play therapists have long recognized the value of family-oriented toys, doll houses, the famous Bobo doll which permits aggressive play, etc. There has been, however, perhaps too much emphasis on a cathartic orientation as if the mere expression of feelings or direct aggressive activities can suffice to deal with inner problems. As Bandura and Walters (1963) have noted, this position has very little justification on the basis of formal scientific research. Instead, it would appear that the use of therapist modeling and of the development of play skills would be most efficacious in providing the child with alternative opportunities for practicing a new kind of behavior and also for finding enjoyable means of dealing with periods of delay or of distress so that there is not an immediate eruption into direct and often self-defeating action. Psychotherapeutic work with adults in the past decade has also increasingly emphasized the importance of imagery in a wide spectrum of efforts at producing personality change or behavior modification (Singer, 1971b). It would seem appropriate that we begin to think in terms of systematic attention to the meaning of fantasy skills for children as well as a means of providing them with an additional resource in their desperate struggle to work out profound experiences of rejection, loneliness, and confusions of identity.

Creativity, Esthetic Experience, and Humor

Make-believe play in childhood is probably best regarded as one aspect of the general capacity for divergent production which is a fundamental human operation. In this sense it clearly has links to what later emerges as creativity in the young adult. We have already noted the work of Schaefer (1969), Schaefer and Anastasi (1968), Anastasi and Schaefer (1969), and Helson (1965, 1967) among others which have called attention to the fact that persons identified as creative during college careers report more daydreaming or imaginary companions in early childhood. To the extent that considerable make-believe activities are part of the growing child's repertory, these form links to a general attitude of "as if" or control over one's products at least in the imaginary sphere. Such predispositions may next become the basis also for an artistic or scientific creative orientation in many young people.

The young Goethe received a puppet theatre as a child and spent long hours playing with it. Fifty years later he indeed became the director of an actual theatre in Weimar. The excitement of wholehearted make-believe play is something that does not disappear for certain great writers. Goethe has written one of his moving poems (appended at the beginning of *Faust*) about how the images of his characters from the past return to haunt him and create a greater reality than his immediate present situation. Dickens is quoted by Groos (1901) as having indicated that when he finished a book he felt as if he were "dismissing some portion of himself into the shadowy world when a crowd of the creatures of his brain are going from him forever.... No one can ever believe this narrative [David Copperfield] in the reading more than I have believed it in the writing [pp. 133, 134]."

The control over one's "characters" may in part be a secondary advantage of make-believe play and at the same time establish the conditions for an esthetic or creative orientation that can be of considerable significance in producing many fine works of art. At the same time, even in persons who do not choose some formal type of creative or scientific expression for their divergent productions, there is considerable value in the "as if" attitude. I have discussed elsewhere (Singer, 1966) the skill that daydreaming can provide for the housewife in organizing her activities, in producing creative reactions in relation to her children and in making her own fairly routine tasks become more exciting and her day more interesting.

As usual, Groos (1901) anticipates much of what one may say about the value of make-believe for the later development of a capacity to appreciate a wide variety of artistic and esthetic experiences. He writes

> ... illusion is essential to esthetic enjoyment in hearing or reading poetic creations. The child who listens absorbedly to a fairy story, the boy for whom the entire external world sinks and vanishes while he is lost in the tale of adventure, or the adult who follows with breathless attention the development of a captivating

romance; all allow the authors' creations to get possession of their consciousness to the exclusion of reality and yet not as an actual substitute for it [p. 134].

Indeed Groos calls attention to the fact that children's eyes may lose their convergence as their interest is absorbed in attending to a fascinating story, a means of detaching themselves from surrounding reality, as he puts it. This same type of observation has led me to formal research. It can actually be demonstrated experimentally that adults engaging in extended daydream activity show a fixation of the eyes or a tendency to focus their gaze at infinity rather than at the stimulus source in their immediate environment (Singer, Greenberg, & Antrobus, 1971).

The excitement of exploring novelty in "as if" or make believe form and the joy of reducing this novelty by seeing its connectedness with other material assimilated from the past provides the basis for a great deal of what we designate as esthetic experience. The ability to appreciate novel approaches to stories, to grasp unusual forms of plot presentation (as in the case of opera or ballet) and to understand some of the experiences that artists in a variety of media are trying to convey may be easier for a child who has had experience with make-believe play. Sociodramatic play therefore establishes an early set which can develop either into more active creative forms of expression of which can make it possible for the child to enjoy a greater variety of artistic expressions. Just as one might argue that playing Policeman, Fireman, Nurse, or Mother all prepare for social roles, it might well be that a general tendency toward varied make-believe play prepares not only for planful behavior, but also for the greater affective range and exploratory quality that makes the enjoyment of artistic endeavor so valuable a part of life.

It would be especially interesting to examine from a research standpoint whether the possibility for early exposure to make-believe increases the child's interest and likelihood of learning to read and to enjoy reading. For all of the increased communication that television and radio have made available to the child, no one yet questions that once one establishes a reading habit there is a tremendous increase in general capacity for intellectual and esthetic development. Reading capacity also leads to the child's having additional resources for "staying out of trouble," that is to say engaging in behavior that is less likely to be disruptive to the world of adults or its peers in which such disruption can lead to extremely negative feedback. The development of the inner dimension of experience through make-believe and fantasizing, reading and the development of esthetic interests may allow for a more exploratory and appreciative attitude toward a new environment.

A Theory of Humor

The importance of the positive emotional experiences associated with make-believe, surprise, interest, and joy cannot be stressed enough. In a sense one can see that much of one's capacity to produce and appreciate humor also takes its beginning in some aspect of make-believe play or in general in the accommodation-assimilation sequence. While much has been said in literature about the origins of humor in conflicts about sex, toilet training, or aggression there has been relatively less emphasis upon the origins of the process through a combination of cognitive and social learning experiences. Bergson long ago proposed that when a man behaves like a machine he evokes a humorous response. When a man falls backward out of his chair his movements look awkward and ungraceful. Perhaps a better way to put it from the standpoint of a cognitive-affective theory would be the following:

> When we perceive a set of movements that are familiar and yet take place in unfamiliar context or that are only crudely like what they ought to be, we are interested and alerted. Then as we understand what is happening (the man is falling off his chair but he is not hurt) there is a sharp reduction in the arousal and a consequent experience of laughter or enjoyment.

Much of this out-of-context or mechanical quality is characteristic of the early effort of children to imitate adults or the novel combinations which arise when they attempt to assimilate phrases or patterns of adult behavior into their own play. One of the 3-year-old children in our observational study of play was overheard reprimanding another child by saying "Don't say Goddam! That means bullshit!" This kind of remark generally evokes a roar of laughter from adults in the vicinity. From the child's standpoint it is a perfectly reasonable attempt to relate two words into a construct of "forbidden language" without really understanding the meaning of either of the phrases. For the adult the awkwardness of the child's performance as well as the titillating quality of the forbidden language evokes an initial novelty and then, as this is assimilated, there follows an affective reaction of enjoyment and laughter.

The next step in this sequence is that the child *overhears* the laughter. While perhaps at first puzzled, the youngster then goes on to consider whether there might not be other such phrases that could evoke laughter. In this sense then there is a social learning component as well as a cognitive one that come together to produce the child's early experiences of humor. Very likely the child will attempt to repeat the humorous phrases or gestures sometimes to the point of annoying adults by repetitive efforts at clowning or assimilative imitation of various phrases.

The cuteness of make-believe play with its awkward simulation of complex adult behavior generally does evoke a good deal of mirth from adults. If such humor is cast in an appreciative and pleasant form the child's inclination to go on with make-believe efforts at evoking such humor will of course be enhanced. If, as too often happens, the adult's humor becomes derisive or humiliating in quality, the child will of course be impeded in more emphasis on make-believe. Where there is an optimal balance of such situations and the child realizes that some kinds of make-believe evoke not only laughter in others but are genuinely humorous, the beginnings of a capacity to generate humor and also to appreciate it are also laid down.

It would be intriguing to know if much of the experiences of well-known humorists, writers or comedians was generated in the course of early attempts at "as if" or make-believe play. We have little doubt from Mark Twain's writings that such was indeed the case for him. The humorist or comedian often learns early to adopt an attitude which involves the shift of a situation from its normal setting to one slightly more bizarre or unusual. The shift of focus should be not too much as to be unassimilable and evoke startle or disgust reaction but just enough so that the interest of listeners is perked up. After a while, when they understand the implications, they respond with laughter. This humorous orientation undoubtedly is based on a pervasive set which approaches each kind of experience from the standpoint of ways it can be altered slightly so as to produce some novel or unexpected turn.

In a Woody Allen movie, *Bananas*, the bumbling hero receives an invitation to dine with the President of a small Latin American country. As he reads the invitation and is thrilled at this opportunity we hear surging up in the background harp music, the kind generally used in movies to express angelic voices or to indicate moments of great emotion. This is humorous enough in itself since the hero is so unromantic and the situation is already mildly ridiculous. But our biggest guffaw comes when the hero walks to a nearby closet, opens it, and finds a harpist inside who apologizes by saying, "I have no place else to practice." Here the complete shift in cognitive orientation from one which by now is familiar, "the typical schmaltzy background music," to the more "as if" and outrageous notion that maybe there really is a harpist there, adds greatly to the surprise and then joy evoked by the scene.

The "as if" play of the child has therefore many routes that lead to humor under appropriately reinforcing conditions. It also prepares us more for appreciating a wide variety of humor and for developing an attitude that makes one aware of the possibilities that do exist in any given behavioral situation. It is this capacity to entertain possibilities and to anticipate or to appreciate the complex interpenetrations of immediate reality with future or past likelihoods that makes the "as if" realm so important a part of adult life.

The early play of the child gives us an insight into what may later become a very significant feature of adolescent and adult behavior. It has been proposed by Chateau (1967) and by Bachelard (1964) that the dimension of the unreal in human experience is a critical feature of man's ultimate reality. That is to say, what is perhaps most truly human about man, what is perhaps his greatest gift in the evolutionary scheme and indeed his greatest resource in his mastery of the environment and of himself, is his capacity to fantasize. To dream makes it possible to examine the alternatives that inhere every moment as we organize our immediate experience. To be able to make-believe gives both the child and the adult a power over the environment and an opportunity to create one's own novelty and potential joy.

In one of his greatest plays Eugene O'Neill showed how stripping men of their illusions led only to despair and greater anguish in surroundings of misery. Our lives are indeed fraught with impending dangers, with horrors and with the inevitability of death. The capacity for "as if" and make-believe is, however, more than an illusion that temporarily helps us escape. It also may serve as an incentive to strive for greater enrichment. It helps create additional possibilities for either momentary esthetic or humorous appreciation of what we do have or for exploring more actively ways of improving what exists for us. The child's world of make-believe starting as it does in the simple effort at imitation and assimilation of the physical and social environment also sets in motion the process which if it is gently fostered as a human skill can make life infinitely richer and more exciting.

Example of Observational Play Instructions and Imaginative Play Predisposition Interview

The Nature of the Project

This study involves three major phases:

Direct Observation of the Spontaneous Play Behavior of Preschool Children

This phase requires a number of careful recordings of exactly what the child does during specific time periods on a number of occasions. The emphasis is upon careful reporting and recording without interpretation or evaluation. The protocol of the play behavior during the sampling period then becomes a basic source of data for further analysis in a number of ways to be described. By having separate observers record the behavior of each child at a given period we increase the chances of accurate recording.

Ratings by Independent Judges of the Protocols of Play

Here the task is to read and reread the protocol also trying to recall (if the rater was also an observer) the actual scene and appearance of the child and then to rate the behavior along certain preestablished dimensions. These rating scales represent schemes for categorizing the natural flow of a child's behavior for purposes of comparision with its behavior at other times under other circumstances, before or after certain experimental interventions, etc. Our goal in setting up these particular ratings is to choose specific behavior categories that may have important theoretical interest. As long as we have the records of the children's behavior in detail from at least two observers we can always go back to them and score them along additional scales as these are developed or suggested by the research of other investigators.

Interview and Psychological Testing

Here the attempt is made to conduct a semistructured interview which can provide some information directly from the child concerning his or her presumed habitual play and thought tendencies. The interview data can then be rated or classified and correlated with the actual observed play behavior, or they can serve a number of other purposes, such as assigning children to experimental groups in a formal study. The psychological tests in the present study are designed to supplement the interview so that our classification on the basis of the child's own statements is not the only basis possible for classification.

Instructions for Observation and Recording

The critical feature in observing and recording is thoroughness. We need as much detail as possible on what the child does and says during the 10-min observation period. The recorder should try to be as impersonal as a camera—this is no time for analysis and interpretation. Psychology is too full of people who jump to interpret without looking carefully at what actually goes on. Recording then should give a moment to moment account of the child's movements around the room, its comments, and the specific emotions displayed. In the case of emotions try to be objective and limited—do not assume that because a child pounds on a block he or she is angry. The child may be laughing and *that* is the emotion to record. The interpretation of underlying anger can come later if at all during ratings. Just indicate if the child laughs, cries, whines, moves slowly, hits another child, breaks a toy apparently intentionally, etc. Examples of *10-min* duration recordings of the same child at the same time by two different observers are appended here as examples. Read them carefully and look at their similarities and differences. The care of recording is important because the protocols may later be rated by persons who have not actually observed the children as you have.

Work in *pairs* so that we always have at least two independent records for each child at each observation period. The child is to be observed a minimum of *four* times, at least *twice* during *unstructured* or free play and at least *twice* during *structured* play. This means you will have to pick up each child on at least two different days during each type of play situation established by the school.

Imaginative Play Research Project
Observational Record

Child's Name _____

Sex _____

Observer _____

Date and Time _____

Location _____

Type of Play   S _____   U _____
                    (structured or unstructured)

Physical Appearance and Clothing

Ten Minute Sample

Time Began _____   Time Ended _____

Start writing here:

(Turn over and also use additional pages if needed)

Write the observations out carefully on the protocol sheets making sure you record the child's name, age, time and date of observation and type of play, *structured-unstructured*. Remember to write your own name on the protocol as well. Use ink if possible since others may be reading your protocol. It would be best if you could retype your protocol afterward, but this will not be required if you are not a good typist. Observe the same child in structured *and* unstructured play on the same day for one rating, and on another day for his second rating.

Go through the class list *once* before beginning your second set of structured-unstructured ratings. Record how he or she is dressed and note general appearance before you begin observing. Important that you and partner observe the *same* child at the *same* time. An example of an actual observation record follows.

Examples of Protocols of the Same Child Recorded
Simultaneously to Establish Interobserver Reliability[1]

Pretraining Protocol of Child A. H. by Observer A

S is sitting in a chair at a table near the door. She stretches her arms over her head and backward. *S* crosses her legs and looks curiously about the room. She looks like she is talking to herself, moving her mouth, but the sounds are inaudible. She jumps up quickly and marches across the room, with her chest thrust outward, with large, almost marching steps, and her arms swinging back and forth. When the teacher calls out, *Where's Brian?*, she calls out *He went for the milk.* She has a loud clear voice. She walks around the room stopping to look at other children and asks several times of various children, *Whatcha doing?* She laughs and smiles fairly frequently. She makes some clowning faces. She walks over to the pile of plastic animals and looks them over. She picks up an elephant and a horse and pushes them together as though they were kissing. She shakes her head and smiles. *You kiss each other, you love each other, now come on.* Then she holds the elephant in her two hands and says to a girl, *This elephant is your husband, you love her.* Then she throws the elephant back to the pile and jumps up giggling. Her whole body is in motion. She turns to the girl next to her and says: *You something else.* She picks up a toy from the floor and says, *You're broken, just have to throw you away.* She throws it on the bottom shelf. She walks over to the house corner and puts on a pair of high heels and prances around the room with her chest thrust out and her hands on her hips.

Pretraining Protocol of Child A. H. by Observer B

This child immediately begins to move around in her chair, stretches her arms over the back of the chair, crosses her legs and then turns her head in various directions looking at all aspects of the room. She makes a few motions with her mouth, but not making sounds. Her whole body moves quickly and agilely. She is somewhat taller and more sturdily built than most of the other children in the room. She marches across the room, making large steps, swinging her arms actively and with great gusto. Whenever questions were asked to the class by the teacher, she peals out the answer in a strong clear voice. During the entire period

[1] From the study by Joan Freyberg, Chapter VI.

she smiled rather frequently. Often she opens her eyes wide and eagerly and she reacts to practically everything happening in the room, frequently asking other children how they are doing or what they are doing. She takes a gray molded elephant and a black horse and pushes their faces together, saying with a brisk shaking back and forth of her head, *Now you kiss each other, you love each other, now come on, come on, there.* Then she took the elephant and turned to her friend saying, *This elephant is your husband, and you love her.* She then gets up swinging her arms back and forth, shaking her head and says to the same little girl, *You something else, you just something else.* She picks up one of the broken wooden toys from the floor and says, *You broken, I just have to throw you away.* She gets up and puts on some high-heeled shoes in the doll corner and swishes back and forth across the room with her hands on her hips.

Instructions for Ratings

There are three types of ratings that are to be done in the initial phase of this study. These call for, first of all, ratings of the protocol on *Imaginativeness, Affect* (or *Emotion*), and *Concentration.* These scales are presented below with definitions of each scale point from 1 to 5 with 5 representing the "high" or "positive" end of the scale. Review the protocol carefully looking for examples of each level. Naturally, the child may change from time to time. We are interested in your evaluation of the overall pattern and predominant direction of its behavior with respect to each dimension. Do not be afraid to use a full range of scores rather than sticking conservatively to the middle. After rating a few protocols you may want to go back and revise earlier ratings based on broader experience with more children in the group. Under no circumstances must you consult with your partner until *after* your rating is set down, however. The ratings must be completely independent. If you do have some strong reservations after both of you have done your ratings, then write a little note and attach it to the rating card.

Scales for First Phase

Imaginativeness

1. Is extremely unimaginative in his play. Introduces no pretend elements into the play situation. Extremely stimulus-bound by the play materials.
2. Is slightly imaginative in his play, occasionally introducing fleeting pretend elements into play situation, but does not stay with any pretend situation for very long. No originality or organization found in pretend situations. A few pretend elements added to otherwise very stimulus-bound play.

3. Shows a moderate amount of pretending in his play, but not very original or removed from the actual stimulus situation. Little organization or consistency of pretense or role-playing. No voice changes or simulated vocalizations. Considerable changing from one activity to another.
4. Shows a substantial amount of pretend elements in his play, spontaneously creating make-believe situations, showing some originality in his pretending, not changing activities very often. Some organization and consistency in pretense or role-playing, including some simulated vocalizations.
5. Shows high originality in the ways he uses toys and play material. A very high number of pretend elements in his play. High organization of activity and role-playing. Is able to go well beyond what the play stimuli in themselves suggest. Resists interruption of play by others.

Affect

(Note that mild surprise, interest, and joy are viewed as *positive* affects and scored high)

1. Shows no interest or pleasure in the toys or play activities; much tangential behavior, conversations with observer, teacher, and others; critical remarks about toys or play activities; no smiling, laughter, or evidence of pleasure in playing.
2. Shows only mild pleasure and interest in toys or play activities; much looking around and/or desultory manipulation of play material. Occasional smiling or laughter.
3. Shows moderate interest, pleasure and enjoyment of activities and toys; talking freely about the play activities; somewhat lost in quiet enjoyment, considerable smiling and/or laughter during activities: some animation.
4. Shows deep pleasure and interest in play activity, smiling or laughing frequently. Expresses frequent pleasure, describing spontaneously or acting out fantasies in play.
5. Shows extreme delight in play; laughing, singing, smiling; thoroughly enjoying self in play, reluctant to leave play situation.

Concentration

1. Shows brief or little attention to or absorption in activities; aimless wandering, high distractibility, many questions to teacher; responding to noises or talk of children in room. Hyperactivity with no real interaction with play material.
2. Engages in superficial play with toys and play material while looking around the room, staring passively, talking to teacher, or wandering aimlessly. Changes toys and/or activities frequently.

3. Responds with moderate interest to the toys or play activities. Changes activities only once during the 5-min segment. Some distractibility and no real loss of self in the play situation. Some response to outside stimuli such as noises and the talk and play of other children.
4. Shows good absorption in play activity; very little response to outside stimuli, no change of activity during 5-min segment; no tangential behavior or conversation pertaining to activities other than the one at hand.
5. Shows intense absorption in play activity; stays with one activity for a long period of time; oblivious to outside stimuli, may not even respond to direct questions from teacher or children not included in the play situation at hand.

The scales for affect and concentration were based on those used effectively by Pulaski (1971) in her study of children's play.

Second Phase

Mood Checklist

The rating of the child's mood is somewhat more difficult and unusual. There are *eight* moods to be evaluated. Since each child's moods may fluctuate from time to time and vary widely in even 10 min, it is important to rate each child *on each mood* for the observation period. Note that a rating of 1 indicates *minimal* occurence of the mood and a rating of 5 indicates a strong manifestation of the mood. Try to rate in terms of the intensity as well as frequency of the mood. Thus, if a child seems sad and downhearted to the point of tears for 1-2 min but then cheers up for the balance of the observation period, you would still rate him 4 or 5 on the scale. You could also rate him 4 or 5 if for the balance of the 10 min he is laughing and joking. It is not likely you will get such extremes. Remember to rate each child on all moods, however. Wherever possible try to give the highest weight to the most predominant mood.

Third Phase

The final rating you will be required to make at this point will be of *Aggression*. Please note that we are interested in direct, overt aggressive behavior, not merely play that involves make-believe attacks. The definition of aggression is the intentional delivery of a harmful stimulus to another person or to personal property. If the child plays a game in which monsters attack spacemen and a battle ensues (all with blocks or plastic figures, etc.) but no child is hurt or property damaged, this would not count as *aggression* for this scale. If the child attacks its own toy, e.g. punches a doll, this is scored as aggression with a rating of 2.

For this rating go through the record and evaluate the overall degree of aggression shown. You can make it easier by taking every minute and rating that separately on the 0-4 scale, then using the average of the 10 scores to give you a

Mood Checklist

Mood	Score				
	1 not at all	2 slightly	3 moderately	4 very	5 extremely
Angry— annoyed		shrug, tsk-like comment	frowns	stamps feet, bangs table, shrill voice	clenched jaw, clenched fist, red face, menacing posture, glaring, yelling
Fearful— tense		pacing up and down, tapping feet or fingers	biting nails, wringing hands, pale, eyes wide	cold, sweaty squirming	facial trembling, body trembling, body rigid, hair erect, tremulous or quavering voice
Lively— excited		whistling, humming	high color, flushed face, eyes sparkling	jabbering, giggling, wriggling	skipping, jumping, dancing, bounding about
Elated— pleased		smiling	broad grin	joking, jesting, clapping hands	laughing, hugging

Sad–down-hearted	looking down at floor	frowning, pouting, droopy mouth	lips quivering, voice quivering, drooped shoulders, hunched position	crying, sobbing
Ashamed–contrite	looking quickly away, eyes averted	head down	shrinking posture, blushing, lowered voice, begging pleading voice	hiding one's face
Contemptuous–disgusted	looking askance	turn up nose, turn back on, point at	sneering, smirking, lips curled, shuddering	booing, hissing, hooting, snarling
Fatigued–sluggish	leaning, slouched, whining voice	feet dragging, plodding	eyes half closed, heavy-lidded, yawning	head on table, head bobbing, sprawled out in chair or on floor

basis for a final summary rating (using a whole number from 0-4). If there is a clear-cut and extreme case of aggression, even if it lasts only a minute or so, give the child a maximum score. That is, if a child strikes another and then assumes a relatively nonaggressive game he still gets a score of 4.

The attached material presents examples of aggression scores for different types of toys with which a child might play. These may not at all be used by specific children. Take these samples only to help you form a judgment for the material you see the children actually using.

Initial Aggression Scale (Biblow Study)

Activity	Score
Nonaggressive activity; child just works on his own project	0
Child makes mild comment reflecting annoyance such as *Oh darn it*; child mutters under his breath; child makes tsk-like sounds of annoyance	1
Child makes faces or sticks tongue out at frustrator; child makes disparaging remarks such as *Get away, stupid,* or aggressive remarks such as *I'll really smack you if you don't leave me alone* toward frustrator; child slams a game piece down	2
Child makes menacing or threatening gestures toward the frustrator; child pushes the frustrator away, actively thwarting the frustrator's interference.	3
Child hits the frustrator; child throws game pieces at the frustrator or at another child; child kicks, punches, etc.	4

Final Aggression Scale: Examples of Degrees of Aggressive Play with Different Types of Games

Targetland	*Score*
Nonaggressive; examines blow-gun or target; watches others shoot	0
Child blows darts at target in ordinary manner	1
Child blows darts not at target but not involving another child or another child's toy	2
Child blows darts at another child's toy	3
Child blows darts at another child	4
Punching Doll	
Nonaggressive; walks or dances with doll, rests on it, embraces it, watches another child punch it	0
Child punches doll in ordinary manner	1
Child punches doll viciously	2
Child interferes with another child playing with the doll	3
Child hits another child with the doll	4

Fort Apache

Nonaggressive; child watches another child playing, examines pieces of equipment	0
Child manipulates pieces in ordinary war maneuvers	1
Child physically knocks over or dismantles his own soldiers or equipment	2
Child knocks over playmates soldiers or equipment	3
Child hits, pushes, strikes, etc. his playmate as part of the game	4

Clay

Nonaggressive; child watches other play or makes objects with clay	0
Child pounds clay on table	1
Child sticks clay on objects in the room not involving another child	2
Child sticks clay on another child's toy	3
Child hits another child with clay, throws clay at another child	4

Silly Faces

Nonaggressive; child watches another child play; child disguises himself, looks in mirror	0
Child makes "monster face"	2
Child makes "monster face," advancing upon another child	3
Child pulls disguise off another child's face or forcibly places disguise on another child	4

Doll Play

Nonaggressive; child watches or plays nonaggressively	0
Child scolds his own doll	1
Child hits his own doll	2
Child hits another child's doll	3
Child hits another child with the doll	4

Aggression Summary Score

Nonaggressive activity	0
Child plays with aggressive toy in normal manner not involving another child; child makes mild comments reflecting annoyance not directed at another child	1
Child directs aggression at his own toy or at inanimate objects in the room; child directs disparaging remarks at another child or another child's toy with no accompanying physical aggression	2
Child directs physical aggression at another child's toy; child menaces or threatens another child; child annoys another child	3
Child directs physical aggression at another child	4

Score 0, 1, 2, 3, or 4 for each 60-second interval

1. _____		6. _____	
2. _____		7. _____	
3. _____		8. _____	
4. _____		9. _____	
5. _____		10. _____	

Imaginative Play Predisposition Interview: Instructions for Interview

This is a semistructured interview. Begin by making a few pleasant remarks to the child and by identifying yourself by name. Then proceed to ask each question initially as written on the sheet. Repeat the question if you do not appear to be understood. If the child replies too tersely, ask him a question such as *Tell me just how you play it?* or *How do you do it?* If the child's answer is at once clear, there is no need to pursue the question. For example, if a child answers Question I by saying *blocks,* we need to know whether the emphasis is on sheer construction or whether there's a "make-believe" component. A game like "marbles" or "ball" needs little further elaboration as it probably does not have a fantasy element. Write down the child's answer verbatim and also note if a further question was asked by writing (a) before the child's reply.

Do not be discouraged if you get relatively brief answers from such young children. This is to be expected; in examining protocols we find that we are getting sufficient material for rating purposes.

Imaginative Play Interview Schedule

> Subject Name _____
>
> Code # _____
>
> Date of Interview _____
>
> Age _____

Imaginative Play Questions

1. What is your favorite game? What do you like to play the most? (Write verbatim answer. Query if not enough information to score.)
2. What game do you like to play best when you're all alone? What do you like to do best when you're all alone? Do you ever think things up?
3. Do you ever have pictures in your head? Do you ever see make-believe things or pictures in your mind and think about them? What sort of things?
4. Do you have a make-believe friend? Do you have an animal or toy or make-believe person you talk to or take along places with you?

Interview

1. What kinds of things do you do with your parents?
2. Who do you like best, father or mother or like both the same?
3. What kinds of games do you play with parents?
4. Do your parents ever read to you or tell you stories? Who? (mother, father, both?)
5. How many children in family? Who is oldest?
6. How much time do you spend watching TV? Favorite programs?

References

Altschuler, R. H., & Hattwick, L. W. *Painting and personality: A study of young children.* Chicago: Univ. of Chicago Press, 1947.

Ames, L. B., & Learned, J. Imaginary companions and related phenomena. *Journal of Genetic Psychology,* 1946, 69, 147-167.

Ames, L. B., Learned, J., Métraux, R., & Walker, R. *Child Rorschach Responses.* New York: Hoeber-Harper, 1952.

Ames, L. B., & August, J. Rorschach responses of Negro and white five- to ten-year-olds. *Journal of Genetic Psychology,* 1966, 109, 297-309.

Anastasi, A., & Schaefer, C. E. Biographical correlates of artistic and literary creativity in adolescent girls. *Journal of Applied Psychology,* 1969, 53, 267-273.

Aries, P. *Centuries of childhood.* New York: Vantage, 1962.

Atkinson, J. W. (Ed.), *Motives in fantasy, action and society.* Princeton, New Jersey: Van Nostrand-Reinhold, 1958.

Auden, W. H. As it seemed to us. *New Yorker,* April 3, 1965, 159-192.

Ausubel, D., & Ausubel, P. Ego development among segregated Negro children. In A. Passow (Ed.), *Education in depressed areas.* New York: Teachers College Publication Series, 1963. Pp. 109-141.

Axline, V. *Dibs: In search of self.* Boston: Houghton Mifflin, 1965.

Bachélard, G. *The psychoanalysis of fire.* Boston: Beacon Press, 1964.

Bandura, A. Behavioral modification through modeling procedures. In L. Krasner and L. P. Ullman (Eds.), *Research in behavior modification.* New York: Holt, 1965. Pp. 310-340. (a)

Bandura, A. Vicarious processes: A case of no-trial learning. In L. Berkowitz (Ed.), *Advances in experimental social psychology,* Vol. 2. New York: Academic Press, 1965. Pp. 1-55. (b)

Bandura, A. *Psychological modeling.* New York: Aldine-Atherton, 1971.

Bandura, A., & McDonald, F. J. The influence of social reinforcement and the behavior of models in shaping children's moral judgments. *Journal of Abnormal Social Psychology,* 1963, **66,** 274-281.

Bandura, A., Ross, D., & Ross, S. A. Transmission of aggression through imitation of aggressive models. *Journal of Abnormal and Social Psychology,* 1961, **63,** 575-582.

Bandura, A., & Walters, R. H. *Social learning and personality development.* New York: Holt, 1963.

Barker, R. G., Dembo, L., & Lewin, K. Frustration and regression: An experiment with young children. *University Iowa Studies in Child Welfare,* 1941, **18,** No. 386.

Barron, F. Threshold for the perception of human movement in inkblots. *Journal of Consulting Psychology,* 1955, **19,** 33-38.

Beck, J. *How to raise a brighter child: The case for early learning.* New York: Trident Press, 1967.

Beller, E. K. Exploratory studies of dependency. *Transactions of the New York Academy of Science,* 1959, Series II, **21,** 414-426.

Berkowitz, L. The expression and reduction of hostility. *Psychological Bulletin,* 1958, **55,** 257-283.

Berkowitz, L. *Aggression: A social psychological analysis.* New York: McGraw-Hill, 1962.

Berkowitz, L. The effects of observing violence. *Scientific American,* 1964, **210,** 35-41.

Berkowitz, L., & LePage, A. Weapons as aggression-eliciting stimuli. *Journal of Personality and Social Psychology,* 1967, **7,** 202-207.

Berkowitz, L., & Rawlings, E. Effects of film violence on inhibitions against subsequent aggression. *Journal of Abnormal and Social Psychology,* 1963, **66,** 405-412.

Berlyne, D. E. Laughter, humor, and play. In G. Lindzey & E. Aronson (Eds.), *The Handbook of Social Psychology,* Vol. 3, 2nd ed. Reading, Massachusetts: Addison Wesley, 1969. Pp. 795-852.

Berlyne, D. E. Children's reasoning and thinking. In P. Mussen (Ed.), *Carmichael's manual of child psychology.* New York: Wiley, 1970.

Blatt, S. J. Object representation in psychosis. *Journal of the American Psychological Analytical Association,* 1972, in press.

Blatt, S. J., & Ritzler, B. A. Some order in thought disorder. *Journal of Abnormal Psychology,* 1972, in press.

Breger, L. Function of dreams. *Journal of Abnormal Psychology Monograph,* 1967, **72,** (Whole No. 641).

Broadbent, D. E. *Perception and communication.* New York: Pergamon, 1958.

Bronfenbrenner, U., & Ricciuti, H. N. The appraisal of personality characteristics in children. In P. H. Mussen (Ed.), *Handbook of research methods in child development.* New York: Wiley, 1960.

Brown, B. R. The relationship of language development to social class and intelligence. *Teachers Journal,* spring 1964.

Bruner, J. S. On cognitive growth: I and II. In J. S. Bruner, R. R. Olver, & P. M. Greenfield (Eds.), *Studies in cognitive growth.* New York: Wiley, 1966.

Bühler, K. *The mental development of the child.* New York: Harcourt, 1930.

Buss, A. *The psychology of aggression.* New York: Wiley, 1961.

Carrigan, P. M. Extraversion-introversion as a dimension of personality: A reappraisal. *Psychological Bulletin,* 1960, **57,** 329-360.

Chateau, J. *L'enfant et le jeu.* Paris: Scarabée, 1967.

Church, J. (Ed.) *Three babies: Biographies of cognitive development.* New York: Random House, 1966.

Colvin, R. W. An experimental analysis of attitudinal determinants underlying behavior to color stimuli in psychoneurotic subjects. Unpublished doctoral dissertation, Duke University, 1953.

Cronbach, L. J., & Meehl, P. E. Construct validity in psychological tests. *Psychological Bulletin,* 1955, **52,** 281-302.

Dattner, R. *Design for play.* Princeton, New Jersey: Van Nostrand-Reinhold, 1969.

Davidson, H., & Greenberg, J. *School achievers from a deprived background.* New York: Assoc. Educational Services, Div. Simon & Shuster, 1967.

Davis, F. B. *Educational measurements and their interpretation.* Belmont, California: Wadsworth Publishing, 1964.

Deutsch, M. Social and psychological perspectives on the development of the disadvantaged learner. *Journal of Negro Education,* summer, 1964. (a)

Deutsch, M. Some psycho-social aspects of learning in the disadvantaged. In *Mental health and educational achievement.* Englewood Cliffs, New Jersey: Prentice-Hall, 1964. (b)

Deutsch, M. Facilitating development in the preschool child: Social and psychological perspectives. *Merrill-Palmer Quarterly,* 1964, **10,** 249-263. (c)

de Mille, R. *Put your mother on the ceiling: Children's imagination games.* New York: Walker & Co., 1967.

Dollard, J., Doob, L., Miller, N., Mowrer, O., & Sears, R. *Frustration and aggression.* New Haven: Yale Univ. Press, 1939.

Doob, L. W. Eidetic imagery: A cross cultural will-o-the-wisp? *Journal of Psychology,* 1966, **63,** 13-34.

Downing, G., Edgar, R. W., Harris, A. J., Kornberg, L., & Storm, H. F. *The preparation of teachers for schools in culturally deprived neighborhoods.* (The Bridge Project.) Flushing, New York: Queens College, 1965.

Dworkin, E. S., & Efron, J. S. The angered: Their susceptibility to varieties of humor. *Journal of Personality and Social Psychology,* 1967, **6,** 223-236.

Edwards, A. L. *Experimental design in psychological research.* Revised ed. New York: Holt, 1962.

Edwards, A. L. *Experimental design in psychological research.* Revised edition. New York: Holt, Rinehart & Winston, 1962.

Eifermann, R. R. Social play in childhood. In R. Herron & B. Sutton-Smith, (Eds.), *Child's Play.* New York: Wiley, 1971.(a)

Eifermann, R. R. *Determinants of children's game styles.* Jerusalem: Israel Academy of Sciences and Humanities, 1971.(b)

Ekman, P., Friesen, W. V., & Ellsworth, P. *Emotions in the human face: Guidelines for research and a review of findings.* New York: Pergamon, 1971.

Ekstein, P. *Children of time and space, of action and impulse.* New York: Appleton, 1966.

El'Konin, D. Symbolics and its function in the play of children. *Soviet Education,* 1966, **8** (No. 7), 35-41. Also in R. Herron & B. Sutton-Smith (Eds.), *Child's Play.* New York: Wiley, 1971.

Erikson, E. H. Studies in the interpretation of play. *Genetic Psychology Monographs,* 1940, **22,** 557-671.

Erikson, E. H. *Childhood and society.* New York: Norton, 1963.

Escalona, S. K. *The roots of individuality.* New York: Basic Books, 1968.

Eysenck, H. *The scientific study of personality.* London: Routledge & Kagan Paul, 1952.

Feffer, M. H., & Gourevitch, V. Cognitive aspects of role-taking in children. *Journal of Personality,* 1960, **28,** 383-396.

Feshbach, S. The drive-reducing function of fantasy behavior. *Journal of Abnormal and Social Psychology,* 1955, **50,** 3-11.

Feshbach, S. The catharsis hypothesis and some consequences of interaction with aggressive and neutral play objects. *Journal of Personality,* 1956, **24,** 449-462.

Feshbach, S. The stimulating versus cathartic effects of a vicarious aggressive activity. *Journal of Abnormal and Social Psychology,* 1961, 63, 169-175.

Feshbach, N. D., & Feshbach, S. The relationship between empathy and aggression in two age groups. *Developmental Psychology,* 1969, 1, 102-107.

Fineman, J. Observations on the development of imaginative play in early childhood. *Journal of the American Academy of Child Psychiatry,* 1962, 1, 167-181.

Foster, J. C. Play activities of children in the first six grades. *Child Development,* 1930, 1, 248-254.

Foulkes, D. *The psychology of sleep.* New York: Scribners, 1966.

Foulkes, D., Larson, J. D., Swanson, E. M., & Rardin, M. Two studies of childhood dreaming. *American Journal of Orthopsychiatry,* 1969, 627-643.

Foulkes, D., & Shepherd, J. Manual for a scoring system for children's dreams. Laramie: Department of Psychology, Univ. of Wyoming, 1971 (Mimeographed).

Frankenstein, C. School without parents. *Megamoth,* 1962, 12, 3-23. (In Hebrew).

Freud, A. *The ego and the mechanisms of defense.* London: Hogarth, 1937.

Freud, S. *Beyond the pleasure principle.* London: International Universities Press, 1922.

Freud, S. Creative writers and daydreaming. In J. Strachey (Ed.), *The standard edition of the complete psychological works of Sigmund Freud,* Vol. IX. London: Hogarth, 1959. Pp. 141-154. (Original publication in 1908.)

Freud, S. Formulations on the two principles of mental functioning. In J. S. Strachey (Ed.), *The standard edition of the complete psychological works of Sigmund Freud.* Vol. XII. London: Hogarth, 1958. (Originally published in 1911.)

Furfey, P. H. Pubescence and play behavior. *American Journal of Psychology,* 1929, 41, 109-111.

Furfey, P. H. *The growing boy.* New York: Macmillan, 1930.

Gardner, R. *Therapeutic communication with children: The mutual storytelling technique.* New York: Science House, Inc., 1971.

Garrison, C. *Permanent play materials for young children.* New York: Scribners, 1926.

Gerard, R. M. Differential effects of colored lights on psychophysiological functions. Unpublished doctoral dissertation, Univ. of California, Los Angeles, 1958.

Gergen, K. J. *The concept of self.* New York: Holt, 1971.

Gerst, M. D. Symbolic coding processes in observational learning. *Journal of Personality and Social Psychology,* 1971, 19, 7-17.

Getzels, J. W., & Jackson, P. W. *Creativity and intelligence: Explorations with gifted students.* New York: Wiley, 1962.

Gilmore, J. B. The role of anxiety and cognitive factors in children's play behavior. Unpublished doctoral dissertation, Yale Univ., 1964.

Gilmore, J. B. Play: A special behavior. In R. N. Haber (Ed.), *Current research in motivation.* New York: Holt, 1966. Pp. 343-355.

Goldstein, K. *Human nature in the light of psychopathology.* Cambridge, Mass.: Harvard University Press, 1940.

Gottlieb, S. Modeling effects on fantasy. Unpublished doctoral dissertation. City University of New York, 1968.

Green, G. H. *Psychoanalysis in the classroom.* New York: Putnam, 1922.

Green, G. H. *The daydream: A study in development.* London: Univ. of London Press, 1923.

Green, H. *I never promised you a rose garden.* New York: Signet, 1964.

Greenacre, P. Play in relation to creative imagination. *Psychoanalytic Study of the Child,* 1959, XIV, 61-80.

Griffiths, R. *Imagination in early childhood.* London: Kagan Paul, 1935.

Groos, K. *The play of man.* New York: Appleton, 1901.

Gross, R., & Gross, B. Let the child teach himself. *New York Times Magazine,* May 16, 1965, p. 34.

Guilford, J. P. The structure of intellect. *Psychological Bulletin,* 1956, **53**, 267-293.

Guilford, J. P. *Personality.* New York: McGraw-Hill, 1959.

Guilford, J. P. *The nature of human intelligence.* New York: McGraw-Hill, 1967.

Gump, P., & Sutton-Smith, B. Activity-setting and social interaction: A field study. *American Journal of Orthopsychiatry,* 1955, **25**, 96-102. (Reprinted in Herron & Sutton-Smith, 1971).

Haber, R. N., & Haber, R. B. Eidetic imagery, I. Frequency, *Perceptual and Motor Skills,* 1964, **19**, 131-138.

Hall, G. S. *Youth.* New York: Appleton, 1906.

Harlow, H. F. Mice, monkeys, men and motives. *Psychological Review,* 1953, **60**, 23-32.

Harlow, H. F. The nature of love. *American Psychologist,* 1958, **13**, 673-685.

Hartley, R. E., Frank, L., & Goldenson, R. *Understanding children's play.* New York: Columbia Univ. Press, 1952.

Hartmann, H. *Ego psychology and the problem of adaptation.* New York: International Universities Press, 1958.

Hebb, D. O. Concerning imagery. *Psychological Review,* 1968, **75**, 466-477.

Helson, R. Childhood interest clusters related to creativity in women. *Journal of Consulting Psychology,* 1965, **29**, 353-361.

Helson, R. Personality characteristics and developmental history of creative college women. *Genetic Psychology Monographs,* 1967, **76**, 205-256.

Herron, R. E., & Sutton-Smith, B. *Child's play.* New York: Wiley, 1971.

Hoffman, M. L., & Hoffman, L. W. *Review of Child Development,* Vols. I and II. New York: Russell Sage Foundation, 1964 (Vol. I), 1966 (Vol. II).

Holt, R. R. The development of the primary process: A structural view. In R. R. Holt (Ed.), *Motives and thought.* New York: International Universities Press, 1967.

Holtzman, W. Holtzman inkblot technique: Group administration by slide projection. *Journal of Clinical Psychology,* 1963, **19**, 433-453.

Holtzman, W., Thorpe, J. S., Swartz, J. D., & Herron, W. *Inkblot perception and personality.* Austin, Texas: Univ. of Texas Press, 1961.

Hudson, L. *Contrary imaginations.* New York: Schocken, 1966.

Huizinga, J. *Homo ludens.* Boston: Beacon, 1950.

Hurwitz, I. A developmental study of the relationship between motor activity and perceptual process as measured by the Rorschach test. Unpublished doctoral dissertation. Clark Univ., 1954.

Isaacs, S. *Social development in young children.* London: Routledge, 1933.

Izard, C. E. *The face of emotion.* New York: Appleton, 1971.

Izard, C. E., & Tomkins, S. S. Affect and behavior: Anxiety as a negative affect. In C. Spielberger (Ed.), *Anxiety and behavior.* New York: Academic Press, 1966.

Jersild, A. T., & Markey, F. V. Conflicts between preschool children. *Child Development Monographs.* New York: Teachers College, Columbia Univ., 1935.

Jersild, A. T., Markey, F. V., & Jersild, C. L. Children's fears, dreams, wishes, daydreams, likes, dislikes, pleasant and unpleasant memories. *Child Development Monographs.* New York: Bureau of Publications, Teachers College, Columbia Univ., 1933.

John, V. The intellectual development of slum children: Some preliminary findings. *American Journal of Orthopsychiatry,* 1963, **33**, 813-822.

Johnson, D. W. Role reversal: A summary and review of the research. *International Journal of Group Tensions,* 1971, in press.

Jung, C. G. *Psychological Types.* London: Routledge, 1959. (Originally published in 1921.)

Kagan, J. Acquisition and significance of sex typing and sex role identity. In M. Hoffman and L. W. Hoffman (Eds.), *Review of Child Development,* Vol. I. New York: Russell Sage, 1964. Pp. 137-167.

Kagan, J. Reflection-impulsivity: The generality and dynamics of conceptual tempo. *Journal of Abnormal Psychology,* 1966, 71, 17-24.

Kagan, J., & Kogan, N. Individual variation in cognitive processes. In P. Mussen (Ed.), *Carmichael's manual of child psychology,* Vol I. New York: Wiley, 1970.

Karon, B. Problems of validities. In A. I. Rabin (Ed.), *Projective techniques in personality assessment.* New York: Springer, 1968.

King, G. F. An interpersonal conception of Rorschach human movement and delusional content. *Journal of Projective Techniques,* 1960, 4, 161-163.

Klein, G. Peremptory ideation: Structure and force in motivated ideas. In R. R. Holt (Ed.), *Motives and thought.* New York: International Universities Press, 1967.

Klein, M. *The psychoanalysis of children.* New York: Grove Press, 1960.

Klinger, E. Modeling effects on achievement imagery. *Journal of Personality and Social Psychology,* 1967, 7, 49-63.

Klinger, E. Development of imaginative behavior: Implications of play for a theory of fantasy. *Psychological Bulletin,* 1969, 72, 277-298.

Klinger, E. *Structure and functions of fantasy.* New York: Wiley, 1971.

Kohlberg, L. A cognitive-developmental approach to socialization-morality and psycho-sexuality. Paper presented at the Midwestern Meeting of the Society for Research in Child Development, Bowling Green State University, Bowling Green, Ohio, 1966.

Korchin, S. J., Mitchell, H. E., & Meltzoff, J. A critical evaluation of the Thompson Thematic Apperception Test. *Journal of Projective Techniques,* 1950, 14, 445-452.

Kris, E. On preconscious mental processes. In D. Rapaport (Ed.), *Organization and pathology of thought.* New York: Columbia Univ. Press, 1951. Pp. 474-493.

Leask, J. Haber, R. N., & Haber, R. B. Eidetic imagery in children, II. Longitudinal and experimental results. Unpublished manuscript, Univ. of Rochester, 1968.

Lerner, B. Rorschach movement and dreams. *Journal of Abnormal Psychology,* 1966, 71, 75-86.

Lesser, L. An experimental study of the drive-reducing function of imagination and fantasy in young children. Unpublished doctoral dissertation, New York Univ., 1962.

Lewin, K. *A dynamic theory of personality.* New York: McGraw-Hill, 1935.

Lewin, K. *Field theory in social science.* New York: Harper, 1951.

Libby, W. L., Jr. Reaction time and remote association in talented male adolescents. *Developmental Psychology,* 1970, 3, 285-297.

Lieberman, J. N. Playfulness and divergent thinking: An investigation of their relationship at the kindergarten level. Unpublished doctoral dissertation, Columbia Univ., 1964. *Journal of Genetic Psychology,* 1965, 107, 219-224.

Lorenz, K. *On aggression.* New York: Harcourt, 1966.

Lukas, J. A. How Mel Allen started a lifelong love affair. *New York Times Sunday Magazine,* September 11, 1971. Pp. 37-38.

Luria, A. R. *The nature of human conflicts.* New York: Liveright, 1932.

McClelland, D. C., Atkinson, J. W., Clark, R. A., & Lowell, E. L. *The achievement motive.* New York: Appleton, 1953.

McCully, R. S. Human movement in the Rorschach materials of a group of pre-adolescent boys suffering from progressive muscular loss. *Journal of Projective Techniques,* 1961, 25, 205-211.

McCurdy, H. G. The childhood pattern of genius. *Horizon,* 1960, 2, 32-38.

McGrath, J. E., & Altman, I. *Small group research.* New York: Holt, 1966.

McKellar, P. *Imagination and thinking.* New York: Basic Books, 1957.

Maddi, S. Motivational aspects of creativity. *Journal of Personality,* 1965, **33,** 330-347.

Markey, F. Imaginative behavior in preschool children. *Child Development Monographs,* 1935, **18.**

Marshall, H. Relations between home experiences and children's use of language in play interactions with peers. *Psychological Monographs,* 1961, **75,** 5.

Marshall, H., & Doshi, R. Aspects of experience revealed through doll play of preschool children. *Journal of Psychology,* 1965, **61,** 47-57.

Marshall, H., & Hahn, S. C. Experimental modification of dramatic play. *Journal of Personality and Social Psychology,* 1967, **5,** 119-122.

Matterson, E. M. *Plan and playthings for the preschool child.* Baltimore, Maryland: Penguin Books, 1967.

Megargee, E. I. A comparison of the scores of white and Negro male juvenile delinquents on three projective tests. *Journal of Projective Techniques and Personality Assessment,* 1966, **30,** 530-535.

Meichenbaum, D. H. *The nature and modification of impulsive children: Training impulsive children to talk to themselves.* Waterloo, Ontario: Department of Psychology, Univ. of Waterloo, Research Report No. 23, 1971. (a)

Meichenbaum, D. H. *Cognitive factors in behavior modification: Modifying what clients say to themselves.* Waterloo, Ontario: Department of Psychology, Univ. of Waterloo, Research Report No. 25, 1971. (b)

Meichenbaum, D. H., & Goodman, J. Training impulsive children to talk to themselves. *Journal of Abnormal Psychology,* 1971, **77,** 115-126.

Michael, D. N., & Maccoby, N. Factors influencing the effects of student participation on verbal learning in films: Motivating versus practice effects, "feedback", and overt versus covert responding. In A. A. Lumsdaine (Ed.), *Student response in programmed instruction.* Washington, D.C.: National Research Council, 1961.

Millar, S. *The psychology of play.* Harmondsworth, England: Penguin, 1968.

Miller, D. R. Motivation and affect. In P. H. Mussen (Ed.), *Handbook of research methods in child development.* New York: Wiley, 1960.

Miller, G., Galanter, E., & Pribram, K. *Plans and the structure of behavior.* New York: Holt, 1960.

Minuchin, P., Biber, B., Shapiro, E., & Zimiles, H. *The psychological impact of school experience.* New York: Basic Books, 1969.

Mischel, W. *Personality and assessment.* New York: Wiley, 1968.

Moreno, J. L. *The theatre of spontaneity.* Beacon, New York: Beacon House, 1947.

Mowrer, O. H. *Learning theory and symbolic behavior.* New York: Wiley, 1960. (a)

Mowrer, O. H. *Learning theory and personality dynamics.* New York: Wiley, 1960. (b)

Murphy, G. *Personality.* New York: Harper, 1947.

Murphy, L. *Methods for the study of personality in young children.* New York: Basic Books, 1956.

Mussen, P. (Ed.), *Handbook of research methods in child development.* New York: Wiley, 1961.

Mussen, P., & Rutherford, E. Effects of aggressive cartoons on children's aggressive play. *Journal of Abnormal & Social Psychology,* 1961, **62,** 461-464.

Nowlis, V. Research with the mood adjective check list. In S. S. Tomkins & C. E. Izard (Eds.), *Affect, cognition, and personality.* New York: Springer, 1965. Pp. 352-389.

Opie, I., & Opie, P. *The lore and language of school children.* Oxford: Oxford Univ. Press, 1959.

Opie, I., & Opie, P. *Children's games in street and playground.* Oxford: Oxford Univ. Press, 1969.

Opie, P., & Opie I. Games (young) people play. *Horizon,* 1971, **XIII,** 16-19.

Page, H. Studies in fantasy-daydreaming frequencies and Rorschach scoring categories. *Journal of Consulting Psychology,* 1957, **21,** 111-114.

Paivio, A. Mental imagery in associative learning and memory. *Psychological Review,* 1969, **76,** 241-263.

Paivio, A. On the functional significance of imagery. *Psychological Bulletin,* 1970, **73,** 385-392.

Parten, M. Social play among preschool children. *Journal of Abnormal & Social Psychology,* 1933, **28,** 136-147.

Patterson, G. R. A nonverbal technique for the assessment of aggression in children. *Child Development,* 1960, **31,** 643-653.

Patterson, G. R., Littmen, R. A., & Bricker, W. Assertive behavior in children: A step towards a theory of aggression. *Monograph of the Society for Research in Child Development,* 1967, **32** (5 and 6).

Pedersen, F. A., & Wender, P. H. Early correlates of cognitive functioning in six-year-old boys. *Child Development,* 1968, **39,** 185-193.

Peller, L. Libidinal phases, ego development and play. In *Psychoanalytic study of the child,* Vol. 9. New York: International Universities Press, 1959.

Phillips, R. Doll play as a function of the realism of the materials and the length of the experimental session. *Child Development,* 1945, **16,** 123-143.

Piaget, J. *The language and thought of the child.* New York: Harcourt, 1932.

Piaget, J. *The moral judgement of the child.* New York: Macmillan, 1955.

Piaget, J. *Play, dreams and imitation in childhood.* New York: Norton, 1962.

Piaget, J., & Inhelder, B. *Mental imagery in the child.* New York: Basic Books, 1971.

Pines, M. Why some three-year-olds get A's—and some get C's. *New York Times Magazine,* July 6, 1969.

Piotrowski, Z. The movement score. In Rickers-Ovsiankina (Ed.), *Rorschach psychology.* New York: Wiley, 1960.

Pitcher, E. G., & Prelinger, E. *Children tell stories.* New York: International Universities Press, 1963.

Pulaski, M. A. S. *Understanding Piaget.* New York: Harper, 1971.

Pytkowicz, A. R., Wagner, N. N., & Sarason, I. G. An experimental study of the reduction of hostility through fantasy. *Journal of Personality & Social Psychology,* 1967, **5,** 295-303.

Rapaport, D. The structure of psychoanalytic theory: A systematizing attempt. *Psychological Issues,* **2,** No. 2. New York: International Universities Press, 1960. (a)

Rapaport, D. On the psychoanalytic theory of motivation. In M. R. Jones (Ed.), *Nebraska symposium on motivation,* Lincoln, Nebraska: University of Nebraska Press, 1960. (b)

Reese, H. W. Imagery and contextual meaning. *Psychological Bulletin,* 1970, **73,** 404-414. (a)

Reese, H. W. Imagery in children's paired-associate learning. *Journal of Experimental Child Psychology,* 1970, **9,** 174-178. (b)

Reese, H. W. Implications of mnemonic research for cognitive theory. Paper read at Southeastern Conference on Research in Child Development, Athens, Georgia, 1970, (mimeographed). (c)

Reppucci, N. D. Antecedents of conceptual tempo in the two-year-old child. Unpublished doctoral dissertation, Harvard Univ., 1968.

Reppucci, N. D. Individual differences in the consideration of information among two-year-old children. *Development Psychology,* 1970, **2,** 240-246.

Richardson, A. *Mental imagery.* New York: Springer, 1969.

Riess, A. A study of some genetic behavioral correlates of human movement responses in children's Rorschach protocols. Unpublished doctoral dissertation, New York Univ., 1957.

Riessman, F. The overlooked positives of disadvantaged groups. *Journal of Negro Education*, 1964, **33**, 225-231.

Roberts, J. M., & Sutton-Smith, B. Child training and game involvement. *Ethnology*, 1962, **1**, 166-185.

Roe, A. *The making of a scientist.* New York: Dodd, Mead, 1952.

Rohwer, W. D., Jr. Social class differences in the role of linguistic structures and paired associate learning: Elaboration and learning proficiency. Final Report, Bureau of Research, Office of Education. Berkeley, California: Univ. of California (mimeographed), 1967.

Rohwer, W. D., Jr. Images and pictures in children's learning: Research results and educational implications. *Psychological Bulletin*, 1970, **73**, 393-403.

Rorschach, H. *Psychodiagnostics.* Berne: Hans Huber, 1942.

Sarason, I. G., & Ganzer, V. J. An observational learning approach to the modification of juvenile behavior. In D. Krumholtz & C. Thoresen (Eds.), *Behavioral counseling: Cases and techniques.* New York: Holt, 1969.

Sarbin, T. R., & Juhasz, J. B. Toward a theory of imagination. *Journal of Personality*, 1970, **38**, 52-76.

Scarr, S. Genetic factors in activity motivation. *Child Development*, 1966, **37**, 663-673.

Schachtel, E. G. *Metamorphosis: On the development of affect, perception, attention and memory.* New York: Basic Books, 1959.

Schachter, S. *The psychology of affiliation.* Stanford, California: Stanford Univ. Press, 1959.

Schaefer, C. E. Imaginary companions and creative adolescents. *Developmental Psychology*, 1969, **1**, 747-749.

Schaefer, C. E., & Anastasi, A. A biographical inventory for identifying creativity in adolescent boys. *Journal of Applied Psychology*, 1968, **52**, 42-48.

Schafer, R. *Aspects of internalization.* New York: International Universities Press, 1968.

Schafer, R. Playing grownup. *Horizon*, 1971, **XIII**, 20-23.

Schonbar, R. Differential dream recall frequency as a component of "life style." *Journal of Consulting Psychology*, 1965, **29**, 468-474.

Scott, J. P. *Aggression.* Chicago: Chicago Univ. Press, 1958.

Sears, P. S. Doll-play aggression in normal young children: Influence of sex, age, sibling status, father's absence. *Psychological Monographs*, 1951, **65**, No. 6.

Sears, R. R. The influence of methodological factors on doll play performance. *Child Development*, 1947, **18**, 190-197.

Sears, R. R., Maccoby, E. E., & Levin, H. *Patterns of child rearing.* Evanston, Illinois: Row, Peterson, 1957.

Sears, R. R., Whiting, J. W., Nowlis, V., & Sears, P. S. Some child-rearing antecedents of aggression and dependency in young children. *Genetic Psychology Monographs*, 1953, **47**, 135-234.

Segal, S. J. (Ed.) *Imagery: Current cognitive approaches.* New York; Academic Press, 1971.

Sharef, M. R. An approach to the theory and measurement of intraception. Unpublished doctoral dissertation. Harvard Univ., 1959.

Sheffield, F. D. A drive-induction theory of reinforcement. In R. N. Haber (Ed.), *Current research in motivation.* New York: Holt, 1966.

Siipola, E., & Taylor, V. Reactions to inkblots under free and pressure conditions. *Journal of Personality*, 1952, **21**, 22-47.

Singer, D. L. Aggression arousal, hostile humor, catharsis. *Journal of Personality & Social Psychology Monograph Supplement,* 1968, **8,** 1-14.

Singer, D. L., & Whiton, M. B. Ideational creativity and expressive aspects of Human Figure Drawing in kindergarten age children. *Developmental Psychology,* 1971, **4,** 366-369.

Singer, J. L. Delayed gratification and ego-development: Implications for clinical and experimental research. *Journal of Consulting Psychology,* 1955, **19,** 259-266.

Singer, J. L. The experience type: Some behavioral correlates and theoretical implications. In M. R. Rickers-Ovsienkina (Ed.), *Rorschach Psychology.* New York: Wiley, 1960.

Singer, J. L. Imagination and waiting ability in young children. *Journal of Personality,* 1961, **29,** 396-413.

Singer, J. L. *Daydreaming: An introduction to the experimental study of inner experience.* New York: Random House, 1966.

Singer, J. L. Research applications of projective methods. In A. I. Rabin (Ed.), *Projective techniques in personality assessment.* New York: Springer, 1968.

Singer, J. L. Drives, affects, and daydreams: The adaptive role of spontaneous imagery or stimulus-independent mentation. In J. S. Antrobus (Ed.), *Cognition and Affect.* Boston, Massachusetts: Little, Brown, 1970.

Singer, J. L. The influence of violence portrayed in television or movies upon overt aggressive behavior. In J. L. Singer (Ed.), *The control of aggression and violence.* New York: Academic Press, 1971. (a)

Singer, J. L. Imagery and daydream techniques employed in psychotherapy: Some practical and theoretical implications. In C. Spielberger (Ed.), *Current topics in clinical and community psychology.* New York: Academic Press, 1971. (b)

Singer, J. L, & Antrobus, J. S. A factor-analytic study of daydreaming and conceptually related cognitive and personality variables. *Perceptual and Motor Skills.* Monograph Supplement 3-V17, 1963.

Singer, J. L, & Antrobus, J. S. Daydreaming, imaginal processes, and personality: A normative study. In P Sheehan (Ed.), *The function and nature of imagery.* New York: Academic Press, 1972.

Singer, J. L., Greenberg, S., & Antrobus, J. S. Looking with the mind's eye: Experimental studies of ocular motility during daydreaming and mental arithmetic. *Transactions of the New York Academy of Sciences.* 1971, **33,** 694-709.

Singer, J. L, & Herman, J. Motor and fantasy correlates of Rorschach human movement responses. *Journal of Consulting Psychology,* 1954, **18,** 325-331.

Singer, J. L., & McCraven, V. Some characteristics of adult daydreaming. *Journal of Psychology,* 1961, **51,** 151-164.

Singer, J. L., & McCraven, V. Patterns of daydreaming in American subcultural groups. *International Journal of Social Psychiatry,* 1962, **8,** 272-282.

Singer, J. L., Meltzoff, J., & Goldman, G. D. Rorschach movement responses following motor inhibition and hyperactivity. *Journal of Consulting Psychology,* 1952, **16,** 359-364.

Singer, J. L., & Opler, M. K. Contrasting patterns of fantasy and motility in Irish and Italian schizophrenics. *Journal of Abnormal & Social Psychology,* 1956, **53,** 42-47.

Singer, J. L., & Rowe, R. An experimental study of some relationships between daydreaming and anxiety. *Journal of Consulting Psychology,* 1962, **26,** 446-454.

Singer, J. L., & Schonbar, R. A. Correlates of daydreaming: A dimension of self-awareness. *Journal of Consulting Psychology,* 1961, **25,** 1-6.

Singer, J. L., & Spohn, H. Some behavioral correlates of Rorschach's experience type. *Journal of Consulting Psychology,* 1954, **18,** 1-9.

Singer, J. L., & Streiner, B. F. Imaginative content in the dream and fantasy play of blind and sighted children. *Perceptual & Motor Skills,* 1966, **22,** 475-482.

Singer, J. L., & Sugarman, D. Some Thematic Apperception Test correlates of Rorschach Human Movement Responses. *Journal of Consulting Psychology*, 1955, **19**, 117-119.

Singer, J. L., Wilensky, H., & McCraven, V. Delaying capacity, fantasy, and planning ability: A factorial study of some basic ego functions. *Journal of Consulting Psychology*, 1956, **20**, 375-383.

Smilansky, S. *The effects of sociodramatic play on disadvantaged preschool children.* New York: Wiley, 1968.

Spivak, G., & Levine, M. *Self-regulation and acting-out in normal adolescents.* Progress Report for National Institute of Mental Health Grant M-4531. Devon, Pennsylvania: Devereaux Foundation, 1964.

Stainbrook, B., & Siegel, M. A comparative group Rorschach study of southern Negro and white high school and college students. *Journal of Psychology*, 1944, **17**, 107-115.

Staub, E. The learning and unlearning of aggression. In J. L. Singer (Ed.), *The control of aggression and violence.* New York: Academic Press, 1971.

Stein, A., Friedrich, L. K., & Vondracek, F. Television content and young children's behavior. In *Television and social behavior*, Vol. II. Report to Surgeon-General's Committee on Television and Social Behavior. National Institute of Mental Health, 1972.

Storr, A. *Human aggression.* New York: Atheneum, 1968.

Sullivan, H. S. *Clinical studies in psychiatry.* New York: Norton, 1953.

Sutton-Smith, B., & Rosenberg, B. G. Manifest anxiety and game preferences in children. *Child Development*, 1960, **31**, 307-311.

Sutton-Smith, B., & Rosenberg, B. G. The dramatic boy. *Perceptual & Motor Skills*, 1967, **25**, 247-248.

Tayler, C. W. (Ed.) *Creativity: Progress and potential.* New York: McGraw-Hill, 1964.

Tomkins, S. S. *Affect, Imagery, Consciousness.* Vols. I and II. New York: Springer, 1962, 1963.

Tomkins, S. S. Affect and the polarity of knowledge. In S. S.Tomkins & C. Izard (Eds.), *Affect, cognition and personality.* New York: Springer, 1965.

Torrance, E. P. (Ed.), *Education and talent.* Minneapolis: Univ. of Minnesota Press, 1960.

Torrance, E. P. *Guiding creative talent.* Englewood Cliffs, New Jersey: Prentice-Hall, 1962.

Torrance, E. P. *Education and the creative potential.* Minneapolis, Minnesota: Univ. of Minnesota Press, 1963.

Torrance, E. P. Torrance Tests of Creative Thinking, Verbal, Forms A and B. Princeton, New Jersey: Personnel Press, 1966.

Torrance, E. P., & Arsan, K. Effects of homogeneous and heterogeneous grouping on individual behavior in small groups. Paper presented to *Third Minnesota Conference on Gifted Children*, Center for Continuation Study, Univ. of Minnesota, October 10-12, 1960.

Townsend, J. K. The relation between Rorschach signs of aggression and behavioral aggression in emotionally disturbed boys. *Journal of Projective Techniques & Personality Assessment*, 1968, **31**, 13-21.

Van Alstyne, D. *Play behavior and choice of play materials of pre-school children.* Chicago, Illinois: Univ. of Chicago Press, 1932.

Vernon, M. D. The development of imaginative construction in children. *British Journal of Psychology*, 1948, **39**, 102-111.

Wallach, M. Creativity. In P. Mussen (Ed.), *Carmichael's manual of child psychology*, Vol. I, Third Edition. New York: Wiley, 1970.

Wallach, M. *The intelligence/creativity distinction.* New York: General Learning Press, 1971.

Wallach, M. A., & Kogan, N. *Modes of thinking in young children.* New York: Holt, 1965.

Wallach, M., & Wing, C. W. *The talented student: A validation of the creativity-intelligence distinction.* New York: Holt, 1969.

Weisskopf, E. A. A transcendence index as a proposed measure in the T. A. T. *Journal of Psychology,* 1950, **29,** 379-390.

Welker, W. I. An analysis of exploratory and play behavior in animals. In D. W. Fiske & S. Maddi (Eds.), *Functions of varied experience.* Homewood, Illinois: Dorsey, 1961.

Werner, H. Motion and motion perception: A study on vicarious perception. *Journal of Psychology,* 1945, **19,** 317-327.

Werner, H. *Comparative psychology of mental development.* New York: Science Editions, 1948.

Werner, H. *Comparative psychology of mental development,* rev. ed. New York: International Universities Press, 1957.

Wheeler, J. Temporal experience and fantasy. Unpublished doctoral dissertation, City Univ. of New York, 1969.

White, R. W. Motivation reconsidered: The concept of competence. *Psychological Review,* 1959, **66,** 297-333.

White, R. W. Competence and the psychosexual stages of development. In M. R. Jones (Ed.), *Nebraska symposium on motivation.* Lincoln, Nebraska: Univ. of Nebraska Press, 1960.

White, R. W. Ego and reality in psychoanalytic theory. *Psychological Issues,* 1964, **3,** Monograph 11.

Whiting, B. B. (Ed.). *Six cultures: Studies of child-rearing.* New York: Wiley, 1963.

Wickes, F. G. *The inner world of childhood.* New York: Appleton, 1966.

Wilt, M. E. *Creativity in the elementary school.* New York: Appleton, 1959.

Winnicott, D. W. *Therapeutic consultations in child psychiatry.* New York: Basic Books, 1971.

Wundt, W. *Volkerpsychologie,* 10 vols. Liepzig: Engelmann, 1911-1929.

Yarrow, L. J. Interviewing children. In P. H. Mussen (Ed.), *Handbook of research methods in child development.* New York: Wiley, 1960.

Zigler, E., & Child, I. L. Socialization. In G. L. Lindzey & E. Aronson (Eds.), *The handbook of social psychology,* Vol. III. Reading, Massachusetts: Addison-Wesley, 1969.

Author Index

Subject Index

B 5
C 6
D 7
E 8
F 9
G 0
H 1
I 2
J 3